REFERENCE

P9-BTY-417

BLAIRSVILLE SENIOR HIGH SCHOOL
BLAIRSVILLE, PENNA.

Encyclopedia of

MULTICULTURALISM

Encyclopedia of

MULTICULTURALISM

Volume 3

Ethnic and minority group names – Inner city

Editor

SUSAN AUERBACH

Marshall Cavendish
New York • London • Toronto

Published By
Marshall Cavendish Corporation
2415 Jerusalem Avenue
P.O. Box 587
North Bellmore, New York 11710
United States of America

Copyright © 1994, by Marshall Cavendish Corporation
All rights in this book are reserved. No part of this work may be used or reproduced in any manner whatsoever or transmitted in any form or by any means, electronic or mechanical, including photocopy, recording, or any information storage and retrieval system, without written permission from the copyright owner except in the case of brief quotations embodied in critical articles and reviews. For information address the publisher.

∞ The paper in these volumes conforms to the American National Standard for Permanence of Paper for Printed Library Materials, Z39.48-1984.

Library of Congress Cataloging-in-Publication Data

Encyclopedia of multiculturalism / editor, Susan Auerbach.
   p. cm.
  Includes bibliographical references (p. 1767) and index.
  Contents: v. 1. A. Philip Randolph Institute–Business and corporate enterprise; v. 2. Mother Cabrini–Estonian Americans; v. 3. Ethnic and minority group names–Inner city; v. 4. Daniel Ken Inouye–Mythology, American Indian; v. 5. Names and name changes–Six Nations; v. 6. Slavery–Zoot-suit riots.
   ISBN 1-85435-670-4 (set : alk. paper). — ISBN 1-85435-673-9 (v. 3 : alk. paper)
   1. Pluralism (Social sciences)—United States—Encyclopedias. 2. Multiculturalism—United States—Encyclopedias. 3. Ethnology—United States—Encyclopedias. 4. United States—Ethnic relations—Encyclopedias. 5. United States—Race relations—Encyclopedias.
I. Auerbach, Susan, 1956-   .
E184.A1E58   1993
306.4′46′0973—dc20

93-23405
CIP
AC

Second Printing

PRINTED IN THE UNITED STATES OF AMERICA

Contents

Ethnic and minority group names—history and controversy 611
Ethnic folk music 616
Ethnic heritage revival 622
Ethnic jokes 623
Ethnic journalism 624
Ethnic restaurants 629
Ethnic slurs 631
Ethnic studies movement 631
Ethnicity 632
Ethnocentrism 636
Eu, March Kong Fong 636
Evangelical and Pentecostal congregations—African American 636
Evers, Medgar W. 638
Exclusion acts 638
Exploration and explorers of the New World . . 638

Factory work 649
Fair Employment Practices Act 650
Fair Labor Standards Act 651
Fair Share Refugee Act 651
Family life 651
Family planning services 655
Farmer, Fannie Merritt 660
Farnham, Marynia 661
Farrakhan, Louis Abdul 661
Fashion 662
Federal assistance programs 665
Feliciano, José 669
Female Labor Reform Association 669
Feminism 669
Feminism—cultural 674
Feminism—radical 675
Feminism—socialist 675
Ferraro, Geraldine 676
Ferrer, José 677
Festival of Our Lady of Guadalupe 677
Festival of the Flowers 677
Fetterman Massacre 677
Fiction writers and fiction 677
Fifteenth Amendment 682
Filipino Americans 686
Filipino Federation of Labor 690
Finnish Americans 690
Fisk University 693

Fitzgerald, Zelda Sayre 693
Five Civilized Tribes 693
Flamenco dance and music 697
Flappers 697
Flores, Thomas Raymond 697
Folk art 697
Folk dance 699
Folk music 700
Folklore 702
Folklórico 709
Fonda, Jane 709
Fong, Hiram Leong 709
Food and cooking 710
Football 718
Foreign-language press—history 719
Forty-eighters 720
Fossey, Dian 720
442nd Regimental Combat Team 721
Fourteenth Amendment 721
Franklin, Aretha 724
Franklin, John Hope 725
Fraternities and sororities 725
Free Soil Party 726
Freedmen's Bureau 726
Freedom Rides 727
French Americans 727
French and Indian War 730
French Canadians in the U.S. 730
Friedan, Betty 734
Friends of the Indian 734
Frontier wars and African Americans 734
Fugitive Slave Act 735
Fuller, Margaret 737
Funk music 737

Gadsden Purchase 739
Galarza, Ernesto 739
Gall [Pizi] 739
Gangs and crime 739
Garifuna 744
Garment industry 744
Garvey, Marcus 748
Gavin, John 749
Gay and lesbian activism 749
Gay and lesbian rights movement 753
Gay and lesbian studies programs 758

General Federation of Women's Clubs 760
Genocide 761
Genthe, Arnold 762
Gentlemen's Agreement 763
German Americans 763
German Jews 766
Geronimo [Goyathlay] 767
Gerrymandering 767
Ghetto 768
Ghost Dance religion 768
Gibson, Althea 769
Gilman, Charlotte Perkins 769
Ginsburg, Ruth Bader 769
Girl Scouts of America 770
Glass ceiling 770
Goizueta, Roberto C. 770
Gold Mountain 770
Gold Rush 771
Goldman, Emma "Red Emma" 771
Gonzales, Pancho 771
Gonzáles, Rodolfo "Corky" 772
Gordy, Berry, Jr. 772
Gospel music—African American 772
Graffiti 773
Graham, Katherine 774
Graham, Martha 775
Grandfather clause 775
Gray Panthers 776
Great Awakening 776
Great Britain, Treaty of Peace with 779
Great Depression 779
Great Migration 780
Greek Americans 781
Greer, Germaine 784
Gregory, Dick [Richard Claxton] 785
Grimké, Angelina, and Sarah Grimké 785
Griswold v. State of Connecticut 786
Guadalupe Hidalgo, Treaty of 786
Guatemalan Americans 788
Gullah 791
Gutiérrez, Horacio 791
Gynecology 792
Gypsies 793

Hadassah 795
Haitian Americans 795
Hale, Sarah 798
Hale House 798
Haley, Alex Palmer 798
Hamer, Fannie Lou 798

Handy, W. C. [William Christopher] 799
Hansberry, Lorraine 799
Hanukkah 799
Harlem Globetrotters 800
Harlem Renaissance 800
Harpers Ferry, W.Va. 805
Hasidism 806
Hatcher, Richard Gordon 806
Hate crimes 806
Hate-speech codes 811
Hawaiian ethnic diversity 811
Hawaiian natives and the sovereignty
    movement 814
Hawaiian Sugar Planters' Association 814
Hayakawa, Sessue 815
Hayakawa, S. I. 815
Hayes, Ira 815
Hayworth, Rita 815
Head of household, female 816
Head Start 820
Health and medicine 821
Health and medicine—American Indian 824
Health and medicine—women's 827
Heart Mountain Fair Play Committee 832
Hebrew language 832
Hebrew Union College 833
Hellman, Lillian 833
Henry Street Settlement 834
Henson, Matthew Alexander 834
Hepburn, Katharine 834
Higher education 834
Hill, Anita Faye 838
Hindus 838
Hip-hop culture 839
Hirabayashi v. United States 840
Hispanic Chamber of Commerce 841
Hispanic Heritage Week 841
Hispanic Policy Development Project 841
Hispanic Society of America 841
Hmong Americans 842
Hobby, Oveta Culp 845
Holiday, Billie "Lady Day" 845
Holidays and festivals 845
Holocaust, the 851
Homelessness 856
Homestead Act 857
Homesteaders and exodusters 858
Homophobia 858
Honduran Americans 859
Hong Kong, Chinese Americans from 860

CONTENTS

Hongo, Garrett Kaoru 866
Hopis 866
Horne, Lena 867
Housework 868
Howard University 872
Howe, James Wong 872
Howe, Julia Ward 872
Huerta, Dolores Fernandez 873
Hughes, [James Mercer] Langston 873
Huguenots 874
Hull House Association 874
Hungarian Americans 874
Hurston, Zora Neale 877
Hutchinson, Anne 879
Hutterites 879
Hwang, David Henry 879

Icelandic Americans 881
Immigration—illegal 882
Immigration Act of 1917 886
Immigration Act of 1924 887
Immigration Act of 1990 887
Immigration and Nationality Act of 1952 887

Immigration and Nationality Act of 1965 887
Immigration and Naturalization Service 887
Immigration legislation 888
Immigration Reform and Control Act
  of 1986 898
Immigration Restriction League 898
In Re Ah Moy, on Habeas Corpus 898
Indentured servants 899
Independent living movement 899
Indian Citizenship Act of 1924 899
Indian hobbyist movement 900
Indian Removal Act of 1830 901
Indian Reorganization Act 901
Indian Rights Association 902
Indian rights movement 902
Indian Self-Determination and Education
  Assistance Act of 1975 905
Indian Territory 906
Indian Wars 906
Indochina Resource Action Center 910
Indonesian Americans 910
Industrial Revolution 911
Inner city 915

Encyclopedia of

MULTICULTURALISM

Ethnic and minority group names—history and controversy: Minority groups in the United States have been referred to by a host of different names over time. Some derogatory names, known as ETHNIC SLURS, are quite old while others are as new as the latest slang. The polite, accepted names for minority groups have changed over time according to both outsiders' and insiders' perceptions of the group and sociopolitical trends. For example, in the 1950's and early 1960's, the term "Negro" was considered respectful while the term "colored" was considered old-fashioned and demeaning, yet "Negro" would soon be supplanted by "black," "Afro-American," and "African American." Such shifts are among the landmarks of multiculturalism in the United States, marking moments when the role and voice of certain minorities became more prominent in mainstream American society.

Ethnic Group Names in the 1990's. Until the late twentieth century, the names for minority groups were generally determined by the views of the dominant

"Older Americans" prefer to be called such to place them in an active, mainstream context. (Skjold)

culture. There was little concern for the connotations that such names might have for the members of such groups themselves. For example, people of Asian ancestry were formerly lumped together as "Orientals"— a term that differentiated them from Caucasians and Westerners, marking them as "the other" according to a now-outmoded worldview. The preferred term in the 1990's is "Asians," a reference to the proper name for their continent of origin.

Since the civil rights struggles of the 1960's, group names reflecting distinctive ethnic pride and group identity have increasingly come into vogue. For example, in the CHICANO MOVEMENT, people of Mexican ancestry, particularly younger people or those born and reared in the United States, promoted the proud term "Chicano" rather than "Mexican American," with its immigrant connotations, to describe their unique place in American culture. Similarly, the BLACK POWER MOVEMENT told the world that "Black is beautiful" and spread acceptance of the term "Black" or "black" for those formerly called Negroes. The term "Native American" similarly underscored the role of Indians as the "first Americans." By the time of the ethnic heritage revival of the 1970's, many nationality groups were appending "American" to their names, as in "German American" or "Arab American," as a badge of ethnic identity combined with American patriotism—the rise of the so-called hyphenated American.

As the new names of ethnic identity took hold and found their way into official government designations, such as census forms, many Americans began to reconsider the appropriateness of the terms. Black people, doubly inspired by their African roots and by the hyphenated American trend, began to call themselves Afro-Americans and then African Americans. Some people of Latin American background objected to the "Spanish-surname" designation as too limiting and the name "Hispanic" as connoting a direct connection to Spain that most of them did not have; they preferred the broad term "Latino" to emphasize the common heritage and common cause of all people of Latin ancestry. Both "Hispanic" and "Native American," widely used in government, came to seem like outsiders' impositions to some members of these groups; Indians when speaking among themselves, still used the terms "Indians," "American Indians," or, more likely, their specific tribal name, such as "Navajos."

Ethnic group names have continued to be controversial in debates on multiculturalism, both within minority communities and in the broader culture. Some people of Latin American ancestry, for example, reject the name "Latino" as being associated with progressive political movements and prefer what they see as a more neutral "Hispanic." Better yet, they say in opinion polls, are names that precisely describe their ethnicity, such as Cuban American or Puerto Rican. American Indians and Asian Americans also often prefer the more specific terms such as "Cherokee" or "Vietnamese American," the exception being individuals who feel a common cause with a broad minority group. Both Pacific Islanders and native peoples of Alaska bristle at being lumped into the categories of "Asian/Pacific Islander" and "American Indian/Aleut/Eskimo," as on forms of the U.S. Census. Furthermore, activists in the multiracial movement argue that many Americans fit into no convenient category because they come from a variety of racial and ethnic stocks; these activists seek to forge a new multiracial identity and label that will become part of how the country measures its population.

By the 1990's, there was no clear mandate on ethnic group names, although there was consensus among many people in the scholarly community who dealt with the implications of such names. To understand minority group members' sensitivity to certain names, it is helpful to know more about the history of such terms, especially the legacy of ethnic slurs.

African Americans. There appear to be more names or labels attached to black Americans of African descent than to any other major group; more than fifty names or variations can be documented. Most of them can be categorized as derogatory (nigger); jocular (inky-dink); neutral (nonwhite) or euphemistic (colored people). Some focus on physical features (domino), assumed ancestry (Zulu), or mixed blood (mulatto) and are or were used with or without derogatory intention. Some group members may perceive certain names as unflattering while others do not, often depending on their social class, education, or regional background.

"Negro" is a Spanish word, known since 1555, meaning black. The term is inherently neutral, though by the late 1960's it was considered a "slave word" by some. "Darky," heard in 1775, became colloquial in the United States around 1840. "Blackbirder" was reported in South Carolina, especially for a slave merchant, but also was used for anyone of foreign background. "Nap" or "nappy" took its name from hair texture. Names noting a lighter skin color include "high yellow," while "octoroon," "quadroon," and "mulatto" refer to people of varying degrees of mixed black and white ancestry. The term "Creole" officially means, in the U.S. Gulf states, French-speaking whites descended from French and Spanish settlers as well as French-speaking persons of mixed French or Spanish and black ancestry; contemporary CREOLES are

Harriet Beecher Stowe's Uncle Tom's Cabin *familiarized readers with the stereotypical black "Mammy."* (Library of Congress)

particularly sensitive about what they should be called. Among black Americans, "peola," "tush," "pink-toes," "brown polish," and the obsolete "charcoal nigger" have also connoted light skin at various points in history. "Nigger" is a corruption of Negro and is derogatory, although it may be used in a teasing manner among blacks. "Jigaboo" and some variant forms also referred disparagingly to blacks in the early 1900's.

Several labels are associated with Harriet Beecher STOWE's antislavery novel *Uncle Tom's Cabin* (1850), in which blacks are portrayed as subservient to whites. The female counterpart to a passive, smiling Uncle Tom is Aunt Thomasina; a slang version of the 1950's

was "handkerchief-head," suggestive of the plantation "Mammy" and her "pickaninny" children, (probably derived from the 1653 Portuguese word *pequeniño*, or little child); a more recent label is Aunt Jemima, from an advertising symbol for a brand of pancakes. The term "boy," also found in the novel, was reportedly used as early as 1764 and referred to a black male of any age. Other common nineteenth century terms in the South were "Russian" (a black who "rushed up" to the North to avoid work); "coon" (from raccoon, which southern blacks supposedly enjoyed hunting and eating); and "Geechee," thought to be from the GULLAH dialect.

"Jim Crow," presumably referring to the black color of the bird, was used before 1838 in a song. It denoted one who is dexterous, tricky, or double-dealing. A Jim Crow car was a train car set aside for blacks, and JIM CROW LAWS instituted official segregation in the South in the late 1800's.

Some names were associated with certain kinds of work or activity, such as "scuttle" (1929) for black taxi passengers and "satch," (short for "satchel-mouth") for a wide-mouthed person, such as a black jazz musician. "Skillet" (1942), used by blacks for themselves, was presumably associated with the color of the iron skillet; "stove-lid" was also heard. Other names of unclear and possibly disparaging origin include "Buck" (c. 1800), "buffalo" (especially in the western states), "seal," "shiny," "squasho," and in 1956, "spaginzy" and "spade."

Latinos. "Hispanic," or "Hispanic American," referring to Americans from Spanish-speaking countries, derives from Hispania, the Iberian peninsula of Spain (c. 1584) and has come to include all Latin Americans. Many Hispanic Americans prefer to be called Latinos to stress their Latin American origin. Around 1946, "hispano" denoted a descendant of Spaniards who had lived in the southwestern United States before its annexation.

Latinos are the largest language minority and the second largest ethnic minority group in the United States. They represent a mixture of several cultural and racial backgrounds, notably European, African, and American Indian. Most Mexican Americans, for example, are *mestizos*, people of mixed white (mostly Spanish) and American Indian ancestry. Some of their Indian progenitors were living in the American Southwest when the Spaniards arrived.

Many Mexican Americans also call themselves Chicanos, a term that was used as early as 1954. Originally the word was a slang, derogatory term suggesting clumsiness. During the 1960's, however, it took on a positive connotation of cultural pride.

Other names have sprung up over time, some unflattering, others neutral. Since 1840, *hombre* has referred to a man of Spanish or Mexican ancestry, along with other Spanish-language terms. About 1832, "dago" referred to a person of Spanish or Italian birth or descent, usually disparagingly. Other early labels include "greaser" (1848) for one of Mexican descent and "spick," dating to 1900, for any Spanish-speaking person. "Dino" (1949) referred to Mexican or Italian railroad hands who worked with dynamite, and "adobe-maker" was a derogatory term for a Mexican American based on stereotypes.

Asian Americans. This diverse and fast-growing population has been called by various names, usually according to nationality group. The Chinese were among the earliest of the Far Eastern immigrants to the United States and, in spite of discrimination, played an important role in building the country. Prior to exclusion laws, notably in 1882 and 1924, which resulted in decreased numbers of Chinese Americans, several names with varying degree of offensiveness appeared. By 1765 "Chinaman" was common, and in 1849, when Chinese worked gold claims abandoned by white prospectors, the phrase "not a Chinaman's chance" was coined, meaning no chance at all. "Chinee" and "chink," both negative, followed. Between 1900 and the 1930's, "chino," "chinkie," and "chinki-chonks" were used; the latter was not limited to Chinese. During the World War II period, "slant-eye" and "slopie" emerged.

As the Chinese presence gave way to more Japanese immigrants, terms such as "slant-eye" transferred to them. Also during the World War II period, Japanese was shortened to "Jap," and "Nip" was short for Nipponese (from *Nippon*, the Japanese word for Japan). "Tojo" was associated with the Japanese military general of that name.

As the Asian population in the United States has diversified, more names have appeared. For example, the neutral term "Amerasian" developed to refer to children born to American military men and Asian women overseas. Some recent Asian immigrants do not relate to the broad term "Asian American" and prefer to be called "Taiwanese" or "Cambodian American."

European Americans. General terms for this group are recent phenomena brought on by comparisons to people of color in the United States. In the Southwest and among some Latinos, the term "Anglo" is used for anyone who is a non-Latino white. Yet this term connotes Anglo-Saxon or English ancestry, which only accounts for some white Americans. The same limitation holds for European Americans when it comprises such groups as Arab Americans. Although they have generally experienced less discrimination than people of color, the group-specific names for European Americans often reflect a heritage of prejudice.

Names for JEWISH AMERICANS vary: some are related to religion, while others refer to geographical, cultural, or other characteristics. "Hebrew," "Israelite," or "Semite" are examples of seemingly neutral terms that refer to ancient conditions and might appear insensitive to modern Jews. Nicknames that spin off of such names may be used with a disparaging intention. For example, "hebe," heard around 1939, is mildly derogatory, as is "yid" (1951), from the Yiddish language spoken mostly by immigrant Jews of eastern European ancestry. "Abie," for Abraham, spiritual leader of the ancient Jews, refers to a Jewish male and is not necessarily derogatory. "Shonnicker," a Jewish pawnbroker, may have derived from *schon*, meaning "fine."

Some other common names for Jews have negative connotations. "Sheeny," (c. 1824, common between 1910 and 1925), refers to untrustworthiness or putting one's own interest ahead of that of others. "Kike," originally referring to an uncouth Jewish merchant, came out about 1924, and "geese" and "mockie" followed in the 1930's. Dates are uncertain for such labels as "Christ-killer," "dark stranger," and "porker"; the latter is especially offensive to observant Jews who abstain from eating pork according to kosher laws.

As early as 1807, before the immigration of thousands of Irish people precipitated by the potato famine, "Irisher" was being used as a neutral name for this group. "Paddy" (c. 1850's), from the common Irish name Patrick, was obsolete by about 1920. "Mick," a short form of Michael, emerged around 1872. It was disparaging only in that it denoted a poor, unskilled Irish immigrant. Other sources associate Mick with the prefix "Mc" common to many Irish names. "Biddy," a diminutive of Bridget, a common Irish female name, was heard around 1858. The term "harp" (early 1900's) refers to the musical instrument on the Irish flag, dear to most Irish people. The phrase "Irish nightingale" came to describe a tenor who sang with an Irish accent. IRISH AMERICANS were also

What's more paralyzing is the way he gets treated.

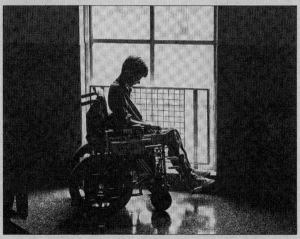

The hardest part about having a disability is being constantly reminded that you have one. Sometimes that happens when people stare at you. Or point at you. Or don't even think of including you in every day activities. Maybe it's time to start treating people with disabilities like people.

Easter Seals

This advertisement expresses the humiliation that name-calling can provoke. (National Easter Seal Society) called "shamrock," while "Irish shanty" described a poor person of Irish descent.

Most of the names that Americans associate with Germans were used not for GERMAN AMERICANS, but for German soldiers in World War I ("boche," "Fritz," "Heinie") and World War II ("superman," "Nazi," "krauthead"). During the 1920's, however, prize-fighters of both German and Dutch descent were called "woodenshoes"; "Dutchie" was also used for both groups. The label "Turner," given to members of a German immigrant fraternal and athletic society called The Turners, has its origin in the 1854 German word *turnen*, meaning to perform gymnastic exercises.

ITALIAN AMERICANS were called by names also used for Latinos, especially Mexicans, such as "dago" (1887). In 1901, it was noted that, while the word probably came from the Spanish *diego*, it was usually applied to Italians; likewise for the "dino" who used dynamite for railroad work, and "spaghetti." In 1885, "guinea" described an Italian American; at first de-rogatory, it became less so with time. In 1924, "wop" designated an illiterate day laborer of Italian descent. By 1939, "ginzo" applied to Italian Americans as well as to any foreign-born individual.

In the 1600's, William Shakespeare spoke dispar-agingly of the "polack," a person of Polish descent, and the label still stands. Two other disparaging names, "bohunk" and "hunkie" (Bohemian plus Hun-garian), were used for immigrant laborers from central Europe such as Hungarians, Slavs, Poles, or Lithuani-ans.

Nonethnic Minority Groups. The names of other marginalized groups have also undergone transforma-tion as a result of their push for more rights and rep-resentation in American society. Organizations repre-senting these groups consistently declare their preference for certain labels, some of which may seem euphemistic to outsiders.

People over the age of sixty-five were once called "the old," "old folks," or more formally, "the elderly." Then "senior citizens" or "seniors" became terms of respect, and continue to be commonly used, as in sen-ior citizens' centers or ticket discounts. In the 1990's, however, the AMERICAN ASSOCIATION OF RETIRED PERSONS believed that "senior citizens" suggests "re-tirees" on the fringes of society. They prefer the term "OLDER AMERICANS," which places older people within an active, mainstream context, using the term "the elderly" only for those over age eighty-five.

A more dramatic case of name changes came as the result of education and agitation by the disability rights movement. People who were once known as "crippled" or "retarded" became known as physically or mentally "handicapped." This term remains in gen-eral usage, although it has been supplanted by at-tempts at greater neutrality in "disabled" or even "dif-ferently abled." By 1990, disability rights groups had specific terms that they preferred for each type of dis-ability, and they stressed the importance of putting people first (as in "people with disabilities") rather than a condition (as in "the disabled").

Terms applied to gays and lesbians have undergone similar changes. "Homosexual," literally simply the opposite of "heterosexual," came into use in the late nineteenth century. However, because the term carried a strong stigma (and because it had been abbreviated and turned into the slur "homo"), "gay" began to be widely used in the late 1960's as a preferred, less-freighted term. "Lesbian" came into use around the beginning of the twentieth century. Whereas lesbian refers only to women, gay is often used to encompass homosexual people of both sexes. The slang term "queer" began to be commonly used as a slur against gays by the mid-1920's; it was embraced many years later by some gay activists (notably the radical Queer Nation) in the 1980's.

SUGGESTED READINGS. For further study, see *Words, Words, Words* (1970) by Eric Partridge, who discusses offensive words related to nationality in one chapter. In his *Words in Sheep's Clothing* (1969), Mario Pei includes a useful chapter on the vocabulary of racial relations. *New Dictionary of American Slang* (1986), edited by Robert L. Chapman as a revised edition of *The Dictionary of American Slang* (1966), which was compiled and edited by Harold Wentworth and Stuart Flexner, is one of a number of reference works that provide etymological help. See also *The Ethnic Alma-nac* (1981) by Stephanie Bernardo.—*Victoria Price*

Ethnic discrimination. *See* **Discrimination—ethnic**

Ethnic diversity, Canadian. *See* **Canadian ethnic di-versity**

Ethnic folk music: Traditional music shared and trans-mitted within a given ethnic group. Though the meaning of "folk" is difficult to define in an urbanized, multicul-tural, and ostensibly classless society such as the United States, folk music generally has its origins in a nonpro-fessional, noncommercial music tradition, passed orally from one generation to the next. Many folk songs are very old, but folk music is inherently changeable. Folk musicians continually adapt their style and repertoire to maintain the vitality and usefulness of the tradition.

The three best-known types of folk musics in the United States are American Indian, European American, and African American. Nearly every ethnic group in the United States, however, maintains a folk music tradition. Most large cities have formal or informal venues and occasions for the performance of Latin American, Irish, Greek, Chinese, and other folk musics. The northern Midwest supports active German and Polish folk music cultures; Texas is the site of

the United States, practicing and transmitting their traditions.

American Indian Folk Music. The folk music of AMERICAN INDIANS is less well known than the music of European immigrants and African Americans. The Indian musical tradition has been somewhat isolated by reservationism and restricted performance contexts. Nevertheless, music plays a central role in American Indian culture in worship, healing, annual and life cycle events, and social occasions. There is a wide variety of performance styles, varying by tribe and region, that generally emphasize voice, drums, rattles, and scrapers.

Afghan and European Americans play traditional instruments in a concert to preserve Eastern arts. (Cleo Freelance Photo)

norteño music, blending Mexican musical styles with those of German settlers in the area; many Southeast Asian musics are maintained in the Los Angeles area. Folk musicians live in both rural and urban areas of

Indians do not distinguish between "folk" and other kinds of music. All music is orally transmitted, and though ceremonial specialists may lead certain musical activities, musicians are generally considered participants rather than performers. While many other folk musics have become commercialized, American Indian music has retained folk values that emphasize participation and cultural function.

European American Folk Music. Early European settlers brought British, French, and Spanish folk musics to the United States. Of these, the British tradition has been the most widely practiced. Though religious ranged hymns in the European art tradition.

Early Anglo American secular folk music consisted of ballads, lyric songs, and instrumental dance music. Many ancient ballads, dating back to Celtic bards, survived in the United States, particularly in the Northeast and Appalachia, after dying out in the British Isles. Sung by a solo voice without instrumental accompaniment, these ballads narrated stories, some-

American Indians chanting and drumming at a 1990 powwow. (James L. Shaffer)

sanctions and the rigors of pioneering curtailed folk music practice during the early days of British colonization, the tradition reasserted itself to become the "mainstream" folk music of white Americans.

The first musical practice among British settlers was religious. Having rejected the elaborate, composed religious music of the Catholic church, the PURITANS practiced a folk style of psalm singing called "lining out," in which a leader sang lines for the often illiterate congregation to imitate. This practice continued into the late 1700's, when a move toward musical literacy in church music resulted in composed and ar-

times quite long and often tragic. The ballad singer could vary the tune or the words with each rendition, and songs might change significantly over time. In the United States, ballad singers began to sing new songs in the old British style, adapting the tradition to their current circumstances. Many new songs also addressed occupational themes, such as the railroad, the sea, mining, farming, and cowboy life.

Though ballads were slow and text-oriented, instrumental dance music was lively. String bands of fiddle, guitar, mandolin, and later banjo, harmonica, piano, accordion, and double bass, accompanied jigs, clogs, reels, and square dances. Dance music usually consisted of repeated phrases, or "strains," that the dancers could recognize easily.

With the invention of the phonograph and the rise of the recording industry, Anglo American folk music became known as "hillbilly music." Hillbilly recordings during the 1920's and 1930's included traditional closely harmonized vocals. The increasing influence of the recording industry on hillbilly music distanced the style from folk tradition, as performers changed their repertoires and styles in search of commercial success.

FRENCH AMERICAN folk music, practiced by French settlers in Canada and Louisiana, shares many char-

Musicians performing zydeco, a Creole tradition that uses mixed French and English texts. (Martin A. Hutner)

ballads and dance music, as well as new styles. From the vocal ballad tradition came mountain harmony, pioneered by the Carter Family of Virginia. This style drew on traditional songs, harmonizing them in the manner of church music and adding instrumental accompaniment, primarily guitar. Many of the Carter Family songs are well known today and appear in contemporary folk song books. African American blues also began to influence Anglo American folk music, producing the "blue yodel" style of Jimmie Rodgers, and leading ultimately to the Nashville sound of country and western music. Out of string band music came western swing, which blended traditional dance music with jazz music styles and instrumentation, and bluegrass, which emphasized instrumental virtuosity and

acteristics with British American dance music. The best-known genre is the Cajun music of Louisiana, a dance style using fiddle, accordion, and guitar to play reels, waltzes, and jigs. African American musicians in Louisiana have adapted Cajun music to create zydeco, a more up-tempo style that includes washboard, double bass, and amplified instruments in the ensemble. Both Cajun and zydeco music employ mixed French and English texts.

Though few Spanish people settled directly in North America, immigrants from Latin America to the United States have brought folk music blending Spanish and indigenous traditions. High-pitched vocal style and the use of guitar and harp are typical of Latin American folk music. Some Mexican folk songs, such as "Cielito Lindo" and "La Cucaracha," have been assimilated into mainstream folk repertoire. Other Mexican styles include ranchera and norteño music, narrative corridos, and the lively "son" style most widely known in the United States as mariachi. Popular styles such as salsa and merengue have roots in Latin American folk musics.

African American Folk Music. Music plays an important role in most African cultures, and African slaves brought a diversity of deeply rooted musical traditions to the United States. During two centuries of SLAVERY, various African musics intermingled, adjusted to new contexts and restrictions, and provided a medium for communication among people from different tribes sharing little in the way of language or lifestyle. Denied most of their traditional instruments

by slaveowners, African Americans relied heavily on singing, accompanying themselves with "found" instruments including washboards, jugs, and the human body. The clapping and foot stamping that replaced intricate African drum patterns was a precursor to the "human beatbox" phenomenon of contemporary RAP MUSIC. The permissible contexts for making music during slavery were generally at work and in the Christian church, and these settings provided the primary outlets for early African American folk music.

African slaves were forbidden to practice their traditional religions, and many quickly converted to the PROTESTANT faiths practiced by their owners and promulgated by traveling missionaries. In church, African Americans adapted Protestant hymns with African music performance styles. These included the ad-

W. C. Handy is known as the father of the blues, which was rooted in African American folk music of the antebellum period. (AP/Wide World Photos)

dition of harmony, off-beat phrasing, complicated rhythms, call and response, improvisation, and a more active and emotional performance style similar to that practiced in religious possession ceremonies in many African cultures. Many hymns were sung in slightly different tunings that could be traced back to African scale systems. By adapting familiar cultural practice to fit into new surroundings, African Americans maintained the vitality of their folk tradition.

Other forms of slave-era folk music included work songs, field hollers, and dance songs. Work songs and field hollers shared many characteristics with African American church music, but were simpler in form and less emotional in performance style, to allow for the exertions of manual labor. During their limited opportunities for social music making and dancing, slaves performed plantation dances and cakewalks, sometimes for the amusement of their owners.

Emancipation expanded the contexts for secular folk music, and African Americans adopted European instruments such as fiddle, guitar, double bass, and the military fife and drum. Urban musicians took up brass instruments and began to play the syncopated marches that formed the roots of JAZZ. The best-known folk form of the antebellum period is the BLUES, a solo vocal tradition originating in rural areas, emphasizing poetry and personal expression. Country blues singers, mostly men, utilized simple song forms mixing field hollers with Anglo American ballad and lyric songs. The texts discussed love, work, and travel, and were often couched in poetic metaphors. Musicians accompanied themselves on the guitar with short, repeated harmonic patterns, performing for themselves and for others at local bars and gathering spots.

African American hymns became widely known as "spirituals" after Emancipation, mostly through the tours of professionalized performance groups such as the Fisk Jubilee Singers, who performed in the style of a European concert choir. Some black congregations chose to adopt white European performance styles in this manner, but many retained African folk elements in their musical practice.

In the early 1900's, African American music became increasingly popularized. Traveling minstrel shows, urbanization, and the recording industry all contributed to the commercialization of the blues, plantation dance songs, and spirituals. Popular styles developed out of these folk traditions, including jazz, urban blues, GOSPEL, RHYTHM AND BLUES, and ulti-

mately, SOUL, FUNK, ROCK AND ROLL, and RAP MUSIC. While African American folk music persists, mostly in rural areas, the rich diversity of popular African American musics have overshadowed folk practice.

American folk musics were widely neglected by scholars and musicologists until the late 1800's. Professional musicians and music teachers often favored European art music over oral traditions and sought to ignore or "educate" folk musicians of all ethnic groups. Two books of written transcriptions marked the beginning of folk song study. *Slave Songs of the United States*, published in 1867, documented African American songs, mostly spirituals. *Songs and Games of American Children* (1884) was a collection of orally transmitted British American songs.

Serious folk music collecting began in the 1900's. John Lomax, along with his son Alan, helped to pioneer the use of the phonograph in "field," or on-location, recording of folk musics. In 1928, the Archive of American Folksong was founded as part of the Library of Congress. Today, the archive is supplemented by collections at numerous universities that house recordings and documentation of numerous ethnic folk musics.

Twentieth Century Developments. Throughout the 1930's, increasing urban awareness of American folk musics led to the publication of folk music anthologies. The development of "crossover" popularized folk genres in the recording industry; the use of folk music themes in American concert compositions and a fascination by white urbanites with the Anglo American rural tradition culminated in the folk music revival of the 1960's. Folk musics of many cultures became the subject of serious academic study, resulting in the establishment of university departments of ethnomusicology and folklore. While ethnic folk musics in the United States were originally studied as survivals of faraway cultures, they have come to be viewed as vital American cultural forms, expressive of current cultural and social conditions.

Many contemporary folk musicians have embraced electric instruments, amplification, and studio recording techniques. Some musicians have made folk music their profession, moving beyond the traditional, non-professional bounds of the term "folk." The line where folk music becomes popular music is difficult to draw, particularly in the United States, where recorded and broadcast media are so prevalent.

Perhaps the most significant trend in American folk musics has been the extensive cross-fertilization be-

A Mien American (originally from Southeast Asia) completes work on a ritual drum in Oakland, Calif., 1981. (Eric Crystal)

tween British- and African-derived traditions. White and black folk musicians have traded song forms, styles, and instruments since slavery began. Many musicologists trace rock and roll, a definitively "American" music form, back to a fusion of African American blues and British American hillbilly music. Similar stylistic blending has occurred among the many other ethnic folk musics practiced in the United States, lending a uniquely American identity to each tradition.

SUGGESTED READINGS. For a survey of American folk musics, see Bruno Nettl's *Folk Music in the United States: An Introduction* (3d rev. ed., 1976). In *Cantometrics: An Approach to the Anthropology of Music* (1976), folk song collector Alan Lomax analyzes folk song style as symbolic of social and cultural structures; the book includes cassette tapes for cross-cultural listening. Samuel L. Forcucci chronicles the historical development of American folk music in *A Folk Song History of America: America Through Its Songs* (1984). Stephen Erdely describes the music of American Indians, European settlers, African Ameri-

cans, and national and ethnic groups in "Ethnic Music in America: An Overview" in *Yearbook of the International Music Council* 11 (1979).—*Elizabeth J. Miles*

Ethnic heritage revival: Social and cultural movement that made millions of Americans conscious of their ethnic identity and led them to search for their roots during the 1970's and 1980's. The movement, which advocated CULTURAL PLURALISM, is considered a reaction to the assimilationist policy after World War II. It was believed that the descendants of immigrants from central and southern Europe would gradually assimilate into American society and that ethnic differences would disappear with greater social mobility, interethnic marriage, and distance in time from the original immigrants. With the publication of Nathan Glazer and Daniel Patrick Moynihan's *Beyond the Melting Pot* in 1963, however, academics and popular writers began to question the validity of the ASSIMILATION thesis.

The revival was also a cultural outgrowth of the CIVIL RIGHTS MOVEMENT, the CHICANO MOVEMENT, and other reflections of the ethnic social consciousness of the 1960's. For example, the BLACK POWER MOVEMENT, which taught African Americans to have pride in their cultural heritage, laid the foundation for the ethnic heritage revival by proposing an alternative model of ethnicity.

Led by such strong proponents as Michael Novak and Reverend Andrew Greeley, the descendants of European immigrants began to assert pride in their ethnic heritage in the early 1970's. The movement was further spurred by the publication of Alex HALEY's *Roots* (1976) and the dramatization of the book in a television miniseries by the American Broadcasting Company, which was viewed by an estimated 130 million Americans.

During the 1970's, a variety of ethnic studies programs were added to the curricula in U.S. universities and colleges as well as public schools. Bookstores created sections for books on ETHNICITY and ethnic groups. Radio and television programs emphasized ethnic fashion, behavioral patterns, and names. City governments, religious organizations, and social organizations began to revive ethnic festivals, parades, and other celebrations while museums mounted ethnic history exhibits and chambers of commerce compiled lists of ETHNIC RESTAURANTS. Traditional music, dance, cooking, and crafts flourished as Americans gained a new appreciation for the cultures of their ancestors. Genealogy and ORAL HISTORY became popular topics both inside and outside the academy as people sought to document minority and immigrant cultures. The descendants of immigrants sent requests for birth, baptism, marriage, and death certificates to their ancestors' hometowns to trace their ethnic roots while African Americans examined the plantation records in the National Archives and American Indians lobbied museums for the return of their cultural records and artifacts. The ethnic heritage revival movement also

and 1980's. The ethnic heritage revival also made more Americans sensitive to the issues of race and ethnicity. By the end of the 1980's, as the number of Latino and Asian immigrants dramatically increased, the notion of cultural diversity as a positive value had permeated the United States, setting the stage for debates on multiculturalism.

SUGGESTED READINGS. For the philosophical foundation of the ethnic heritage revival, see Michael Novak's *The Rise of the Unmeltable Ethnics* (1972) and

Young American Indians revive their tribal traditions through dance, music, and dress. (Elaine S. Querry)

influenced government policy in such areas as BILINGUAL EDUCATION, multicultural education, and arts funding.

Critics of the revival argued that the emphasis on ethnic identity would result in ethnic chauvinism and create a rivalry among different ethnic groups. They also claimed that the movement was superficial because it had become a mere hobby to the financially secure third and fourth generations of immigrants. Despite such criticisms, Americans became more conscious of their ethnic heritage throughout the 1970's

Further Reflections on Ethnicity (1977). See Jack Kinton's edited collection *American Ethnic Revival* (1977) for theories and research studies that emerged from the revival. *The Ethnic Almanac* (1981) by Stephanie Bernardo Johns gives a good sampling of the kinds of cultural interests and resources that typify the movement.

Ethnic jokes: Identify and parody the eccentricities and incongruities of a particular ethnic group, relying on stereotypes to provoke laughter. When told by members of the ethnic group, ethnic jokes reinforce the bond among them and assert the group's unique identity. When told by outsiders, ethnic jokes may express social tensions between groups while acknowledging inequality. In the 1980's, American comedians such as Andrew Dice Clay began telling ethnic jokes which aggressively attacked certain ethnic groups, causing outcries from those who believed they were being slandered and victimized by offensive humor.

Ethnic jokes often operate on the assumption that the stereotype of the group in question is already known to the joke's listeners; the presumably culture-specific traits form the basis for the slurs. Thus, Germans are often portrayed as militaristic, English as cold-blooded and aloof in personal relations, French as promiscuous and preoccupied with food, Polish as stupid and clumsy, Scottish as stingy to the point of miserliness, and Americans as selfish and prone to exaggeration. African American ethnic jokes may emphasize the group's origins in slavery and its encounters with prejudice and oppression. When told by whites, these ethnic jokes portray the African American as considerably less than intelligent. When told by blacks, these jokes often show the African American outsmarting his white counterpart.

A typical format for ethnic jokes involves two or more members of various ethnic groups performing the same action, thus highlighting the differences between the groups. Being stranded together on a desert island or trapped in an airplane which is about to crash are common scenarios. In ethnic jokes, both men and women of a given group tend to display the same cultural characteristics. For example, both French males and females in these jokes would be interested only in lovemaking, good food, and good wine. Within each ethnic group, there may also be further breakdown into categories; Jewish ethnic jokes differentiate among Orthodox, Conservative, and Reform Jews, for example. Scholarly research on racial slurs and ethnic humor has demonstrated that character stereotypes remain fairly constant over time.

SUGGESTED READINGS. For additional information on ethnic jokes and humor, consult Alan Dundes' *Cracking Jokes: Studies of Sick Humor Cycles and Stereotypes* (1987), Henry Spalding's *The Encyclopedia of Black Folklore and Humor* (1972), and William Novak, Moshe Waldoks, and Donald Altschiller's *The Big Book of New American Humor: The Best of the Past 25 Years* (1990).

Ethnic journalism: The world of journalism has been a rich and dynamic arena among all cultural groups in the United States since the colonial period. From the founding of German-language newspapers in the eighteenth century to the vitality of Indochinese-language papers in the late twentieth century, virtually all ethnic groups have established voices of their own, at first through the printed word and later via the electronic media.

Ethnic journalism has typically meant general-circulation dailies, weeklies, or monthlies that have paralleled the mainstream mass-circulation newspapers, seeking to serve the needs of a particular community. A large ethnic group often spawns specialized papers or periodicals focusing on specific age, regional, gender, religious, or political cohorts. The functions of ethnic journalism since the eighteenth century have been several. Its primary function has been informational, carrying general news of an ethnic group in its various locations in the United States and overseas. It has also expressed and reinforced a group's cultural heritage, values, and customs. Further, it has helped to educate ethnic Americans, especially immigrants, about the news, values, and expectations of the dominant culture, and has even served to promote ASSIMILATION. Finally, it has reinforced group solidarity, pride, and power.

The survival rate of such publications has been uneven; in some years almost as many newspapers failed as were established. The most vibrant era of multicultural journalism was from 1900 to 1930, as seen in circulation figures as well as in numbers of publications. For example, in 1917, several culturally identifiable groups claimed newspaper circulations among their various papers totaling hundreds of thousands. In 1930, more than a thousand individual foreign-language papers were published in the United States, with additional newspapers appearing among ethnically distinct English-speaking groups such as the Irish, African Americans, and others.

Foreign-language press circulation figures and numbers of papers dipped after 1930 because of restrictive immigration quotas. In the 1960's, however, these figures rose again because of a revised immigration policy drawing new immigrant groups to the United States from Asia, Latin America, the Middle East, and the Caribbean. Among them were Vietnamese, Salvadoran, Iranian, and Haitian immigrants. A second reason for the resurgence of multicultural journalism was the ETHNIC HERITAGE REVIVAL of the 1970's, in

Greek American editor keeps up with the news from the homeland in his native language. (Odette Lupis)

which various groups of Americans sought to reinvigorate their respective heritages. This interest in "roots" also made possible the development of unprecedented multiethnic publications such as the *Ethnic News* of Seattle, Washington.

European Newspapers. The first ethnic newspaper in North America was the *Philadelphische Zeitung*, published in German by Benjamin Franklin in Philadelphia in 1732. It failed after a few issues. With *Der Hoch-Deutsch Pennsylvanische Geschichts-Schreiber*, begun in 1739, Christopher Sauer founded the most complex foreign-language publishing concern in the United States. A major German paper has been the *Staats-Zeitung*, which began publishing in New York in 1834. It became an influential Democratic paper before the Civil War under German political refugee editors. Another significant paper published by German Americans was the *Illinois Staats-Zeitung*, which appeared from 1848 to 1922. It was originally the voice of the "FORTY-EIGHTERS" who fled after the failed revolutions in central Europe. The most influential product of GERMAN AMERICAN journalism was Joseph Pulitzer, who began as a reporter on the *Westliche Post* in St. Louis in 1868 and became a major figure in the shaping of modern American journalism. German American newspapers enjoyed a large readership because of the size and scope of the German community in the United States until its decline after World War I.

Newspapers have been published in several languages to serve the various cultural and linguistic needs of American Jews. The leading Jewish newspaper has been the *Forverts*, founded in New York in 1897, which became the most important Yiddish newspaper in the world. Its colorful editor, Abraham Cahan, an immigrant from Lithuania, guided the paper and its readership toward support of the New Deal of Franklin D. Roosevelt and encouraged assimilation. Under Cahan's editorship, the paper initiated departments that the mass circulation dailies copied, such as the "Bintl Brief," a column of letters from immigrant readers on personal and adjustment problems that became a model for American advice columns. Contemporary Jews can choose from several national magazines and periodicals of major Jewish organizations, as well as from local newspapers in major cities, most of which are now published in English.

The Italian press also offered a large number and variety of publications. *Il Progresso Italo-Americano*, the longest-lasting Italian newspaper in the United States and the one with the greatest readership, was founded by an entrepreneur named Carlo Barsotti in New York in 1880 and is still published today. Between the two world wars, the paper's editorial stance was sympathetic to Italy's Mussolini government. Another important newspaper has been *L'Italia*, which was published in San Francisco from 1887 until 1966. It was the major Italian-language newspaper on the West Coast.

Among Scandinavians, the leading Danish newspaper, *Den Danske Pioneer*, has been published in the Midwest since 1872 in various cities. Its most important editor was Sophus F. Neble, who favored the American system of representation and attacked Denmark as having too authoritarian a political structure. The leading Norwegian newspaper in the United States was the *Skandinaven*, published from 1866 to 1941 in Chicago. Its longtime editor, John Anderson, promoted the Republican Party, women's rights, temperance, public schools, and free land for settlers.

Most other European ethnic groups in the United States have produced their own newspapers, both long-lasting and ephemeral. There has been a pattern of large national BENEVOLENT societies sponsoring monthly papers or magazines for their ethnic membership in English. Where newspapers have proved unfeasible, some European groups have sponsored weekly commercial foreign-language radio programs with a format featuring music and a calendar of events rather than strict news.

Asian Newspapers. Immigrants from Asia have also established their own lively world of journalism. Chinese Americans on the West Coast and in New York established newspapers that tended to be caught up in the politics and nationalistic fervor of their homeland. For example, *Sai Gai Yat Po* was published by the Reform Party in San Francisco under various names from 1892 to 1969. *Young China* for most of its history has been published in San Francisco under a number of names since its founding in 1909. It initially supported the policies of Sun Yat-sen and favored the overthrow of the Chinese imperial government. In later decades, Chinese papers on both coasts attacked one another over support for or opposition to the Guomindang regime of Chiang Kai-shek and the People's Republic of China.

The Japanese began to publish newspapers in Hawaii and on the West Coast in the late nineteenth century. Their thriving publications were destroyed by the internment of JAPANESE AMERICANS during World War II, but revived after the war, with some of the same newspapers being reestablished. Leading papers have been *Rafu Shimpo*, a Los Angeles paper established at the start of the twentieth century, *Kashu Mainichi*, a Los Angeles newspaper begun in the 1930's, and *Hokubei Mainichi*, one of two Japanese papers published in San Francisco.

Japanese newspapers since the interwar period have been published in cities throughout the United States. Young Japanese Americans have promoted the rise of English-language publications that deal with broad issues of Asian American identity, politics, and culture on the local and national level.

The first FILIPINO AMERICAN newspaper began publication in 1921 in Salinas, California, under the editorship of Luis Agudo, as the *Philippine Independent News* and eventually became *The Philippines Mail*. Most Filipino newspapers have published in English and have been located on the West Coast, where the population is clustered. *The Philippine News*, which in the 1980's claimed the largest circulation of any in this group, has benefited from the influx of Filipino immigrants since 1965.

Other Asian groups that have immigrated in large numbers since that time, such as Koreans, Thais, Vietnamese, and Cambodians, have also established newspapers as part of the process of strengthening their communities. These publications keep new immigrants informed of major events in their homeland, laws and issues in the United States that impact their community, local social and cultural events, the work of local ethnic organizations, and the accomplishments of ethnic youth and prominent individuals. Like all ethnic newspapers, Asian papers include ads for Asian businesses at the local or national level.

Latino, African American, and American Indian Newspapers. Spanish-speaking Americans have created their own journalistic worlds, whether Puerto Rican in New York and other eastern and midwestern cities or Cuban in Florida. The MEXICAN AMERICAN press offers the oldest and most visible journalistic presence among these groups. More than a hundred newspapers geared to readers of Mexican heritage appeared in the nineteenth century. These numbers more than doubled in the twentieth century as a result of the growing influx of immigrants from Mexico and the rise of the CHICANO MOVEMENT in the 1960's. *La Opinión* of Los Angeles has been the longest-lasting Mexican American newspaper, having begun publication in 1926. *La Raza*, published from 1967 to 1975

in Los Angeles, was one media voice of the Chicano movement.

African American newspapers have provided blacks with a means of expression starting with newspapers such as Frederick DOUGLASS' *The North Star* before the Civil War. They began to thrive in the late nineteenth century. For example, the *Free Speech and Headlight* appeared in the 1890's in Memphis, Tennessee, and was edited by Ida WELLS-Barnett until she was forced to flee the South over her campaign against LYNCHING. T. Thomas Fortune of the *New York Age* was one of the most famous black journalists of that era. The most prominent African American newspapers in the North have been the *Pittsburgh Courier*, the *Baltimore Afro-American*, and especially the *Chicago Defender.* Published since 1905 under the guidance of the legendary Robert S. Abbott, the *Chicago Defender* became virtually a national newspaper for African Americans through its regional editions. Various newspapers in the early twentieth century encouraged African Americans to migrate to the North, and they used their pages to speak out against discrimination, racism, and second-class citizenship. As African Americans became more powerful in American society, they founded national publications such as *Ebony* magazine, founded in 1945.

Journalistic efforts by AMERICAN INDIANS have been more sporadic. The first Indian newspaper was the bilingual *Cherokee Phoenix*, founded in 1828 by Elias Boudinot (Cherokee) and missionary Samuel A. Worcester. Contemporary tribal newspapers have been inspired by the general Indian cultural revival and American INDIAN RIGHTS MOVEMENT. Indians and Alaska natives have also made use of radio, an especially useful way of reaching people who live in remote areas such as some reservations.

Trends and Electronic Media. Ethnic newspapers typically have a life span that depends on the pace of ASSIMILATION or degree of marginality of the group. As long as a group maintains a sense of identity, its ethnic newspapers tend to thrive. When a group loses its distinctiveness, its need for its own voice declines. Newspapers then often begin to feature more general news and to publish in English in an effort to retain readership. Such papers may revive if renewed immigration occurs or if political events stimulate the group's need for solidarity. Usually, however, the newspapers cease to exist if and when a group becomes absorbed into the mainstream or when the older immigrant generation dies. The rise of the ethnic elec-

Latina glances through Spanish-language magazines at this California newsstand. (Robert Fried)

tronic media may signal a change in this pattern as certain groups assert their identity through the powerful medium of television.

Members of ethnic and minority groups have been quick to take advantage of new opportunities in the electronic media. A number of commercial radio stations throughout the country have long been oriented to and staffed by African Americans or Latinos and have proved important in multicultural advertising campaigns. While commercial radio programs featuring foreign-language popular music and ads have been common for years in large American cities, more ethnic groups, such as those from Central America, have become involved in independent or community-based radio stations to promote more controversial cultural and political perspectives. In the 1970's and 1980's, various ethnic groups used local community access cable television to publicize everything from festivals to public grievances. The late twentieth century has seen the development of entire cable networks devoted to African American and Latino programming. In the early 1990's, Los Angeles had two commercial Spanish-language television stations and one multilingual station that targeted new immigrants with multilingual news, information, and educational programming in mostly Asian and Middle Eastern languages.

SUGGESTED READINGS. Sources on this subject are relatively scarce. The standard work until recently has been Robert E. Park's *The Immigrant Press and Its Control* (1922, repr. 1970). More contemporary books are Lubomyr R. Wynar and Anna T. Wynar's *Encyclopedic Directory of Ethnic Newspapers and Periodicals in the United States* (1976) and Sally M. Miller's edited work, *The Ethnic Press in the United States: A Historical Analysis and Handbook* (1987). Journalistic histories of a few particular groups are available, such as Robert A. Karlowich's *We Fall and Rise: Russian-Language Newspapers in New York City, 1889-1914* (1991) and Frank Del Olmo's "Chicano Journalism: New Medium for a New Consciousness," in *Readings in Mass Communication* (1974), edited by Michael C. Emery and Ted Curtis Smythe.— *Sally M. Miller*

Ethnic press. *See* **Foreign-language press—history**

Ethnic restaurants: Restaurants that specialize in preparing and serving food of an ethnic group's native culture. Ethnic restaurants are most common in urban areas where ethnic populations tend to cluster. Wherever ethnic groups exist in high concentration and in great variety, such as New York City, Los Angeles, and Chicago, there also exist a great variety and concentration of ethnic restaurants.

Ethnic restaurants serve important social, cultural, and economic functions. They are a means of preserving the traditional foodways and festive customs of an ethnic community, serving as the hallmark of ethnic

Advertisement for an Argentinean restaurant in San Francisco, Calif. (Robert Fried)

neighborhoods and as gathering places for weddings, holidays, and other important occasions. As highly visible and accessible symbols of an ethnic group, ethnic restaurants also serve as cultural ambassadors that introduce other Americans to unfamiliar tastes, customs, and cultures in a pleasant, nonthreatening way. Moreover, ethnic restaurants offer important opportunities to workers and entrepreneurs of ethnic groups, especially new immigrants.

come such a staple of twentieth century American life that some are of the fast-food variety, serving Mexican tacos or British fish and chips.

Other restaurants offer less common fare. Greek restaurants might have *gyros*, a sandwich of spicy roast lamb, tomato, and onion on pita bread; *baklava*, a confection of honey, filo dough, and nuts; and Greek salads with feta cheese and olives. Spanish restaurants serve savory *tapas*, small snack-size portions of a va-

African American youth enjoys pizza at an Italian American restaurant. (James L. Shaffer)

Ethnic restaurants serve both well-known and exotic foods associated with the ethnic group's country of national origin. Chinese restaurants specialize in stir-fry dishes, Mexican restaurants feature tortillas and beans, and Italian restaurants are known for their pasta and tomato sauce-based dishes. French restaurants are known for gourmet items such as *escargots* (snails) and frogs' legs, rich sauces, sophisticated atmosphere, and expensive menus. Such ethnic restaurants appear in virtually every part of the United States, and have become so familiar that they may no longer seem ethnic. Indeed, ethnic restaurants have be-

riety of foods, or gazpacho, a cold, tomato-based vegetable soup, followed by the main dish of *paella*, a saffron-based rice and seafood dish. As more Asian, Latino, Caribbean, and Middle Eastern immigrants have settled in the United States and opened restaurants, other Americans have been introduced to Vietnamese pho (beef noodle soup), Salvadoran pupusas (savory turnovers), Jamaican jerk chicken (marinated and highly spiced), and Iranian fesenjon (chicken stew with walnuts and pomegranate juice). Increasing numbers of restaurants also feature traditional African American dishes such as sweet potato pie or African and Afro-Caribbean specialties.

The foods served in ethnic restaurants use spices and special ingredients popular in that culture. For example, Spanish cooking relies heavily on cumin and saffron, Indian on saffron and curries, Hungarian on paprika and garlic, and Thai on chilis and peanuts.

Just as French dining is considered an experience of the French way of life, so it is with other less formal ethnic restaurants. Many try to evoke the atmosphere of their native country not only with food but with interior decoration, the dress (and/or nationality) of the staff, background music or entertainment.

SUGGESTED READINGS. *Eating Out: Fearless Dining in Ethnic Restaurants* (1985) by John F. Mariani is an entertaining and informative guide; *The Art of Eating* (1976) by M. F. K. Fisher blends stories of travel with commentary on various foods. General sources on ethnic cuisine include *Food and Culture in America* (1989) by Pamela Goyan Kittler and Kathryn Sucher and *The Melting Pot* (1986) by Jacqueline M. Newman. In addition, local guidebooks of ethnic restaurants are published for many metropolitan areas.

Ethnic slurs: Insulting terms for groups or individuals based on their race, ethnicity, national origin, or religion. Ethnic slurs are generally considered a reflection of prejudice or racism as they tend to be based on stereotypes; they are also part of some ethnic humor. Such disparaging terms have a long history in the multicultural society of the United States, with one of the first, "redskin," appearing in writing in 1699. By the late 1900's, the use of an ethnic slur was considered sufficiently serious to cause public figures from baseball managers to presidential candidates to have to apologize or resign.

Ethnic slurs are derived from five broad categories of ethnic experience: the proper name of a group; real or supposed physical traits; cultural or religious beliefs and practices; mocking use of a group's native language; or sexual habits or preferences, real or imagined. Each of these categories is seen from the perspective of outsiders, often members of the dominant culture.

Slurs based on a group's name focus on actual or supposed traits, such as the term "Mexican breakfast," for a cigarette and glass of water, referring to the poverty of many Latino immigrants or "African golf," implying the supposed propensity of African Americans for the dice game of craps. A "Chinese fire drill" describes a disorderly or confused situation, to "Jew down" suggests intense bargaining, and to "gyp"

(from Gypsy) means to cheat or swindle.

Physical traits, real or stereotyped, have provided "redskin," "red man," and "red devil" for American Indians, and "white eyes" and "paleface" for whites. Asian Americans have endured "slant eyes" and "slope head," responding with "round eyes" as an insult for non-Asians. African Americans have been called "spade," "darky," "dinge," and "shade," using themselves "whitey," "pink toes," and "white buckra" for whites in reply.

Cultural or religious traits have provided a source of slurs, such as "mackerel snapper" for Roman Catholics. A subcategory plays on names typically associated with ethnic groups, such as Mick for the Irish, Hymie for Jews, Sambo or Aunt Jemima for African Americans, all of which evoke painful stereotypes for the groups involved.

Non-English languages provide the chance for deliberate mispronunciations as in "Ay-rab" or "Eye-talian," while other slurs come from misheard or misunderstood foreign words. For example, the insulting term for Italian Americans, "wop," is said to come from guappo, which means "strong and handsome" in Sicilian dialect.

Sex and sexual orientation have always been a rich source of slurs. Both men and women are identified by crude reference to their sexual organs. Homosexuals have been called "dyke," "homo," "fag," and "queer," responding with the label "breeder" for heterosexuals.

SUGGESTED READINGS. Any study of ethnic slurs must start with Raven McDavid's abridged edition of H. L. Mencken's *The American Language* (1963). Irving Lewis Allen's *Unkind Words* (1990) is a brief but thorough study. Three works by Stuart Berg Flexner provide additional material: *The Dictionary of American Slang* (1975), edited with Harold Wentworth; *I Hear America Talking* (1976); and *Listening to America* (1982).

Ethnic studies movement: Movement beginning in the 1960's to encourage formal teaching about the history, cultural heritage, and contemporary concerns of various ethnic groups. Early vocal proponents of ethnic studies included African Americans and American Indians, who demonstrated that standard public school education focused too heavily on white European Americans. This approach, they argued, shortchanged everyone, especially the children of excluded ethnic groups, who were not able to learn about their own people. In 1972,

Congress passed the American Ethnic Heritage Bill to fund ethnic heritage education and research in public schools. Hundreds of colleges and universities also set up separate African American, American Indian, Asian American, and Chicano studies programs.

Ethnicity: Cultural distinctiveness of a social group sharing common heritage, values, language, and behavior. A sense of common descent and history underlie this distinctiveness, which in turn, forms part of an individual's perception of self-identity. Ethnicity is present in both stratified and unstratified societies and has often been examined in conjunction with race, minority group status, and nationalism, as concepts used in discussing the status and role of groups within society.

Ethnicity is a distinctive component of the population profile of the United States. The variety of ethnic groups represent the diverse cultures and geographical regions that have contributed to American life. Aware of this diversity and sensitive to its overwhelmingly nonindigenous origins, the U.S. Bureau of the CENSUS has been collecting information on ethnicity since 1850. Thirty years later, in recognition of the large proportion of second-generation immigrants, data on the origins of parents were solicited. More recent census questions on ethnicity have focused on eliciting people's self-identity, rather than actually tracing roots, which have become extremely complex over the generations, reflecting intermarriage between ethnic groups.

Ethnic diversity and views on ethnicity have also shaped intergroup relations in American society. These issues underlie the dominance of some groups and the minority status of others. The foundations of these relationships were established by the earliest European immigrant groups and reinforced by various conditions that attended the development of the nation. Intergroup relations have been driven by the competing forces of ASSIMILATION and CULTURAL PLURALISM. Assimilation, often described in terms of the "MELTING POT" THEORY, really involved conformity to Anglo American standards without any significant attempt to absorb cultural aspects of other ethnic groups, especially those of non-Europeans. Most groups of European origin assimilated to the Anglo American pattern in varying degrees over time. Non-European groups such as Chinese, Mexicans, and African Americans, among others, experienced some of the oppression long faced by American Indians and contributed to the growth of the theory of cultural pluralism in which ethnic distinctions are both tolerated and celebrated.

Historical Background. The first European immigrants to the United States, including English, Scottish, Irish, French, Dutch, German, and Spanish people, encountered an indigenous population with whom they shared no common cultural features. This population was collectively labeled "Indians" by the settlers despite the variety of distinctive native cultures with varied levels of development, separate languages, and different types of social organization. The tribes were distinctly different in appearance and culture from the Europeans, and this cultural clash resulted in a series of European assumptions as to the ability or fitness of the tribes to control the land they inhabited. Over time, these assumptions were to constitute the basis of a policy that led to INDIAN WARS, massacres, removal and relocation, and the relegation of Indian groups to minority status.

During the first phase of European settlement, towns functioned as outposts of European cultural expansion through the introduction of the political, social, and economic institutions that were to shape American society. In the ensuing period of struggle and competition, each culture sought to establish its

U.S. Population by Ethnic Background

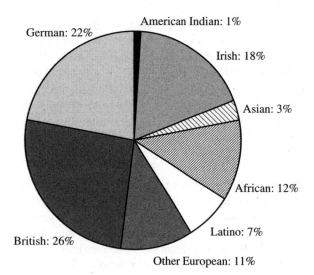

Source: From William C. Lowe, *Blessings of Liberty: Safeguarding Civil Rights.* Human Rights series, p. 62. Vero Beach, Fla.: Rourke Corp., 1992.

Religious organizations like this black Catholic church help to preserve ties in ethnic communities. (James L. Shaffer)

presence in the New World, with British culture eventually dominating and English prevailing as the language of the Colonies. Anglo American ethnicity became the model to which other European groups adapted with varying degrees of success. Efforts to assimilate the indigenous population to this model were less successful for a variety of reasons including resistance on the part of both Anglos and Indians.

The growing prosperity of the nation was fueled by the development of agriculture and by westward expansion. A shortage of labor was compensated for by importing indentured servants from Europe and eventually slaves from Africa. Africans were introduced in large numbers and subjected to severe controls that did not apply to any other ethnic group. Ethnicity, in this instance, as in the case of the American Indians, became a justification for oppression and minority status.

The construction of railroads to facilitate westward expansion in the mid-1800's also required the importation of labor, this time from China. Later, in order to meet the needs of industrial development, European immigration to the cities was encouraged. Mexican and Japanese workers were sought to replace the Chinese in agriculture after the passage of the CHINESE EXCLUSION ACT (1882-1943). Thus, the introduction of many cultural groups into the population was impelled in part by a shortage of workers.

While most immigrants experienced some discrimination and prejudice during their first arrival, some groups continued to experience intensified prejudice over several generations. This prejudice was further compounded by institutionalized discrimination.

The Growth of Ethnic Communities. Official policies have significantly influenced the ethnic composition of the American population. Restrictive immigration legislation limited the size of some groups while liberal policies benefited others. Notwithstanding official encouragement of immigration to fill labor needs, newcomers continued to encounter legal and social barriers. For example, some California laws were designed to discourage the pursuit of occupations such as mining by the Chinese, while in New York, some professions such as banking, law, and medicine were closed to them as well. The JAPANESE AMERICAN INTERNMENT during World War II was based solely on ethnic origin. The distinctive appearance and small population size of the JAPANESE AMERICANS were factors in isolating them, but these alone do not explain the exemption of German Americans from similar treatment as wartime enemies.

The abolition of SLAVERY and the granting of full citizenship to minority groups, in conjunction with the extension of fundamental rights to all Americans regardless of race, color, national origin, or religion, were official measures designed to achieve integration. Yet legislation was no guarantee of altered behavior, and discriminatory practices continued to mark American social relations.

The ethnic composition of the population was determined by other factors besides official policies. The process of territorial expansion through conquest and annexation of lands led to the acquisition of ethnic communities as diverse as the Inuits (Eskimos) and the Mexicans. Variable fertility rates, birth rates, and death rates in these groups affected their size and distribution. Length of stay in the region, availability of economic opportunities, and community ties also played a part in the spatial distribution of ethnic groups.

External forces such as social change in other parts of the world also had an impact on the size and source of as well as the impetus for immigration among various groups. Famine, civil war, political unrest, and religious dissent were some of the forces underlying the large-scale migration of refugees and others. Europe continued to contribute the most until it was surpassed by Asia and Latin America after the lifting of national origins quotas in 1965.

Ethnic Organizations. Social and religious organizations designed to preserve cultural roots and protect the group from discriminatory practices emerged in most ethnic communities. Ranging from MUTUAL AID SOCIETIES to church groups and CIVIL RIGHTS organizations, these institutions helped to define the level of cultural distinctiveness that was to be preserved and

provided a focus for ethnic identification. The preservation of native language, important at first, gave way eventually to celebrations of religious occasions and holidays, the revival of traditional cuisine, and other customs that provided a general sense of community. There are thousands of such ethnic organizations at both the national and local levels, representing virtually every ethnic culture and subculture.

Some ethnic organizations have played a crucial role in bringing about social change and improving intergroup relations. The NATIONAL ASSOCIATION FOR THE ADVANCEMENT OF COLORED PEOPLE (NAACP), for example, helped to draw attention to and address discrimination toward African Americans and sponsored CIVIL RIGHTS LEGISLATION that benefited other groups as well. Similarly, organizations such as the AMERICAN JEWISH COMMITTEE have worked to raise public awareness of issues important to Jewish communities and to foster policies supportive of CULTURAL PLURALISM.

The FOREIGN-LANGUAGE PRESS and ETHNIC JOURNALISM have long provided an alternative to the mainstream media by focusing on group-specific issues, promoting language competence, and encouraging links with cultural traditions and the home country. More numerous during the early years of a group's arrival in the United States, these newspapers, magazines, and broadcast programs continue to present a diverse and unique perspective on events.

Social Impact. The history of settlement in the United States has shown the importance of ethnicity as a determinant of social status and economic power. The pattern of Anglo American dominance that was established during the earliest phase of settlement continued well into the twentieth century. One development was the distribution of population by ethnicity into separate residential enclaves. Many American Indians were already isolated from the rest of the population on RESERVATIONS set aside for them, generally lacking a major economic base. In urban areas, ethnicity underlay the development of enclaves such as CHINATOWNS, Little Italys, Latino BARRIOS, and Jewish and African American GHETTOS. Reflecting both socioeconomic realities, housing discrimination such as restrictive covenants, and cultural comfort zones, these patterns of spatial distribution reflected the problems of ASSIMILATION encountered by the diverse groups.

Accompanying these patterns of SEGREGATION were JIM CROW LAWS and behavioral norms that reinforced separation of racial and ethnic groups in public transport, educational institutions, restaurants, and other public facilities. Attitudinal changes did not always occur with legislative intervention or desegregation orders.

A reverse condition prevailed in cases where ethnicity contributed to one's dominant status in society. A variety of choices and opportunities were available

or Mexican Americans. At times, celebrations have succeeded in breaking down ethnic cultural distinctions, as in THANKSGIVING dinners, which are broadly accepted by Americans of diverse origins. Alternatively, some holidays such as Orthodox EASTER (Greek and Russian), Diwali (South Asian), and Juneteenth (African American) remain unique to an ethnic group.

The Mexican festival Cinco de Mayo has come to be celebrated by Americans of many backgrounds, rather than by Mexican Americans alone. (Robert Fried)

to members of ethnic groups identified with the Anglo American mainstream. Control over the political process, in conjunction with access to educational, economic, and social options provided these groups with a greater measure of security.

Cultural Impact. The presence of ethnic diversity in American society has contributed to a rich tradition of HOLIDAYS AND FESTIVALS. Many ethnic festivals such as ST. PATRICK'S DAY and CINCO DE MAYO have come to be celebrated by the community at large rather than exclusively a specific group such as Irish

While many components of ethnicity have not survived the passage of time, distinctive ethnic foods and cooking as well as music have permeated American culture. The popularity of ethnic dishes such as tacos and pizza in fast-food establishments is itself remarkable. The growing visibility of Middle Eastern pita bread and of Japanese tofu in American stores is a further example of the comfortable coexistence with and wide acceptance of ethnic food in the American diet.

Similarly, JAZZ and GOSPEL music are considered

all-American forms, although they were essentially developed by African Americans. Some musicologists argue that all American popular music is really African American in origin. ETHNIC FOLK MUSIC and FOLK DANCE have come to be widely appreciated as symbols of community and diversity.

Both ethnic cuisine and ethnic arts were strongly promoted by the ETHNIC HERITAGE REVIVAL movement of the 1970's. Spurred by the CIVIL RIGHTS MOVEMENT and Alex HALEY's *Roots: The Saga of an American Family* (1976), many Americans began researching their genealogies and collecting ORAL HISTORIES of their communities. Numerous organizations and publications emerged during this period in which ethnicity was proclaimed as a positive attribute to unite groups of individuals and extend their empathy for members of other ethnic groups. By the 1990's, however, critics of MULTICULTURALISM charged that strong ethnic identities were being used to divide American society and reject a common culture. The role of ethnicity in the lives of groups and individuals remains controversial in American life.

SUGGESTED READINGS. *Multiculturalism in the United States: A Comparative Guide to Acculturation and Ethnicity* (1992), edited by John D. Buenker and Lorman A. Ratner, has several excellent essays on the adaptation process of many of the ethnic groups that comprise American society. Stephen Steinberg's *The Ethnic Myth: Race, Ethnicity, and Class in America* (1981) focuses on the social origins of ethnic values and trends. In *Beyond the Melting Pot* (1963), Nathan Glazer and Daniel P. Moynihan approach the issue of integration from a liberal perspective. James W. Vander Zanden's *American Minority Relations* (1963) argues that American racial attitudes are too deeply rooted in the structure of society for easy solutions.— *Sai Felicia Krishna-Hensel*

Ethnocentrism: Attitude that one's own ethnic group or culture is innately superior to others. Under ethnocentrism, people judge members of other groups by the standards and values of their own group. The term, coined in the early 1900's, was used in the late 1900's to characterize most American textbooks and school curricula, which critics maintained were specifically Eurocentric in outlook, neglecting minority experiences and perspectives. Ethnocentrism is the opposite of CULTURAL RELATIVISM, which sees the inherent value of all cultures and respects their differing perspectives, as well as the general thrust of MULTICULTURALISM.

Eu, March Kong Fong (b. Mar. 29, 1922, Oakdale, Calif.): Health worker, educator, and politician. After receiving her education from the University of California at Berkeley, Mills College, and Stanford and Lincoln universities, Eu worked as a dental hygienist in Oakland public schools. She served in the California legislature from 1966 to 1974 and in 1975 became the first woman of Asian descent elected secretary of state of California. Her many honors include the Outstanding Woman Award from the Women's Political Caucus in 1980. In addition to participating in state Democratic politics, Eu has taken an active interest in social issues and WOMEN'S ISSUES and has been involved in numerous social, economic, educational, and medical organizations in the Bay Area and statewide.

Evangelical and Pentecostal congregations—African American: Religious organizations dating primarily from the early 1900's. Initially three forces combined to shape the conservative religious movement among African Americans: African religions, early Methodism, and the American Holiness movement.

Africans were transported in large numbers to the United States in the seventeenth and eighteenth centuries through the transatlantic slave trade that had grown out of the European-controlled slave industry that had begun in the 1400's. Newly arrived Africans continued to practice their own religious beliefs. African folk religion had no written creeds, liturgies, or holy books and was passed on by oral tradition from one generation to the next through folktales, myths, and legends among the enslaved Africans. The participants in early African American religion were expected to take an active role in the ceremonies. A tradition known as call and response developed in which the storyteller and the audience spoke to one another during a religious ceremony that stressed music and dance. Unlike Western Protestantism, which stresses individual salvation, the African systems stressed that an individual's relationship to God depended on the relations among God, spirits, ancestors, and the community.

Methodism had its origin in England during the 1700's under the leadership of John Wesley and grew in the United States through the efforts of itinerant preachers and the popularity of revival meetings. Charles F. Parham, who established a school in Houston, Texas, in the early 1900's, contributed to METHODIST doctrine by promoting the theological view of total annihilation for sin and the view that individuals

California Secretary of State March Fong Eu at a 1986 press conference. (AP/Wide World Photos)

grow in grace to overcome sin as a result of gaining the Holy Spirit. The latter was considered evidence that an individual was saved.

Parham became a teacher of an African American named William Joseph Seymour, who emerged as the father of the Pentecostal movement. Seymour established the Azusa Mission of Los Angeles, California, in 1906 after experiencing discrimination in Parham's organization and failed attempts to integrate several Holiness churches across the country. The Azusa Mission established a newspaper, *The Apostolic Faith,* in 1906 and spread the movement to more than fifty nations. Seymour's vision was to establish a multiethnic religious movement based on the gifts of the Holy Spirit including speaking in tongues and the sanctification of the saved.

The Evangelicals emerged in the United States in 1942 with the creation of the National Association of Evangelicals. Theologically, evangelicalism differs from Pentecostalism on the issue of the authority of the Bible; Pentecostalists believe that the spirit expresses the living word. The African American experience with Pentecostalism and Evangelicalism, as well as the fundamentalist and charismatic movements, combined traditional European American theology with aspects of African religion and culture, resulting in distinct congregational forms. Because of racism, African American religious denominations developed apart from white denominations.

In 1991, seven out of eight African American church members were either Baptists or Methodists, and there were more than eight million members of black Pentecostal/Apostolic, Holiness, and Deliverance denominations. Two of their denominations, The Church of God in Christ and the United House of Prayer for All People—Church on the Rock of the Apostolic Faith, claimed four million members each.

SUGGESTED READINGS. For further study, see Iain MacRobert's *The Black Roots and White Racism of Early Pentecostalism in the USA* (1988). For the history of modern evangelicalism, see Harry S. Stout's *The Divine Dramatist* (1991). Other useful works are Albert J. Raboteau's *Slave Religion: The Invisible Institution in the Antebellum South* (1978) and John S. Mbiti's *African Religions and Philosophy* (1969).

Evers, Medgar W. (July 2, 1925, Decatur, Miss.— June 12, 1963, Jackson, Miss.): African American civil rights leader. For a decade before his assassination, Evers helped lead the fight in Mississippi to end racial injustice. After service in World War II and graduation from Alcorn A&M College, he began energizing the NATIONAL ASSOCIATION FOR THE ADVANCEMENT OF COLORED PEOPLE (NAACP) as state field secretary in 1954. He publicized civil rights violations and organized boycotts, mass meetings, sit-ins, and demonstrations in Jackson, Mississippi. Evers' activism offended some blacks, and many whites. After an ambush at his home took his life, Evers became an important symbol of struggle in the growing CIVIL RIGHTS movement.

Exclusion acts: Series of state and federal laws that severely limited Chinese immigration to the United States. The CHINESE EXCLUSION ACT of 1882 prohibited the entry of Chinese laborers into the United States for a period of ten years. This act marked the first time that a group had been denied the right to immigrate to the United States on the basis of race or ethnicity. Subsequent legislation extended the ban on Chinese laborers and added new restrictions. These restrictions on Chinese immigration set the pattern for discriminatory immigration legislation restricting arrivals from other Asian countries. The Chinese Exclusion Act was not repealed until 1943, and not until the IMMIGRATION AND NATIONALITY ACT OF 1965 were discriminatory immigration quotas for Asian immigrants abolished.

Exploration and explorers of the New World: Early on the morning of October 12, 1492, Rodrigo de Triana, a sailor on the *Pinta,* shouted from the forecastle, "Land! Land!" After carefully picking their way through the reefs, the captains of the *Pinta, Niña*, and *Santa María* anchored their ships offshore, and Christopher COLUMBUS led a landing party onto the beach of what is now part of the Bahamas. He named the island San Salvador and claimed it for Ferdinand and Isabella, monarchs of Castile. Thus began four centuries of European exploration and settlement of the New World.

Numerous European explorers sought adventure, fame, and fortune in the Americas. But their voyages

Anti-Chinese editorial cartoon from 1883. (Asian American Studies Library, University of California, Berkeley)

went beyond mere geographical exploration. Many involved biological investigation. The flora and fauna of America differed greatly from those of the Old World. Explorers from Columbus to Meriwether Lewis and William Clark encountered species unknown to Europe, from the mighty grizzly bear and the buffalo to foodstuffs such as maize. Exploration also represented a philosophical and religious challenge to accepted beliefs. European theologians and scholars wrestled to understand explorers' discoveries in light of biblical authority, even though the Bible seemed mute about the Americas. Encounters with AMERICAN INDIANS forced Europeans to rethink their definitions of human nature and civilization. Although some Europeans argued for the basic humanity of the native population, the explorers and their successors too often treated the continent's original inhabitants as something other than human. Only with great difficulty did the explorers discard classical and Christian teachings regarding natural slavery and barbarism. Yet the unfolding of America's multiracial, multicultural societies was an inevitable legacy of New World exploration.

Pre-1492 Exploration. In certain respects 1492 did not mark the discovery of America, nor did exploration of the Western Hemisphere begin with Columbus' first voyage. For tens of thousands of years after crossing from Siberia to Alaska via the Bering Strait, proto-Mongoloid immigrants and their descendants had explored and settled the American continents. To these peoples, the AMERICAN INDIANS, the new lands became home, something needing no discovery. The Indians created great civilizations in Mexico, Central America, and the Andes mountains. They adapted to the plains of North America and the pampas of Argentina; to the tropics of Brazil and the Caribbean; to the arid deserts of the Southwest and the woodlands of the East. They developed crops which after 1492 became dietary staples throughout the world, including maize, potatoes, tomatoes, beans, and peanuts.

Other Old World travelers may have preceded Columbus to the New World, although such claims are generally controversial. The identification of Negroid characteristics in the monumental sculpture of the Olmec civilization of Mesoamerica has led some scholars to speculate that the culture's rise depended in part on transatlantic contact with Africa. Other investigators have pointed to possible links between East Asia and the Olmecs or the roughly contemporaneous Chavín culture in the Andes. More radical theorists

have attempted to link the Americas to Phoenicia, Egypt, remnants of Alexander the Great's expedition, the lost island of Atlantis, and the Ten Lost Tribes of Israel. There is no conclusive proof, however, for these theories of cultural diffusion. To counter the diffusionists, isolationists have emphasized the unique contributions of American Indian culture and discounted evidence suggesting significant transoceanic cultural exchange.

Even if the roots of American Indian culture are native to the New World, there was likely some contact with outside cultures. Chinese documents, for example, record voyages to a land called Fu-sang beyond Japan in the Pacific. A large expedition headed by Hui-shen in 499 C.E. reported visiting a place where the inhabitants ate beans and wore bark clothing. Certainly the Chinese were aware of the Pacific currents, which would have facilitated such expeditions, and may have had adequate sailing vessels and navigational skills for the voyage. Diffusionist scholars point to similarities between Asian and American Indian religious images and art forms, as seen, for example, in Cambodian and Maya temple architecture. Yet Chinese accounts tell almost nothing of any visits made to America, and it is difficult to assign the Asians any significant role in the development of American Indian civilization.

One well-documented example of pre-1492 European exploration of the Americas is the Norse voyages. Norse sagas tell of the Vikings' settlement of Iceland and Greenland and visits to more hospitable lands even farther westward. Around 985 C.E. a storm pushed the ship of Bjarni Herjolfsson to the North American coast, although the voyagers did not land. When Herjolfsson finally reached Greenland, his original destination, he described the discovery to Erik the Red, colonizer of Greenland, and his son, Leif Eriksson. In 992 the latter led an expedition to explore the new lands. They spent the winter there, attracted by the abundance of lumber, salmon, and grass for pasturage—all in short supply back in Greenland. Part of their discovery they called Vinland. Another Norse expedition, led by Thorvald, Leif's brother, met American Indians, whom the Norse called *skraelings*. Archaeological excavations at L'Anse aux Meadows, Newfoundland, have revealed unmistakable signs of Viking presence. On the other hand, the Kensington Stone and the Vinland map, which purported to prove Norse presence in North America, were hoaxes. Irregular and superficial Norse contact with North

AMERICUS VESPUTIUS

Italian explorer Amerigo Vespucci (1454-1512) concluded that North and South America were continents and not islands off the coast of Asia; thus, they were named after him. (Library of Congress)

America probably lasted into the fourteenth century but ended around 1350 with the demise of the Greenland settlements.

Some historians have claimed that English and Portuguese ships also reached the Americas prior to Columbus. Fishermen from Bristol sailed westward to locate the legendary Irish Island of Brasil and perhaps reached Newfoundland in 1481. Portuguese expeditions down the coast of Africa may have also revealed the existence of Brazil, but if so they kept it quiet. Even if these discoveries took place, neither had the dramatic consequences of Columbus' first voyage.

Understanding Columbus' Discovery. COLUMBUS set foot on San Salvador on October 12, 1492, convinced that he had reached an island off the coast of Asia. Before his death in 1506, he sailed throughout the Caribbean, searching for the Great Khan and stubbornly refusing to acknowledge his discovery of the New World. Driven by a desire for wealth, power, and adventure, Columbus also had a mystical faith that he was the Christ-bearer, believing that God directed his life and voyages to help Christians acquire the resources and allies needed to expel the Muslims from the Holy Land. He explored most of the main Caribbean islands and visited long stretches of northern South America and Central America. Columbus did not reach North America. His reports, however, inspired an irreversible tide of European exploration, conquest, and settlement in the Americas.

The notion that Europeans were exploring Asian waters off Cipangu (Japan) and Cathay (China) was not easily set aside in the first years after 1492. Most early explorers assumed that the newly discovered lands were parts of Asia previously unknown to Europeans. Backed by Henry VII and assisted by Bristol seamen, the Italian explorer John Cabot sailed to Newfoundland in 1497, perhaps continuing as far south as New England. Nevertheless, he believed the lands to be part of Asia. Setting sail in 1498 with five ships carrying trade goods for Asia, Cabot hoped to follow the coast he had discovered southward until he reached the Spice Islands. He perished and four of his ships were wrecked in a storm. Around 1500, João Fernandes and the Corte Real brothers of Portugal also explored the Newfoundland coast, where they were most impressed with the cod fisheries. While leading a fleet to India in that same year, Pedro Álvars Cabral sailed far enough west in the Atlantic to reach and claim northeastern Brazil for Portugal. Cabral may have had instructions to claim publicly lands which the Portuguese already knew existed.

Gradually, however, some explorers and cartographers began to see the discoveries as a New World rather than Asia-in-the-West. Columbus' own discovery of the mighty Orinoco River during his third voyage indicated that they were sailing along a continent; a mere island could not have produced such a river. Although he concluded that he had discovered the Earthly Paradise, which, according to Saint Isidore, lay in southeastern Asia, others gradually began to think that an unknown continent blocked access to Asia. Voyages by Juan de la Cosa, Alonso de Ojeda, and the Florentine agent and geographer Amerigo Vespucci added knowledge about the eastern and northern contours of South America.

Meanwhile, European geographers and cartographers tried to make sense of the discoveries and descriptions flooding back across the Atlantic. Vespucci wrote insightful reports about the great land mass in the south. In Spain, Rodrigo de Santaella published *Libro del famoso Marco Paulo veneciano* (1503), in which he declared the discovered islands not part of Asia. The following year, Vespucci's *Mundus Novus* appeared in print. Although probably not written by the Florentine, it was likely based on his correspondence and reports and argued that the southern continent was "a new world" and not part of Asia. At roughly the same time, Nicolo Caneri produced a world map which showed not only South America but also Florida, the Yucatán, and the Gulf of Mexico. None were part of Asia. In 1507 at Saint-Dié in Lorraine, under the guidance of printer Martin Waldseemüller, scholars synthesized reports of the explorations to produce a globe, a large world map, and a geographical treatise. The maps depicted northern and southern New World continents with imaginary western shores. Waldseemüller and his associates named the southern continent America in honor of Vespucci, although they omitted it in later charts. This map, printed in an edition of one thousand, strongly contributed to the rejection of Columbus' Asia-in-the-West theory while suggesting a name for the new lands.

Searching for a Passage to the East. When Europeans began to understand the discoveries as new continents rather than part of Asia, the question immediately arose as to whether there existed a passage through which ships could reach Asia. The promise of rich profits in Asia still outshone anything seen in the New World. For a while, the Spanish hoped to find a passage westward from the Caribbean, but each returning expedition made such hope more forlorn. In 1513, Vasco Núñez de Balboa crossed over the Isthmus of Panama, and for the first time Europeans saw the immensity of the Pacific, which Balboa called the South Sea. Some Spaniards decided that the best approach to an Asian route might be to construct ships on the western coast of the new continents. In fact, Spain conducted most of its trade with Asia by such a system. Beginning in 1565, the Manila Galleons plied the waters between the Philippines and Acapulco.

Some thought a southwesterly route around the Americas seemed most likely to reach the Moluccas or Spice Islands. The Spanish crown authorized the expedition of the Portuguese Fernão Magalhães, which departed in 1519 with five ships and a largely Spanish crew. Magalhães, or Magellan, proved the southwest passage possible, passing in late 1520 through the strait which now bears his name at the southern tip of present-day Argentina. Although Magellan died in a skirmish in the Philippines, the Spaniard Sebastián del Cano assumed command and brought a single surviving vessel back to Spain in 1522, loaded with cloves.

Meanwhile, the search for a passage to Asia through North America continued. Portugal already had its route to the Spice Islands via the Cape of Good Hope. Spain was diverted by the riches discovered by Hernán Cortés, Francisco Pizarro, and others. Northern Europeans, however, especially the French, sought a Northwest Passage to Asia to counterbalance the southwestern route pioneered by Magellan. In 1524 the French crown dispatched Italian Giovanni da Verrazano to look for such a passage in the North American mainland. He surveyed the coast from the Carolinas to Nova Scotia and reported that the vast stretches of the Albemarle and Pamlico Sounds seemed a likely route. Whether Verrazano believed his own report is debatable: He seemed more impressed by the majesty of the lands he surveyed and directed his next expedition to Asia via the Cape of Good Hope.

In 1525 Spain launched its only serious effort to discover the Northwest Passage on the Atlantic coast. The crown sent Portuguese Estevão Gómez to explore the waters north of Florida, which the Spaniard Juan Ponce de Leon had already traveled in 1513 and 1521. After ten months and voyaging as far north as the great fishing banks, Gómez returned disappointed. At about the same time, Lucas Vázquez de Ayllón led a group of settlers from Hispaniola to South Carolina, spurred on by the tales of an Amerindian named Francisco Chicora. The group disintegrated because of poor planning, Ayllón's death in 1526, and the failure to find anything that could be turned to profit.

English explorations at this time are poorly documented, making them more mysterious. The *Mary Guilford*, under the command of John Rut, appeared in the Spanish Caribbean in 1527, and its crew told of searching for a Northwest Passage through the icy North Atlantic. Turned back by the ice, the English sailed southward along the Atlantic coast until passing through the Florida Strait and entering the Caribbean.

Europeans lacked knowledge about the width of North America, but during the next two decades they began to realize the vast dimensions of the continent. Between 1534 and 1542, French expeditions under Jacques Cartier explored the gulf and river of St. Lawrence as far as the native town of Hochelaga (Montreal). The French traded for furs and thought they had found gold, but it was only the mineral pyrites. Cartier concluded that the St. Lawrence would not provide access to Asia. The French Wars of Religion largely extinguished that nation's explorations in North America until the seventeenth century and the arrival of Samuel de Champlain.

Spanish Exploration of the North American Interior. In the mid-1530's, the Spanish hoped to find other wealthy civilizations like those of the Nahuas of Central Mexico and the Incas of the Andes. The tales of Álvar Núñez Cabeza de Vaca spurred Spanish exploration of the North American interior. Cabeza de Vaca had been a member of Pánfilo de Narváez's disastrous expedition to the northern Gulf of Mexico in 1528. Landing near Tampa Bay, Narváez and his men pillaged their way north and west. Disease and poor discipline led to the expedition's demise, and the survivors withdrew to the coast. They built rafts and attempted to make their way westward to Mexico, but most perished.

Wrecked on the coast of Texas, Cabeza de Vaca and several others, including a black slave named Estebán, wandered through present-day Texas, New Mexico, and perhaps Arizona before turning south into Sonora. They finally met other Spaniards in 1536. Cabeza de Vaca's trek had taken him from Florida almost to the Pacific coast. His account spoke of rich civilizations, and his listeners imagined golden plunder to rival that of Mexico and Peru.

Cabeza de Vaca went to Spain in 1537 to seek King

A portrait of Christopher Columbus, painted in 1512. (AP/Wide World Photos)

Charles V's permission to explore the interior of the continent. The king, however, had just granted the governorship of Cuba and license to undertake the exploration and conquest of Florida to Hernando de Soto, a wealthy conquistador fresh from plundering Central America and Peru. The invasion of North America became a competition between Soto, the Mexican viceroy Antonio de Mendoza, and Hernán Cortés. After prolonged preparation, Soto landed at Tampa Bay in 1540. Meanwhile, Cortés had desisted, and Mendoza had appointed his young friend Francisco Vásquez de Coronado to lead a large force to investigate Cabeza de Vaca's report.

While Coronado was readying his expedition, Mendoza sent Friar Marcos of Nice and the slave Estebán into the American southwest to verify Cabeza de Vaca's claims. Estebán reached the Zuni city of Hawíkuh and was killed. Following behind, Marcos perhaps only reached the southern border of Arizona but reported he had reached an important civilization, which he fancifully called the Seven Cities of Cíbola. Encouraged by the friar, Coronado's expedition departed for the north in 1540. With it went several hundred Mexican Indian recruits, who also participated in the exploration. Hernando de Alarcón sailed up the Gulf of Mexico to supply and reinforce Coronado's men. Although Alarcón went all the way north to the mouth of the Colorado River, he lost contact with Coronado.

Coronado's force met with little but disappointment. Deceived by Marcos' report, they forced their way into Hawíkuh. Men under García López de Cárdenas trekked northwest to explore the Grand Canyon. Then the force moved eastward near the headwaters of the Rio Grande and wintered around Tiguex among the Pueblos. By this time Coronado was desperate to find treasures to justify the expedition. He let himself be enticed by an Indian whom the Spaniards called Turk, who told of a golden land of Quivira to the east. With Turk to guide them, Coronado led a small force through the Texas panhandle and into Oklahoma and Kansas. They saw the Plains Indians and buffalo but found no gold. Turk paid for his lies with his life. The Spaniards returned to Tiguex and with great disappointment made their way back to Mexico.

In Kansas, Coronado was perhaps only three or four hundred miles from Soto's expedition, although neither was aware of the other. Soto had marauded in northwest Florida and then turned to the northeast. Making its way through Georgia to the Savannah River, his expedition met the queen of Cofitachequi and took freshwater pearls from Indian burial offerings. They were poor plunder but the richest booty Soto was to discover. The force continued into the western Carolinas and Tennessee and south through Alabama, nearly to Mobile Bay. The Creek, Mississippian, and Choctaw cultures were sufficiently advanced that they led Soto to believe that rich civilizations might lie ahead. Soto consequently turned his force north once again, afraid that if he pressed forward to the Gulf of Mexico, his men would desert. Seizing food, porters, and women as they went, the Spaniards marched and fought their way into northern Mississippi. Then they turned west and on May 8, 1541, reached the great river, which they named for the Holy Spirit. Soto crossed the Mississippi River and wandered out into Arkansas before turning southeast again. The group wintered in central Arkansas until Soto finally decided to abandon the quest, despite his reluctance to admit defeat. They rejoined the Mississippi in Louisiana, where Soto died of fever in May, 1542. After a futile attempt to reach Mexico overland through Texas under the command of Luis de Moscoso, the men returned to the Mississippi, built rough boats, and floated downstream into the Gulf. In September, 1543, they reached Pánuco in Mexico.

The Coronado and Soto expeditions dampened Spanish enthusiasm for further exploration of the North American interior. Juan Rodríguez Cabrillo's voyage along the California coast in 1542-1543 likewise found little of enticement. The Spaniards worried when the English under Francis Drake appeared off the coasts of Mexico and California during his circumnavigation of the globe (1577-1580). The Spaniards also wondered how to protect the rumored strait of Anian, which allegedly ran from the Atlantic to the Pacific, from interlopers such as Drake. Florida was nothing more than a strategic outpost. Only in the 1580's did Spanish attention turn again toward the upper Rio Grande Valley, when several small expeditions of missionaries, explorers, and prospectors returned to New Mexico. They were followed by a larger force in 1598 under the command of Juan de Oñate, who was named royal governor of the area. He explored the regions visited by Coronado, including Quivira, and in 1604-1605 made his way down the Colorado River to its mouth. Along the Pacific coast, Sebastián Vizcaíno discovered Monterey Bay in 1602. The Spaniards still failed to find the riches necessary to attract further colonization. The New Mexican settlements soon dwindled, although they did not die out completely.

The Renewed Search for a Northwest Passage. By the late 1500's, the commercial possibilities of a Northwest Passage fascinated the English, spurring further Arctic exploration. In 1576 English investors hired Martin Frobisher to find the passage to China.

Walter Raleigh founded Roanoke on the Outer Banks of North Carolina in 1585, after having explored the area a year earlier. The settlement failed when the attack of the Spanish Armada prevented Raleigh from resupplying the colonists.

Interest in the Northwest Passage reached its high point with the voyages of the English navigator Henry

Illustration that depicts Hernán Cortés (1485-1549) brutally conquering Mexico. (Library of Congress)

Approaching Baffin Island, he entered Frobisher Bay but believed that it was a strait. He concluded that the land to the south was America, while that on the north must be Asia. Frobisher's expedition met and observed Inuit and found what they hoped was gold-bearing ore. The mistaken promise of mineral wealth inspired two more voyages by Frobisher, the last of which attempted but failed to establish a mining colony. Sir Humphrey Gilbert, John Davis, and George Waymouth added knowledge about the northern waters in succeeding years. Eager not only to explore but also to establish strategic settlements in North America,

Hudson. Hired by the English Muscovy company, he first tried to reach Cathay by the northwest (1607) and then by sailing north of Scandinavia (1608). While in the employ of the Dutch East India Company, he explored the Hudson River (Verrazano had discovered its mouth) as far as Albany (1609). His final voyage, again for English investors, led to his discovery of Hudson's Strait, Hudson's Bay, and James Bay. His remarkable discoveries caused his crew great suffering, however, and they mutinied in 1611, abandoning the explorer in James Bay. Upon returning to England, the mutineers claimed that they had found the Northwest Passage. The report buoyed English investors for a while. It proved false, and the northern Europeans concluded that the Far East was more easily reached around the Cape of Good Hope.

English, French, and Dutch Penetration of the Interior. By this time, other Europeans had embarked on the colonization of North America, an enterprise which led to renewed exploration of the Atlantic interior. English interests established colonies at Jamestown (1607) and Plymouth (1620). The latter received great assistance from Squanto, an American Indian seized by George Waymouth's expedition and taken to England, where he lived for several years before returning to America. The settlers also benefited from the information gathered about New England by John Smith. Following up Hudson's voyage and another by Adriaen Block, Dutch investors established posts on Manhattan Island and upriver at Fort Orange (Albany) in 1624-1625. By trading with the Algonquin and especially the Iroquois tribes, the Dutch penetrated the interior.

The French also returned to the St. Lawrence, and eventually explored the Great Lakes and the Mississippi basin. While searching for furs, passage to Asia,

This illustration from a sixteenth century German history book erroneously depicts the character of American Indians, reflecting centuries of misinformation and misunderstanding. (Library of Congress)

and American Indian allies between 1603 and 1615, Samuel de Champlain ventured into northern New York and the Huron territory. He frequently relied on maps drawn by his Algonkian allies. Under Champlain's direction, Étienne Brulé visited all of the Great Lakes except Lake Michigan, reaching the western tip of Lake Superior. He also trekked through Pennsylvania down the Susquehanna to the Chesapeake Bay. Around 1634 Champlain also sent Jean Nicolet westward from Lake Huron to search for another great freshwater lake, which Champlain hoped would offer access to Asia. Nicolet was the first explorer to pass into Lake Michigan and then up the Fox River toward the Mississippi before finally returning. Later in the century, other Frenchmen explored north and south from the Great Lakes. Louis Jolliet and Father Jacques Marquette reached the Mississippi in 1673, aided by a map which Marquette's Indian friends provided. It showed the length of the river and the different peoples dwelling along it. The party traveled down the Mississippi to its juncture with the Arkansas. Convinced that the river emptied into the Gulf of Mexico rather than the Pacific, they then returned to Canada. Meanwhile, from 1669 to 1687 René-Robert Cavelier, Sieur de La Salle, explored the Great Lakes (except Lake Superior); discovered the Ohio River and set up fur trading operations there; made and lost several fortunes; journeyed down the Mississippi to its mouth; and finally died while trying to establish a French colony on the Gulf coast at Matagorda Bay.

Exploration in the Eighteenth Century. Exploration of North America languished during the first half of the eighteenth century, as the European powers consolidated their colonies and as France, Spain, and Great Britain fought to expand their New World possessions. Expelled from New Mexico by the Pueblo Revolt of 1680, the Spaniards soon reoccupied the region. Occasionally, small expeditions of friars and soldiers set up new missions and military outposts in the southwest, especially in the late 1700's. Father Junípero Serra helped lead the effort in Upper California, with the aim not only of converting the American Indians but also of preventing British or Russian occupation of the territory. By 1776 he and his co-workers had established a line of missions all the way to San Francisco. In that same year, fathers Francisco Atanasio Domínguez and Silvestre Vélez de Escalante explored central Utah in search of a route that would link Santa Fe with Monterey. Accompanying them was Bernardo Miera y Pachecho, who made detailed topographical maps of the intermountain West up to the forty-first parallel.

Meanwhile, the Russians, already interested in Siberia, were exploring Alaska and the Pacific coast down to California. Hired by the czar, Danish explorer Vitus Jonassen Bering sailed through the Bering Strait in 1728. In 1741 he and Aleksey Chirikov led a voyage from the Kamchatka Peninsula to Alaska. Grigory Shelekhov founded a permanent settlement on Kodiak Island in 1784 to service the fur trade. Russian influence extended as far south as Fort Ross in northern California.

The British, too, were venturing into the Canadian Northwest, having expelled France from North America in the French and Indian War (1754-1763). Agents of the Hudson's Bay Company had begun to survey the area as early 1690. In 1771-1772 the company sent Samuel Hearne, aided by Chippewa guides, to explore further. The party reached the Arctic Ocean overland by way of the Coppermine River. Competition among fur companies led to more expeditions westward. Scotsman Alexander MacKenzie and French Canadians explored from Lake Athabasca to Great Slave Lake and finally to the Arctic in 1789. In 1792-1793 MacKenzie crossed the continental divide and reached the Pacific coast of Canada. Years later, from 1807 to 1811, David Thompson led a group southwest from Fort Saskatchewan to the Columbia River, establishing Hudson's Bay and British claims to the territory.

Americans to the West. Thompson had been preceded in the Oregon territory by the expedition of Meriwether Lewis and William Clark, sent out by Thomas Jefferson to explore the Louisiana Purchase. The explorers departed from St. Louis in May, 1804, and moved up the Missouri River to its headwaters. Peacefully received by most of the tribes they encountered, Lewis and Clark used the Shoshone guide SA-CAGEWEA, who participated in the journey from the Rockies to the Pacific. Clark took his African American slave York with him. The explorers also drew upon the valuable knowledge of woodsman George Drouillard, who was of French and Shawnee ancestry. Crossing through the Lemhi Pass in mid-1805, Lewis and Clark reached the Salmon River and followed it to the Columbia and the ocean. They returned through the Rockies and reached St. Louis in 1806, bringing valuable information about the geography, flora, fauna, and American Indians of the region.

Other Americans were soon exploring the Rocky

Mountains and the Southwest. In their search for beaver pelts, trappers learned and revealed much about the extent of the great mountain range. Manuel Lisa of Spanish Louisiana organized an American fur company in 1807 for trapping in the Upper Missouri drainage. One of his men was John Colter, who had been a member of the Lewis and Clark expedition. Wandering through Idaho, Montana, and Wyoming, Colter was the first white man to see the wonders which later became Yellowstone National Park. In 1812-1813 Robert Stuart discovered South Pass in central Wyoming. In 1824 Jedediah Smith and other trappers found a good wagon route through the pass. This action opened the way for the Oregon, Mormon, and California trails used by pioneers. In 1824 Jim Bridger visited the Great Salt Lake, although the Domínguez-Escalante party knew of its existence, and trapper Étienne Provost may have seen it earlier. Besides the Americans, trappers from the British North West Company and Hudson Bay Company also continued to roam through the region.

Americans also explored the Spanish Southwest. Zebulon Pike traversed the headwaters of the Arkansas and Red Rivers in 1806-1807, discovered the peak named for him in Colorado, and wandered south in Texas. A scientific party led by Major Stephen Long also investigated the southern prairies in 1819-1821. William Becknell blazed the Santa Fe trail a year later. In 1827 Jedediah Smith, the greatest American trapper and explorer, traveled southwest from the Great Salt Lake to San Diego and then returned by crossing the Sierra Nevada and the salt desert of the Great Basin. In the 1840's Captain John C. Frémont led exploratory parties in the Great Basin and California. Frémont mapped the Oregon Trail in 1842. Frémont could be called the last of the explorers of areas that were eventually included in the continental United States.

SUGGESTED READINGS. Good general surveys of the early exploration of America are David B. Quinn's *North America from Earliest Discovery to First Settlements: The Norse Voyages to 1612* (1977) and Samuel E. Morison's *The European Discovery of America* (1971-1974). Ray Allen Billington and Martin Ridge discuss exploration and offer a massive bibliography in *Westward Expansion: A History of the American Frontier* (1982). Nigel Davies' *Voyagers to the New World* (1979) judiciously considers pre-Columbian contacts between the Old and New Worlds. On Columbus, see William D. Phillips, Jr., and Carla Rahn Phillips' *The Worlds of Christopher Columbus* (1992). Noteworthy for its maps and illustrations as well as excerpts from explorers' own accounts is *The Exploration of North America 1630-1776* (1974) by W. P. Cumming, S. E. Hillier, D. B. Quinn, and G. Williams. Carl O. Sauer, an eminent historical geographer, published two valuable studies of North American exploration: *Sixteenth Century North America: The Land and the People as Seen by the Europeans* (1971) and *Seventeenth Century North America* (1980).—*Kendall W. Brown*

F

Factory work: Factories have traditionally provided a welcome source of employment for immigrants to the United States and, since the world wars, for women and racial or ethnic minorities. They have also been the site of exploitation and danger, a battleground for struggles between labor unions and management, and an inspiration for various types of PROTECTIVE LEGISLATION. Through its development of factories, the United States became the world's premier manufacturing nation during the WORLD WAR I era.

Factories where goods are produced in large quantities are a product of the INDUSTRIAL REVOLUTION. Before the early 1800's, most work was done at home or in small workshops. Mechanization and URBANIZA-TION both facilitated the growth of factories. Machines and a large labor force allowed for the division of labor, in which the manufacturing process was broken down into a series of repetitive steps, each performed by a different worker or set of workers. Early American factories, for example, made clothing and armaments. By the early 1900's, Henry Ford had pioneered the assembly line system for making cars.

Because they hired large numbers of people, in and near cities, factories became, in many cases, a reflection of American diversity. The LOWELL MILL GIRLS in Massachusetts in the early 1800's were an instance of an industry dominated by young women, much like factories of the GARMENT INDUSTRY in New York a

American factories have traditionally provided employment for immigrants of various nationalities. Here, two workers operate a stamping press in a Detroit automotive factory. (Jim West)

century later. Certain industries, such as northeastern steel mills, tended to employ immigrants of certain nationalities; such work was convenient because it did not necessarily require English or job skills so much as brawn and endurance. Factories also drew disaffected farm hands of various backgrounds from the country to the city for work, changing American demographic patterns. After RECONSTRUCTION and especially during the GREAT MIGRATION and WORLD WAR II, many African Americans saw defense factory work as their ticket to equal economic opportunity. Yet many women and blacks hired during the world wars either lost their jobs or found that they were relegated to the most menial positions when peace came and white male workers returned.

In the early years, American factory workers, including children under ten years of age, worked as long as sixteen hours a day, six days a week. Until the early 1900's, their workplaces were often poorly lit, poorly ventilated firetraps posing considerable health and safety risks. One of the events that galvanized the American LABOR MOVEMENT was the TRIANGLE SHIRTWAIST COMPANY FIRE of 1911 in New York that left more than one hundred workers dead. Union leaders and other reformers pressed for shorter working hours and better working conditions, gradually winning through national protective legislation even if they lost particular strikes or work disputes. Some highlights of reform that affected American factory workers were the Keating-Owens Act (1916) to outlaw the abuse of child labor, the SOCIAL SECURITY ACT (1935), the FAIR LABOR STANDARDS ACT (1938), and the Occupational Safety and Health Act (1970), as well as various pieces of CIVIL RIGHTS LEGISLATION.

Factory work has important implications for ideas of CLASS in the so-called "classless" United States. Factory workers are generally labeled working class or blue collar, regardless of their level of skill, because they work with their hands. Yet by the 1970's and 1980's, the higher-skilled among them were securely middle-class in terms of their earning power, with incomes that matched or exceeded those of many people who had better educations or white-collar jobs. In 1989, some 31 million Americans were classified as blue-collar workers, even as the nation's traditional industrial heartland had begun to decline.

The late 1900's saw tremendous changes in factory work. Shifts in the world economy and frequent recessions led to the closure of plants that had once been the lifeblood of a community, creating jobs not only within the factory but also around it in businesses that supplied factory workers with goods and services. As the high-technology and service sectors grew, large manufacturing industries in the Northeast and upper Midwest simply shut their doors, creating virtual ghost towns. Increasing numbers of companies merged with others, moved abroad, or "downsized" their operations, laying off thousands of workers. For example, the end of the COLD WAR and reductions in defense spending struck a blow to aerospace factories in Southern California beginning in the late 1980's, leading to massive unemployment and a state budget crisis. Economists, politicians, and union leaders agreed that "Rust Belt" workers needed retraining and the defense economy needed restructuring to develop peacetime uses of technology.

Factory work, whether packaging potato chips or making computer chips, continues to be important for many Americans, especially the young, new immigrants, and members of ethnic minorities. While the basic repetitiveness and monotony of the job remains, some workers and management have experimented with greater participation of workers in decision making, job rotation, and even workers' stock options to motivate employees and improve the workplace environment.

SUGGESTED READINGS. *Work, Culture, and Society* (1985), edited by Rosemary Deem and Graeme Salaman, compares factory work with other jobs and analyzes the U.S. labor market. See also *Women of Steel: Female Blue-Collar Workers in the Basic Steel Industry* (1983) by Kay Deaux and Joseph C. Ullman. Works on labor unions, such as *The Decline of Organized Labor in the United States* by Michael Goldfield often include discussions of factory work.

Fair Employment Practices Act (1964): Title VII of the CIVIL RIGHTS ACT OF 1964 states that employers, employment agencies, and labor organizations cannot hire, fire, adjust salaries, change conditions of employment, or exclude from membership anyone on the basis of the person's "race, color, religion, sex, or national origin." It also established a five-person EQUAL EMPLOYMENT OPPORTUNITY COMMISSION, appointed by the president and confirmed by the Senate, to oversee its implementation and to set forth procedures for individuals seeking redress for violations. Existing laws giving employment preference to veterans and Indians living on or near reservations are still valid.

Fair Labor Standards Act (1938): Established a minimum wage for workers employed in interstate commerce, a maximum number of hours per week they could work, and a formula for overtime wages. The act defined "oppressive child labor" to mean children working under the age of sixteen or those between sixteen and eighteen employed in hazardous occupations. It established a Wage and Hour Division with an administrator within the Department of Labor to oversee compliance. Certain agricultural occupations were exempted. Individual states could require a higher MINIMUM WAGE or shorter work week than those set forth by this act.

Fair Share Refugee Act (1960): Amended the IMMIGRATION AND NATIONALITY OF ACT OF 1957 concerning alien refugees or escapees. It empowered the attorney general to parole them into the United States if they applied while living in a non-Communist country, as long as they were not citizens of the country from which they applied and were "within the mandate of the United Nations High Commissioner for Refugees." The number admitted was determined by how many refugees had resettled in countries other than the United States between July 1, 1959, and June 30, 1960. The provisions ended July 1, 1962.

Family life: The basic unit of social interaction in the evolution of the human species is the family. In the modern United States, the definition, structure, and function of the family have changed in response to social, economic, and political factors, but its very survival and adaptability attest the importance of family life.

Definition. The question of what defines a family has only arisen with the liberating social influences of the mid-twentieth century. Nevertheless, certain factors are almost universally accepted. In basic terms, a family is two or more people living in or coming from the same household, often related by blood, marriage, or law. Two mates and any children form a nuclear family, while the extended family includes members of related nuclear families such as grandparents, aunts, and uncles.

Within this broad definition, various factors can be added or substituted. These include a shared residence; economic cooperation and interdependence; frequent and intimate communication; shared beliefs, traditions, and attitudes; and trust and love. None of these elements, however, characterizes all families; nor does the absence of any of them disqualify a group of individuals from being considered a family. Rather, the concept of family responds to people's innate need for inclusion and identity; as such, each individual ultimately defines his or her own family.

Families fulfill four primary functions. They satisfy sexual and emotional needs; they form a basic economic unit; they maximize reproductive capability and success; and they provide the means for educating the next generation. Family life refers to the activities, choices, and decisions that characterize the individual's relationship to other family members, and how membership in a family unit shapes and influences the individual's identity. Family life is not determined solely by blood or marital relationships, but also by the complex web of external forces acting upon individual families and society as a whole.

Humans have always established pair bonds: one adult male and one adult female joined for the purposes of mutual protection, shared labor, and the begetting of offspring. Pairs were formed as economic interactions between families. It is only since the chivalric tradition developed in the aristocratic court of thirteenth century France that romantic love has played a key role in forming marriages and families.

As civilized societies became more sophisticated and labor functions more specialized, modern gender roles developed within the family. Males tended to focus on the family's dealings with the external economic world, while females assumed a more submissive role, remaining in the internal world of household and family. The INDUSTRIAL REVOLUTION changed the nature of work, by putting more people in the employ of others at workplaces farther from their homes. Thus, during the nineteenth and twentieth century in the United States, men's and women's specific gender roles were in many ways institutionalized. By the 1950's, the basic nuclear family unit came to be defined as a father, a mother, and their biological offspring. Since that time, both gender roles and the nuclear family have been questioned and adapted.

Family Variations. While the nuclear family is the reality for many families and the ideal for some, it is far from the norm in modern American society. Rather, there are millions of families that are vastly different from this conventional standard; they continue to fulfill the needs of their members and form a strong social unit.

While marriage is traditionally the centerpiece of the family, it is by no means valued equally among the various cultures that comprise the United States. Among the traditional INUITS of north Alaska, for ex-

An important aspect of family life involves educating the next generation. Here, an African American family gathers to help their daughter with her homework. (James L. Shaffer)

ample, marriage is not necessarily viewed as a permanent arrangement. Though the practice is no longer common, on their westward trek across the United States during the nineteenth century, the Mormons incorporated polygamy—the taking of several wives by one husband—as optimal for peopling a new community. Going even further, some Utopian communities, such as the Oneida Community formed in 1848, sought to establish communal marriages involving all adults of the community. In the late 1900's, rising divorce rates, stepparent and single-parent families, especially those with a female head of household, have radically changed the picture of the conventional marriage-based family.

Very different from communal families, though often satisfying the same needs, are extended families. An individual's extended family includes his or her grandparents, grandchildren, aunts, uncles, nieces, nephews, and cousins, as well as their nuclear families. Members of an extended family often fulfill essential family functions. In many Asian cultures, for example, grandparents are revered for their experience and wisdom and granted special privileges and respect. Elders' stories are a traditional connection with the past among African American families. Among Latinos, children often have godparents—usually aunts or uncles—who are deeply involved in their rearing and welfare. Some ethnic groups, including African Americans, American Indians, and Inuits, favor fostering kinship with nonrelated people for the effective education and socialization of children.

In some families, the parent-child relationship does not fit the conventional formula because of circumstances or health. Individuals who are biologically unable to reproduce may become parents through the ADOPTION of children. In 1986, some 104,000 children were adopted in the United States. Some were orphans, came from troubled homes, or had been put up for adoption in their own best interest by single mothers. Beginning with the adoption of Korean War orphans and American Indian orphans in the 1950's, adoption across racial and cultural lines has become commonplace. In 1991, some 9,000 children of foreign birth were adopted. Relationships in adoptive families, while seemingly unconventional, fulfill all the basic functions of family life for both parents and children.

Modern Developments in Family Life. The ever-increasing complexity of modern American society has had profound effects

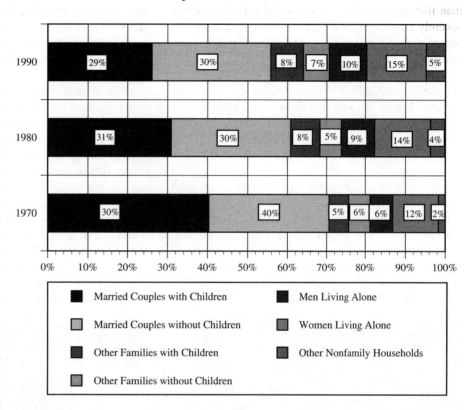

Family Households: 1970-1990

Legend:
- Married Couples with Children
- Married Couples without Children
- Other Families with Children
- Other Families without Children
- Men Living Alone
- Women Living Alone
- Other Nonfamily Households

Source: Adapted from Carol Foster, ed. *Women's Changing Role.* Figure 1.4. Wylie, Tex.: Information Plus, 1992.

on family life. Many changes in family life are related, directly or indirectly, to contemporary FEMINISM and the WOMEN'S LIBERATION MOVEMENT which, since the 1960's, have led both women and men to question traditional gender roles in the family. The legalization of ABORTION in 1973 and the development of BIRTH CONTROL AND FAMILY PLANNING methods have expanded women's options. More women than ever have entered the workplace, and the traditional model of the American household—father as breadwinner, mother as homemaker—has been replaced by the two-income family, in which both partners work and children are often left with relatives or child care providers. In 1980, more than half of American mothers with children under the age of five held full-time jobs, twice the figure for 1970. By 1991, that figure had increased to nearly 70 percent.

For more than a century, the economic forces that traditionally encouraged large families have been changing. The shift from an agricultural to an indus-

trial and service-oriented economy, as well as the expanded educational process mandated by the complexity of modern society, have made large families much less desirable. As a result, between 1790 and 1974, the average household size in the United States decreased from 5.7 persons to 3.4. In 1991, the average household size decreased to 2.63 persons.

The institution of MARRIAGE has also come into question. With the social liberation movements of the twentieth century, premarital sex, once cause for outrage and scandal, has become normative and tolerated. In 1945, the marriage rate for American women was two hundred per thousand; by 1980, it had fallen to half that level. The average age at the time of marriage has also risen for most groups, especially for European Americans between 1960 and 1980. In short, relatively fewer Americans are marrying, and they are marrying later in life.

Marital disruption affects families much more frequently than ever before. DIVORCE rates have risen steadily in the United States during the twentieth century. In 1980, there were 1.2 million divorces, or more than fifty divorces for every hundred marriages. Once severely condemned, divorce has become a more accepted part of family life in most sectors of American society.

Marital instability is especially high among certain populations, including African Americans, American Indians, Puerto Ricans, and Hawaiians. One half of first marriages of African American women in 1980 were likely to be disrupted within ten years. Conversely, Asian American marriages have much higher success rates.

The result of these trends has been an increase in single-parent households, especially among lower-class, urban, and minority populations. In 1960, 10 percent of American families were headed by women; by 1971, the figure had risen to 17 percent. Estimates for 1991 show a total of 8.7 million single-parent households headed by women; of that figure, 3 million were headed by African American women and slightly more than 1 million were headed by Latinas. Of children born to unmarried mothers in 1980, 83 percent were African American. There are also high rates of single MOTHERHOOD among some Latino groups, especially Puerto Ricans, and a remarkable rise in teenage pregnancies, especially among LATINAS, since the 1980's.

High divorce rates have led to an increase in remarriage. As a result, many families consist of a complex pattern of relationships, including stepparents, stepchildren, and half-siblings. Many individuals have not one but several nuclear families, which can either create family stress or offer more possibilities for the satisfaction of family needs.

The cultural diversity of the United States has resulted in a steady increase in families that bridge different communities and ethnic groups through INTERMARRIAGE. By 1988, more than 30 percent of American Jews who married did so with non-Jews, up from 2 percent in 1900. In 1990, more than 3 percent of births were to multiracial couples.

Latino culture encourages close ties between extended family members. This San Antonio, Tex., family includes a grandfather, a father, a mother, and three children. (James L. Shaffer)

Other variations in family patterns are found in homosexual communities. The GAY AND LESBIAN RIGHTS MOVEMENT has demanded the validation of same-sex partnerships and recognition of their legitimate functions. While homosexual marriages have not been recognized anywhere in the United States, increasing numbers of homosexuals have openly established households, often based on the traditional heterosexual model. They adopt children or beget them through outside sexual partners, and some jurisdictions legally recognize such partnerships for purposes of custody, inheritance, or medical insurance.

Contemporary American lifestyles have imposed other stresses on family relationships. Improved communications and transportation combine with employment and educational opportunities to disperse even members of conventional nuclear families. In such families, traditional family occasions, such as weddings, births, baptisms, confirmations, bar mitzvahs, graduations, reunions, and funerals, assume an even greater importance in maintaining and strengthening family ties.

Public Policy and Politics. During the 1980's and 1990's, the issue of the role of the family in American life and "traditional family values" entered the realm of political debate. Concerned over growing social problems such as crime, drug abuse, and teenage pregnancy, many people—especially members of the religious right—lay blame on the breakdown of the traditional nuclear family unit and the loss of the values they believed it encouraged.

The "family values" cited in political debate included the institution of heterosexual monogamous marriage; respect for parental authority; clearly defined, traditional gender roles; the strict instilling of religious and moral values; and stability. Proponents of these values have opposed sexual liberation, the women's movement, DIVORCE, the GAY RIGHTS MOVEMENT, freedom of artistic expression, open marriage, and certain forms of legislation.

Under President Jimmy Carter, 1980 was proclaimed the Year of the Family. The White House Conference on the Family subtly redefined its subject from "the family" to "families," thus refocusing the debate from a perceived norm to the relative diversity found in American family life.

During the presidential administrations of Ronald Reagan and George Bush, however, the "family values" debate was defined in largely cultural, categorical terms. The Republican presidents aligned themselves with Christian CONSERVATIVES, fighting against the public funding of potentially offensive art and allegedly antifamily images and characters in the mass media. The REPUBLICAN PARTY took up the "family values" bandwagon during the 1992 presidential election until the DEMOCRATIC PARTY attempted to redefine the debate under candidate Bill Clinton. The Clinton Administration committed itself to developing a new, pro-family policy in the areas of welfare reform, CHILD CARE, education, health care, housing, employment, and, more broadly, the environment.

Proposed legislation dealing with MARRIAGE, sexuality, education, and CHILDREN'S RIGHTS contribute to ongoing redefinitions of family relationships. While family life in the contemporary United States starkly contrasts with its historical precedents or that of families in smaller, nonindustrialized societies, American families in all their variety continue to provide the basic support and sense of identity that all people need.

SUGGESTED READINGS. For further discussion of the family in contemporary American culture, see *The War Over the Family* (1983) by Brigitte Berger and Peter L. Berger; *What's Happening to the American Family?* (1981) by Sar A. Levitan and Richard S. Belous; and *The Changing Family* (1973) by Betty Yorburg. Statistical surveys and discussions can be found in *American Families and Households* (1987) by James A. Sweet and Larry A. Bumpass, based on the U.S. Census of 1980, and *The Nation's Families: 1960-1990* (1992) by George Masnick and Mary Joe Bane.— *Barry Mann*

Family planning. *See* **Birth control and family planning**

Family planning services: Services offered to couples and individuals to assist with both fertility enhancement and BIRTH CONTROL. The main thrust of family planning services is the avoidance of unwanted pregnancies among both married and unmarried women, and the primary services offered include the dissemination of information, counseling, contraceptives, sterilization, and ABORTION.

While primarily a medical concern, family planning touches on economic, racial, sexual, environmental, and moral issues as well. A number of political issues have surrounded family planning services over the years. In the 1960's, many African Americans grew suspicious of what some viewed as the family plan-

Margaret Sanger (center) was a leading figure in the effort to provide family planning and birth control information to American women in the early 1900's. (AP/Wide World Photos)

ning "establishment" because of its white middle-class makeup and its early association with the eugenics movement, whose efforts to breed a superior race smacked of racism. Controversies over the general liberalization of sexual attitudes have caught family planning providers between the need to serve and educate underage and unmarried populations and charges that sex education fulfills a particular liberal political and moral agenda.

History. In colonial America and the early United States, the concept of birth control was considered immoral, even within marriage. The PURITAN tradition rendered any nonprocreative sexual activity unacceptable. Such activity certainly took place, but the nation's religious, governmental, and social institutions officially condemned it.

In 1831, Robert Dale Owen wrote the first American tract on birth control, entitled *Moral Physiology.* In it he envisioned a conventional family with fewer, better-nurtured children. His essay initiated an ongoing national debate on the moral and practical aspects of contraception.

During the nation's early period, ABORTION was not a public or legal issue. Though the first antiabortion statute appeared in Connecticut in 1821, abortions were widely available in the United States through the 1860's. Between 1840 and 1880, the abortion trade became increasingly commercialized. Abortion became a common means for married women to limit family size, and newspapers carried advertisements for clinics, instruments, and abortion inducing substances.

In 1847, the American Medical Association opposed the use of abortion for birth control. By the 1870's, the growing influence of the Catholic church and the declining birth rate among native-born Americans (concurrent with massive waves of European immigration) contributed to widespread concern about the easy availability of abortion and other forms of birth control.

Anthony Comstock, a young Civil War veteran outraged at the proliferation of PROSTITUTION, gambling, drinking, and other vices, began a campaign against obscenity. In 1872 and 1873 he was instrumental in the passage of national laws prohibiting contraceptives and the mailing of obscene matter, including birth control information. The Comstock Laws, which stayed on the books well into the next century, effectively curtailed the public dialogue about family planning. By 1910, every state had laws against abortion.

Margaret Sanger and Planned Parenthood. In 1909,

Margaret SANGER, a thirty-year-old housewife and mother from Hastings-on-Hudson, New York, appeared on the scene. Drawn to New York City, she worked among its poor women and came to know their plight. She became involved in the prewar socialist movement and worked with the well-known anarchist Emma GOLDMAN. Sanger shared Goldman's concern for the sexual emancipation of women, but while the latter promoted a wide agenda of social transformation, Sanger focused on the problems of poor, urban, married women. This led her to champion the need for readily available BIRTH CONTROL.

Flouting the Comstock Laws, Sanger promoted birth control information and materials at public meetings and in 1914 published a pamphlet called "Family Limitation," in which she openly recommended the use of contraceptives. Knowing that poor women must be reached in their own communities, Sanger opened the first family planning clinic, in the Brownsville section of Brooklyn, New York, in 1916. The clinic offered sex counseling and information on birth control techniques. Late in 1916, however, the clinic was closed, and Sanger was arrested. Tried in early 1917, she was sentenced to thirty days of imprisonment.

Her resolve was strengthened, however, and she soon founded the American Birth Control League. As Sanger was not a physician, the medical and scientific basis of her work was a constant source of criticism. In 1918 she struck a precarious alliance with the medical profession, which wanted the income that could be generated from family planning in their private practices, and eugenicists, who were disturbed by the uneven birthrates among the nation's socioeconomic populations. The medical and scientific establishments then conferred upon the American Birth Control League a legitimacy that it could not have attained alone.

In 1923, Sanger convinced Dr. Dorothy Bocker to open a private medical clinic, the Clinical Research Bureau. Over the next decade, the bureau served thousands of patients and offered a model for other such clinics. In 1930, in the heart of the GREAT DEPRESSION, Sanger obtained funding to open a clinic in Harlem, the impoverished African American community in northern Manhattan. Birth control clinics staffed by doctors were opened across the South in the 1930's, again with the support of local white politicians eager to curb the birthrate among poorer African Americans.

In 1938, the American Birth Control League and the Clinical Research Bureau merged to form the Birth

Faye Wattleton (right) was the first African American to serve as president of Planned Parenthood (1978-1992). (Library of Congress)

Control Federation of America. In 1942, the organization's name was changed to the PLANNED PARENTHOOD FEDERATION OF AMERICA, a name less suggestive of sexuality. Though she was the organization's honorary president, Sanger objected to the name change; she had always favored a direct and radical approach.

In the ensuing years, Planned Parenthood grew into one of the major family planning service providers in the country and continued Sanger's fight for more liberal laws and attitudes. In 1986, the organization included two hundred affiliates and an international wing, and it served more than a million American women annually.

Practices and Services. In the 1960's, the emergence of oral contraceptives, the accumulation of sociological data on family size and poverty, and the growing awareness of global overpopulation led to federal funding of family planning services and clinics. The Supreme Court's 1965 decision in *Griswold v. State of Connecticut* asserted the individual's right to privacy in the use of contraceptives. In 1966 and 1969, presidents Lyndon Johnson and Richard

Nixon both endorsed birth control in speeches to Congress, and in 1972 the Supreme Court determined that all individuals, including unmarried people, have the right to family planning information.

Family planning encompasses a variety of procedures and technologies. ABORTION, one of the most common, is usually accomplished through a technique known as dilution and curettage. With advances in technology for increasing the viability of premature infants—even those born as much as three months early—second- and third-trimester abortions are increasingly rare. In 1985, 90 percent of all abortions were performed in the first thirteen weeks of pregnancy.

Contraceptive technology has expanded since the 1960's. The birth control pill has simplified contraception for many women; while causing certain side effects, it is still one of the more popular methods. A "morning-after" pill known as RU-486 was developed in France in the late 1980's and made available in a number of countries, but it encountered strong opposition in the United States. Diaphragms and intrauterine devices are other forms of contraception available to women. With the spread of sexually transmitted diseases, especially the ACQUIRED IMMUNE DEFICIENCY SYNDROME (AIDS) epidemic, during the 1980's and 1990's, the use, acceptance, and availability of traditional condoms have become pervasive.

Tests for both pregnancy and sexually transmitted diseases (STDs) are available from most family planning service providers, augmented by sexual and psychological counseling. Counseling quality is uneven, with private physicians and Planned Parenthood facilities generally offering the best counseling and follow-up.

An increasingly frequent procedure—the most popular among Americans over thirty—is sterilization. For men, this entails a vasectomy, a surgical excision that ties off the excretory ducts of the testes. For women, it is tubal ligation, in which the oviducts or fallopian tubes are tied. Most doctors require spousal consent before performing such operations. Sterilization has the lowest failure rate of all methods of birth control.

Other, more complicated procedures, primarily for fertility enhancement, are offered by specialists. They include artificial insemination, in vitro fertilization, artificial wombs, embryo transfer, and arrangements for surrogate motherhood.

In the United States, family planning services are offered through a variety of channels. Health care in general is primarily provided through private practice physicians, many of them specialists, and family planning services follow suit. In 1985, 53,000 general and family practitioners offered office-based family planning services, and 23,000 obstetrician/gynecologists dealt specifically with women's reproductive health.

The abortion debate has focused attention on the range of family planning services offered at federally funded clinics. Here demonstrators march in support of the proposed Freedom of Choice Act in 1993. (Sally Ann Rogers)

Predictably, private practice physicians are used by middle-class and upper-class clients; women who cannot afford such care—often less educated, urban, unmarried, or minority women—go to family planning clinics. Managed by a variety of organizations and jurisdictions, clinics offer general services or refer patients elsewhere for special needs. Clinics run by public health agencies at the state, county, or municipal level serve 40 percent of family planning patients. Community, neighborhood, and women's centers account for another 21 percent of patients, and Planned Parenthood for 28 percent. Many clinics are located in lower income areas alongside other medical services and provide outreach into the surrounding community.

On the federal level, family planning policy is handled by the Office of Family Planning in the Department of Health and Human Services. The Food and Drug Administration is charged with the testing and approval of contraceptives. In the private sector, family planning service providers are organized in the National Family Planning and Reproductive Health Association, and foundations such as the Population Council and the Population Association of American contribute to policymaking and research.

The Abortion Debate. The prime example of the controversies that have embroiled American family planning services is the question of ABORTION, which has become a divisive social and political issue during the last half of the twentieth century. In the 1950's, the family planning establishment joined with feminist and civil rights groups to push for abortion law reform. In the 1960's, forty-nine states and the District of Columbia still classified abortion as a felony; in New Jersey it was a misdemeanor.

The prohibitions did not prevent abortions, but they did make them more difficult and dangerous. Many women would attempt abortions on themselves; others would resort to abortionists of dubious qualifications. Legitimate physicians who performed abortions did so at great personal and professional risk. Only wealthier women could afford the research, travel, and fees that would guarantee a safe and confidential abortion in this restrictive political climate.

In 1967, Colorado passed legislation allowing abortion in certain circumstances, and North Carolina and California soon followed suit. By 1970, eleven states had legalized some types of abortion. New York, Alaska, Hawaii, and Washington allowed abortion on request; New York became a mecca for women with unwanted pregnancies since it had no residency requirement for the procedure.

In 1973, the Supreme Court decisions in *ROE v. WADE* and the less-publicized *Doe v. Bolton* established a woman's right to terminate an unwanted pregnancy under the privacy rights construed from the Fourth Amendment to the U.S. CONSTITUTION. The decisions, while establishing the judicial legality of abortion, did not clearly articulate reproductive rights, nor did they have the legislative precision of statutory law. Yet Congress has always left this very volatile issue to the courts.

During the 1970's and 1980's, abortion became a central polarizing issue in congressional and presidential campaigns. Organizations grew up on both the "pro-life" and "pro-choice" sides, pitting the conservative, often Christian right against the liberal left and leading to heated debate and encounters. In 1987, 50 percent of American abortion providers and 80 percent of the large urban clinics reported experiencing some form of violence or harassment.

The abortion debate has placed attention and restrictions on the availability of various types of abortion. During the Reagan and Bush administrations, attempts were made to curb the use of federal funding for abortions, the types of counseling offered, and the availability of services to minors. The election of President Bill Clinton in 1992 promised a more liberal approach to abortion policy in the administrative, legislative, and judicial arenas.

SUGGESTED READINGS. An excellent source on the history of American family planning services is James Reed's *The Birth Control Movement and American Society: From Private Vice to Public Virtue* (1978). Likewise, Madeline Gray's biography *Margaret Sanger* (1979) gives a good account of Sanger and the birth control movement. *The Law Governing Abortion, Contraception, and Sterilization* (1988) by Irving J. Sloan and *Pregnancy, Contraception, and Family Planning Services in Industrialized Countries* (1989) by Elise F. Jones et al. are straightforward, highly factual profiles of modern law and practice. Finally, Carole Joffe offers an inside view of family planning services in *The Regulation of Sexuality: Experiences of Family Planning Workers* (1986).—*Barry Mann*

Farm labor. *See* **Migrant workers**

Farmer, Fannie Merritt (Mar. 23, 1857, Boston, Mass.—Jan. 15, 1915, Boston, Mass.): Cookbook author. After attending the Boston Cooking School in 1887, Farmer became assistant principal. In 1896 she published *The Boston Cooking School Cookbook*, which sold almost four million copies. In 1902 she founded Miss Farmer's School of Cookery, offering nutrition and diet advice. In 1904 she published *Food and Cooking for the Sick and Convalescent*. She lectured regularly on nutrition and cooking and wrote a column in *Women's Home Journal*. While her best-selling cookbook made her a household name, Farmer's most important contribution was her emphasis on nutritional value in cooking.

asserts that by leaving traditional family roles, feminists only make themselves and others around them unhappy.

Farrakhan, Louis Abdul (Louis Eugene Walcott, b. May 11, 1933, New York, N.Y.): Leader of the NATION OF ISLAM. Farrakhan, who was reared in a middle-class black family in Boston, converted to the Black Muslim faith in 1955. He steadily rose in the ranks of the Nation of Islam, became Malcolm X's assistant in Boston, and was appointed to replace Malcolm as head of the Harlem mosque. When MALCOLM X left the Nation of Islam,

Louis Farrakhan has attracted many African Americans to the Nation of Islam but has also provoked controversy for his nationalist rhetoric. (AP/Wide World Photos)

Farnham, Marynia (Sept. 29, 1899, Red Wing, Minn.—May 29, 1979, Brattleboro, Vt.): Antifeminist sociologist and psychiatrist. Farnham first set up private practice at the New York Psychiatric Institute. She directed the Traveling Child Health Clinic of the New York State Department of Health (1933-1934); directed psychiatric services at The Children's Village in Dobbs Ferry, New York (1953); and taught psychiatry at Columbia University (1956-1960). She is best known for her antifeminist book, *Modern Woman: The Lost Sex* (1947), written with Ferdinand Lundberg, in which she

Farrakhan bitterly denounced him. After ELIJAH MUHAMMAD's death in 1975, his son Wallace Deen Muhammad transformed the Nation of Islam to conform to traditional Islamic beliefs and opened the sect to all races. Farrakhan maintained his allegiance to the sect's original teachings, became leader of a resurrected Nation of Islam, and began publishing the newspaper *The Final Call*. Although he has alienated many middle-class Americans with his racist and anti-Semitic comments, Farrakhan began to make conciliatory overtures to Jewish leaders and black civil rights leaders during 1993.

Fashion: American fashion varies according to the gender and age, as well as the geographic, ethnic, racial, or class origins of the wearer. Experts agree that a distinctive American style in dress came into existence gradually following the European conquest. Early encounters between Europeans and American Indians influenced the evolution of American fashion, as did the social, political, and religious backgrounds of the successive waves of colonists in the seventeenth and eighteenth centuries. The rigorous demands of pioneer life created fashions that were less formal and restrictive than those of Europe.

While European immigrants of the nineteenth and early twentieth centuries arrived with their ethnic costumes on their backs, their eagerness for ACCULTURATION soon led them to abandon their traditional dress for the latest in New World fashion. With the emergence of the developing nations following World War II, the increase in American tourism to non-European destinations, as well as the increase in immigration from Asia, South America, and the Caribbean, awareness and appreciation of cultural diversity has had a significant impact upon the development of American fashion.

American Indian Influence and the Spanish Southwest. The earliest encounters between Europeans and American Indians produced some adaptations in attire on both sides. While the Spanish explorers of Columbus' maiden voyages encountered members of the Carib tribe whose costume consisted of little more than loincloths, the later conquistadors of Mexico, Central America, and South America encountered the highly advanced civilizations of the Mayas, Aztecs, and Incas, as well as the PUEBLO and NAVAJO nations. The costumes of these people were highly advanced, extremely colorful, and uniquely functional in design. For the most part, they were made of cotton.

From the beginning, many Spanish settlers adopted with some modifications the fashions of the Indians they encountered. By the twentieth century, the evolution of fashion and the movement toward dress reform, moreover, saw the adaptation of many South and Central American tribal fashions by men and women of European extraction, all over the globe, particularly for summer and recreational wear. The "peasant" skirts and blouses of the California Style of the 1940's and later years derive from the dress of Indian women of the Spanish Southwest, as do the sundresses, sandals, and bright colors of contemporary California fashion.

These rodeo spectators have adopted attire stereotypical of the cowboys of the American West—leather boots, ten-gallon hats, and denim blue jeans. (Elaine S. Querry)

Spanish settlers also influenced the evolution of American fashion in the Southwest and in California, as they brought to New Spain fashions influenced by centuries of Moorish dominance. The black lace mantilla or full-length shawl that became an obligatory accessory for young Latino women derives from the Moorish tradition of enveloping single young women in black from head to toe in public. The sombrero, from which the Stetson and "cowboy" hats were adapted in the mid-nineteenth century, is similarly of Spanish origin, dating to late Roman antiquity. Boots were likewise an indication of the Spaniard's station in life and the virtuosity of Cordovan tanners and bootmakers was legendary in the courts of Europe even prior to Columbus. The highly detailed leather incision work of these artisans has been retained in the elegance of modern western "cowboy" footwear, and in the hand-tooled elegance of distinctively "western" belts, wallets, and other leather goods.

French, Cavalier, and Frontier Fashion: The South and Central United States. The first encounters between the American Indians of the Atlantic Coast and the French took place in the maritime provinces of modern Canada in Newfoundland, New Brunswick, and Nova Scotia, and in the Northeast and North Central territories of the present-day United States. As French trappers and traders explored the interior waters of North America, the interaction and exchange of fashion with their Indian hosts accelerated. The French explorers learned native tanning processes and began to adapt French clothing style to leather and fur. Gradually they fashioned what became the frontier style: fringed leather shirt and overcoat; low-slung, wide-brimmed leather or distinctive raccoon-skin hat; fringed leather trousers; and moccasins or boots.

Significantly, the most "American" of all fashion materials, blue denim or *serge de Nimes*, was an early import from France, where it was the fabric of choice of the southeastern French peasantry because of its durability. Denim was itself an improvement upon Genoan fustian (gene or jean). It is an appropriate footnote to the multicultural nature of American style that the German Jewish immigrant Levi Strauss, on his way to the gold fields of California, carried with him a carload of this cheap French material. He designed trousers fashioned after the frontier leggings of the French trappers, riveted together with copper fastenings and stitched with orange thread, thus creating blue jeans, the foremost article of clothing associated with modern American fashion throughout the world.

With the advent of the French, coastal and inland Indians began to adopt European fashions. When the first colonists from England arrived in the 1600's, they encountered many Indians clothed in linen shirts and trousers that had been traded or purchased from the transient French traders and fishermen.

With the arrival of French women colonists, the fashions of Paris came to American shores. French planters and their wives, like their English counterparts on the Atlantic Coast and the Gulf territories, adopted the fashions of the French court and the Cavaliers. Elegance in dress became the rule. French superiority in textile manufacture and cloth-dying led, in turn, to the importation of floral print textiles and Belgian lace, creating a taste for luxury that has always distinguished southern women's fashion. Brocaded vests for men, elaborate cravats or neckties, and elegant shirt design are three vestiges of early French influence upon the fashion preference of many southern men—a style that sets them apart from their counterparts in the North, Midwest, and West.

Finally, the dress of the French peasants of southern France of the seventeenth century affected the dress of the African American slaves of the South of the same period. As fashion conscious as their owners, African Americans modified and embellished their garments to reflect their own fashion preferences and developed as distinctly regional a sense of style as the Europeans and Indians of the South.

New England and the Virginia Territory: The Northeast Experience. The earliest encounters between the indigenous peoples of the Northeast from North Carolina to Maine with the English came later than those with the Spanish and French. Because of their religious beliefs, the English settlers of New England brought with them the extreme Calvinist bias toward fashion that prevailed in the Netherlands, France, and England, where religious dissent was outwardly manifested in simplicity of dress. The seventeenth century in Europe saw the height of monarchical, baroque affluence, which resulted in the elaborate court dress of the French, Spanish, and English courts. This elegance was closely associated with the Roman Catholic church, and dissenters of every class adopted the sober dress associated with the early Pilgrims and PURITANS.

The settlers of the Virginia Company, on the other hand, were Cavalier or Royalist in their sympathies, and they followed French and English Cavalier fashion. Indeed, they imported their clothing directly from Europe until the outbreak of the American Revolution. Their fashion preferences, therefore, conformed almost exactly to those of the French settlers in the Carolinas and Gulf states, as did those of their slaves. Even after the revolution, life in Virginia and the Carolinas imitated, as much as possible, the country life of the English gentry, and fashion tastes evolved accordingly with much focus upon proper dress for the hunt and the assembly.

The Puritans, on the other hand, passed sumptuary laws to protect themselves from the insidious influence of the Cavaliers immediately upon their arrival in New England. Thus they restricted the use of certain materials, such as brocade, silver, and gold, and dictated that all persons be clad in dark colors, white, or gray. They prohibited lace, frills, buckles, and jewels. Similar customs of choice, rather than statute, characterized the fashions of other dissenting immigrant groups such as the QUAKERS and the BAPTISTS. This Calvinist or Protestant conservative fashion taste was the rule among the other Protestant European immigrant groups of the seventeenth and eighteenth centuries who settled along the Atlantic Coast and followed the preferences of the Puritans in dress. In the nineteenth century the MENNONITE and AMISH peoples of Pennsylvania put a voluntary stop to the evolution toward modernity in dress, thus overcoming the descendants of the early English immigrants. Out of this dissenting Protestant tradition of restraint, many fashion historians believe, grew the East Coast preference for dark, staid, conservative dress.

ful mackinaws, headgear, and footwear of their Indian guides, if only for their leisure activities. Variations and assimilation of some of these fashions led, ultimately, to the formation of the "preppy" style.

Twentieth Century Multicultural Fashion Trends. American fashion has continued to develop somewhat along regional lines, absorbing the multicultural influences that characterized it from the beginning of European colonization. For the most part, fashion history

These Amish children of Pennsylvania display the consciously conservative "plain" dress first adopted by their German-born ancestors. (Pennsylvania Dutch Visitors Bureau)

This conservatism in dress prevented settlers in the Northeast from adapting any American Indian fashions for their own, since most of the indigenous tribes dressed in little more than loincloths and ceremonial clothing. Indians who remained in the East had to conform to Puritan sumptuary laws. Not until the nineteenth century when the merchants of Boston trekked to the Maine woods for hunting, fishing, and other outdoor activities did the Puritan rejection of Indian fashion soften. There white people adopted the color-

in the twentieth century has been a study in cultural ASSIMILATION. The great waves of immigrants from southern and Eastern Europe in the late nineteenth and early twentieth centuries cast off their distinctive native costumes for "American" fashions as soon as they could, reserving traditional dress for ethnic national holidays or parades.

With the invention of the motion picture and television, however, the national acceptance of new trends in fashion accelerated. Many new styles sprang from a new multicultural awareness. In the 1960's, for example, the CIVIL RIGHTS MOVEMENT awakened in African Americans an intense interest in African fashion, which had been suppressed when their slave forebears were forced to conform to the dress codes imposed upon them by their owners. Many African Americans

African fashion influences such as a kente cloth headdress and colorful bead necklace complete the outfit of this participant in New York City's annual African American Day parade. (Frances M. Roberts)

ceased such practices as straightening their hair and lightening their skin and began to wear fashions of African derivation, such as dashikis and bold *kente* cloth fabrics. In the 1980's and 1990's, African American HIP-HOP CULTURE produced more distinctive, brightly colored clothing, which also found acceptance outside the black community.

The increase in Asian and Latino immigration after the 1960's coincided with an increasing influence of Asian and Latino styles on mainstream American tastes. Two examples were the popularity of clothing made of handwoven imported Guatemalan fabric, and the intricate *pan dau* needlework made by Southeast Asian refugees that was prized for dress and home

decoration in the 1970's and 1980's. The "ethnic look" remained popular with American fashion designers seeking new directions in the 1990's.

SUGGESTED READINGS. A survey of two hundred years of fashion is presented in Katherine Grier's "Men and Women: A History of Costume, Gender, and Power," in *Journal of American History* 78 (December, 1991), pp. 988-992. For a valuable article on African American fashion history and modern multicultural trends, see Rosemary Bray's "Reclaiming Our Culture," in *Essence* 21 (December 1990), pp. 84-86. A valuable history of fashion in the New World through the 1960's is R. Turner Wilcox's *Five Centuries of American Fashion* (1973). Other sources include *Fashion Power: The Meaning of Fashion in American Society* (1981) by Jeanette C. Lauer and *Changing Styles in Fashion: Who, What, Why* (1989) by Maggie Pexton Murray.—*Barbara Langell Miliares*

Federal assistance programs: The United States has a complex system of 1,288 federal assistance programs administered by fifty one agencies of the federal government. Despite the large number of assistance programs, 36 million Americans (14.2 percent of the population) live at or below the poverty level. POVERTY has a disproportionate impact on minorities: 32.7 percent of African Americans, 28.7 percent of Latinos, and 28 percent of American Indians live in poverty. Poverty is also especially acute among Vietnamese Americans, Samoans, and Alaska Natives. The persistence of poverty reflects the fragmented and uneven structure of public assistance in the United States. The nation has a divided income security system that addresses the needs of some members of the population reasonably well (especially older Americans and the middle class), while failing to provide adequate assistance to other groups (in particular the young, families with a FEMALE HEAD OF HOUSEHOLD, and minorities).

History. The federal government did not become involved in providing assistance to individuals until the 1930's. Assistance to the poor had been the sole responsibility of local governments and private charities since the founding of the country. The nation in its early years was strongly influenced by the Puritan work ethic. Poverty was thought by many to be the result of individual laziness rather than social and economic conditions. In addition, many Americans blamed poverty on alleged poor work habits of immigrants such as the Irish (in the late nineteenth century), and Slavs, Italians, and Greeks (in the late nineteenth and early twentieth centuries). The pattern of attributing poverty to lack of enterprise on the part of individuals, especially immigrants or racial minorities, continues to influence public opinion as well as official policy toward assisting the poor.

As the country became more industrialized, some state governments began to realize that local poorhouses and private charities were not sufficient to meet the needs of the growing number of poor resulting from the periodic recessions and depressions that disrupted the American economy. By 1900, it is estimated that 6.4 million workers were unemployed at some point during the year, and 10 percent of the population lived in poverty. Nevertheless, state governments were reluctant to increase assistance for the poor and raise the necessary taxes to fund such programs without similar actions by all other states. Although some states enacted modest programs for widowed mothers and impoverished older Americans, state aid to the poor was not sufficient to meet the needs of an industrial economy.

The passage of the SOCIAL SECURITY ACT of 1935 marked the entry of the federal government into public assistance policy. Passed by Congress at the height of the GREAT DEPRESSION and signed into law by President Franklin Roosevelt, the act established a federal system of benefits for retired workers, as well as a combined federal-state system of unemployment insurance. The law also included matching grants-in-aid from the federal to state governments to assist states in providing assistance to needy persons in three separate categories: older Americans, blind people, and dependent children (later renamed Aid to Families with Dependent Children or AFDC).

The Social Security Act institutionalized a two-tier system of administration for distributing public assistance that has contributed greatly to the failure of U.S. antipoverty policy. The act has been amended a number of times since its enactment. In 1939, Congress significantly expanded the old-age insurance component by extending monthly benefits to workers' dependents and survivors. In 1956, the Disability Insurance program was added, providing monthly cash benefits to workers who suffered severe disabilities. Congress established both the Medicare and Medicaid programs as part of President Lyndon Johnson's WAR ON POVERTY in 1965. Supplemental Security Income (SSI) was created by combining the programs for needy blind people, older citizens, and people with disabilities in 1972. Many smaller federal and federal-state assistance programs, some of which are described below, were established following the Social Security Act.

Major Programs. The major assistance programs can be grouped into three categories based on the differing functions that the programs perform: social insurance programs; means-tested cash assistance programs; and noncash assistance. Social insurance benefits are paid mainly to the middle class based on

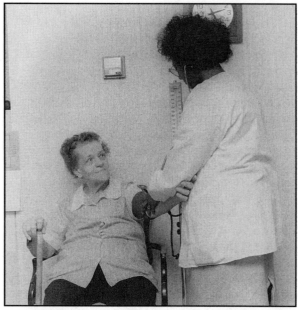

Many elderly Social Security recipients use Medicare to help cover the cost of health care. (Sally Weigand)

past earnings and are not means-tested. Recipients of means-tested assistance must have income and assets below certain standards. Noncash assistance provides goods or services (such as food and medical care) to specific populations, and may or may not be means-tested.

Among social insurance programs, Old Age, Survivors, and Disability Income (OASDI, or Social Security as it is commonly known) is by far the largest income maintenance program in the United States. OASDI provides monthly cash benefits to replace part of the income lost by a worker or the worker's family when the worker retires, becomes disabled, or dies. Unemployment Insurance is a federal-state program that provides partial wage replacement payments to covered workers who lose their jobs involuntarily and continue to be available for work.

Aid to Families with Dependent Children is a federal-state program that provides cash payments to needy families, with need and payment levels defined by each state. In all states, eligible families are those with children under eighteen where one parent (usually the father) is absent or in some cases, out of work. As the federal government matches state expenditures for assistance payments, AFDC payments vary greatly depending on the policy and fiscal capacity of each state. Some states provide monthly AFDC payments that are less than half the amount paid by others. Supplemental Security Income (SSI) provides monthly payments to older or blind persons or persons with disabilities whose incomes fail to meet a certain federally determined minimum. Federal benefit payments and eligibility requirements under SSI are uniform, and all but two states supplement the amount paid by the federal government.

In noncash aid, Medicare covers most medical costs for individuals eligible for Social Security retirement and disability benefits. Medicaid is a federal-state program that covers medical costs for low-income individuals and families, including those eligible for AFDC and SSI. Within broad federal guidelines, each state determines its own eligibility requirements and scope of services provided; therefore, Medicaid programs vary considerably from state to state. The Food Stamp Program provides coupons redeemable at retail food stores to individuals and households meeting nationwide standards for income and assets. The Supplemental Food Program for Women, Infants, and Children (WIC) is a federal nutrition and health assistance program designed to help pregnant and postpartum women, infants, and children. Participants receive vouchers or checks that are redeemable for nutritious supplemental foods at participating retail grocers, are given nutrition education, and have access to health services. All students eating lunches at schools participating in the School Lunch Program pay less than the cost of the meals. Those children determined by local school officials to be unable to pay the established price receive their lunches free. Other types of federal noncash assistance provided by the government include Low-Income Home Energy Assistance, Public and Other Subsidized Housing, and Educational Assistance (which may take the form of loans or grants). There are several small-scale educational assistance programs targeted specifically for minority students.

In addition to the three categories outlined above, the federal government provides a number of programs for special groups. VETERANS of military ser-

Federally funded school programs provide nutritious hot meals for school-age children such as this girl. (James L. Shaffer)

vice may receive disability payments, educational assistance, hospitalization and medical care, survivor and dependents loans, and hiring preference for veterans in certain jobs. In recognition of its central role in creating and perpetuating the POVERTY that affects the American Indian population, the federal government has created a number of assistance programs specifically for American Indians and Alaska Natives. These include health care; housing, social services, and food; education; roads and construction; administration; and employment. Undocumented immigrants who enter the United States illegally do not receive federal assistance payments. REFUGEES (those fleeing political persecution) who are admitted into the country are entitled, however, to receive cash and medical assistance for their first two years in the United States.

Welfare v. Social Security. The SOCIAL SECURITY ACT assigned most social insurance functions to the federal government yet created a public assistance system for the poor that is divided between federal, state, and, in some cases, local government. Programs that are not means-tested, and those that benefit older Americans, enjoy widespread public and political support. Means- tested programs, especially Aid to Families with Dependent Children (AFDC), do not enjoy similarly broad political or public support. Although expenditures on AFDC amount to less than 1 percent of total federal outlays, the program (which is often referred to as "welfare") has been the target of extensive criticism.

Unlike Social Security, AFDC payments are made to racial minorities, especially African Americans and Latinos, in numbers higher than their proportion of the population. Many have tried to blame the persistence of poverty among minorities on dependence on welfare payments rather than on conditions such as institutional RACISM and lack of employment opportunity that especially affect minorities. Welfare has become a racial code word by which minorities are accused of immoral lifestyles and laziness leading to welfare dependency. Welfare recipients are often depicted as unmarried urban women of color who do not work and who elect to have additional children in order

Benefits from welfare programs such as Aid To Families with Dependent Children (AFDC) and the Food Stamp Program were cut in the 1980's, forcing many impoverished single mothers such as this woman to seek help from homeless shelters. (AP/Wide World Photos)

Social Security and other federal aid that benefit older Americans such as this man enjoy broad public and political support. (Skjold)

to increase the amount of benefits that they receive.

The stereotyped conception of the program is contradicted by facts. A survey of all AFDC recipients reveals that 60 percent are white, and 90 percent of all recipients live in suburban or rural areas. The average AFDC family has only 1.9 children, fewer than the average family. The average monthly payment of less than half the poverty rate does little to encourage extended participation, and half of all recipients receive payments for less than two years. Acting in part on the basis of prevailing STEREOTYPES, the Reagan Administration made a number of changes in AFDC (and other assistance programs for the poor) in 1981 that made eligibility more difficult and cut benefit levels. State governments are experimenting with a variety of programs designed to lower the costs of their share of AFDC and to alter the behavior of recipients by including work requirements and penalizing recipients for having additional children while receiving payments.

Although social insurance programs, especially Social Security, account for a much larger share of federal expenditures, they have not been subject to much criticism from either the public or political leaders. Social Security is paid to those sixty-five years of age and older regardless of income and is indexed to inflation, guaranteeing that payments will retain purchasing power. In 1991, $55 billion, more than one-fifth of all Social Security payments, were paid to

José Feliciano displays his 1986 Grammy Award for best Latin Pop performance. (AP/Wide World Photos)

households with incomes of more than $50,000 a year. In the same year, funding for the federal share of AFDC amounted to approximately $19 billion. Data from the Congressional Budget Office indicates that U.S. households with incomes exceeding $100,000 receive slightly more on average in federal cash and in-kind benefits than do those with incomes less than $10,000. The two-tier assistance system in the United States thus leaves one child in every five in poverty but subsidizes older and wealthier families.

SUGGESTED READINGS. *The Catalog of Federal Domestic Assistance* (1989), compiled by the U.S. General Services Administration, Federal Assistance Catalog Staff, contains information on all 1,228 federal assistance programs. For current statistics and descriptions of the major assistance programs, see the quarterly *Social Security Bulletin* (1938-). *Current Population Reports*, Series P-60, *Consumer Income*, published by the Bureau of the Census, provides data on the impact of federal assistance programs on income and poverty. For discussions of the history and structure of federal assistance programs, see David B. Robertson and Dennis R. Judd's *The Development of American Public Policy* (1989), and Andrew W. Dobelstein's *Social Welfare* (1990).—*Scott A. Frisch*

Feliciano, José (b. Sept. 10, 1945, Larez, Puerto Rico): Puerto Rican musician and singer. Feliciano was born to Puerto Rican parents and moved with them to the United States at a young age. Although blind, he learned the guitar while growing up in the Spanish Harlem section of New York City. His debut album, *Feliciano!* (1968), earned him Grammy Awards for Best New Artist and Best Pop Vocalist. Feliciano toured to sellout crowds during the 1970's and was named *Guitar Player* magazine's Best Folk Guitarist in 1973. He appeared in various television episodes and received an Emmy Award nomination for the theme for the television series *Chico and the Man*. He has more than thirty gold albums, including *Los exitos de José Feliciano* (1984), *Escenas de amor* (1982), *Me enamore* (1984), and *Nina* (1990).

Female academies. *See* **Academies—female**

Female head of household. *See* **Head of household, female**

Female Labor Reform Association: Nineteenth century labor organization of women textile mill workers. Sarah Bagley and eleven other female mill workers in Lowell, Massachusetts, organized the group in January, 1845. The main goal of the association was to reduce the workday to ten hours. Within six months, five hundred women joined to support the cause. They faced society's scorn for speaking publicly about rights for women workers. Long before women had the right to vote, this association allied with the New England Workingman's Association to testify on the unhealthy working conditions in the mills and to petition the state legislature for a shorter workday.

Feminism: Ideology and movement that seek equality for women in all areas of human endeavor. Feminism in the United States is a historical phenomenon as well as a contemporary development. American women have achieved some, but not all, of the goals of feminist movements after some 150 years of progress and struggle.

Origins of Feminism. The origins of feminism in the United States are hard to determine with precision. After the AMERICAN REVOLUTION, women had neither full economic rights nor political equality. The first major feminist movement began in the mid-nineteenth century and was linked with women's drive to gain the right to vote (suffrage). Leaders of the early SUFFRAGE MOVEMENT, such as Susan B. ANTHONY and Elizabeth Cady STANTON, are still heroines and role

The women's suffrage movement of the mid-nineteenth century marked the first major feminist movement in the United States. Here, suffragists in 1912 use a quote from Abraham Lincoln in their ongoing struggle to gain the vote for women. (Library of Congress)

models for feminists in the twentieth century. The nineteenth century women's movement was also linked with the ABOLITIONIST MOVEMENT. Women and slaves shared some common problems, especially the lack of the economic and political rights of citizenship. The informal alliance between the abolitionists and the suffragists would later be paralleled in the 1960's in the linkages between the CIVIL RIGHTS MOVEMENT and the WOMEN'S LIBERATION MOVEMENT.

In the early twentieth century, the feminist movement was revitalized in the drive to achieve suffrage. The suffragists were feminists whose main agenda focused on women's right to vote, which was finally granted after World War I in 1920. In the 1920's and 1930's women advanced in opening new career areas, although this progress was limited by the GREAT DEPRESSION.

World War II provided women with an opportunity to demonstrate their abilities. While men were engaged in battle in Europe and the Pacific, women served in special noncombat units and took their places in industrial jobs. "Rosie the Riveter" symbolized the American woman at work during the war, but

"Rosie's" gains were short-lived. Returning veterans received special consideration to complete their education through the G.I. Bill while their wives worked at any available job and raised children in what became known as the postwar "baby boom."

After World War II, feminism was at a low ebb. During the 1950's, the ideal for women was to be a successful mother-homemaker in the suburbs. Although many women were well educated, there was little opportunity for them to exercise their talents outside the home. The back-to-the-home movement for women was endorsed by the media. The new medium of television presented family situation comedies such as *Ozzie and Harriet* and *Father Knows Best* with a competent, loving mother at home and an all-knowing, benign father who returned home at night to resolve difficulties that had arisen during the day. Films in the 1950's also reinforced the image of the full-time housewife and mother, overwhelmed by children, pets, and the problems of maintaining the home while her husband worked long hours in the city, largely cut off from family life. Magazines such as *The Ladies' Home Journal* related tales of suburban housewives whose lives were more fulfilling and challenging than those of their old college friends who were career women.

Behind the happy façade, latent tensions were brewing among American women. Despite their lovely homes and modern conveniences, some felt trapped in suburban residential communities, isolated from the vitality and challenges of the workplace and society.

The Third Wave of Feminism. In 1963, housewife and writer Betty FRIEDAN questioned women's supposedly idyllic life in *The Feminine Mystique*, a book that influenced a generation of women. She talked about the indescribable "malaise" that seemed to plague modern housewives. More than any other single force at the time, her book led many women to reexamine their lives.

The book was published shortly before passage of the CIVIL RIGHTS ACT OF 1964, which attempted to ensure equal employment opportunities for minorities and women. A 1963 law had required equal pay for equal work. Encouraged by the new laws and anxious to ensure their implementation, the National Organization for Women (NOW) was formed by a number of prominent women, including Friedan, in 1966. It soon became the nucleus of a wide-reaching feminist movement.

In 1967 NOW adopted its basic program in the form of a Women's Bill of Rights. In addition to equal employment, NOW advocated legalized ABORTION and a greater political voice for women. In 1973, the U.S. Supreme Court legalized abortion in *ROE v. WADE*, which established norms for allowing abortion in each trimester of pregnancy. Many women consider their "right to choose" abortion or carry a child to term a basic right, although a substantial minority of American women and men consider abortion the killing of an unborn child and an inappropriate alternative in a society where BIRTH CONTROL is readily available. This basic controversy persists in American life, with feminists often labeled "pro-choice" and those who call themselves "pro-life" often considered antifeminist. The fact that there is debate within feminist groups about abortion and within antiabortion groups about women's rights suggests that the pro-choice feminist stereotype does not always apply.

NOW became the single most important feminist organization in the United States. Soon it was joined by the NATIONAL WOMEN'S POLITICAL CAUCUS (NWPC), a bipartisan group that sought to increase women's participation in political life. NOW, NWPC, and other mainstream feminist groups attracted primarily white, urban, middle-class women, both younger and middle-aged. Their message often did not reach working class women, rural women, or women of color—a problem which continued twenty-five years later.

Feminist Betty Friedan, author of The Feminine Mystique, *cofounded the National Organization for Women (NOW) in 1966.* (AP/Wide World Photos)

In the early 1970's, *Ms.* MAGAZINE was established by the journalist Gloria STEINEM, with the support of prominent feminists. It became the unofficial voice of the feminist movement in the United States. Books and articles on feminism proliferated as consciousness grew among women journalists, writers, and scholars, as well as ordinary women in consciousness-raising groups. WOMEN'S STUDIES PROGRAMS, founded at numerous colleges and universities in the wake of the feminist movement, encouraged the spread of feminism and feminist scholarship among younger women.

Women made considerable progress in the 1970's and 1980's as feminist ideas took hold in American society. Some women began combining careers, marriage, and family in a complex juggling act that earned successful women the label "superwomen." When some women found the attempt to "have it all" too stressful, they began to redefine their personal priorities, ranging themselves along the "career track" and the "mommy track."

The Battle for the ERA. In the 1970's, the mainstream women's movement focused on ratification of the EQUAL RIGHTS AMENDMENT to the U.S. CONSTITUTION. Congress passed an Equal Rights Amendment, subject to ratification in three-fourths (thirty-eight) of the states. Women of differing political persuasions joined the ratification battle. More than any other single development, the ERA campaign unified women. Although the amendment secured ratification in thirty-five states over the next decade, time ran out and the amendment died.

In the intervening years, women gained many of the goals sought in the Equal Rights Amendment through legislation. They were employed in more challenging careers, although gender clustering by occupation remained; their salaries increased, though in some fields they still earned less than men; and women strengthened their economic and credit rights, previously denied them in practice, if not in law. Women entered professions such as law and medicine, which had been male strongholds. The number of women in Ph.D. and other graduate programs also increased sharply. Women became more active politically, especially at the state and local levels, serving as state legislators, city council members, and political advisers. They were elected as governors and lieutenant governors of several important states. Congress was a more elusive barrier. By 1990, women constituted only about 5 percent of the House of Representatives, and only two women were Senators.

Since the early 1970's, journalist Gloria Steinem has shaped the editorial content of Ms. *magazine, a leading feminist periodical.* (AP/Wide World Photos)

Despite these gains, the ERA's defeat had a debilitating effect on the women's movement during the 1980's. Feminists seemed unable to unite on an agenda. Younger women were obtaining good jobs without difficulty and were unwilling to jeopardize their positions with activism. Issues such as pornography divided, rather than united, feminists, who could be found on both sides of the freedom of expression issue. For young and middle-aged women, employment conditions and opportunities were undeniably better than a generation earlier, although life had not improved as dramatically for the growing number of urban, poor women.

Class and Racial Dimensions of Feminism. The mainstream women's movement, although nominally open to all, has always had a white, middle-class bias. Although concern was expressed for disadvantaged women, the leadership was principally drawn from white, well-educated, upper-middle-class women. A notable exception was feminist support for Shirley CHISHOLM, the African American member of the House of Representatives from Brooklyn, who in 1972 was the first woman to try to become the presidential nominee of one of the two major parties.

For minority women, the issue of feminism had always been more complex and less clear-cut than for middle-class white women. While a number of well-educated, articulate women of color participated in the feminist movement of the 1960's, most minority women had never been reached. For them, feminism did not seem relevant. Feminism was often perceived as a struggle against powerful male oppressors, but minority men were rarely powerful members of society. Indeed, their situation was in some ways worse than that of women of color. For example, although employed African American males earn more than African American women, those men are also the group in society with the highest rate of unemployment. To attract minority women, the appeals of feminism had to be framed in terms of social justice rather than male-female conflict. Some black women intellectuals had a strong consciousness of the significant role they could play in empowering African American women. Other feminists of color have expressed the view that the mainstream feminist movement itself had racist undertones.

Feminism in the 1990's. For much of the 1980's, the women's movement appeared to lack either momentum or a concrete agenda. By the late 1980's, many feminists were united by a desire to preserve ABORTION rights, as prescribed in *Roe v. Wade*. As the "right to life" movement gained momentum, feminist organizations focused on shoring up abortion rights while other issues were set aside.

Eventually, the women's movement rediscovered a focus as a number of issues converged to form a new agenda. By the early 1990's, there was widespread recognition among women that, although they had advanced significantly since the 1960's, a "GLASS CEILING" prevented them from reaching the upper echelons of management or receiving promotions they believed they had earned. There was a growing consensus that women and children were the most disadvantaged groups in the United States. Feminists' attention turned to social issues, such as POVERTY among women and children, CHILD ABUSE, RAPE, sexual abuse, SEXUAL HARASSMENT, and the need for a national family leave law.

Although some women activists addressed these issues directly, the mainstream feminist movement did not become fully revitalized until 1991, when the U.S. Senate hearings to confirm Clarence THOMAS, a candidate for the Supreme Court, awakened women from their complacency. In the later stages of the televised hearings, charges of sexual harassment were raised against Thomas by his former assistant, Anita HILL, a respected law school professor. The televised proceedings chronicled how the articulate Hill was questioned for hours by an all-white, all-male Senate committee, some of whose members doubted her honesty and sense of reality. Hill became a new symbol of women's continuing victimization and harassment by powerful men. The hearing ceased to be the word of one woman against one man and became the battle of many women against the all-male interrogators in the Senate. The fact that both Thomas and Hill were African Americans further complicated the situation, since all the interrogators were white.

The Thomas hearings had a significant impact on women's consciousness and mobilized women to enter a new stage of activism. In 1992, the so-called YEAR OF THE WOMAN, many women came forward to run for political office. Eleven women ran for, and six were elected to, the U.S. Senate, including Carol Moseley BRAUN, the first African American woman ever elected to the Senate. Many women also won seats in the U.S. House of Representatives, as well as state and local office.

In the 1990's, only a small percentage of American women actively identified themselves as feminists. Yet modern feminism, over the course of a generation, had greatly influenced American ideas, social institutions, and the options pursued by individual women. Without the feminist movement, for example, it is unlikely that so many American women would have been in high corporate or political positions, seeking redress for sexual harassment, or sharing some portion of HOUSEWORK and CHILD CARE with their mates. Feminism spawned new programs in women's health and medicine and new awareness of the feminization of poverty, as well as new branches of academic inquiry such as feminist literary theory, feminist psychology, and women's studies.

Anita Hill's 1991 allegations of Clarence Thomas' sexual harassment revitalized the mainstream feminist movement in the United States. (AP/Wide World Photos)

Each phase of feminism in American history has been triggered by new needs and developments, and impelled by slightly different goals. In the 1990's, feminism entered a new stage after almost a decade of recovering from the defeat of the ERA. Feminist women are no longer willing to settle for anything less than a complete role in society and policymaking. Despite the new movement's momentum, there is less unity among feminists than is generally realized. Issues of CLASS and RACE divide the movement, as does the question of abortion. The future of feminism may well depend on its ability to tolerate diverse perspectives and goals.

SUGGESTED READINGS. For background on the history of American women, see Sara Evans' *Born for Liberty: A History of Women in America* (1989), and Rosalind Rosenberg's *Divided Lives* (1992). To understand the origins of the feminist movement of the 1960's, consult Betty Friedan's *The Feminine Mystique* (1963). Dorothy McBride Stetson offers a good introductory survey in *Women's Rights in the USA* (1991). The story of the ratification of the ERA can be found in Donald Matthews and Jane De Hart's *Sex, Gender, and the Politics of the ERA* (1990) and in Jane Mansbridge's *Why We Lost the ERA* (1989). An interesting brief history of feminism is Barbara Ryan's *Feminism and the Women's Movement* (1992). For a closer examination of the views and activities of minority women, see Patricia Hill Collins's *Black Feminist Thought* (1990) and Lisa Albrecht and Rose M. Brewer's *Bridges of Power: Women's Multicultural Alliances* (1990).—*Norma Corigliano Noonan*

Feminism—cultural: Perspective on women's experience that emphasizes the collective identification of women, rather than political or economic aspects of women's subordination. It took somewhat different forms in the nineteenth century United States than in the "second wave" of feminism since the 1970's. What these strands of feminist theory have in common is the belief that women have different qualities than men, which must be valued. Although equal rights for women is just and necessary, cultural feminists believe that women need to develop their own social bonds and emotional strengths, going beyond the competitive, aggressive orientation of male-centered society and its institutions.

In the nineteenth century, when American women were not accorded civil or political rights, cultural feminists such as Margaret FULLER contended that women needed to develop their own internal abilities

and "electric nature." Women's nature, in turn, could change society itself. Other theorists emphasize the special qualities of mothering and nurturing that early societies embodied in a matriarchal power that was used for human benefit. Only with male domination did war, ignorance, and oppression arise. Charlotte Perkins GILMAN continued this theme by condemning the unnatural economic dependence of women on men, which distorts women's lives and stunts their growth as human beings. In the course of evolution it is the female qualities of cooperation and altruism that will bring about social cooperation and development. Gilman's novel *Herland* (published posthumously in 1979) depicts a female-centered utopia based on her ideas of women's unique qualities.

Some more recent visions of women's special qualities do not assume they are innate but rather that they arise out of women's connection with raising children and being caregivers. Sara Ruddick depicts "maternal thinking," which values the preservation of life, fostering growth and independence, humor and humility

Documentaries such as the one advertised in this poster attempt to portray women's collective experiences that cross cultural and racial lines. (Library of Congress)

in the face of unpredictable, unforseen events. These important qualities need to be developed in both men and women, according to Ruddick. Carol Gilligan describes women's "different voice" which tends toward a morality based on connectedness and care, rather than on competition and impersonal standards of justice.

Some contemporary cultural feminists see women's perspective as intrinsically pacifist and antimilitarist. They seek to form alliances with other women worldwide in order to transcend the narrow nationalist wars fought by men and to promote peace. This kind of understanding between women on opposing sides of national conflicts is based on their shared identity as nurturers and life givers rather than life destroyers.

SUGGESTED READINGS. For a historical perspective, see Josephine Donovan's *Feminist Theory: The Intellectual Traditions of American Feminism* (1985). For an example of women's "difference" see Carol Gilligan's *In a Different Voice: Psychological Theory and Women's Development* (1982).

Feminism—radical: Perspective that emerged during the "second wave" of American feminism in the 1960's. Radical feminists differ from other feminists by emphasizing women's unique capabilities rather than women's common ground with men. Politically active women found that the "New Left" and the CIVIL RIGHTS MOVEMENT in which they participated ignored feminist issues and tended to accord women second-class status. Unlike Marxism or the socialism of the "New Left," which viewed economic CLASS as the primary source of oppression, the radical feminist position views women's subjugation as the root of all other forms of oppression. Women are considered a "sex-class" who are victims of a specific form of oppression rooted in female biology and reproduction. For some radical feminists such as Shulamith Firestone, the only way to "free" women, therefore, is to liberate them from pregnancy and childbearing through technological "test tube" babies.

Even more important is the abolition of the traditional nuclear family. Firestone contended that real love can exist only between equals; dominance of men over women, especially women's economic dependence on men in the family, makes true love between them impossible. The traditional family also came under attack by radical feminists for its psychological orientation, which they charge is grounded in patriarchal (male-centered) gratification at the expense of women.

Other radical feminists focus on the experience of MOTHERHOOD, which is unique to women. Acknowledging that under current social arrangements motherhood is often coerced, both by outright denial of reproductive choice and by more subtle socialization to fulfill expectations, Adrienne RICH contends that the experience of motherhood must be reclaimed by feminists as a source of joy and self-realization.

Another type of radical feminism is the ideology of radical lesbian separatists. They contend that LESBIANS who are woman-identified women have successfully refused to accept social STEREOTYPES about women's limitations imposed by a male-dominated society. Ti-Grace Atkinson pointed out that this most radical form of feminism was also the most directly threatening to men's power over women. (Not all lesbians are radical feminists.)

Radical feminists consider the many forms of violence against women, such as footbinding, RAPE, and genital mutilation, as examples of male domination that cannot simply be explained by economic or political power. For example, rape is used as a systematic form of terror against women both in wartime by invading armies and in everyday situations by some men. Rape, and the fear of rape, may be used by men to control women and to punish "independent" women. Some radical feminists also contend that pornography, by treating women as sexual objects to be used by men, is degrading and leads to further violence against women. By focusing on the prevalence of systematic violence against women, the radical feminist perspective has successfully drawn public attention to laws and attitudes that condone such violence.

SUGGESTED READINGS. For a good discussion of radical feminism see Hester Eisenstein's *Contemporary Feminist Thought* (1983). For an early, thought-provoking example of radical feminist thinking in the women's movement, see Shulamith Firestone's The Dialectic of Sex: The Case for Feminist Revolution (1970). For a radical feminist perspective on motherhood see the poet Adrienne Rich's book, *Of Woman Born: Motherhood as Experience and Institution* (1976).

Feminism—socialist: Explanation of sexual inequality that draws upon SOCIALISM for its critique of economic, or class-based oppression, and of feminist approaches to sex-based inequality. Feminism since the 1970's has been strongly influenced by Marxist analysis of economic exploitation and its vision of social justice, while critical of conventional Marxism's inattention to the dimension of gender.

Socialist feminists argue that class analysis alone is not sufficient to understand women's oppression. Traditional Marxists consider the exploitation of the dominant class—the capitalist or employing class—over the working class to be the key to understanding social relations. In this view, liberation means radically transforming class-based oppression, although both Karl Marx and Friedrich Engels themselves recognized other forms of exploitation, including women's oppression. Engels traced the "world historic defeat of the female sex" to a period in prehistory when men acquired tribal wealth, especially cattle, and used this private property to gain power over women, forcing them into marriages based on men's control over property and male dominance within the family. For traditional Marxists, the solution for women is to become economically independent of men, thereby changing the basis of men's power within the family. For socialist feminists, however, this is an inadequate explanation of women's oppression.

Socialist feminists contend that patriarchy (the domination and control of men over women) is a distinct form of gender-based oppression and cannot simply be reduced to economic forces or capitalism. Even if a society transformed its property relations, women would remain oppressed by men unless women also struggled for their own liberation. Socialist feminists point out that even in socialist countries such as the Soviet Union after the revolution in 1917, or China since its revolution in 1949, women's position, although improved, remained clearly subordinate to men.

Socialist feminist analyses stress various aspects of the interaction of capitalism and patriarchy. For example, Heidi Hartmann pointed out that in the workplace, working-class men earn more than women and have power over women, which is maintained by means of jobs being sex-segregated. Since traditional "women's jobs" pay less than traditional "men's jobs," women are less able to support themselves, are under more pressure to marry, and are therefore more dependent upon men. Men, in turn, benefit by women's exclusion from better-paid skilled jobs and from women's domestic work for them within the home. Other socialist feminists focus on Marx's concept of class consciousness, stressing women's need to understand and oppose the forms of their own oppression.

"Capitalist patriarchy" is the term used by Zillah Eisenstein to emphasize the mutually reinforcing relationship between the CLASS (economic) structure and hierarchy in gender relations.

SUGGESTED READINGS. For a clear socialist feminist analysis see Zillah Eisenstein's *Capitalist Patriarchy and the Case for Socialist Feminism* (1979). For a different emphasis see Michele Barrett's *Women's Oppression Today* (1980).

Ferraro, Geraldine (b. Aug. 26, 1935, Newburgh, N.Y.): Member of Congress and first woman to run for vice president with a major party. From a poor Italian American family in Queens in New York City, Ferraro taught elementary school until she passed the bar exam in 1960. She began her political career in 1974 as an assistant district attorney in Queens and in 1975 helped create a Special Victims Bureau for victims of RAPE, CHILD ABUSE, and domestic violence. In 1978 she was elected to Congress from Queens District, New York, an office she held until 1984, when she ran for vice president alongside Democratic presidential candidate Senator Walter Mondale.

Geraldine Ferraro accepted the Democratic Party's nomination to run for vice president in 1984. (AP/Wide World Photos)

Ferrer, José (José Vicente Ferrer de Otero y Cintron; Jan. 8, 1912, Santurce, Puerto Rico—Jan. 26, 1992, Coral Gables, Fla.): Puerto Rican actor, director, and producer. Ferrer received his A.B. from Princeton University in 1934. His theatrical career, spanning half a century, included dozens of stage plays—as actor and/or director—and a comparable list of films. He debuted on Broadway in 1935 in *A Slight Case of Murder* and became known for such performances as Iago opposite Paul Robeson in *Othello* (1943), the title role in *Cyrano de Bergerac* (1946), and Don Quixote in *Man of La Mancha* (1966). Ferrer received an Academy Award for the film version of *Cyrano de Bergerac* (1950); other notable films include *The Caine Mutiny* (1954), *I Accuse* (1958), and *Lawrence of Arabia* (1962).

Festival of Our Lady of Guadalupe (Dec. 12): Festival commemorating the apparition of Mary, mother of Jesus, seen by an Indian, Juan Diego, at Tepeyac Hill outside Mexico City in 1531. Mary allegedly asked Diego to have a church built on that site, but Bishop Zumarraga refused to believe Diego. In a subsequent apparition, Mary directed Diego to collect flowers, place them in his cloak, and take them to the bishop. Upon opening the cloak, an image of Mary (Our Lady of Guadalupe) was revealed. The image is now in the Basilica of Our Lady of Guadalupe, which was constructed on the site requested. The same image is found in many contemporary Mexican American churches, organizations, homes, and murals, where it is revered as both a religious and cultural symbol.

Festival of the Flowers: Commemorates the Texas victory over Mexican forces at the battle of San Jacinto on April 21, 1836, known as the Battle of the Flowers. San Antonio first celebrated the event in 1891 when President Benjamin Harrison visited the city. Since then the fiesta has grown to a week of festivities. Festival events include the Pilgrimage to Alamo Plaza, Battle of the Flowers parade, River Parade, and Flambeau Parade.

Festivals. *See* **Holidays and festivals**

Fetterman Massacre (1866): Entrapment and killing of more than eighty U.S. soldiers by a band of SIOUX warriors near Fort Phil Kearny on December 21, 1866. The Sioux Indians were infuriated because the U.S. government was attempting to build a road to Bozeman, Montana, through their favorite hunting grounds in the Bighorn Mountains. Chief RED CLOUD led sixteen thou-

Born in Puerto Rico, José Ferrer had a distinguished career in American theater as an actor and director. (AP/Wide World Photos)

sand Sioux warriors in battle to fight the roadbuilding between 1865 and 1867. In late December, 1866, a band of Sioux warriors under Chief High Backbone was responsible for the massacre. Eventually acknowledging defeat at the Second Treaty of Fort Laramie in 1868, the U.S. government agreed to abandon the Bozeman Trail.

Fiction writers and fiction: The explosion of multicultural literature in the United States in the last quarter of the twentieth century was truly remarkable, and nowhere was the change more marked than in popular American fiction. Since the 1960's, fiction by women and writers of color has become a force in every literary market and a fixture on most bestseller lists. Long a bastion of white male professionals, American fiction had by the 1990's become equally the production of a diverse mix of women and minority writers.

Historical Background. Ethnic fiction has existed since almost the beginning of American creative literature. William Wells Brown's *Clotel* (1853) is considered the first African American novel, and John Rollin Ridge's *Life and Adventures of Joaquin Murieta* (1854) was the first novel by an American Indian author. It was not until the latter twentieth century, however, that fiction by people of color began to be felt as a force on the American literary scene. African American novelists were the first to have an impact with Richard WRIGHT's powerful naturalist *Native Son* in 1940 and Ralph Ellison's multileveled *Invisible Man* in 1952—a work still considered by many critics to be the best American novel published in the post-World War II era. Yet African American writers, both male (Jean Toomer, Claude McKay) and female (Nella Larsen, Jessie Redmon Fauset) had been building a presence in American fictional forms since at least the HARLEM RENAISSANCE of the 1920's. Other ethnic literature was more scattered or hidden, as many ethnic groups were still defining their American identity, gaining access to fictional tools, and fighting oppression. The dominant ideological notion of the "MELTING POT" undoubtedly did further damage in keeping writers from the exploration of their own cultures.

Interestingly, American fiction has accommodated the "immigrant" novel since the early 1900's— from Abraham Cahan's *The Rise of David Levinsky* in 1917 and Anzia Yezierska's short stories in *Hungry Hearts* (1920) through more recent Jewish American writers such as Bernard Malamud, Chaim Potok, Philip Roth, or Isaac Bashevis Singer, who often explore their eastern European heritage. Many of these works stressed ASSIMILATION rather than the depiction and preservation of diverse ethnic experiences. Certainly, the "ethnic" novel—fiction celebrating the multicultural richness of nation—was hardly thinkable as a literary genre before the 1960's.

The situation for American ethnic writers was in many ways comparable to the dilemma for women writers. Nathaniel Hawthorne deplored the "mob of scribbling women" with whom he competed in the mid-1800's. Most of these women were dismissed as "popularizers" in the dominant literary canon that prevailed in the literary academies for the next century, a canon that almost exclusively privileged male writers such as James Fenimore Cooper, Edgar Allan Poe, Herman Melville, and Henry James. Yet the most popular works of the nineteenth century—Susan Warner's *The Wide, Wide World* (1850) and Harriet Beecher STOWE's *Uncle Tom's Cabin* (1851)—were

written by women. When scholars and critics began to reevaluate women's literature of the nineteenth century, starting in the 1960's, they discovered much important fiction, including groundbreaking novels such as Rebecca Harding Davis' early realist *Life in the Iron Mills* (1861) or Kate Chopin's disturbingly naturalistic *The Awakening* (1899).

The Rise of Ethnic Fiction. After World War II, a significant shift occurred in American thinking about race, ethnicity, and gender, especially following the Supreme Court decision on SEGREGATION in *BROWN V. BOARD OF EDUCATION* in 1954, when the CIVIL RIGHTS MOVEMENT was symbolically born. Not only for African Americans but also for Chicanos (with the CHICANO MOVEMENT), American Indians (with the

Acknowledged as one of the foremost contemporary Jewish American novelists, Philip Roth is known for incorporating autobiographical details in his novels. (Nancy Crampton)

AMERICAN INDIAN MOVEMENT), women (with the WOMEN'S LIBERATION MOVEMENT), and homosexuals (with the GAY AND LESBIAN RIGHTS MOVEMENT), the 1960's and 1970's were the decades for redefining and celebrating multicultural uniqueness. Out of this cauldron of social and political turmoil, a number of literary movements were born. At the same time, historians began to reevaluate the inherited literary canon and to rediscover women and ethnic writers of the past who had often labored in obscurity.

The year that signaled the change for American fiction was 1968. In that year, the Kiowa writer N. Scott MOMADAY won the Pulitzer Prize for fiction for *The House Made of Dawn* symbolically marking the emergence of the ethnic novel as a force in American fiction. Its presence was confirmed in the next decade by Alex HALEY's *Roots: The Saga of an American Family* and Maxine Hong KINGSTON's *The Woman Warrior*, both works of fictionalized autobiography and history published in 1976, which captured the African American and Chinese American heritage, respectively. These two works encouraged a renaissance of ethnic fiction, a movement that uncovered the cultural roots of most Americans. From its inception, fiction by ethnic writers (and by women as well) has often been close to autobiography. The story that ethnic novelists have to tell—of SLAVERY, of immigration and ASSIMILATION, of American Indian history—has always been a story steeped in, and spilling over into, American social history. To separate ethnic fiction from its origins in American history is impossible, as Haley and Kingston demonstrate.

By the 1980's, writers of color, and particularly women, had become an established force in American fiction. African American Alice WALKER won the Pulitzer Prize in 1982 with *The Color Purple*; Toni MORRISON took the award five years later for *Beloved* (1987). Gloria Naylor, Jamaica Kincaid, Terry McMillan, Paule Marshall, Ishmael Reed, Ernest J. Gaines, John Edgar Wideman, and Charles Johnson were other popular black writers working into the 1990's.

By the early 1990's, almost every ethnic group could claim a real presence in American fiction. American Indian fiction writers of prominence, besides Momaday, included James Welch (*Winter in the Blood*, 1974), David Seals (*The Powwow Highway*, 1979), Paula Gunn Allen (*The Woman Who Owned the Shadows*, 1983), Louise ERDRICH (*Love Medicine*, 1984, *Beet Queen*, 1986, and *Tracks*, 1988), Michael Dorris (*A Yellow Raft on Blue Water*, 1987), and Gerald Vizenor (*The Heirs of Columbus*, 1991).

Latino Writers. The situation for Latino writers has always been more complicated, since Latino writers represent three major but separate ethnic groups—Puerto Rican Americans, Cuban Americans, and Mexican Americans—as well as smaller South American or Caribbean populations. Puerto Rican fiction emerged with Piri Thomas (*Down These Mean Streets*, 1987), Nicky Cruz (*Run, Baby, Run*, 1968), and Nicholasa Mohr (*In Nueva York*, 1977) and continues with Abraham Rodriguez, Jr. (*The Boy Without a Flag:*

Tales of the South Bronx, 1992) and Victor Rodriguez (*Eldorado in East Harlem*, 1992). Cuban American fiction has been slower developing but was in full flower by the late 1980's when Oscar Hijuelos won the Pulitzer Prize for *The Mambo Kings Play Songs of Love* (1989). Other recent Cuban American writers include Elías Miguel Muñoz (*Crazy Love*, 1989, and *The Greatest Performance*, 1991), Christina Garcia (*Dreaming in Cuban*, 1992), and J. Joaquín Fraxedas (*The Lonely Crossing of Juan Cabrera*, 1993).

The Latino fiction with the longest history in the United States is Chicano; in fact, it includes a whole history of literature in Spanish from southwestern territories appropriated by the U.S. government in the nineteenth century. Mexican American fiction was at least fairly well developed by the time of Fray Angelico Chavez' *From an Altar Screen: Tales from New Mexico* (1943) and Josephine Niggli's *Mexican Village* (1945), and continued to grow in the next decades with the work of Raymond Barrio (*The Plum Plum Pickers*, 1969), through Tomás Rivera and Rolando Hinojosa, to Oscar Zeta Acosta (*The Autobiography of a Brown Buffalo*, 1972) and Rudolfo A. Anaya

Authors Louise Erdrich and Michael Dorris have collaborated on several books with American Indian themes. (Jerry Bauer)

(*Bless Me, Ultima*, 1972). Contemporary Chicano writers of note include Arturo Islas (*The Rain God: A Desert Tale*, 1984), Gary Soto (*Living up the Street: Narrative Recollections*, 1985), Alejandro Morales (*The Brick People*, 1988), and Victor Villaseñor (*Rain of Gold*, 1991). Chicana writers have had a similar resurgence, including Sandra Cisneros (short fiction collected in *The House on Mango Street*, 1983, and *Woman Hollering Creek and Other Stories*, 1991), Helena Maria Viramontes (*The Moths and Other Stories*, 1985), and Ana Castillo (*So Far from God*, 1993).

Asian American Writers. Fiction writers of Asian background who became increasingly prolific in the 1980's and 1990's also represent a diverse range of ethnic cultures, from the Korean American Richard Kim (*The Innocent*, 1968), and the Asian Indian American Bharati Mukherjee (*Wife*, 1975, and *Jasmine*, 1989), to Filipino American writer Jessica Hagedorn (*Dogeaters*, 1990). It is impossible to generalize about such diverse talents, the broad term "Asian American" hardly helping in this case. Newer South-

east Asian American writers from Vietnam, Cambodia, and Laos will undoubtedly be emerging in the future to fill in further this diverse Asian American literary canvas.

The two best-known types of Asian American literatures at the end of the 1900's were Japanese American and Chinese American. Hampered by history, including Japanese American INTERNMENT during World War II, Japanese American fiction emerged only after the war in the short stories of Toshio Mori (*Yokohama, California*, 1949) and Hisaye Yamomoto (*Seventeen Syllables*, from 1949 but not collected until 1989), and the novel in John Okada's *No-No Boy* (1957). Distinctive contemporary Japanese American fiction includes Cynthia Kadohata's *The Floating World* (1989) and *In the Heart of the Valley of Love* (1992), Holly Uyemoto's *Rebel Without a Clue* (1989), and Gail Tsukiyama's *Women of the Silk* (1991).

Chinese American fiction has an even longer history, including as it does work done at the beginning of the twentieth century by Winifred Eaton and her

The range of titles displayed here shows the important literary contributions made by contemporary Chinese American authors. (Dawn Dawson)

sister Edith, and the later popular fiction of Lin Yutang (*Chinatown Family*, 1948) and Han Suyin (*A Many-Splendored Thing*, 1951). Contemporary Chinese American fiction includes not only established figures such as Maxine Hong KINGSTON (*Tripmaster Monkey*, 1989) and Frank CHIN (*Donald Duk*, 1991) but also the best-selling authors Amy TAN (*The Joy Luck Club*,

As a novelist and book editor, Toni Morrison has influenced the careers of numerous contemporary African American authors. (Maria Mulas)

1989, and *The Kitchen God's Wife*, 1991), Steven Lo (*The Incorporation of Eric Chung*, 1989), Gus Lee (*China Boy*, 1991), Gish JEN (*Typical American*, 1991), David Wong Louie (the short story collection *Pangs of Love*, 1991), and Fae Myenne Ng (*Bone*, 1993).

The Impact of Multicultural Fiction. American fiction has made a dramatic structural shift, from a fiction dominated by male writers (and a patriarchal criticism that gave precedence to male issues) to a much more egalitarian range of work. Increasingly after the late 1960's, women and ethnic writers came to domi-

nate every mode and genre of American literature, and, in fiction in particular, to produce a number of popular and critical successes. It was difficult to find an area of American fiction in the last quarter of the twentieth century not filled with women writers and women writers of color in particular.

What this has meant is a whole retooling of the production of American fiction and fiction-writing. Publishers, like graduate schools of creative writing, have courted minority writers and touted their work. Publication of one ethnic writer often means recognition of the group, which in turn means that more ethnic writers can aspire to the profession. The economics of the publishing industry notwithstanding, more and more ethnic writers have succeeded in American fictional markets.

Significantly, the opening up of the canon by certain ethnic writers has meant that other writers have been able to claim their own lost heritage. There has been much discussion in fiction of Irish American (Mary Gordon, William Kennedy), Italian American (Mario Puzo, Gay Talese), and other individual European American heritages. Likewise, the success of feminist fiction has meant that gay and lesbian works have become increasingly influential in American writing.

All in all, the gains by ethnic writers and women have meant the revitalization of American literature as a whole. It is impossible to imagine the American novel free of the powerful influences of Ann Beattie, Joyce Carol Oates, Jane Smiley, Anne Tyler, or Bobbie Ann Mason. Likewise, it is increasingly difficult to imagine American fiction free of the influences of Toni MORRISON, Rudolfo ANAYA, Leslie Marmon Silko, or Maxine Hong Kingston. Women and ethnic writers, in short, are hardly token contributors to the contemporary literary scene. The frontiers they have explored have opened up American fiction for all future generations of American writers and readers to explore.

SUGGESTED READINGS. The secondary literature concerning these varied literary movements has barely begun. *Multi-Cultural Literacy* (1988), edited by Rick Simonson and Scott Walker, collects a dozen essays that address issues of the multicultural American canon. Likewise, *Redefining American Literary History* (1990), edited by A. La Vonne Brown Ruoff and Jerry W. Ward, Jr., contains essays on revising the canon, as well as selected bibliographies of half a dozen American ethnic literatures. For a more extensive bibliography, see David Peck's *American Ethnic*

Literatures: Native American, African American, Chicano/Latino, and Asian American Writers and Their Backgrounds, an Annotated Bibliography (1992)— David Peck

Fifteenth Amendment (1870): Amendment to the BILL OF RIGHTS of the U.S. CONSTITUTION which forbade federal or state government from denying people the right to vote based on race, color, or previous condition of servitude. A second section of the amendment grants Congress the power to enforce the provision with appropriate legislation. Though the amendment was ratified in 1870 during the period of RECONSTRUCTION following the American CIVIL WAR, enforcement of its guarantees was halting and incomplete until the passage of the VOTING RIGHTS ACT OF 1965.

Historical Context. Following the defeat of the Confederacy in 1865, the economic, legal, and social system of slavery in the South was formally abolished with the passage of the THIRTEENTH AMENDMENT. The Republican-controlled Congress began to enact a series of radical reform measures to protect the citizenship rights of the freedmen (emancipated slaves). These measures included the Freedmen's Bureau Act of 1866, the Civil Rights Acts, the FOURTEENTH AMENDMENT (which nationalized civil rights), and the Reconstruction Act of 1867. The Fifteenth Amendment was introduced in 1869 after it became clear that existing laws were inadequate to protect the voting rights of African Americans. The Republicans intended the amendment as a conclusive step in Reconstruction, the North's military occupation and supervision of state political processes in the South.

The Fifteenth Amendment added fuel to violent white opposition to the suffrage rights and the civil and political equality of African Americans. In response, Congress passed two Enforcement Acts in 1870 and 1871, which provided for extensive national supervision of state elections, including the punishment of private interference with the right to vote. This latter measure was directed against the terrorism and intimidation conducted by the KU KLUX KLAN in states such as Alabama, Mississippi, Georgia, and South Carolina. While initially the federal government enforced its CIVIL RIGHTS reforms with vigor, by the early 1870's Northern opinion was growing weary of Reconstruction policy. Federal judges retreated from a broad interpretation of Congress' enforcement power. In *U.S. v. Reese* (1876), the U.S. Supreme Court stated that the Fifteenth Amendment did not grant a right to vote per se but was directed at state actions that were intended to deny voting rights on racial grounds.

During the Reconstruction period, African Americans in the South voted freely and won political office. They served in state legislatures and in most elective executive offices below the level of governor. In addition, African Americans from several former confederate states served in the U.S. Congress.

This progressive political trend ended by the early 1880's as conservative forces in the Southern states regained control and set up the "JIM CROW" system of state-sponsored racial SEGREGATION and DISFRANCHISEMENT. Conservative southern Democrats were able to reestablish a racial caste system because only a minority of Northerners felt any genuine enthusiasm for the radical Republicans' program of equal civil and political rights for the races. Indeed, in 1894 Congress repealed the Enforcement Acts of 1870 and 1871, paving the way for state deprivations of the right to vote through extralegal coercion and violent intimidation or by devious legislative subterfuge.

Application and Interpretation of the Amendment Prior to 1965. Terrorist acts and vote fraud had prevented electoral participation by African Americans in the South since the end of RECONSTRUCTION. By the 1890's, white political leaders in states such as Mississippi, Louisiana, South Carolina, Alabama, Virginia, and Texas sought to "legalize" this exclusion of African Americans from the political process. Through a series of amendments to the state constitutions, devices such as poll taxes, LITERACY TESTS, burdensome residency and registration requirements, and white primaries were enacted to disfranchise African Americans. For example, between 1889 and 1902 all eleven former Confederate states required voters to pay a fee, thus erecting an economic obstacle to voting by blacks and poor whites.

Many states adopted these direct measures to get around the restrictions of the Fifteenth Amendment and applied them in a racially discriminatory manner. Thus, the discretion of county registrars ensured that black applicants were disqualified if the written responses on their voter registration forms were not "letter perfect." Likewise, in administering the literacy tests—which often included copying and interpreting sections of the state constitution—registrars gave white applicants illegal assistance. An even more overt means of discrimination was the "GRANDFATHER CLAUSE" exemption. According to the Oklahoma constitution, for example, descendants of citizens who were entitled to vote in 1866 were not required to prove their ability to read and write in order to register. Most African Americans could not qualify for this exemption, and so were subject to the capricious requirements of the literacy test.

Some states' exclusionary measures were blatantly racial in design. A Texas law authorized the prohibition of African Americans from participating in the Texas Democratic Party primary on the grounds that ries" as unconstitutional abridgements of the right to vote. In response, states such as Texas repealed all laws regulating the Democratic Party, thus making the party a private organization without connection to the state. The party could exclude African Americans from membership and refuse to give them ballots in the primary, but without the presence of "state action," no violation of the Fourteenth or Fifteenth Amendments could exist. This situation persisted until 1944, when the Court concluded in *Smith v. Allwright* that the

Despite constitutional guarantees of their right to vote, many African Americans, such as these southern sharecroppers in 1932, were still excluded from voting by discriminatory measures. (AP/Wide World Photos)

the party was a private association whose actions were free from constitutional restraints. Since winning the Democratic primary election in the one-party South was tantamount to winning the general election, excluding African Americans from the primary totally weakened their voting power.

Not all these measures survived the scrutiny of the federal courts. The first to be invalidated as a violation of the Fifteenth Amendment was the grandfather clause. In 1915, in *Guinn v. U.S.*, the U.S. Supreme Court struck down Oklahoma's law, since its obvious effect was to impose the literacy test solely on former slaves and their descendants. Next, a series of Supreme Court rulings struck down the "white prima-

party's "public function" of administering elections rendered it an "agent of the state" and therefore subject to the Fifteenth Amendment.

Despite this progress toward the enforcement of Fifteenth Amendment protections, the Supreme Court generally upheld the constitutionality of both literacy tests and poll taxes through the 1950's. These tests and taxes were, by far, the most serious and widespread barriers to African American electoral participation. In 1957 and 1960, the first federal civil rights acts since RECONSTRUCTION authorized the Justice Department to seek injunctions against state interference with the right to vote and allowed federal courts to appoint referees to supervise and enforce voting registration. While these measures encouraged African American aspirations for political equality, they were weak and incomplete ways to enforce the Fifteenth Amendment.

While the Supreme Court and the Eisenhower Administration were becoming more receptive to claims of racial DISFRANCHISEMENT, racial bars to voting continued to operate in the South. African Americans who pursued their right to register and vote were subject

The Gerry-mander.

A new species of *Monster*, which appeared in *Essex South District* in January last.

This political cartoon satirizes the practice of gerrymandering, by which politicians manipulate district boundaries to dilute the voting strength of certain racial and ethnic groups—an issue that continued to make political headlines in the early 1990's. (Library of Congress)

to economic coercion and intimidation by White Citizens Councils, locally organized segregationist groups composed of prominent officials and businessmen. Where blacks could not be kept from the polls—for example, in large cities—the impact of their vote was often minimized or diluted in the ways that electoral districts were decided. One technique was the gerrymander, a manipulation of district boundaries to exclude black residential areas or submerge them within white majority areas. Also employed was the at-large electoral system, which provided for multimember

districts in which the (white) majority could determine an entire slate of candidates. Such devices ensured that African Americans' votes were "wasted," or had little or no effect on electoral outcomes. The discriminatory nature of this type of racial vote abridgement was examined by the Supreme Court in *Gomillion v. Lightfoot* (1960). In a blatant case of exclusionary gerrymandering, the state of Alabama had redrawn the city boundaries of Tuskegee so as to exclude most of the city's black population from the city limits and thus from municipal elections. Citing the Fifteenth Amendment, the Court invalidated this scheme to deprive a minority of all its voting power.

Contemporary Voting Rights Enforcement. Meanwhile, an increasingly active CIVIL RIGHTS MOVEMENT was pressuring the federal government for the passage of an effective voting rights enforcement act. Following the Mississippi Freedom Summer of 1964, the deaths of three civil rights workers attempting to register black voters, and the upheaval of the demonstrations and marches in Selma, Alabama, the Johnson Administration secured the passage of the VOTING RIGHTS ACT OF 1965. This most far-reaching of all the enforcement acts was intended to make real the promise of the Fifteenth Amendment.

The act's constitutional validity as a broad enforcement measure was affirmed by the Supreme Court in two separate rulings in 1966. The act shifted the burden of proof from the plaintiff challenging a discriminatory electoral practice to the jurisdiction defending its use. Further, the act not only suspended the use of literacy tests, but it outlawed English-only literacy requirements as discrimination against Spanish language-educated Puerto Rican citizens. Most important, the act provided for automatic federal supervision of jurisdictions where such literacy tests had been in place and where voter registration rates had been low. Most of the areas covered were Southern states but certain counties of New York, California, and Arizona were also included later.

The act's coverage of these non-Southern jurisdictions was in response to the use of GERRYMANDERING tactics to dilute the Mexican American, American Indian, and Puerto Rican vote. Initially, there was a question about whether Latinos were covered by the Fifteenth Amendment's protections. Since the amendment forbids denial of the right to vote on the basis of "race or color," its intended beneficiaries had been assumed to be non-white racial minority groups. Yet the Census Department—and many Latinos themselves—classified Latinos as white. Congress skirted the contentious issue by extending protections against discrimination in voting to specified "language minorities." Accordingly, in 1973 in *White v. Regester* the Supreme Court held unconstitutional Texas' use of a multimember electoral district because of its dilution of the voting power of Mexican Americans.

Most voter discrimination cases after 1966 have been statutory; however, an important constitutional

distinct cultural group, they are not a protected minority in terms of the Fifteenth Amendment or the Voting Rights Act. This case raised a difficult question of CULTURAL PLURALISM and representation rights: how to facilitate the political representation of diverse racial, ethnic, and cultural interests within the American electoral system. It is a problem for which the Fifteenth Amendment provides little guidance.

SUGGESTED READINGS. For a discussion of the his-

Before the Voting Rights Act of 1965 was passed in order to enforce the provisions of the Fifteenth Amendment, civil rights groups sponsored voter education programs such as this class to prepare blacks to take southern voter registration tests. (Library of Congress)

question was raised in the 1977 case of *United Jewish Organizations of Williamsburg v. Carey.* A group of Hasidic Jewish plaintiffs challenged a New York legislative districting plan which divided their community between districts in the effort to guarantee the voting strength of African Americans. The Hasidic plaintiffs alleged that such race-conscious districting violated their Fifteenth Amendment rights. The badly split Supreme Court rejected their constitutional claim, arguing that Congress may require states to take race into account in redistricting in order to prevent dilution of minority voting power. Although the Hasidim are a

torical context of the Fifteenth Amendment's passage and early application, see Herman Belz's *Emancipation and Equal Rights* (1978), and Kenneth M. Stampp's *The Era of Reconstruction, 1865-1877* (1965). For accounts of the struggle to secure the political equality of African Americans, see Frank R. Parker's *Black Votes Count: Political Empowerment in Mississippi after 1965* (1990), and Charles S. Bullock III and Charles M. Lamb's *Implementation of Civil Rights Policy* (1984). On the general problem of remedying racial vote dilution, see Abigail M. Thernstrom's *Whose Votes Count?* (1987).—*Nancy Maveety*

Filipino Americans: Filipinos, sometimes referred to as "Pilipinos," make up the second largest Asian American ethnic group, outnumbered only by Chinese Americans. About 740,000 Filipinos, or roughly half of the American Filipino population, are concentrated in California. Another 170,000 live in Hawaii. The Chicago area is also home to a fairly large number of Filipinos. The remainder are dispersed throughout the states, often thoroughly integrated into American neighborhoods and workplaces.

The term "Filipino" refers to someone who comes from the Philippines, or whose ancestors are from the Philippines, a nation composed of more than seven thousand islands across the China Sea from mainland Southeast Asia. The majority of Filipinos are primarily Malays, related to the people of Malaysia and Indonesia, although over the centuries Filipinos have intermarried with Chinese, Spanish people, Americans,

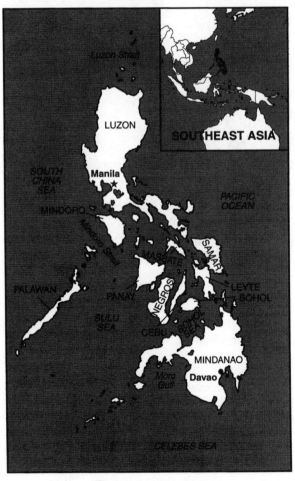

PHILIPPINES

Asian Indians, and other nationalities. The people of the Philippines speak about two hundred dialects classified into eight major language groups, but the TAGALOG LANGUAGE, spoken in the capital of Manila, is spoken and understood by the majority of Filipinos.

Historical Background. The first Filipinos to settle in the United States made their homes in southern Louisiana in the 1830's and 1840's. Most of these pioneers were probably seamen who deserted their ships in the port city of New Orleans, but it is not clear how the men managed to bring their families across the ocean. After the Filipino fishing village of St. Malo was destroyed by a hurricane in the 1890's, the Filipino seaman Quentin de la Cruz founded a second colony, Manila Village, about forty miles south of New Orleans near the mouth of the Mississippi River. By 1933, Manila Village had a population of about fifteen hundred people, most of whom lived by shrimping, fishing, and fur-trapping. Although Manila Village has disappeared, many of the old Filipino families of the New Orleans area retain a sense of their heritage, and they try to preserve their culture through social clubs and Catholic religious organizations.

Apart from this one instance, virtually all of the migration from the Philippines to the United States has occurred in the twentieth century. This migration resulted from the American conquest, occupation, and colonization of the smaller country, which created close and complicated ties between the two countries.

From about 1570 to 1898, the Philippines was a colony of Spain. During this three hundred-year period, Catholicism became the religion of most Filipinos, although the Muslims in the south successfully resisted Spanish control and Spanish efforts at conversion. Philippine languages adopted many Spanish words, and most Filipinos took Spanish names.

In the late nineteenth century, the people of the Philippines rose against foreign domination. At the same time, another Spanish colony, Cuba, began a similar struggle for independence. Public feeling in the United States, stirred up by newspaper reporting, favored the Cuban rebels. American businessmen in Cuba also strongly favored Cuban independence, and a number of American military men and politicians favored war as a means of transforming their country into a world power. In 1898, after a mysterious explosion that sank an American naval ship in Havana harbor, the U.S. declared war on Spain.

As part of the SPANISH-AMERICAN WAR, a U.S. na-

During the 1940's, many Filipino farm workers found employment harvesting crops in California. (Library of Congress)

val fleet, on secret orders from Assistant Secretary of the Navy Theodore Roosevelt, attacked and defeated the Spanish navy in Manila Bay. At first the Filipinos, who had already set up their own independent government welcomed the Americans. The United States, however, for reasons that are still debated, decided to keep the Philippines for itself. The Filipino fighters for independence resisted, and the U.S. government sent its soldiers into a full-scale war of conquest that is still ignored by many American history textbooks. Between 200,000 and 500,000 Filipinos died as a result of the invasion.

Once the Filipinos had been defeated, the new colonial power proceeded to govern its subjects with a mixture of RACISM, profit-seeking, and democratic idealism. The natives of the Philippines were treated as second-class citizens in their own country, and their economy was dominated by American investors. At the same time, though, the Americans built roads, schools, universities, and public buildings. Filipino political institutions were established on the American model. The use of English in high schools and the screening of Hollywood films in theaters brought American culture into the Philippines even before

large numbers of Filipinos settled in the United States.

In World War II, Filipino soldiers fought against the invading Japanese, either in the American army or as guerrillas. The experience of having faced a common enemy, combined with an intimate familiarity with American popular culture, created a special affinity among Filipinos with the large country across the ocean. This situation also raised questions of identity, since the Filipinos were caught between their identification with the United States and their membership in a unique Asian society. The Filipino American community, therefore, grew in the midst of complex relations between the two countries, and the two cultural identities of the community remain intricately woven together.

Migration to the United States. Scholars generally divide migration from the Philippines into three periods. The first period, from 1906 to the beginning of World War II, resulted from the U.S. demand for cheap agricultural labor. Sugar plantations dominated the economy of Hawaii early in the century, and plantation owners were interested in finding hardworking field hands who would work for low wages. The HA-WAIIAN SUGAR PLANTERS ASSOCIATION began recruiting in the Philippines, and by 1946 it had brought more than a quarter of a million Filipinos to Hawaii. California, with its own demands for seasonal agricultural workers, was the home of more than thirty-one thousand of the forty-six thousand Filipinos living in the mainland United States in 1940.

The second migration period lasted from 1946, when the Philippines became politically independent, through 1964. The U.S. government had established large military bases in the foreign colony, and many Filipino women married to American servicemen were admitted to the United States. Filipinos who had become naturalized American citizens after the war were also able to petition to have family members enter the United States, so that most immigrants in this period came as a result of marriage or family connections.

The third migration period began in 1965, when Congress passed the IMMIGRATION AND NATIONALITY ACT OF 1965 that ended the discrimination against Asians in all previous immigration legislation. The result was a rapid growth in the Asian American population in general and in the Filipino American population in particular. The latter grew by roughly 100 percent in each ten-year period from 1960 to 1990: from 176,000 in the Census of 1960 to 343,000 in 1970, 775,000 in 1980 and 1,407,000 in 1990.

Filipinos in American Society. The third wave of Filipino immigrants differs greatly from the earlier waves. While immigrants before 1965 were mostly laborers from rural parts of the Philippines, immigrants after 1965 tend to be highly educated, urban professionals, such as doctors, nurses, teachers, and engineers. This may create "brain drain" problems for the Philippines, since it loses many of its professionals, executives, and technicians to the United States, but it has been a benefit to the American economy. Filipino doctors and nurses are on the staffs of many American hospitals, and teachers from the Philippines are employed in many American schools.

As a result of the generally high level of education of Filipino Americans, they have very high rates of employment. Unlike Korean Americans, who also arrived in large numbers after 1965, Filipinos in the United States tend not to be owners of small businesses. They are more likely than the rest of the American population to work at white-collar jobs.

Although most members of this ethnic group are born overseas, they have become American citizens in large numbers. More than 60 percent of Filipino immigrants who have completed the necessary five

As part of a large population of highly educated professionals, these Filipino American nurses salute their heritage in a Philippine Independence Day Parade in New York City. (Richard B. Levine)

years of residence in the United States have become naturalized citizens. The attempt to maintain both Filipino and American identities may be seen in the use of language. While most Filipinos in the United States speak English well and use English in their places of employment, the majority of them speak a Filipino language at home, according to the U.S. Census.

Cultural Contributions. In the large urban areas of California and in Hawaii, where there are sizable Filipino communities, Filipino Americans have retained much of their distinctive culture. TAGALOG and Cebuano, the two principal Filipino languages, may often be heard in the ethnic neighborhoods of Los Angeles and San Francisco. In these ethnically concentrated districts with intimate ties to the Philippines, residents maintain close-knit, extended families.

Nonfamily members are often included in Filipino American family through the *compadrazgo*, or "godparent," system. When a child is baptized, a number of friends of the parents will be asked to become *comadres* and *compadres* to the child. These words are usually translated as "godmothers" and "godfathers," but they literally mean "comothers" and "cofathers," for the *compadrazgo* system is a way of making the rearing of children a community responsibility. There are strong, familylike bonds between parents and the *comadres* and *compadres*, as well as between these godparents and their godchildren.

The many Filipino Americans who do not live in ethnic neighborhoods are usually very similar to other Americans: They maintain lifestyles that are outwardly indistinguishable from those of their non-Filipino neighbors, live in nuclear families (families composed only of a father, mother, and children, without grandparents or other relatives in the house), and fit into a variety of American workplaces and communities. Nevertheless, even those who have apparently been "melted in the MELTING POT" seem to hold to some of their distinctive cultural values. For example, Filipino Americans often report that *utang na loob*, a phrase that might be translated as "the heartfelt debt," remains an important value for them. This means that they feel a special sense of obligation to anyone who has helped them. The subtle survival of norms and customs may also be seen in the intense sense of hospitality felt in Filipino households. When guests arrive at a Filipino American's house, the host will usually offer them food and insist that the guests take food home with them.

In addition to bringing Filipino traditions to the United States, Filipinos have enriched American culture through their contributions to literature. Perhaps the greatest Filipino American writer was Carlos Bu-

LOSAN. Born in the Philippines in 1914, Bulosan left for California in 1931. Largely self-educated, he initially worked as a fruit-picker on California farms and then became a hobo and traveled on freight trains through the country, later returning to California to become a labor leader. During these wanderings, he wrote several books of poems and short stories that expressed the Filipino American's sense of exile and experience of poverty and discrimination. In 1946, ten years before his death, Bulosan published his best-known work, the autobiography *America Is in the Heart.*

Other important Filipino American writers include Juan Cabreros Laya, whose major theme is the Filipino American's feeling of not fitting into either American or Filipino society, and N. V. M. Gonzalez and Oscar Penaranda, both of whom are writing teachers in American universities as well as novelists. Poet and novelist Jessica Hagedorn's best-selling novel *Dogeaters* (1990) achieved wide recognition and critical

These Filipino Americans run a market that caters to the appetite for ethnic foods. (Gail Denham)

praise. Among the numerous Filipino American poets whose works have appeared in books and journals are Virginia Cerenio, Al Robles, Alfredo Encarnacion, and Vince Gotero.

SUGGESTED READINGS. Readers interested in the Filipino American experience can find Carlos Bulosan's *America Is in the Heart* (1946) in many libraries. Stanley Karnow's *In Our Image: America's Empire in the Philippines* (1989) provides a fascinating overview of relations between the United States and the Philippines. Luis Mangiafico, an American of Filipino ancestry and a high-ranking U.S. diplomat, examines Filipino immigration in *Contemporary American Immigrants: Patterns of Filipino, Korean, and Chinese Settlement in the United States* (1989). Antonio J. A. Pido's *The Pilipinos in America* (1985) is an excellent description of Filipinos as an American minority.—*Carl L. Bankston III*

Filipino Federation of Labor: Labor union organized in 1919 to improve the lives of sugarcane workers in Hawaii. The federation was founded by Pablo MAN-LAPIT, who had come to Hawaii from the Philippines in 1910. He organized Filipino workers in Hawaii and tried to make sure that Filipinos who were thinking about coming to Hawaii knew that working and living conditions were poor. The workers struggled to stay organized and fight together, even after several defeats and new beginnings. In 1932, the group took the name Filipino Labor Union. It continued to have some influence—and many defeats—in Hawaii. Meanwhile, the urge to unionize spread to the mainland. In 1927, the federation became a registered labor union in California.

Finnish Americans: Finnish Americans make up a small but culturally distinct community of European immigrants to the United States. Although some Finns settled in the New Sweden colony on the Delaware River in the mid-seventeenth century, the first significant migration of Finns to the United States did not come until 1865. Finnish immigration reached its height during the period 1890-1920. In the latter year, persons born in Finland made up 1.1 percent of all foreign-born persons in the United States (150,000 out of 13.7 million). Immigration from Finland slowed thereafter because of general restrictions enacted by the United States. By 1980, persons born in Finland made up only .2 percent of all foreign-born persons in the United States (29,000 out of 14 million). Finnish Americans, the descendants of the Finnish immigrants, cannot be numbered with

exactitude from census data, but they probably represent about .5 percent of the total U.S. population.

Historical Background. Throughout the Middle Ages, Finland was a prize in the struggle for power between Sweden and Russia. Sweden gradually conquered the land in the 1100's and 1200's, converted the Finns to Christianity, and later introduced Lutheranism. After several wars with Sweden during the 1700's, Russia occupied Finland in 1809, turning it into a grand duchy under the Russian czar.

During the great age of nationalism in the 1800's, educated Finns, who previously had spoken Swedish, began to take pride in their own Finnish language. Finland's national epic, the Kalevala, was written down. Writers celebrated Finnish life in their works, and composers used Finnish folk melodies. After seventy years of relative peace, repressive Russian policies such as compulsory military service led to discontent and the growth of socialist parties. The czarist policy of "Russification" after 1899 generally attempted to make Finland an indistinguishable part of Russia, thereby increasing Finnish resentment.

Finland took advantage of the Russian revolutions of 1917 to declare its independence but almost immediately fell into a civil war between the socialists and the conservatives. The conservatives won, and they dominated Finnish politics until World War II. After 1945, Finland pursued a policy of neutrality, maintaining good relations with both the Soviet Union and the Scandinavian countries.

Why Emigrants Left Finland. There are two primary factors involved when people migrate to a new land: the "push" factors that cause them to leave one place, and the "pull" factors that draw them to another. In the case of Finnish immigrants to the United States, the "push" factors relate to economics and politics, while the "pull" factors relate to the availability of work, prior knowledge of the destination, and the climate.

The "official" count of emigrants from Finland during the period from 1893 to 1920 numbered more than 273,000. Two thirds came from the northern provinces of Oulu and Vaasa, known for their thin and stony soil, short growing season, and harsh winters. From 1862 to 1868 there had been constant hardship for Finnish farmers, and although the situation had improved, the specter of famine was ever present. Most rural Finns were tenant farmers, landless cottagers, and day laborers who subsisted on low wages and a sparse diet of black bread, potatoes, and fish.

While economic necessity provided the main stimulus for emigration, political problems determined its timing. Many immigrants to the United States left Finland in order to evade the draft. Others engaged in clandestine political agitation against Russification and had to flee from the czarist secret police.

The most popular destinations for the emigrants were Canada—which had about 2,000 Finnish-born persons in 1900, and almost 60,000 in 1971—and the United States. Of prime importance was the American reputation for high wages and cheap land, which appealed to rural, landless Finns. A daily wage of $1.25 in the 1890's was much more than a laborer could hope to earn on the farm back home. Like other immigrants, most of the Finns planned to earn money in the United States and then return to the Old Country. (Only about 20 percent actually managed to make the return journey.) About half of the Finns set themselves up as farmers; many others found work in mining, logging, and fishing.

A second "pull" factor was the common practice of "letters home." Immigrants who wrote back to their home villages to describe their new lives often had their letters published in newspapers. Almost five-sixths of the Finnish immigrants who came to the United States between 1907 and 1920 were joining friends or relatives, and a third came with prepaid tickets.

The Finnish Experience in the United States. There were two distinct waves of immigration from Finland, and two distinct kinds of immigrants: those who came before and after 1900. The first wave was more conservative, both politically and socially, than the second wave, reflecting the fact that the rise of socialist and other radical parties in Finland came after 1900.

There were also religious differences among the immigrants. The vast majority were LUTHERAN, which was the state church of Finland. Among them were followers of Laestadianism, which emphasized ecstatic revivalism, trances, and preaching, leading to a sudden realization of joy at having one's sins forgiven by Christ. Laestadianism was brought to the United States early, appearing in Michigan, Minnesota, and Wisconsin in the 1870's. In Finland, this movement remained within the state church, but in the United States it led to schism. Because there was no American state church, denominations tended to be narrower and less willing to comprehend diversity. Hence Finnish American Lutheranism divided into three groups: the Suomi Synod, the National Church, and the Apostolic

Church. The Suomi Synod eventually amalgamated with the Lutheran Church of America in 1963 and represents the mainstream Protestant strand of Finnish Lutheranism. The National Church amalgamated with the Lutheran Church Missouri Synod in 1964 and represents the conservative, fundamentalist strand. The Apostolic Church, which evolved out of Laestadianism, is fundamentalist in its theology but is too ecstatic in its worship for Missouri Synod-style Lutheranism.

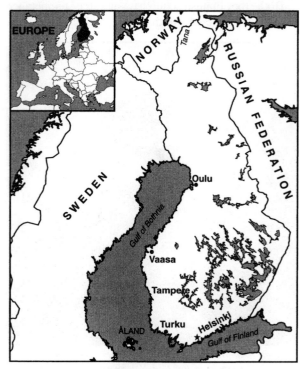

FINLAND

The Finnish churches cooperated in forming temperance societies, which were ubiquitous in Finnish communities until the end of Prohibition. These societies functioned as community social centers in the isolated villages of Michigan, Wisconsin, and Minnesota. In addition, they operated as agents for suppressing what the local church authorities and employers considered to be "deviant" or undesirable behavior. Finns had a reputation for the abuse of alcohol, perhaps because many lived in transient communities in which men outnumbered women.

Finnish temperance societies published newspapers, operated lodges, and served as self-help clubs. Lodge meetings consisted of singing, FOLK MUSIC, poetry reading, the auctioning of needlework, and simple flirtation between young men and women, as well as the more serious temperance lectures. Besides entertainment and edification, the temperance societies provided social benefits unavailable elsewhere. They supplemented the local schools by operating libraries of popular and inspirational literature, which often were made available to nonmembers. The societies also set up insurance and death funds, and paid out benefits to members too ill to work as well as to the families of deceased members.

Both the Finnish churches and the temperance movement suffered controversy, factional splinters,

Finnish immigrants such as this farmer were drawn to the rural environment of the Old Northwest, establishing communities in Michigan, Wisconsin, and Minnesota. (Library of Congress)

and competition from other movements from the mid-1890's onward. One serious conflict was between the temperance movement and SOCIALISM.

Starting in the late 1890's, a new breed of immigrant began arriving from Finland: the socialist or "Red Finn" who imported socialist ideas and organizations. Socialists believed that temperance was only one plank in a platform of economic and social change leading to the redistribution of wealth. In contrast, the temperance lodges believed that the consumption of alcohol was the main abuse in society. A further source of conflict came from the close relations between the temperance lodges and the churches, which distrusted socialism as an antireligious movement.

Finnish settlements in the cranberry region of Massachusetts and the timber lands of the Pacific Northwest also saw similar conflicts among different varieties of Finnish Lutheranism, between liberal and conservative temperance men, and between "Church Finns" and "Red Finns."

Finnish American lifestyles began changing with the DEPRESSION OF THE 1930'S. Young people from the farming communities began moving to large cities in search of better-paying work. Finns from Michigan's Upper Peninsula moved to Detroit, attracted by the automobile industry, while Wisconsinites moved to Duluth, Minnesota, and to Milwaukee. The demands of the growing defense industry in the late 1930's encouraged further migration. The new city dwellers imported Finnish organizations such as the church and the fraternal lodge and patronized Finnish-oriented taverns and dance halls. The Finnish community in Detroit, for example, supported thirty-two taverns in one four-block strip and four commercial saunas, as well as Finnish restaurants, shops, and dance halls.

In the 1950's, urban Finns began moving to the suburbs, as did many other American ethnic groups. This move had the effects of dispersing Finns over a wide area, reducing the significance of ethnic institutions such as taverns and churches and hastening the process of ASSIMILATION. By the end of the twentieth century, some distinctive Finnish communities continued to exist primarily in rural areas.

Cultural Contributions. Finnish Americans brought many customs with them from the Old Country, the sauna probably being the most familiar to non-Finns; they were also sympathetic to European-wide trends such as SOCIALISM. Like other immigrant groups, the Finns supported a lively ETHNIC PRESS. The first Finnish-language newspaper commenced publishing in 1876, and more than 350 such newspapers and magazines appeared in the United States during the following hundred years. (Four survived by 1979 in Massachusetts, New York, Minnesota, and Wisconsin.) Some were religious in nature; others were socialist or temperance. They created a spirit of community and mutual help, which allowed the immigrants to survive in a new environment. They educated newcomers in how to get along in the United States and helped to build self-confidence against the attacks of ethnocentrists who were prejudiced against immigrants in general and Finns in particular.

Finns were in the forefront of the American cooperative movement, forming credit unions, dairy and grain cooperatives, grocery stores, and many other endeavors. Most of the cooperatives were to be found in rural areas, but large retail stores were established in Massachusetts, Minnesota, and Wisconsin.

Finally, in education, the Finns established Suomi College. Located in Hancock, Michigan, the college was affiliated with the Suomi Synod and served as that synod's theological school. It continued in existence after the Suomi Synod's merger in 1963, and it is one of the major centers of Finnish American studies in North America.

SUGGESTED READINGS. John H. Wuorinen's pioneer study *The Finns on the Delaware, 1638-1655: An Essay in American Colonial History* (1938) documents the early presence of Finns in New Sweden. The forty years that saw the height of Finnish immigration to the United States are surveyed in A. William Hoglund's *Finnish Immigrants in America, 1880-1920* (1960). The earlier period is covered in Reino Kero's *Migration from Finland to North America in the Years Between the United States Civil War and the First World War* (1974). Carl Ross treats the role of the Finns in United-States Labor history in *The Finn Factor in American Labor, Culture, and Society* (1978). *Finnish Diaspora* (1981), edited by Michael G. Karni, is an indispensable two-volume collection of papers given at an international conference on Finnish emigration.—*D.G. Paz*

Fisk University (Nashville, Tenn.): Historically black university. Fisk University opened its doors in 1866 as a result of the work of the American Missionary Society and Clinton B. Fisk of the FREEDMEN'S BUREAU of Tennessee. Originally founded to educate African Americans, the nondenominational, coeducational school now enrolls students of all races. Charles Spurgeon Johnson became the school's first African American president in 1948. The university offers two programs: the Basic College, which covers freshman and sophomore courses, and the College of Higher Studies, which offers bachelor's degrees in numerous areas. Fisk also offers master's degrees in eight subjects. Its Jubilee Singers are world-famous.

Fitzgerald, Zelda Sayre (July 24, 1900, Montgomery, Ala.—March 11, 1948, Asheville, N.C.): Writer. Her life was enmeshed with that of writer F. Scott Fitzgerald, whom she married in 1920. In 1924 the Fitzgeralds became expatriates in the south of France. Here Fitzgerald wrote six sketches about the lives of young women,

including one published in *The Saturday Evening Post* in 1929 under her husband's name. She suffered a series of nervous breakdowns beginning in 1930, after which time she wrote a novel, *Save Me the Waltz* (1932), and produced a large number of paintings and drawings. She spent the rest of her life in and out of a mental hospital, where she died in a fire in 1948.

Five Civilized Tribes: CHEROKEE, CHOCTAW, Chickasaw, Creek, and Seminole Nations of American Indians, who were grouped together under this designation after the Indian Removal Act of 1830. The title distinguished these tribes concentrated in the eastern half of INDIAN TERRITORY (now Oklahoma) from the buffalo-hunting Southern Plains tribes who were relocated in the western regions of the area. Distinct cultural groups with their own individual cultures, histories, beliefs, and governances, the Five Civilized Tribes originally shared geographic proximity in the American Southeast: Cherokees in North Carolina and Georgia; Choctaws and Chickasaws in Mississippi; Creeks in Alabama; and Seminoles in Florida. Additionally, these nations were among the first to experience contact with white explorers and colonists, and each had developed a complex, stable, and sophisticated form of social organization, assimilating (and influencing) the European immigrants with whom they had long maintained a tense but peaceful coexistence. After their removal to Oklahoma via the TRAIL OF TEARS, they continued to be bound by even greater proximity, as well as by some distinct aspects of their relations with the federal government. For example, they held their lands under patented title like that of white citizens and unlike the treaties reached between the United States and most other Indian nations and tribes.

Conflict. White encroachment on the traditional lands of Indians of the Southeast was inevitable after the establishment of the southern colonies and the expansion that led to statehood after the American Revolution. Tensions between the Five Civilized Tribes and their neighbors grew. The struggling states frequently coveted the prosperity and social stability of what they increasingly thought of as their heathen and culturally inferior predecessors, and Indians felt mounting resentment toward physical and social infringement by invaders who treated them with both disdain and envy. Particularly with the discovery of gold on Cherokee lands in 1823, frictions increased. Cherokees had an established and complex township system, embracing prosperous plantations under an enlightened and democratic governmental philosophy, while citizens of the American states were still struggling to maintain their control of their newly evolved society.

With the election in 1828 of President Andrew Jackson, an infamous Indian-fighter and frontiersman, the scales tipped in the states' favor, for Jackson had a public disdain for native cultures and strongly op-posed the traditional treaty system. Even before his inauguration, the southern states began enacting a variety of repressive and savage laws against Indians within their boundaries (those of Georgia were not repealed until 1962). The Indians tried to work within the systems of the fledgling nation, fearing the worst,

The Five Civilized Tribes were known for establishing stable governments and promoting Indian literacy. Sequoya, a Cherokee of mixed descent, is shown here displaying the written syllabary he developed for the Cherokee language. (Smithsonian Institution)

and in 1831 in *The Cherokee Nation v. Georgia,* their sovereignty was affirmed by the Supreme Court. This landmark case, bolstered by the Court's subsequent ruling in 1832 with *Worcester v. Georgia*, confirmed the tribes as "domestic dependent nations" whose "relation to the United States resembles that of a ward to his guardian." Reportedly, Jackson responded: "John Marshall has made his decision; now let him enforce it." Jackson approved removal legislation in 1830 which violated Indian sovereignty, yet this illegal action was allowed to progress unimpeded.

Removal. The peaceful CHOCTAWS were the first to be forced from their traditional lands to the alien environment beyond the Mississippi, the majority relocating between 1830 and 1833. As their treaty allowed, almost a third chose to remain behind, establishing individual farms. Governmental corruption and wholesale neglect of protective statutes, however, soon forced the survivors to flee to the new nation in the West. The Creeks voted in 1829 to resist the loss of their territory, but a forced treaty in 1832 made them surrender their Alabama homelands. On arrival in INDIAN TERRITORY, they had lost 24 percent of their numbers, having already been reduced by 45 percent from civil wars that erupted and continued until their capitulation to the federal program in 1836. The Chickasaws were subjected to a series of treaties beginning in 1832, and removed in 1837-1838 without resistance. They received more favorable terms than did any other tribe, finally paying the Choctaws to settle on their new lands.

The other two nations experienced an even more divisive and damaging transition. As the most numerous, prosperous, politically sophisticated, and envied (and thus resented) tribe, the CHEROKEES had tried unsuccessfully to use the federal courts as recourse. By 1834 their national unity was crumbling and the nation was split between those loyal to the resistant Chief John Ross and those favoring the so-called Treaty Party, led by the powerful Ridge family, a faction convinced of the inevitability of removal and concerned with maintaining whatever could be salvaged in the coming displacement. In 1835, the federal government wrote a treaty with the Ridge faction that was subsequently rejected by the full tribal council, and Ross was imprisoned. After his release and while he was on a delegation to Washington, the New Echota Treaty was signed in his absence. In 1838 a reluctant General Winfield Scott was sent with seven thousand soldiers to stockade all Cherokees who had not already trav-

eled west, to seize all their property and holdings, and to remove them forcibly. Of the eighteen thousand people who went to the Territory after 1835, four thousand died in the stockades or en route on the Trail of Tears. In Oklahoma in 1839, members of the antitreaty party assassinated Major Ridge, his son, and journalist Elias Boudinot in retaliation (STAND WATIE, later a Confederate general, was marked for death but escaped), plunging the newly reformed nation into division for many years. Several hundred Cherokees hid in the North Carolina mountains, forming the core of what today is the Eastern Band of Cherokees, which was eventually granted reservation status in that state.

Tricked into a treaty agreement, the Seminoles of Florida refused to leave their lands. The ensuing Seminole War was more costly to the United States in terms of both lives and money than any Indian war in its history. The resistant nation fled to the protective Everglades, led by several chiefs, including OSCEOLA, who was eventually captured and who died in prison. Any possible formal governmental removal was complete by 1842, merging the transplanted Seminoles with the Creeks in Oklahoma by the terms of an 1839 treaty. Warfare in Florida continued, reducing the Seminole population by 40 percent, until the government finally gave up and let the survivors remain in their traditional homelands. There they were finally recognized and granted support in 1962. The Seminoles in Oklahoma adjusted to their displacement poorly, adapting to the new environment far less quickly and successfully than the other nations; a treaty in 1856 purchased land for them from the Creeks and established a school fund, but their progress toward integration was interrupted by the CIVIL WAR.

The Civil War. Surrounded by the Confederacy, the Five Civilized Tribes believed that their only chance for continued survival was to support the South. As a result, new treaties in 1861 resulted in the withdrawal of all federal support for the tribes, although Cherokee Chief Ross led a movement for neutrality. Conservatives among the Creeks, Seminoles, and Cherokees insisted on honoring the original treaties with the United States, provoking civil wars within those nations, although all five eventually allied with the rebels. There were Choctaw-Chickasaw, Creek-Seminole, and Cherokee delegates to the Confederate Congress throughout the war, a right promised Indians since the Delaware Treaty of 1778 but consistently withheld. Indian regiments also fought with distinction; STAND

Unhappy about the Cherokees' treatment at the hands of the U.S. government, Stand Watie recruited a tribal regiment of mounted riflemen to serve in the Confederate Army during the Civil War. (Library of Congress)

WATIE was, indeed, the last Confederate general to surrender. Following the war, the nations were subjected to the general punitive terms imposed on the southern states. The treaties of 1866 represented a range of severe restrictions and losses, including land. With the franchises granted to the railroads through INDIAN TERRITORY, the region lost its fragile protected isolation forever.

Manifest Destiny. The Five Tribes recovered internally with surprising speed, but other nations, both refugees and exiles, were rapidly appearing in the Territory. Realizing that their lands were increasingly being coveted from without, the Five Tribes advised the newcomers to adopt a position of peace and agricultural progress. In 1870, the officially sanctioned Okmulgee Council was convened, with fourteen nations represented, to consider a variety of postwar concerns. By 1879, more than twelve thousand whites were living in the Five Tribes' area, and beginning in 1885, a series of bills was introduced in Congress to open land for homesteading; the only possible options soon seemed to be either forced sales or seizure.

Bowing yet again to the seemingly inevitable, the Creeks and Seminoles were the first to act, selling 3,000 square miles to the government. Thousands of homesteaders eagerly staked claims during the 1889 OKLAHOMA LAND RUNS. More than 100,000 more people joined the land run in 1893 after the Cherokee Outlet was sold to the United States. Greed and corruption soon became the most formidable foes the nations had yet encountered.

Although the Five Tribes and a few others, by virtue of holding their land under patented titles, were initially exempted, the DAWES ACT of 1887 struck a fatal blow to the tribes and soon pauperized virtually all American Indians. The act demanded the division of tribal lands into individual allotments, a concept foreign to most Indian cultures, making Indians easy prey for the unscrupulous. Each person had to be individually enrolled, and those so recorded, if heads of families, could receive 160 acres to be held in trust for twenty-five years (provisions emended to the detriment of Indians in 1906 and twice again as expiration dates approached). Of the 19.5 million acres that belonged to the Five Tribes in 1898, 1.5 million remained in 1934 and only 316,902 by 1956. The Curtis Act in 1898 expanded allotment, mandated the division of national property, terminated tribal governments, and seized control of school systems. Citizenship was generally conferred in 1901, and in 1907, when the Indian Territory was joined with the Territory of Oklahoma and admitted to the Union, only 5.3 percent of the population of the new state was Indian. Although the Indian Reorganization Act of 1934 prohibited further allotment and again permitted the formation of tribal governments, brutal legislation continued to mount, culminating in 1953 with House Concurrent Resolution 108, followed a few days later by Public Law 280, terminating the trust status between the federal government and the Indian nations and allowing the states to extend their laws over reservations.

More positively, reaction against the wholesale exploitation of Indians began early in the twentieth century. The Meriam Report of 1928 detailed a litany of shocking statistics and questionable practices, launching a sincere Senate investigation and awakening many Americans to the degraded and deteriorating situation of Americans Indians. The second half of the century witnessed a resurgence in the social and cultural vitality of the Five Tribes, and the more recent governmental policy of self-determination holds much promise for the continued health and prosperity of the Cherokee, Choctaw, Chickasaw, Creek, and Seminole peoples.

SUGGESTED READINGS. A standard study is Grant Foreman's *The Five Civilized Tribes* (1934). Much can also be added by more recent and focused histories, such as Grace Steele Woodward's *The Cherokees* (1963), and general historical studies such as Angie Debo's *A History of the Indians of the United States* (1970). Debo has also authored *The Five Civilized Tribes of Oklahoma* (1951), *The Rise and Fall of the Choctaw Republic* (2d ed., 1961), *The Road to Disappearance: A History of the Creek Indians* (1941), and *History of the Choctaw, Chickasaw, and Natchez Indians* (1962).—*Rodney Simard*

Flamenco dance and music: First performed by GYPSIES in southern Spain. Flamenco dancing exists both in a folk form and in a version for stage performance. Originally dancers were guided by singing and accompanied by the clapping of hands and the stamping of feet. Later guitars were added. Musicians provide a repetitive yet varied rhythm to which the dancers improvise and add personal interpretations. Movements often include finger snapping and heel stamping. Flamenco dances may be performed by a single person, a couple, or a large group. Colorful costumes and much vocal participation contribute to the excitement of the performance. Spanish Americans have kept the flamenco style alive as a FOLK-DANCE tradition.

Flappers: Young, often upper-class women of the 1920's who symbolized a shift to the modern age. In contrast to their foremothers, flappers represented a free view of sexuality, individualism, and consumption. In style, the flapper cut her hair short, traded in her corsets for shorter and looser clothing, wore cosmetics, enjoyed dancing and jazz, and smoked cigarettes. She generally abandoned the social concerns of the suffragist generation to focus on herself and her appeal to men as a sex object. The problems of gender antagonism of the nineteenth century drifted beyond view as the flapper embraced men as friends and partners.

Flores, Thomas Raymond (b. Mar. 21, 1937, Fresno, Calif.): Latino football player and coach. After earning his B.A. degree from the University of the Pacific in 1958, Flores began his professional football career when he was drafted by the Calgary Stampedes of Canada. He

played for the Washington Redskins before joining the Oakland Raiders in 1960 as quarterback. Flores moved to the Buffalo Bills in 1967 and to the Kansas City Chiefs in 1968. After retiring as a player, he was assistant coach for the Bills in 1971 and for the Raiders from 1971 to 1978, becoming the Raiders' head coach in 1979. Flores led the Raiders to Super Bowl victories in 1981 (from Oakland) and 1984 (from Los Angeles). He was named Latino of the Year for the City of Los Angeles in 1981 and National Football League Coach of the Year in 1982. In 1989, he was hired by the Seattle Seahawks as the team's president and general manager; he became their head coach in 1992.

Tom Flores was the first Latino to rise within the National Football League to become general manager of a professional football team. (Seattle Seahawks)

Folk art: Visual expression that takes a variety of forms, according to several competing definitions. Artists, art historians, museum professionals, collectors, folklorists, and the general public all have their own fiercely defended ideas of what folk art is. Most agree that it differs from fine art in terms of the training of the artist and the function of the object. The three main definitions, roughly summarized, treat folk art as a naïve artifact, a community-based tradition, or a visionary creation.

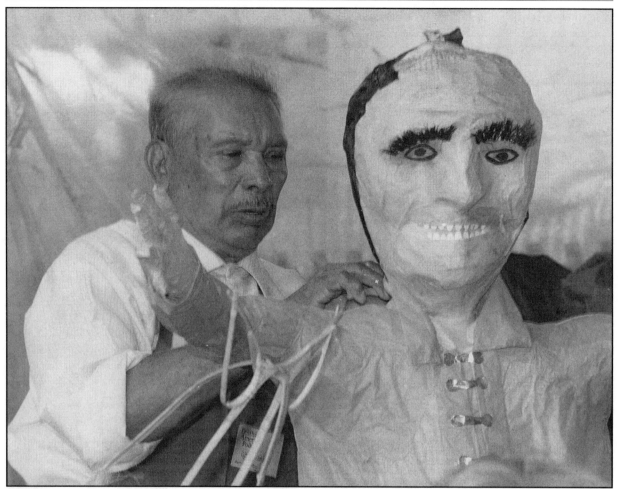

A Mexican American toy maker demonstrates his craft at the Festival of American Folklife in Washington, D.C. (Smithsonian Institution)

For most of the twentieth century, folk art meant the work of untrained painters, sculptors, and craftspeople, whose objects were often described as "simple," "primitive," or "naïve." Examples in the United States ranged from the charming rural scenes painted by Grandma Moses to American colonial samplers and weathervanes. Such folk art was often synonymous with artifacts, decorative arts, or Americana. These works were appreciated as objects in and of themselves, with little interest in their makers (who were often unknown) or their cultural environments—both of which were far from the world of art schools, museums, and galleries.

By contrast, folklorists became increasingly concerned with the cultural context of traditional objects, especially functional objects known as crafts. Their research found that these objects derived their meaning and much of their aesthetic style from the community in which they were made, notably communities based on ethnicity, occupation, or region. Folklorists maintained that crafts and other things previously dismissed as folk art were not only functional but also beautiful and often complex in conception and technique. Thus, folklorists attempted to debunk negative STEREOTYPES of folk art and replace them with a more glorified notion of these objects as expressions of community values and aesthetics, as conveyed through an individual's distinctive style. Examples include African American quilts, Mexican American religious wood carvings called *santos*, Hmong American embroidery, Ukrainian American Easter egg decoration, loggers' chainsaw sculptures, and a host of traditional American Indian arts and crafts. Such types of folk art were not fixed, immutable forms, but changed and adapted to new circumstances and outside artistic influences.

The folklorists' view was reinforced in the 1970's by the federal government's establishment of the American Folklife Center at the Library of Congress and the Folk Arts Program in the National Endowment for the Arts (NEA). The NEA funded projects such as folk art apprenticeships, in which master artists passed on their skills, and state folk art exhibitions that collected and documented an astonishing array of traditional visual objects from every ethnic and regional group. National Heritage Awards were given to exemplary makers of folk art, such as Japanese American bonsai artists or Pomo Indian basketmakers. These efforts furthered the notion that folk art is a vital part of everyday life in the United States rather than a product of preindustrial times or faraway places. NEA projects also gave artistic credibility and respect to traditional arts, even if the makers of the objects often did not see themselves as artists.

Since the mid-1900's, yet another type of visual expression has come to be called folk art by museums and collectors, though folklorists prefer to call it "visionary art" or "folk art environments." This refers to the creations of untrained artists, often older or isolated people, who produce assemblages or worlds of their own ambitious imaginations, often from recycled objects. One well-known example is the Watts Towers in Los Angeles, a striking complex of three tall towers made of steel and bits of glass, tile, crockery, and mirrors, constructed singlehandedly by an Italian American stonemason named Simon Rodia over a period of thirty years. Such unusual places can be found across the country in both rural and urban areas, though they are often in danger of being razed as eyesores.

Folk art from around the world has influenced many well-known, innovative nineteenth and twentieth century artists, such as Pablo Picasso and Paul Klee. Ethnic traditional arts continue to shape the direction of contemporary visual art and artists in the United States, as in the assemblages made by Amalia Mesa-Baines that are inspired by Catholic Mexican American home altars.

SUGGESTED READINGS. For an overview of the definitional debate on folk art and its meaning in different settings, see *Folk Art and Art Worlds* (1986), edited by John Michael Vlach and Simon J. Bronner. Information on the folklorists' view is summarized in "Folk Art" by Henry Glassie in *Folklore and Folklife: An Introduction* (1972), edited by Richard Dorson, and Kenneth L. Ames's *Beyond Necessity: Art in the Folk Tradition* (1977).

Folk dance: Celebratory, communal forms of dance that are traditional to certain national, ethnic, or regional groups. Folk dance falls under the broader heading of FOLKLORE. As such, it is typically passed on from one generation to the next by example, informal instruction, and participation, rather than being learned from books or in formal training. It is anonymous in origin and exists in many different forms. Like the term "FOLK MUSIC," the term "folk dance" makes a distinction between these forms and the more complex styles of classical dance such as ballet that are associated with formal training and elite audiences.

Folk dance has been found in all times, cultures, and places, from the satyr dances that accompanied ancient Greek comedies to the line dance *syrto* danced at modern Greek American weddings. Some folk dances, such as Anglo American square dances, may reflect traditional courtship rituals as they mime the perennial drama of attraction, rejection, pursuit, and conquest. Other types of folk dances relate to hunting, work, vegetation/fertility, and friendship—often the most basic concerns of a society. Some folk dances have magical, supernatural, religious, or mythic overtones.

As different as many folk dances are in style and meaning, they are alike in that they are typically celebratory in nature, designed to bring people together physically and spiritually, to promote positive feelings of fun, friendship, kinship, and community. In this respect the Macedonian and Croatian *kolos* are characteristic folk dances. Performed at weddings, family gatherings, or any festive occasion, *kolos* feature a joining of hands (literal and symbolic unity), a circular configuration (one of the most basic folk dance patterns, possibly suggestive of life's cyclical nature), and joyous exclamations from participants.

In the twentieth century, folk dances that were originally participatory are also performed at formal occasions such as ethnic HOLIDAYS or multicultural city FESTIVALS. For example, young Mexican Americans dance in FOLKLÓRICO troupes to share their culture with others, while Irish American children drilled in the rigorous style of Irish step dancing take part in competitions as well as performances. The ETHNIC HERITAGE REVIVAL of the 1970's greatly increased the interest in folk dance among all ethnic groups. Some modern dance choreographers have consciously incorporated folk dance elements, as when Katherine DUNHAM introduced her African American dance troupe to Haitian styles. There is also a recreational folk dance

This folklórico dancer demonstrates the characteristic steps of Mexican folk dance. (James L. Shaffer)

movement in which people of all backgrounds learn and participate in international dances.

SUGGESTED READINGS. A good general introduction to the subject is found in *Funk and Wagnalls Standard Dictionary of Folklore, Mythology, and Legend* (2 vols., 1949-1950), edited by Maria Leach, which presents a detailed discussion of both folk and primitive dance across various cultures. David C. Laubach's *Introduction to Folklore* (1989) considers folk dance in relation to folk music and to the broader field of folklore. Ted Sarella's *Balance and Swing: A Collection of Fifty-five Savares, Contras, and Triplets in the New England Tradition with Music for Each Dance* (1982) and Robert G. Dalsemen's *West Virginia Square Dances* (1982) provide examples of American regional folk dances.

Folk music: Traditionally, music characteristic of a national, ethnic, or other group that is passed down by word of mouth and whose composer usually remains anonymous. Folk music must be acceptable to members of a group in order to survive; it binds communities together in a common heritage. Because it exhibits great variety and has changed considerably in the twentieth century, folk music is difficult to define. It is often stereotyped as the simple, amateur, unchanging music of poor or marginalized rural groups, or romanticized as the voice of the common people. Yet scholars have found that folk music undergoes great variation over time, and urban folk singers since the 1960's have brought professional standards to some American folk music.

One useful way to look at folk music is in contrast to both the classical music of the elite and the popular music of the masses. Unlike the former, most folk music does not rely on professionally trained composers and performers; unlike the latter, folk music is not usually transmitted by the mass media. Yet folk music styles have influenced classical composers such as

William Grant Still and popular performers such as Linda RONSTADT. Likewise, folk music may evolve into more popular forms, as when the African American field holler led to country and urban BLUES, or when immigrant groups began to use modern nonacoustic instruments and cassette recordings to transmit their songs. It is important to remember, however, that not all ethnic music is folk music. For example, most Asian American groups have popular music (Vietnamese American rock bands) and classical music (for Korean court dance) as well as folk music (for Japanese American Bon Odori celebrations).

Traditional American folk music serves various functions and takes many different forms. It accompanies folk dance, ritual, and calendric and life cycle celebrations such as weddings. For example, Croatian Americans dance to the rapid tempo music of the plucked *tamburitsa* lute; Cherokee Baptist choirs sing their own style of hymns; Sephardic Jews sing special songs at the circumcision ceremony of their sons. Folk song can range in mood from the sweetness of a love song, as in a Filipino American serenade, to the vigor of a work song, as in one of the chain gang songs of renowned African American folksinger Huddie Ledbetter (known as Leadbelly). Folk ballads that tell a story are important in many areas, from the famous Child ballads of Appalachia that are related to similar songs in the British Isles, to the topical CORRIDOS sung in Spanish in the Southwest. Certain instruments are a hallmark of certain types of folk music, such as the button accordion that is used in the Cajun music of Louisiana and the *musica norteña* of Mexican Americans, or the banjo of early African American folk music that is still heard in much Anglo American country music. There are also regional styles of American folk music, such as the scores of different types of fiddle music that can be heard from the French Canadian Americans in New England to the Athabascans in Alaska.

In a multicultural society, there is great exchange between different types of music, which mutually influence one another. African American folk music, for example, has had a powerful effect on many other kinds of American music with its syncopated rhythms, call and response patterns, and stress on improvisation. Ethnic groups have perpetuated their folk music through the formation of singing groups and the support of instrumental musicians for community events; for example, one of the first acts of the early Welsh settlers was to establish choirs and song contests. The ETHNIC HERITAGE REVIVAL of the 1970's also encour-

Popular singers such as Linda Ronstadt, seen here with her 1988 Grammy Award, have made the folk music of their heritage known to a wider audience. (AP/Wide World Photos)

aged many Americans to rediscover their traditional musical roots.

Often, American folk music is associated with songs of social protest that address current issues. Activists in the early LABOR MOVEMENT and CIVIL RIGHTS MOVEMENT, for example, adapted folk songs or made up new ones that passed into oral tradition in order to voice their concerns. The urban folksingers of the folk revival in the 1960's, such as Pete Seeger and Joan BAEZ, brought these and other folk songs to a large audience in both new and traditional versions.

SUGGESTED READINGS. For a general discussion, see *The Story of Folk Music* (1976) by Melvin Berger. John Greenway, in his *American Folksongs of Protest* (1970), discusses the political history of folk music. One good illustrated encyclopedia that emphasizes the folk revival of the 1960's is *Folk Music: More Than a Song* (1976) by Kristin Baggelaar and Donald Milton. Especially useful for tracing the influence of African American blues on folk music is Nicholas Tawa's *A Sound of Strangers: Musical Culture, Acculturation, and the Post-Civil War Ethnic American* (1982).

Folk music, ethnic. *See* **Ethnic folk music**

Folklore: Often refers to the traditional customs, arts, tales, and other expressions of an ethnic, religious, or regional group. These expressions are usually learned informally and passed on orally from one generation to the next. Folklore can be most simply understood when it is broken down into its components of "folk" and "lore." The "folk," once seen as backward or illiterate people, today refers to members of any group who share something in common, most notably ethnicity, religion, family, occupation, or region, but also such things as a disability, as in the special sign language-based jokes that are part of the folklore of deaf people. There are many examples of types of lore shared by a group: beliefs such as superstitions, objects such as crafts, practices such as folk medicine, stories such as legends, events such as HOLIDAYS AND FESTIVALS. FOLK MUSIC, FOLK DANCE, and FOLK ART are generally contrasted to classical styles of music, dance, and visual art done by professionally trained musicians or to popular styles disseminated by the mass media. Yet folk expression has become increasingly less isolated and distinct from other styles with modern communication and URBANIZATION.

Folklore is also a field of academic study concerned with various kinds of "folk" and their lore. Originally in the eighteenth century, folklore study was associated with the relics of ancient or primitive cultures, which the English called "popular antiquities." The term "folklore" was coined in the mid-1800's to describe European peasant culture, such as the folk tales collected in Germany by the Grimm brothers. The American Folklore Society was established in 1888 with an early interest in the lore of Anglo Americans (such as the long Child ballads from the British Isles that thrived in Appalachia), French Americans, Mexican Americans, American Indians, and African Americans.

Gradually, American folklorists expanded their interest beyond texts and "verbal art" to other forms of expression and the cultural contexts in which they were found. By 1949, the *Standard Dictionary of Folklore, Mythology, and Legend* listed twenty-one definitions of folklore. Contemporary folklorists may study everything from methods of fishing in the New Jersey Pine Barrens to uses of the image of the Statue of Liberty to the "Xeroxlore" (cartoons, fictitious memos, slogans) that is created by and circulated among contemporary office workers. Folklorist Elliott Oring prefers to speak of an "orientation" rather than a definition for what folklorists study. This is characterized by a focus on that which is communal, informal, ordinary, marginal, personal, and traditional in aesthetic forms, beliefs, behaviors, and events.

Folklore is commonly misunderstood or denigrated as something untrue or outmoded, as in the phrase, "that's just folklore." Yet folklore, in the sense meant by folklorists, is not a relic of distant times and places. Rather, it is marked by variation and change, and new folklore is always being invented. The break dancing moves and GRAFFITI styles that were pioneered and polished by many young Americans in the 1980's, for example, are examples of modern urban folklore.

The abundance and diversity of folklore in the United States reflects the experiences of the many peoples within "the people." Between its two coasts, as culturally different as the empires that colonized them, and its two national borders, the United States has fostered the evolution of a variety of regional cultures. The deserts of the Southwest, the hill country of Appalachia and the Ozarks, the badlands, farmlands, and urban centers all have their distinctive folklore. Language reflects this variety of American expressions. English is mixed liberally with German influences in Pennsylvania, French in Louisiana, Spanish in the old Mexican territory of the Southwest, African languages in the South, and various tongues in immigrant enclaves. The folklore of immigrant ancestors remains vital, though it has changed through the generations with ASSIMILATION and exposure to other peoples. A few common folklore genres are discussed below.

Rites of Passage. Custom directs the poignant ceremonies that hail the milestones of individual lives. Events such as birth, marriage, and death are universally celebrated and are steeped in folkloric traditions. Most Jewish American families, for example, still practice the ancient tradition of a ritual circumcision, called brit milah or bris, which symbolizes God's covenant with the descendants of Abraham. To soothe the baby, it is traditional to give him sweet wine; to soothe the adults present, it has become customary to tell bris-related jokes. Other forms of folklore associated with birth include certain verbal expressions or the placing of amulets near a newborn to ward off the "evil eye" that may bring harm to a baby, as practiced by some Arab Americans, Greek Americans, and Italian Americans. Yet another form in the area of material culture are the cradleboards traditionally made by American Indians to carry infants.

A range of folk traditions are maintained at celebrations such as this annual street procession for Our Lady of Guadalupe in New York City. (Odette Lupis)

Since the ETHNIC HERITAGE REVIVAL of the 1970's, weddings have increasingly become an occasion for asserting one's ethnic identity through the maintenance or reincorporation of discarded customs. For example, some African American couples in the 1990's included "jumping over the broom" at their weddings in an evocation of an old slave practice, while folk klezmer bands, once common in eastern Europe, were increasingly in demand at Jewish weddings in the United States. From Armenian Americans to Cuban Americans, newlyweds and their families often choose to feature traditional foods, music, and dance at lavish celebrations, regardless of their level of assimilation in daily life.

The types of elaborate dress, social ritual, and feasting that have grown up around the religious ceremony of a Mexican American QUINCEAÑERA (coming-of-age celebration for fifteen-year-old girls), as well as a Jewish American BAR MITZVAH or BAT MITZVAH, have often made these events as impressive and expensive as a wedding. Ethnic markers at weddings combine with mainstream American customs, such as the bride and groom cutting the first slice of a multitiered wedding cake and feeding it to each other, or the bride throwing her bouquet to a cluster of single women to predict who will marry next.

Death customs may also reveal combinations of mainstream practices, such as embalming or a brief religious service at the graveside, and distinctive ethnic or regional traditions, such as merry Irish American wakes and New Orleans funeral processions with live jazz music. Folk traditions often reveal a celebratory or ironic view of death, which is treated as an inevitable part of life rather than as a taboo subject. For example, the DAY OF THE DEAD has been practiced by Mexican American families in the Mexican border states since before the acquisition of the territory by the United States. Mass is said for those who have died, and the community turns out for a day lacking the morbid dread often associated death. Cemeteries are cleaned, trimmed, and weeded, and graves are decked with flowers, food, and other offerings. A family picnic often follows among the resting places of loved ones.

Folk Belief and Religion. The Hawaiian belief in *mana*—the essential, individual force of all things, animate or inanimate—has provided the English-speaking world with a term for that which cannot be violated without the gravest of consequences—"taboo." The term today is indiscriminately applied to all sorts of superstitions, from the European prohibition against proceeding where a black cat has passed to the Chinese custom of waiting until a child is a month old before risking a gift.

Before modern science won credence, the nature of the universe was explained by concepts similar to the Hawaiians' *mana*, as well as myth and religion. Answers were sought in the arrangement of stones and shells, the behavior of animals, the appearance of birthmarks, and the imagery of dreams. For example, some American Indian tribes encouraged young people to go on a "vision quest" as part of their initiation into adulthood. Aid was to be found in the use of herbs, the concoction of charms, and the invoking of spirits, as in the shamanism practiced by various American groups.

Yet myth and superstition do not merely precede science; they persist in spite of or alongside scientific knowledge. The new age movement revived some of the herbal remedies that have been used by ethnic minorities and older Americans for generations; scientists have researched some of these products for their beneficial chemical effects. Similarly, the same women who undergo high-tech prenatal tests in a hospital listen attentively when their elders speculate about the sex of the fetus according to the shape of the pregnant woman's stomach.

Folk religion, too, coexists alongside more official, mainstream practices. According to folklorist William Clements, the folk church in the United States tends to exist on the margins of society among poor or pe-

A Chinese American practices an important folk tradition as he does Chinese palm readings for visitors at a Washington, D.C., folklife festival. (Smithsonian Institution)

Haitian immigrants brought their African-derived religious faith—voodoo—to the United States. Here, women perform a voodoo ceremony at the 1989 Festival of American Folklife. (Smithsonian Institution)

ripheral groups. It is often characterized by informality, emotionalism, egalitarianism, isolation, evangelism, and an orientation in the past. Instances include the speaking in tongues, divine healing, and testifying that are part of worship in some Baptist and Pentecostal congregations. The black folk church has long been a center and support of many African American communities, in both rural and urban areas. It combines West African and Protestant influences and reflects aspects of the experience of slavery and discrimination. Among its folklore products are SPIRITUALS, GOSPEL MUSIC, baptism customs, and various preaching styles, which folklorists have studied for their remarkably effective rhetoric and rhythm.

The Spanish conquest brought Catholicism to the Americas; the slave trade brought Africans. The result was the superimposition of African gods on Christian saints, as in the Afro-Cuban religion called SANTERÍA. It thrives in Latino communities, especially in Miami, New York City, and Los Angeles. From Haiti comes another African-derived religion: voodoo. Its North American (and largely Protestant) sister cult, hoodoo,

arose under similar circumstances of forced conversion and is still practiced widely in the South. The powerful influences of hoodoo, voodoo, and Santería are sought for healing and hexing, antihexing and ensuring good luck, for fertility and sudden death, for finding and keeping love—all the standard complaints for which folklore everywhere has always attempted to provide a cure.

Every religion, whether folk, mainstream, or in between, has its own folklore. One rich source is the tales and customs of MORMONS, who have always considered themselves a people apart from others. They share an unusual heritage of the practices of polygamy, pioneer struggles, and the fight against anti-Mormon prejudice. Young Mormons who have completed the required two years of missionary work have distinctive tales to tell about their experience. Mormons also share songs, cuisine, holidays, and jokes that poke fun at themselves. Among other religious groups, Latino CATHOLICS in the Southwest make or collect beautiful wooden *santos* (carved figures of saints) while Catholics everywhere like to trade stories of their days

African American artist Palmer C. Hayden used the folk legend of John Henry as the basis for a series of paintings, including this one of John Henry's death. (National Archives)

in parochial schools; Jews do Israeli FOLK DANCES and eat fried foods at HANUKKAH; and BUDDHISTS bring holiday offerings of food to their saffron-robed monks, who bless them with holy water.

Tales. Folktales are primarily oral entertainments springing from the experience of a folk group and perpetuated by the imagination, memory, and narrative abilities of the tellers.

Isolation and illiteracy have frequently contributed to the preservation of folktales. In the Ozarks, where poverty and poor soil conditions long prevented inhabitants from keeping pace with the changing world, early American folklorists discovered a rich vein of lore. The "hillfolk" of the Ozarks are the descendants of English immigrants who settled in the southern Appalachians but were pushed west in the 1830's and 1840's as planters and more prosperous farmers claimed the better land. The story of the Arkansas Traveler describes the inhospitable reception a pas-

serby receives in an isolated cabin until he helps its occupant finish a fiddle tune. The popularity of this tale was established by 1850, and its currency demonstrated by Arkansawyer Bill Clinton's 1992 presidential election victory speech, in which he announced the "arrival" of the Arkansas Traveler.

American folktales rarely depict straightforward nobility or plain honesty. The Traveler's rustic host withholds his generosity and conceals his shrewdness until the stranger in some way demonstrates his own worth, according to regional standards. The New England Yankee is often an unscrupulous salesman, but he is also a figure of common sense as economical with his words as with his wallet and possessing an almost fierce self-reliance. The Hoosier is portrayed as an irrepressible braggart, boasting the wonders of his home state's beef—yet the punchline never besmirches the reputation of the bovine from Indiana. A culture's traditional virtues are present, though usually buried be-

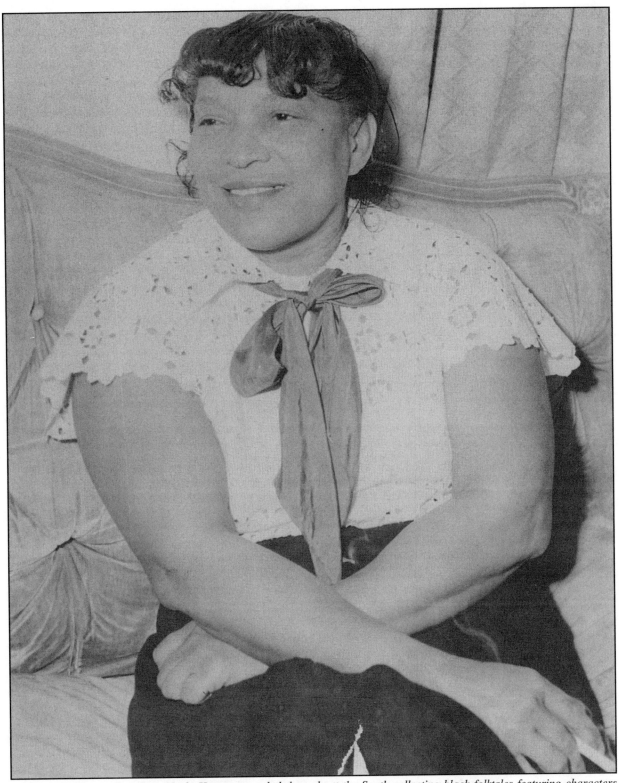

African American author Zora Neale Hurston traveled throughout the South collecting black folktales featuring characters such as Br'er Rabbit. (AP/Wide World Photos)

neath an ironic twist or unfavorable stereotype.

The Flying Fool and the Flying African are two popular African American folktales. In the first, a deceased black man is rejected at the gates of Heaven but succeeds in slipping in and appropriating a pair of wings until an outraged Saint Peter discovers the intruder and casts him back to earth. Relating his adventure to friends he boasts, "They may not let any colored folk in, but while I was there I was a flying fool." In the second tale, a plantation's exhausted slaves lift their arms and fly back to Africa. Such tales offered obvious inspiration to an oppressed people. The more familiar animal tales, however, were to a large degree brought from Africa rather than originating in conditions of slavery or segregation.

The trickster is a familiar character in folklore all over the world. Too full of mischief to be a hero and too full of charm to be a true villain, he usually appears in tales that offer no moral, justice, or even a predictable outcome. Trickster is no more likely to succeed in his trickery than he is to be out-tricked by his annoyed victim. Trickster tales offer universal entertainment, and it is not surprising that versions of the most famous of Br'er Rabbit's exploits—his entanglement with the tar baby and his escape through the briar patch—are found throughout North America. There is a Spanish American variant in which Sis Fox and Br'er Coyote, trickster figures of the Southwest, become stuck to a wax doll for essentially the same reasons (and with essentially the same outcome) as the African Americans' Br'er Rabbit. The Pine Gum Baby is a favorite folktale among southeastern tribes.

Often, but not always, a trickster, Coyote is as ubiquitous in American Indian folklore as his animal counterpart is in the American landscape. In the Northwest, he is the greatest of the animal people, and his role in diverting the Columbia River is told in a poignant creation tale. Coyote falls in love with the daughter of a powerful chief who advises him to win her heart. Coyote creates a private bathing pool for the chief's daughter by turning the river and screening it with a waterfall, thus winning her heart. Two gossiping grandmothers then humiliate Coyote's betrothed, who throws herself in the river, followed by Coyote. The two lovers are turned into little ducks that forever look back toward the river's westernmost cascade.

American history is haunted by the many tribes that disappeared as European American settlements spread across the continent. MANIFEST DESTINY left a legacy of tales describing courage and bloodthirst, courtesy and treachery, from both Anglo and Indian perspectives. Historical persons such as Daniel Boone, Kit CARSON, Buffalo Bill Cody, GERONIMO, and CRAZY HORSE became glorified in folktales despite the documentary evidence of their lives.

More folktales have been introduced by each new influx of immigrants, including humorous stories of "greenhorns" eating an entire banana, peel and all, as part of their adjustment to American life. Among the most recent groups with a rich body of lore are the Hmong Americans, who, while in refugee camps in Thailand, wove "storycloths" depicting traditional Hmong life and the ravages of war in Laos. In time, the Tiger figure of the Hmong may be as familiar to American children as the African American's Rabbit or the American Indian's Coyote.

Folktales such as those described above may not be frequently told outside of certain ethnic enclaves. Nearly all Americans, however, have told or heard tales in the form of personal narratives about their own family's history, customs, and personalities. These change with each rendition, like other folklore, and may be the center of social interaction at family reunions, holidays, and other occasions. Another familiar modern folktale is the urban legend, bizarre stories in realistic urban settings that are told as if they are true and circulated as often by the mass media as by informal communication.

In some of these legends, pet baby alligators flushed down toilets grow to huge proportions in the dark, forbidding sewers of New York City, or rats frequently topple into the batter of fast-food chicken vendors, only to be served to the friend of a friend of adolescent storytellers across the country. These legends are thought to reflect the fears and divisions of modern urban life and the technological age.

Mass communication has to a large degree replaced the community storyteller as the distiller of tales; it can be used to convey the cultural legacy of one people to others. Yet new folklore forms continue to emerge and old ones flourish as part of the vitality of the nation's many cultures.

SUGGESTED READINGS. For an overview of American folklore forms and folklore study, see the *Handbook of American Folklore* (1983), edited by Richard M. Dorson. A more recent, analytical approach to the field may be found in two books edited by Elliott Oring, *Folk Groups and Folklore Genres: An Introduction* (1986) and *Folk Groups and Folklore Genres: A Reader* (1989). *A Treasury of American Folklore*

(1944), edited by B. A. Botkin, is a massive classic collection of ballads, riddles, and tales from all over the United States. A classic compilation of African American lore is Zora Neale Hurston's *Mules and Men* (1935), while a good modern collection is Daryl Cumber Dance's *Shuckin' and Jivin': Folklore from Contemporary Black Americans* (1978). Women's folklore is explored in *Women's Folklore, Women's Culture* (1985), edited by Rosan A. Jordan and Susan J. Calik. For a survey of American Indian Coyote tales as well as a sampling of the work of three of the great earlier folklorists, see *Coyote Wisdom* (1938; facsimile edition, 1965), compiled by Frank J. Dobie, Mody C. Boatright, and Harry H. Ransom. Jan Brunvand has written several books on urban legends, including *The Vanishing Hitchhiker: American Urban Legends and Their Meanings* (1981).—*Ivy Potts*

Folklórico: Term derived from the word "folklore" that is most commonly applied to Mexican folk dances, or *baile folklórico*. Each region in Mexico is known for its distinctive traditional dances and costumes. Today these are studied, preserved, and practiced by numerous amateur and professional groups in Mexico and the United States. In Mexican American communities, *folklórico* classes and performances are a popular way of passing on cultural heritage to the young and representing Mexican culture to other communities.

Jane Fonda accepts an Oscar on behalf of her father, Henry Fonda, for his performance in the 1981 film On Golden Pond. *(AP/Wide World Photos)*

Fonda, Jane (b. Dec. 21, 1937, New York, N.Y.): Actor, producer, and political activist. Fonda's earlier films include *Barbarella* (1968) and *Cat Ballou* (1965), in which she played stereotyped female roles. During the Vietnam War she formed the Anti-War Troupe with Donald Sutherland and visited Hanoi, North Vietnam. Three films came out of this period. She began producing in the late 1960's and 1970's and is known for her serious films on women's issues. Some of these titles include: *A Doll's House* (1973), *Julia* (the story of Lillian Hellman, 1977), *Nine to Five* (1980), and *Women Coming of Age* (1984). She expresses her antinuclear sentiments in the 1979 film *China Syndrome* and in *The Morning After* (1986).

Fong, Hiram Leong (b. Oct. 15, 1906, Honolulu, Hawaii): Politician. The young Yau Leong Fong changed his name to Hiram in honor of the nineteenth century missionary Hiram Bingham. Reared in Honolulu by Chinese-born parents, Fong earned his law degree from Harvard University in 1935 and went to work in the Honolulu city attorney's office. Elected as a member of the Republican Party, Fong served in the Hawaiian territorial legislature from 1938 through 1954. After Hawaii achieved statehood, Fong served in the U.S.

Hiram Fong served as the first U.S. senator of Chinese descent when he represented Hawaii in the U.S. Senate between 1959 and 1977. (Library of Congress)

Senate from 1959-1977. In his government service as well as his private practice, Fong always kept in mind the ethnic diversity of the Hawaiian population and was instrumental in recommending qualified persons of Asian and Hawaiian ancestry to serve as judges and political officials. He has traveled throughout Asia and has received awards from the Republic of Taiwan and South Korea.

Food and cooking: The term "MELTING POT," used in describing the variety of newcomers streaming to American shores since the nineteenth century, might also symbolize the cuisines that were adapted and adopted from indigenous ingredients in the United States. Peoples around the globe have contributed to the joys of cooking and eating, with dishes such as bouillabaisse from France, pastas from Italy, couscous from Morocco, blini from Russia, moussaka from Greece, enchiladas from Mexico, sushi from Japan, piri piri from Mozambique, and arroz con pollo from Puerto Rico. All these, plus the influences of American Indian and African American cultures, have whetted Americans' varied palates and created unity from diversity, making foods and cooking a virtual ambassador of MULTICULTURALISM.

The stereotyping of "American" foods as consisting only of hamburgers, hot dogs, and apple pie is passé. From its beginnings, colonial America assimilated a variety of cultural influences such as British, American Indian, Spanish, and French. The immigration stream soon became a flood, and men and women from around the world brought their customs of cooking and eating into American kitchens.

Food and Culture. It is often through food that Americans are introduced to one another's cultures. Many people are drawn to ethnic FESTIVALS and ethnic neighborhoods by the lure of exotic foods and find the sampling of new dishes in these settings to be positive, tension-free encounters with cultural diversity. Even before the advent of MULTICULTURAL EDUCATION, schools taught children about certain cultures and HOLIDAYS through the common denominator of food. Americans of all backgrounds seem to be better able to appreciate one another when sharing recipes or delicious food.

If food has the potential to bring Americans together, it also serves to keep American ethnic and cultural groups distinct. Food remains one of the strongest aspects of cultural identity. For example, although many children and grandchildren of immigrants tend to abandon the language, customs, and religious practices of their ancestors, they are likely to preserve and take pride in certain culinary traditions, at least on holidays or special occasions. Even if NORWEGIAN AMERICANS do not actually eat the gelatinous lutefisk at Christmas, they know what it is and enjoy joking about it. Preferred types of foods and cooking methods are also absorbed unconsciously within families and communities.

One of the reasons food figures so positively in memory and tradition is its associations with the history, celebrations, rituals, and values of a cultural group. Not only what people eat but also how, when, where, why, and with whom they eat help shape ethnic identity. These are the foodways studied by folklorists, exhibited at occasions such as African American family reunions, Jewish Passover seders, and Plains Indian powwows—the stories and lore behind foods such as Mexican Christmas tamales, Chinese mooncakes, and Tennessee barbecue.

In studying the foods and cooking of the multicultural United States, it is important not to STEREOTYPE ethnic and racial groups according to the so-called typical foods of their culture. For example, many middle-class African Americans do not eat the traditional southern fare of grits and black-eyed peas and wish to disassociate themselves from that image of African American culture. Outsiders are usually only familiar with a few of the most popular foods of another cultural group; insiders not only eat a variety of traditional dishes but plenty of "typical" American foods as well. While a CAMBODIAN AMERICAN grandmother might try to eat the same combinations of rice and vegetables in California that she did in her homeland, her daughter might adapt traditional dishes to American ingredients. Her grandson might insist on hamburgers, pizza, and tacos. Thus, the food preferences of groups and individuals are constantly in flux as part of the processes of ASSIMILATION, CULTURAL PLURALISM, and the definition of one's ethnicity.

African Americans. The nearly thirty million AFRICAN AMERICANS come from a variety of cultural groups, and their food habits are similarly diverse. Those who came from West Africa virtually revered the transported yam, which became a metaphor for survival during and after slavery. Some contemporary African immigrants still consider the yam the designated vegetable to mark births, deaths, weddings, and recovery celebrations. Other food products indigenous to Africa and now part of the American diet include cassava, palm and coconut oils, coconuts, peanuts, and spices that were imported from the East Indies by the Dutch. From Mozambique came cashew nuts, recipes with curry, and piri-piri sauce containing chilies and lemon juice for chicken, prawns, and shrimp. Malaysian saté (spiced sauce) imported into Africa and exported to the United States is used in many American restaurants today.

Foods and cooking traditions from the South, often dating back to plantation culture, continue to shape the diet of many African Americans throughout the United States.

These customers of an Atlanta, Ga., cafeteria are enjoying its traditional southern-style soul food. (Jean Higgins, Unicorn Stock Photos)

They often favor cooking or frying in lard, barbecuing, or stewing. Salt pork and corn, once provided by the pre-Civil War slaveowners, are still used in the South, as are okra, cow peas (black-eyed peas), salted fish, molasses, collard greens, grits (coarsely ground cornmeal), filé (powdered young leaves of sassafras used to thicken soups or stews), hoecakes (cakes of cornmeal traditionally baked on the back of a hoe in a fire), gumbo z'herbes (from the Congo) and greens (leafy vegetables), and ham and pork with pan bis-

cuits. Salt cod, popular with many African Americans from the West Indies, appeals to Puerto Ricans as well. Fish remains a preferred food for blacks from many cultures, prepared southern-style by coating with cornmeal and deep-frying in lard, similar to southern-fried chicken. Blacks from Jamaica favor curried goat, pork and pork products, while some Southern blacks prefer chitterlings (hog intestines) or spare ribs.

Since the popularity of Alex HALEY's *Roots* (1976) in the 1970's and growing interest in the African diaspora, there has been a revival of appreciation of traditional African American foods and food-related customs as well as a greater awareness of the diverse cuisines of black cultures.

Caribbean Americans. The foods of Puerto Rico, Jamaica, Cuba, and other Caribbean islands continue to influence foods and cooking in the United States. Some recipes from the Caribbean remain essentially the same, with variations from the Spanish influence of frying in lard and the French preference for butter. Curry was brought to the islands by the East Indians and by the Dutch slave traders. Molasses, too, was often processed into rum, especially by Jamaicans.

Caribbean Latinos particularly favor rice, beans, cassava, and pork or beef that are often fried in lard or olive oil. Almost a million Puerto Ricans live in New York City. Their culture and cuisine are essentially Spanish. PUERTO RICANS enjoy rice and kidney beans, and sofrito (a mixture of sweet chilies, cilantro, tomatoes, garlic, and onions fried in lard). Plantains, a kind of banana, are fried and eaten plain or stuffed with spicy beef or fried pork rinds (chicharrones). In Florida, CUBAN AMERICANS consume yellow rice and black beans and enjoy picadillo (beef hash, olives, raisins, hot chilies, and Caribbean tomatoes) served with plantains. Another Cuban dish is chicharrones de pollo (chicken marinated in lime juice and soy sauce, breaded, and fried in lard). Cuban foods and restaurants have become popular with the non-Cuban population as well in areas such as Miami.

JAMAICAN AMERICANS favor chicken fricassee, oxtail stew, corned spare ribs, and beans in addition to curried goat. Flavorings from this island include ginger, jalapeño peppers, garlic, curry powder, coconut milk, and peanut oil. Transplanted Caribbean cuisine includes yams, starchy vegetables, sancocho (a Dominican Republic pork intestine stew), and "mountain chicken" (frog from Dominica), as well as seafood dishes of sea urchins, green turtles, and flying fish from Barbados. Salt cod is a typical food throughout the Caribbean.

Chinese Americans. Chinese immigration to the United States began in the 1850's when the Chinese came to California as miners and railroad workers and subsequently opened restaurants and laundries. The CHINESE EXCLUSION ACT, effective from 1883 to 1943, stopped the flow of immigrants, while the IMMIGRATION AND NATIONALITY ACT OF 1965 encouraged it. The 1990 U.S. Census reported 1,645,472 Chinese residents in the country.

The Chinese immigrants brought with them centuries of respect for gastronomy. At the end of the Middle Ages, Chinese cuisine was already 3,500 years old, with cooking flourishing as an art. Food historians such as Jean-François Revel cite a huge and unique gastronomical literature in China—the only country in which poets, scholars, political thinkers, and philosophers wrote tracts on food and collected recipes. Eight thousand codified recipes exist, many of them written on silk or bamboo. The Chinese believe that a successful cuisine depends both on the master chef and on the educated taste of the consumer. The finest of Chinese food preparations hinge on careful juxtaposition of textures and consistencies—the blend of condiments and sauces and the mixture of crisp with soft vegetables. The Chinese interest in the balance of the complementary forces of yin and yang also affects the blending of fan (grain foods including rice and dumplings) and ts'ai (cooked meats and vegetables).

Rice, an indispensable staple in Asia, has seven thousand varieties, according to food specialists. The Chinese prefer a long-grain white variety, which is eaten fried or steamed. Soybeans are another mainstay of Chinese cuisine. Bean curd (tofu) is popular, as are black beans with ginger. Chow mein and chop suey are not authentic Chinese dishes. One theory is that the terms originated with the food provided for Chinese railroad workers in the western United States.

In the United States, the Chinese enjoy ts'ai (meat or seafood with vegetables). Popular fish are carp, tripe, tuna, sturgeon, salmon, and perch; other seafood includes conch, shrimp, squid, abalone, crab, and shark's fin. Legumes made popular by the CHINESE AMERICANS vary from broad beans, mung beans, cowpeas, and peapods to split peas, soy beans, and red kidney beans. Other common vegetables in the Chinese diet include bamboo shoots, cabbage (known as bok choi and napa), eggplant, lotus roots and stems, lily blooms, a variety of mushrooms, snowpeas, water chestnuts, and seaweed—all familiar to diners at Chinese restaurants.

Chinese food is cooked rapidly by stir-frying in a wok, a hemispheric pan of iron or steel containing oil that has been heated. Woks and stir-frying became popular with Americans of various backgrounds after the 1970's for reasons of health and convenience, as well as taste. For wok cooking, food is cut into small pieces and fried quickly. Other Chinese methods of cooking include steaming, deep-frying, and simmering.

Americans enjoy traditional northern Chinese specialties such as Peking duck or mu shu pork wrapped in Mandarin wheat pancakes. From the southern Chinese provinces comes the spicier Szechwan-Hunan cuisine, characterized by fagara (a Szechwan pepper), garlic, and chilis. This region inspired hot and sour soup and tea-smoked duck. Yunnan province popularized Chinese dairy dishes, especially yogurt, cheese, and fried-milk curd, as well as foods with hot and spicy flavors. Many Americans are familiar with Cantonese cuisine, which features dim sum (meaning "dot the heart"), small samples of food that are usually some form of fried or steamed dumplings with meat or seafood stuffing. In American CHINATOWNS, it is customary to eat dim sum for brunch, selected from trays wheeled around the restaurant. Chinese restaurants of all types have become ubiquitous in the American landscape, from small towns to big cities.

Creole and Cajun (Acadian) Americans. In Louisiana, Alabama, and parts of Florida, but especially in New Orleans, the French influence on foods and cooking is definitive. In 1803 the Louisiana Territory was formally transferred from Spain to France and soon afterward sold to the United States. In Louisiana, French is the language of cooking. French influence is notable in CREOLE and Cajun cooking, in which it is combined with the many contributions of AMERICAN INDIANS, AFRICAN AMERICANS, the Spanish, and ACADIANS.

The Cajuns or Acadians were French settlers who emigrated from Acadia (Nova Scotia, New Brunswick, and Prince Edward Island) in Canada and settled in the Louisiana bayous and the Delta marshlands.

Cajun cooking is heavily influenced by the fish and shellfish found in the Gulf of Mexico and the rivers and bayous of Louisiana: shrimp, crabs, crayfish, oysters, redfish, and pompano. In Louisiana, bouillabaisse is a fish stew, compared to the French bouillabaisse, which also contains meat and sausage. Gumbo, a favorite dish, supposedly brought to the New World by

These participants at New York City's Indian Street Festival prepare a traditional dish called paan. (Richard B. Levine)

the Spanish, is a thick and spicy soup, containing varieties of seafood, meat, and vegetables. Another famous Creole dish is jambalaya, containing rice, ham, sausage, chicken, shrimp, and oysters, seasoned with herbs. For both gumbo and jambalaya, the base is roux, a typically French thickening agent consisting of flour cooked in butter or fat drippings.

Key Cajun cooking ingredients include Louisiana rice, red beans, eggplant, chayote squash, tomatoes, spicy hot sauce, and pork products. Other Cajun fare includes pork stew, boudin (sausage), cracklings, coush-coush (fried cornmeal dish with seasoning or with syrup, hot milk, and rice). Tabasco sauce, a hot concoction, is produced in the south Louisiana bayous from fermented chili peppers, vinegar, and spices, and exported throughout the world. The Cajun dishes appear simpler than the Creole ones, with the Cajuns preferring pungent and peppery white rice. Their menus feature crab chops, resembling pork chops, and head cheese (jellied meat from hogs' heads).

Although Cajun and Creole cooking share many of the same ingredients and techniques, Creole cooking is to Cajun cooking as French grand cuisine is to provincial cooking in France, according to some cooking experts. Creole cooking is most evident in New Orleans and in nearby Teche County. Its genesis is complicated but stems partly from descendants of Africa, India, Spain, and France in the West Indies. After slavery was abolished in the West Indies, several decades before the U.S. emancipation, there was a need for labor; therefore, Chinese and East Indians were imported, along with their native cuisines. When West Indian immigrants settled in Louisiana and mingled with the diverse population there, a unique culture and style of cooking developed. Today Creole cooking is no longer derivative but a distinctive cuisine with a soul of its own.

Creole cooking is renowned for its subtle blends and sauces. Roux with herbs and spices (and a measure from a stock-pot with a base of shellfish) as well as fish, meat, and poultry are specialties. Rice is favored by the southern parishes, with cornbread preferred in the north of Louisiana. Jambalaya is readily available throughout the state, and the bayou country is famous for its delectable choice of oysters, jambalaya, gumbo, and crabs. Louis ARMSTRONG, the well-known jazz trumpeter, was a connoisseur of Cajun and Creole food; he generally signed his letters with the two ingredients central to the cooking of New Orleans: "Red beans and ricefully yours."

Parts of Florida and Alabama also feature both Cajun and Creole cuisine. Since the 1980's, many American restaurants far from the South have been preparing fish the Cajun or Creole way and enthusiastically adopting other Cajun and Creole recipes.

Hot green tea is a popular accompaniment to traditional Chinese cuisine. (Gail Denham)

Asian Indian Americans. In 1990, according to census figures, there were 815,447 Asian (East) Indians in the United States. This population uses short-grain Basmati rice as a staple as well as ghee, cucumber, lentils, plantains, yogurt, coconut, and eggplant. Curries are complexes of many spices such as coriander, turmeric, cinnamon, cumin, chilies, cloves, and ginger root. The spices result in a subtle blend of fragrances and flavors. Biryani is a traditional dish consisting of saffron rice with chicken, lamb, or beef. Asian Indians enjoy an astonishing variety of fried breads from the puffy nan to the flat, crisp pappadam made with lentils. Beans and legumes are common in various forms of dahl. Vindaloo is a chicken stew with cloves, cinnamon, turmeric, cayenne, mustard seed, paprika, ginger, and garlic. Asian Indians also cook meat tandoori style in a cylindrical clay oven heated with charcoal, a technique developed by several Asian nations. Chutney, a condiment made of acid fruits with raisins, dates, onions, and spices, often accompanies the main course.

Despite the complexity of preparing this type of cuisine, many ASIAN INDIAN AMERICANS preserve it in their homes and community organizations, especially on special occasions. Indian restaurants grow ever more numerous in the United States, serving a great variety of regional dishes and often catering to vegetarians.

Japanese restaurants in the United States use traditional grilling and steaming techniques to prepare foods at the customers' tables. (Betts Anderson, Unicorn Stock Photos)

Japanese Americans. In 1990 the U.S. Census reported 847,562 JAPANESE AMERICANS in the United States. Seventy percent resided in California or Hawaii. In Japanese tradition, food is respected as an essential product of nature. Japanese cuisine is prized by gourmets for its aesthetic presentation, the result of a subtle blending of color, texture, and shape.

Fish is central to the Japanese diet because the coasts of Japan teem with many varieties; Japanese Americans continue to eat abundant fish. Soybean, king of the Japanese kitchen, is often combined with nori (seaweed), steamed rice, a variety of mushrooms, and white curd. Japanese cooking methods stress grilling, frying, broiling, and steaming rather than baking or roasting.

The number of Japanese restaurants in the United States has burgeoned with the rise of Japan as a world economic power and the establishment of American branches of famous Tokyo eateries. American diners select from typical dishes such as tempura (shrimp or vegetables deep-fried in light batter and oil); sushi (balls of vinegared rice and raw seafood, or rice with vegetables, seaweed, or egg); sashimi (sliced raw fish); chicken teriyaki (in a soy-based sauce); miso soup (made from fermented soybean paste); and sukiyaki (beef stew with clear rice noodles). In many recipes, the Japanese are flexible and may substitute shrimp, crab, lobster, or any white fish. There is little filleting of fish, since the skin and the bones provide particular flavors.

Special Japanese ingredients include an array of mushrooms from the large matsutake prized by gourmets to the smaller shiitake. Fresh ginger root is often used, together with white radishes, water chestnuts, rice vinegar, and seaweed. The notorious fugu (globefish) can be deadly if the fish's liver and ovaries are not extracted; eating globefish is safer, however, only if a licensed fugu chef prepares the fish. This dish is expensive but is enjoyed by many because of the taste and the fish's presentation—some chefs arrange it like a chrysanthemum flower or a crane. The Japanese have provided the United States with another rice product—sake (rice wine), served hot in a diminutive porcelain cup.

Japanese cuisine has become so integrated into American life that teriyaki dishes may be served in institutional cafeterias and fast food franchises as well as elegant Japanese restaurants. Sushi was considered the trendy, fashionable food of the 1970's and 1980's.

Mediterranean Americans (French, Greeks, Italians, and Spanish). The French consider themselves the grand masters of cuisine. Ever since the thirteen American colonies were formed, the French influence has affected American foods and cuisine. Long before he became the third president, Thomas Jefferson had been a gourmet who reveled in French cuisine. During his presidency, the dinners at the White House featured French-inspired foods made by Julien Lemaire, a renowned French chef.

For many connoisseurs, French influence is most apparent in methods of preparation and in high standards of cooking. French classic cuisine blends color, flavor, and texture with sauces such as roux, velouté, and bechamel. French cooking aims for subtle flavors, making sauces from stocks that simmer for hours to release their essences.

French culinary influence is found today in some American regional cuisines, such as Creole cookery in Louisiana, and in fine restaurants throughout the country. French fare ranges from the Burgundy style of food cooked in a sauce of wine, shallots, butter, marrow, tomato, and cèpes (large, plump mushrooms), such as beef bourguignon (beef stew with red wine), to the southern Provençal use of olive oil, garlic, tomatoes, and spices, as in bouillabaisse (spicy fish stew) or ratatouille (a stew of zucchini, tomatoes, and eggplant).

Italian cookery relies heavily on pasta and rice, which may have been brought to Italy by the Muslims. Food historians often credit Thomas Jefferson for smuggling rice from Italy into the United States. Northern Italian cooking uses cream sauces and pasta made from eggs, shaped like flat ribbons, while southern Italian cooking prefers tomato sauces and pasta without eggs shaped like tubes, such as macaroni. Rome exported fettucini Alfredo (long egg noodles, mixed with butter, cream, and parmesan cheese), while Bologna specialized in lasagne and tortelline (egg pasta stuffed with meat, eggs, and cheese). Gnocchi (potato dumplings with egg and flour) and ravioli are two other common imports. Polenta (cornmeal mush, originally made from semolina wheat) is typically Italian, though less well-known. Garlic, parsley, and olive oil are "givens" in Italian cooking.

All of these foods are now consumed with gusto in American homes and restaurants. Pizza, originating in Naples, is an essential part of the American diet and, like various forms of pasta, has been adapted to new forms by venturesome American chefs.

The Spanish influence on American foods and cooking is also unmistakable after centuries of conquest and settlement in the Americas. Chorizo (sausage of spicy beef or pork) is typical of Spanish cuisine. A classic dish is paella (saffron rice with chicken, shrimp, sausage, mussels, tomatoes, and peas). Spanish-speaking Americans also enjoy cocido (stew of garbanzo beans, vegetables, and meats); gazpacho (a cold puréed vegetable soup); and zarzuela (stew of fresh seafood). The Spanish also contributed aioli,

made with pulverized garlic, eggs, olive oil, salt, and lemon juice, resembling mayonnaise in consistency. Some Spanish culinary traditions shaped popular Mexican cuisine.

Greece, another Mediterranean country, is considered European, but its cuisine is reminiscent of the Middle East. GREEK AMERICANS, along with immigrants from other Middle Eastern/European nations, contributed pita bread (flat, round bread with a hollow center) and filo (any paper-thin pastry that is filled with meat or cheese). Another export of the Greeks is souvlaki, thin slices of lamb layered on a rotisserie and grilled. Shish kebab, another Greek dish, consists of meat grilled on skewers; the meat is alternated with tomato, onion, and sweet peppers. Rice pilaf, a long-grain variety of rice, is served with meat, perhaps with feta cheese (a moist, salty, white cheese from sheep's or goat's milk). Dolmas are grape leaves stuffed with rice or meat, flour, spices, and oil. Lamb is widely used throughout the Middle East. A traditional Greek dish popular in the United States is moussaka, a casserole of olive oil, eggplant, lamb, bread crumbs, tomato sauce, and spices.

Close to the cuisine of Greece is the food of Middle Eastern countries such as Lebanon, Iran, Yemen, Iraq, and Kuwait. These nations, too, use yogurt, kuku (broiled omelettes), ghee or samneh (clarified butter), lentils, raisins, mint, roasted seed and nut oils, together with filo pastry and tahini (a sauce made from crushed sesame seeds).

Mexican Americans. Mexicans have lived in the present-day United States since the days of the Spanish Empire. Originally, the states of Texas, Arizona, New Mexico, and parts of Nevada, Colorado, and California were part of the Mexican Territory. After three hundred years of Spanish rule, Mexico became independent in 1820. In the 1990's, MEXICAN AMERICANS numbered approximately eight to ten million, part of the fast-growing Latino population.

In Mexican American cooking, chilies are frequently used as well as beans, cocoa, tomatoes, and corn. These ingredients also formed the basis of the cooking of Aztec Indians before the Spanish arrived. Tortillas, the round flat "bread" of Mexico, are made from cornmeal or wheat flour, cooked on a griddle, and served with every meal.

The Spanish who occupied Mexico contributed cinnamon, wheat, sugar cane, onions, garlic, and later pork to the diet of the Mexican Indians. Combining with indigenous ingredients, Mexican cuisine evolved

Mexican foods include (clockwise from upper left): tortilla chips, salsa, flan (custard), quesadillas, fajitas, tacos, enchiladas. Refried beans and Spanish rice commonly accompany these foods. (Dawn Dawson)

in many directions. Many foods are served with salsa, a spicy sauce consisting of tomatoes, jalapeño peppers, wine vinegar, onions, and green peppers. Characteristic foods include frijoles refritos, sometimes called "refried beans" but actually beans that are boiled and later fried in lard. There are also popular "stuffed" foods such as tacos (sandwiches made of tortillas rolled up with or folded over a meat or bean filling); enchiladas (tortillas on which filling is spread then rolled up, and baked in a chili-seasoned tomato sauce); and tamales (cornmeal, chopped meat, and hot pepper wrapped in a cornhusk and steamed). Another Mexican import is guacamole, a blend of mashed avocado, lime juice, salsa, cumin, scallions, and coriander that is used as a dip or a salad dressing.

Less familiar Mexican foods can be found in immigrant homes, restaurants, and community centers, especially at HOLIDAYS AND FESTIVALS. One dish usually only appreciated by "insiders" is menudo, a soup of tripe, green chilies, and onions often consumed late at night or as an early-morning hangover remedy.

Mexican food has seized the palates of many people throughout the United States through the fast-food in-

dustry. In the Southwest, people of various ethnic backgrounds commonly prepare and enjoy Mexican foods in their homes and patronize regional restaurants.

American Indians. Without the help of many indigenous Indian tribes, the Puritans and other early European settlers would never have survived. The Indians contributed beans, squash, corn, cranberries, and maple syrup to their diet and taught the European transplants simple and practical methods of both growing and cooking food in the New World. For example, the Indians taught the Pilgrims how to prepare the clambake, Boston baked beans, succotash, roasted peanuts, codfish cakes, and cranberry sauce.

When Columbus arrived, the Indians were already using two thousand different types of wild and cultivated foods. In the Southwest, many Indians, including the Pima, Pueblo, and Zuni tribes, were farmers who cultivated beans, squash, chilies, melons, and corn. The APACHES and NAVAJOS, mostly itinerant hunters and gatherers, raised the sheep imported by the Spanish. Blue, yellow, and black corn were traditionally used in tortillas, pozole (hominy), and tamale-like chukuviki (dough packets stuffed with cornmeal).

AMERICAN INDIANS contributed the peanut, now spread throughout the world and a key factor in the economy of many African nations. The Indian "food triad" refers to three vegetables: beans, squash, and maize (Indian corn).

Modern Indian tribes number in the hundreds and have diverse culinary traditions. There is much fish in the Indian diet as well as corn, game, beans, and sweet potatoes, all of which have influenced cooking in the Southwest. Restaurants use mesquite wood to add flavor to their grilled fish, beef, and chicken, a method directly attributable to the Indians. At their own community "feeds," modern Indians may serve fry bread, Indian tacos, and traditional stews.

The ancient Indian reverence for life, to be lived in harmony with nature and the universe, also extended to foods, which assumed importance in seasonal rituals. Today the legacy of the early Indians remains, calling succeeding generations back to a simplicity and a practicality in the selection and the preparation of foods. For example, nutritional studies of a high rate of diabetes and obesity among the Pimas of Arizona have suggested that tribal members have suffered from adopting a conventional modern "American" diet and should instead return to healthier traditional eating habits.

By learning about and enjoying the foods of their ancestors, present-day Americans can better understand the infinite variety of their multicultural society.

SUGGESTED READINGS. *Food and Culture in America: A Nutrition Handbook* by Pamela Goyan Kittler and Kathryn Sucher (1989) is a valuable source of information on the history and cuisine of American ethnic groups. *The Melting Pot: An Ethnic Foods and Nutrition Handbook* by Jacqueline M. Newman (1984) provides an introduction to cultures and cuisine, with an annotated bibliography. M. F. K. Fisher compiled five of her published books in *The Art of Eating* (1976); her travels provide a setting for food commentary in witty prose. See also Cynthia Roberts' *Cultural Perspectives on Food and Nutrition* (1992) and Charles Camp's edited volume *American Foodways: What, When, Why, and How We Eat in America* (1989)—*Julia B. Boken*

Football: Contact sport played throughout the United States and, to a lesser degree, in Canada at the high school, college, and professional level. It is derived from soccer and rugby and is second only to BASEBALL in attendance in the United States. The violent nature of the sport leads to many injuries, but the game's contact nature is responsible for its popularity. The professional championship game, the Super Bowl, is held every January and usually attracts television's largest audience.

The first American football game was a college match in 1869 between Rutgers and Princeton. It grew into a game for elite northeastern college men seeking rugged action. By the late twentieth century, the game was played mostly by middle-class and lower-class youth seeking not only glory but also scholarships to colleges and high pay offered by the professional National Football League (NFL).

In the early years of pro football's growth, many of the leading players were Caucasians of eastern European descent, and many came from the coal-mining towns of Pennsylvania. Indian sports hero Jim THORPE was the first president of the NFL's ancestor, the American Professional Football Association. The first African Americans to play in modern professional leagues were Marion Motley and Bill Willis in the All-American Football Conference and Woody Strode in the now-dominant NFL, all in 1947. Blacks who starred in the 1950's included Buddy Young, Lenny Moore, Emlen Tunnel, and Dick "Night Train" Lane. By the 1960's, many black players were among the game's brightest stars, among them Jim Brown, Ernie Davis, Charley Taylor, and Alan Page, now a Minnesota State Supreme Court justice. African American football greats from the 1970's included O. J. Simpson, Walter Payton, and Willie Lanier.

For many years, African American players had been relegated to certain positions that emphasized strength and speed. By the 1980's, however, they were also playing positions that emphasized leadership and quick thinking, such as quarterback. In 1988, African American quarterback Doug Williams led the Washington Redskins to the Super Bowl championship. In 1989, Art Shell of the Los Angeles Raiders became the first African American head coach in the NFL, followed by Dennis Green of the Minnesota Vikings in 1992.

The Jewish American Sid Luckman of the Chicago Bears was a standout quarterback in the 1930's. Among notable Latinos in the 1980's were linemen Anthony Munoz and Max Montoya, and coach Tom FLORES.

Despite the prominence of minorities on the field, institutional RACISM in professional football, as in other sports, has been an issue of wide discussion. In 1962, the Washington Redskins (whose very name caused protests by American Indians) hired its first black player, Bobby Mitchell, only after the intervention of the John F. Kennedy Administration, which

O. J. Simpson parlayed his fame into a lucrative second career as a sports announcer and commercial spokesperson. (AP/Wide World Photos)

threatened to deny the team use of a federally funded stadium unless it integrated. The lack of minority coaches was an issue well into the 1990's.

SUGGESTED READINGS. The issue of racism in football is discussed in parts of sportscaster Howard Cosell's *What's Wrong with Sports* (1991) and Jim Brown's autobiography *Out of Bounds* (1989). An exposé of the seamy side of professional football's economics and politics can be found in David Harris' *The League: The Rise and Decline of the NFL* (1986).

Foreign-language press—history: The foreign-language press is an integral part of the culture of the United States. Benjamin Franklin was the publisher of the first foreign-language newspaper in the United States, the German-language Philadelphia *Zeitung* ("Journal" or "Gazette"), which appeared in 1732 but was shortly abandoned. The earliest foreign-language newspapers in the United States to enjoy great popularity were the Germantown *Zeitung* and the *Wöchenliche Philadelphische Staatsbote* ("Weekly Philadelphia Public Post"), both of which were printed in German and were highly religious in tone and content. The first foreign-language daily was the Philadelphia *Courrier Français,* printed

in French from 1794 to 1798. The first French-language and German-language Sunday editions appeared in 1841 in New Orleans.

The foreign-language press showed no major increase in circulation or popularity until the 1830's, when the large influx of German immigrants inspired the founding of newspapers. By 1850, there were 133 German-language publications in the United States; a decade later that number had practically doubled. The *New Yorker Staats-Zeitung,* founded in 1834, became the foremost American German-language daily. No other nationality had so many newspapers in this country, although French, Italian, Spanish, Dutch, and Swedish-language papers were printed. Joseph Pulitzer, the youthful immigrant who later would usher in a new era in journalism, began his career as a reporter for the leading German-language newspaper in the United States, the St. Louis *Westliche Post.* By 1940, there were 237 foreign-language newspapers published in New York City alone. More than one thousand newspapers and periodicals were printed in languages other than English, and they enjoyed a combined circulation of almost seven million.

Between 1940 and 1945, however, 165 foreign-language publications, approximately 15 percent of the total, ceased publication. During World War I, the 1917 Trading with the Enemy Act had authorized censorship by requiring all foreign-language newspapers and magazines to file sworn translations of their printed material. Additionally, the 1918 Sedition Act, an amendment to the 1917 Espionage Act, allowed the postmaster to impound any foreign-language materials printed in "any language" that might be suspected of "disloyalty" to the government of the United States. During World War II, censorship of foreign material, on which foreign-language newspapers depended for information, and restrictive rules of broadcasting and publication caused further decline in foreign-language newspapers. Even more destructive to the ethnic press, however, was the increased desire on the part of immigrants to appear assimilated into American culture and society.

The interest in foreign-language newspapers never returned to its original vitality. The foreign-language press did, however, become considerably more diverse with the rise of national and local papers in Spanish as well as in various Asian and Middle Eastern languages to serve the new immigrant communities of the post-1965 era.

SUGGESTED READINGS. For additional information

consult Frank Mott's *American Journalism: A History, 1690-1960* (1962), Richard Polenberg's *One Nation Divisible: Class, Race, and Ethnicity in the United States Since 1938* (1980), and Peter Stoler's *The War Against the Press* (1986).

Forty-eighters: German immigrants who fled from Germany to the United States after the failed revolution of 1848. In many parts of Europe, there were revolutions in 1848 as liberals attempted to overthrow outdated, repressive governments. Most of these revolutions, in-cluding one in Germany, were unsuccessful. The forty-eighters were generally cultured and well-educated and were therefore prepared to rise as leaders in the German American community. They opposed slavery, supported the arts, and led political discussions. The first German American senator, Carl Schurz (elected in 1869), was a forty-eighter.

Fossey, Dian (January 16, 1932, San Francisco, Calif.—December 26, 1985, Ruhengeri, Rwanda): Anthropologist. Fossey was best known for her work with the

Dian Fossey's 1983 autobiography, Gorillas in the Mist, *became the basis of a popular feature film.* (AP/Wide World Photos)

mountain gorilla, an endangered species in the Virungas range of East Central Africa. She spent a total of seventeen years beginning in 1967, at the Karisoke Research Centre. She lived in almost complete isolation, often observing the habits of the gorillas on her hands and knees. In 1983 she documented her experience in *Gorillas in the Mist,* which was later made into a feature film. On December 26, 1985, Fossey was found dead near the center, probably killed by poachers of the gorillas she spent her life trying to protect.

442nd Regimental Combat Team: One of three groups of second-generation Japanese Americans (NISEI) who fought for the United States during World War II. Its soldiers were taken from INTERNMENT camps in the United States and sent to fight in Italy and France. The 442nd performed very well and received more medals than any other combat unit of its size. It also suffered many casualties. The bravery and loyalty of these soldiers helped to counteract anti-Japanese prejudice during and after the war. Nevertheless, many veterans of the 442nd reported that they faced DISCRIMINATION IN HOUSING AND EMPLOYMENT even after they returned from the war as heroes.

Fourteenth Amendment (1868): Amendment to the U.S. CONSTITUTION defining citizenship and citizens' rights. It was one of three post-Civil War amendments which significantly changed the nature of the U.S. constitutional system. The THIRTEENTH AMENDMENT abolished slavery. The Fourteenth Amendment provided the first clear definition of national citizenship and established that citizens had rights enforceable by the national government against abridgement by state and local governments. The FIFTEENTH AMENDMENT gave the vote to black males.

These amendments were unprecedented developments. Before 1860, very few white Americans believed in the equality before the law that the amendments promised. No state accorded African Americans the same rights as whites. Furthermore, no real concept of national citizenship existed before 1860. Few citizens looked to the national government for the protection of their rights. An amendment which would have allowed the national government to protect citizens against state limitations on their rights had been rejected by Congress in 1791. This position was reaffirmed in 1833 when the Supreme Court ruled in *Barron v. Baltimore* that the provisions of the BILL OF RIGHTS did not apply as limitations on state and local governments.

The Amendment's Provisions. The amendment consists of five sections, only two of which, sections one and five, are relevant today. Section one defines national, as well as state, citizenship: "All persons born or naturalized in the United States and subject to the jurisdiction thereof, are citizens of the United States and of the State wherein they reside." It also contains three great rights clauses, two of which eventually became the basis for redefining the relationship between citizens and the national government. States are prohibited from abridging "the privileges or immunities of citizens of the United States"; from denying any person "life, liberty, or property, without due process of law"; and from denying any person "the equal protection of the laws." Section five empowers Congress to enforce the amendment's provisions by "appropriate legislation." This became one of the constitutional bases for much of the CIVIL RIGHTS LEGISLATION passed immediately after the Civil War and beginning again in the 1960's.

Sections two, three, and four mainly deal with issues relevant to the aftermath of the CIVIL WAR: Congress' reducing the representation of states that denied the vote to black males; the qualifications for voting and officeholding of former Confederate officeholders; and the validity of the public federal debt. Significantly, in section two, the word "male" was inserted in the Constitution for the first time in history, contributing to a split between the advocates of women's rights and African American rights.

Early History. The Fourteenth Amendment was approved by Congress in June, 1866, partly as a reaction against President Andrew Johnson's RECONSTRUCTION program of 1865. Under that program, the old white planter class was put back in power in the South and a penal labor system was installed for the recently freed slaves under the infamous BLACK CODES. Johnson and the Southern states denounced the proposed Fourteenth Amendment, which became the focus of the congressional elections of 1866. Republican proponents of the amendment won the elections and used their electoral mandate to secure ratification of the Fourteenth Amendment; grant black men the right to vote; and require the formation of new Southern governments based on universal male suffrage under their program of "Radical" Reconstruction.

There has never been a consensus on exactly what the passage of the Fourteenth Amendment meant. The language was a compromise yet the central principle is clear—a national guarantee of equality before the law. Most of the Republican supporters assumed the amendment would be subject to changing interpretation and wanted to allow Congress and the courts flexibility in combating the injustices being done to Southern blacks after the CIVIL WAR. Most supporters also thought the amendment would incorporate the provisions of the BILL OF RIGHTS and make them applicable to the states at a time when the Southern states were systematically violating such rights.

The Supreme Court, however, gave a much more restrictive interpretation to the amendment in a series of cases in the 1870's, most notably the *Slaughterhouse Cases* and *Bradwell v. Illinois* (1873). Ironically, neither of these cases involved African Americans. *Slaughterhouse* dealt with small butchers fighting an economic monopoly in New Orleans, while *Bradwell* concerned a woman denied admission to law practice by the State of Illinois.

clause, the Court said that it was primarily meant to apply to the newly freed slaves and refused to extend it to other constituencies such as small proprietors and women. In spite of this, the 1896 decision of *PLESSY V. FERGUSON* upheld the newly instituted system of racial segregation in the South. Not until the 1950's did the CIVIL RIGHTS MOVEMENT and the Supreme Court begin to use the equal protection clause to promote equality before the law for African Americans.

In addition, the Court also refused to incorporate the Bill of Rights in the amendment and apply it to the states until after 1925. Later, principally in the 1930's and 1960's, the Court used the due process clause to incorporate most of the Bill of Rights, so that now it serves as a limit on the national as well as state and local governments.

Finally, in the *Civil Rights Cases* of 1883, the Court narrowly read the enforcement powers of section five of the amendment as limiting Congress' ability to en-

As Reconstruction-era reforms gave way to restrictive Jim Crow laws, African Americans who were concerned about their rights as U.S. citizens held special meetings like this 1873 Equal Rights Convention. (Library of Congress)

The Court decided that most of the privileges and immunities of citizenship were part of an individual's state, not national, citizenship. The Court also limited the meaning of the due process clause to the traditional concept of procedural protections, not more substantive considerations of fairness.

In interpreting the amendment's equal protection

act CIVIL RIGHTS LEGISLATION. This contributed to the failure of Congress to pass another major civil rights law for almost a century.

The Due Process Clause. This clause was the focus of constitutional interpretation of the Fourteenth Amendment until the 1930's. A flexible concept that eludes precise definition, it suggests that government will deal fairly with individuals. Due process has traditionally been concerned with how the government must act rather than with what it must do.

down hundreds of state laws over the next forty years in the areas of rate setting, price regulation, and wages and hours legislation.

During World War II, Americans of Japanese ancestry living on the West Coast were incarcerated against their will in direct violation of their Fourteenth Amendment rights as American citizens. (National Japanese American Historical Society)

Ironically, between the 1870's and 1890's, the Supreme Court transformed its narrow procedural reading of due process for individuals into a basis for protecting property rights against state regulation. It examined what states chose to regulate rather than how they regulated, often invalidating state laws. This became known as the doctrine of substantive, as opposed to procedural, due process.

The Court first used this doctrine to strike down a state law in *Chicago, Milwaukee & St. Paul Railway Co. v. Minnesota* (1890), deciding that the courts should have the final say on the fairness of railroad rates. In the 1897 case *Allgeyer v. Louisiana* the Supreme Court used the due process clause to protect the contractual freedom of corporations and businesses. Relying on these doctrines, the Court struck

The GREAT DEPRESSION and NEW DEAL, however, created conditions that turned political forces against the Court's doctrines. In a series of dramatic decisions in 1936-1937, the Court reversed its position and largely abandoned its role in economic policymaking. By 1941 the Court had unanimously decided that economic legislation was left to the judgment of Congress and the states.

Yet the due process clause retained its vitality. It not only became the foundation for the selective incorporation of the Bill of Rights, but also was used as one basis for a new kind of substantive due process that protected individual rights. Some rights were so fundamental, "implicit in the concept of ordered liberty," the Court said in *Palko v. State of Connecticut* (1937), that states had to protect them under the requirements of due process.

The Court has applied this new form of due process mainly in matters of personal choice and privacy. For example, the landmark 1965 decision in GRISWOLD V. STATE OF CONNECTICUT struck down a state law forbidding the use of birth control devices on the basis of privacy as a fundamental right protected by the Constitution. The Court also rested the 1973 ROE V. WADE decision granting a woman the right to an abortion based on the right to privacy derived from the word "liberty" in the due process clause.

The Equal Protection Clause. The equal protection clause was not used to protect individual rights until the mid-1900's. Since then, it has become the most litigated clause in the Constitution and the basis for extending formal legal equality to African Americans, aliens, and women. The guarantee of equal protection prohibits arbitrary or capricious discrimination against a classified group. Until the 1940's, the Supreme Court used a rationality standard to determine if such classifications were permissible. Under this standard, the Court normally deferred to the judgment of a governmental body if a reasonable basis could be shown for the classification.

In the 1942 case *U.S. v. Carolene Products*, however, the Court indicated that it would apply a higher level of scrutiny to certain governmental classifications including those directed against "discrete and insular" minorities. Thereafter the Court began to apply the strict scrutiny standard to racial classifications. In the Japanese American INTERNMENT case of KOREMATSU V. UNITED STATES (1944), the Court declared race to be a suspect category of classification requiring a heightened level of judicial scrutiny. Yet the Court did not use this approach consistently until the CIVIL RIGHTS MOVEMENT's claims on behalf of African Americans in the 1950's. Only in 1967 did the Court expressly declare all racial classifications to be "inherently suspect."

As early as 1886 the Court held that the Fourteenth Amendment protected aliens as well as citizens, but it then applied the traditional rationality standard to uphold most statutes challenged for discriminating against aliens. It did not begin applying a heightened level of scrutiny to laws classifying aliens until 1948, and it only explicitly categorized such classifications as inherently suspect in 1971.

Women had to wait even longer than African Americans and aliens to enjoy the guarantee of equal protection. In the 1970's the Supreme Court began to use a "middle-tier" or "mid-level" scrutiny standard when assessing claims of gender discrimination. While not as demanding as the strict scrutiny standard used for other classifications, this new standard meant a major step forward for equal treatment of men and women before the law. Under this standard, however, certain inequitable laws, such as those that exclude women from the military draft, have continued to be upheld based on societal beliefs about gender roles.

Two other groups—gays and lesbians and the poor—have tried to claim the guarantees of the equal protection clause without much success. Discrimination based on wealth has been held to violate the Constitution only when the poor are denied basic rights such as access to the courts, the right to travel, or the right to vote. The Court has denied efforts to extend such protection to access to education, health care, and housing. It has only required the states to show a rational basis for their legal distinctions between the rich and the poor. Gay and lesbian claims for equal protection from discrimination were rejected by the Supreme Court in the 1986 case of *Bowers v. Hardwick* when it again used a rationality standard to uphold Georgia's sodomy law.

The Fourteenth Amendment had promised a revolution in the relationship between individuals and government when it was ratified in 1868. It did not fulfill this promise until the 1950's, when it began to be used to provide most Americans with the constitutional protection of equality before the law.

SUGGESTED READINGS. Eric Foner offers a comprehensive account of the events surrounding the passage of the Fourteenth Amendment in *Reconstruction: America's Unfinished Revolution, 1863-1877* (1988). Legal developments in civil rights are covered in C. Herman Pritchett's *Constitutional Civil Liberties* (1984); Henry Abraham's *Freedom and the Court: Civil Rights and Liberties in the United States* (1988); and Melvin I. Urofsky's *The Continuity of Change: The Supreme Court and Individual Liberties, 1953-1986* (1991).—*Carl Swidorski*

Franklin, Aretha (b. Mar. 25, 1942, Memphis, Tenn.): African American singer. A preacher's daughter who assimilated the electrifying GOSPEL choir tradition along with the blues sound of her mentor Ray CHARLES, Franklin became the warm, natural "Queen of Soul." She moved from Memphis to Detroit as a young child and sang on the gospel circuit. She got her big break with Atlantic Records in 1966. Her career in the 1970's and 1980's included a European tour, a performance for the

Aretha Franklin incorporated her gospel and rhythm-and-blues background into popular music, earning the title of "Queen of Soul." (AP/Wide World Photos)

Queen of England, and a new contract with Arista records. Aretha has had twenty-one gold records and has won ten Grammy Awards.

Franklin, John Hope (b. Jan. 2, 1915, Rentiesville, Okla.): African American historian and educator. Franklin is a distinguished author whose specialty is the role of blacks in United States history. After taking degrees at FISK UNIVERSITY (A.B. 1935) and Harvard University (A.M. 1936, Ph.D. 1941), he taught history at Howard, Fisk, Brooklyn College, the University of Chicago, and the Duke University Law School. Franklin's long list of books spans four decades; one famous study is titled *From Slavery to Freedom: A History of American Negroes* (1947). For many years he worked on his prize-winning book *George Washington Williams: A Biography* (1985). Franklin has also been an editor for the University of Chicago Press.

Fraternal organizations. *See* **Benevolent and fraternal organizations**

Fraternities and sororities: Usually associated with colleges and universities as social Greek letter societies. The first fraternity established in the United States was Phi Beta Kappa at the College of William and Mary in Virginia in 1776. Many of the social fraternities and sororities grew to become an integral part of college and university life, but encountered criticism in the late twentieth century.

Fraternities developed from older literary or academic associations connected with colleges and universities. Many of these were secret societies with admittance based largely on social class or standing. The turn to social fraternities caused these early associations to lose prestige and quickly dissolve. Debating clubs, for example, no longer held the high status they once enjoyed and became separated from the term "society" as strictly academically based. Just as most colleges were for men only, so, too, were the early societies. In 1851, the first sorority (an organization for women) was established as the Adelphian Society at Wesleyan College in Macon, Georgia.

Contemporary controversy and criticisms surrounding fraternities and sororities have to do with selective admission—the exclusion of lower-income students and DISCRIMINATION based on race, color, and creed. Other concerns focus on member initiation rituals, which have sometimes resulted in injury and death. In response to these criticisms, many fraternities and sororities began to stress a goal of community service,

John Hope Franklin has enjoyed a distinguished career as a leading historian of the African American experience. (AP/Wide World Photos)

which is similar to the original philosophy of Phi Beta Kappa. Some fraternities have been formed specifically to serve members of racial and religious minorities, with members serving as role models of success for other students. Some universities have banned the societies from their campuses; Princeton, for example, has banned fraternities and sororities since the latter part of the nineteenth century.

Modern fraternities and sororities are not purely social in nature. There are professional fraternities for students and faculty who pursue interests and studies in a particular field, such as law, medicine, education, music, agriculture, business, and foreign languages. Honor societies are extensions of fraternities that recognize qualities of leadership and talent as well as excellence in academics.

SUGGESTED READINGS. Henry D. Sheldon's *Student Life and Customs* (1901, repr. 1969) gives a detailed historical account of fraternities and sororities, such

For contemporary views on the Greek system, see essays in *Fraternities and Sororities on the Contemporary College Campus* (1987), edited by Roger B. Winston, Jr., William R. Nettles II, and John H. Opper, Jr.

Free Soil Party: Political party influential in the United States between 1848 and 1854. The Free Soil Party's declared goal was to keep slavery out of territories gained during the war with Mexico. Composed largely of antislavery Democrats called Barnburners and antislavery Whigs called Conscience Whigs, members adopted the slogan "Free Soil, Free Speech, Free Labor, and Free Men." In 1848, they nominated Martin Van Buren for president; although he lost, they did elect nine congressmen. Party membership increased following passage of the Compromise of 1850, but in 1852, their presidential candidate also lost. When Free-Soilers realized they had insufficient resources to fight the slavery issue, most allied with the REPUBLICAN PARTY.

The Freedmen's Bureau was instrumental in establishing schools to educate newly freed slaves. (The Associated Publishers, Inc.)

as their origins, transformations, problems, and status. Another early study dealing instead with black fraternities and sororities is Charles H. Wesley's *The History of Alpha Phi Alpha: A Development in Negro College Life* (5th ed., 1948). An account of discrimination in Greek letter societies may be found in Alfred McClung Lee's *Fraternities Without Brotherhood: A Study of Prejudice on the American Campus* (1955).

Freedmen's Bureau: Established by Congress on March 3, 1865, it helped former slaves during RECONSTRUCTION. Headed by Major General Oliver Otis Howard, the bureau was to provide federal relief to those displaced by the Civil War, both loyal white southerners ("refugees") and former slaves ("freedmen"). One of the original goals had been to distribute to these groups land that had been confiscated during the war. When President Andrew Johnson granted amnesty to most former Confederates in May of 1865, however, there was much less land to redistribute. Instead, the bureau focused on immediate relief, primarily for freedmen, and later, with the 1866 extension act, tried to help former slaves to become self-supporting citizens. The organization located lost family members, established hospitals and schools, provided food rations, protected the civil rights of freedmen, and drafted labor contracts for them. The Freedmen's Bureau closed in 1872.

Freedom Rides: Civil rights protests that sent groups of black and white people, including many college students, on buses into the Deep South in the early 1960's. Freedom Rides were sponsored by the CONGRESS OF RACIAL EQUALITY (CORE) after the U.S. Supreme Court ruled that desegregation in interstate carriers included waiting rooms in bus terminal facilities (*Boynton v. Virginia*, 1960). Riders planned to speak at rallies along the way. At some stops, the riders suffered violent beatings while crowds and law enforcement officers looked on. Between May and November of 1961, more than one thousand people participated in Freedom Rides. The program was seen as a success, and it helped CORE achieve national prominence.

French Americans: Understanding the role that French-speaking communities have played in the multicultural development of the United States requires looking at North American history before the Declaration of Independence. The search for religious freedom, so important in explaining the arrival of diverse European peoples to American shores, played a key role in the establishment of at least a small number of French Protestant communities on the Atlantic seaboard as early as the seventeenth century. For example, New Rochelle, New York, was founded following the violent persecution of the HUGUENOTS in Rochelle, France. French place names in key regions of the United States, particularly the northern states, attest that much of the early exploration of frontier territories was undertaken by the French. Well-known names such as Detroit, Des Moines, and St. Louis all derive from original French settlements.

French explorers of North America were motivated by the same factors driving other European rivals, namely the rich fur trade. Behind individual French traders and trappers, however, international political concerns loomed important, at least until the period of the FRENCH AND INDIAN WAR (1756-1763). These concerns pitted British and French colonial interests against each other on several continents. The French loss of the war would have major significance for the development of North America. French settlers who had hoped for a victory in Canada would see key French-speaking provinces, especially Québec, fall under the political, economic, and cultural control of British imperial authorities. After the watershed date of 1763, the movement of French people from Canada and other zones of French colonial influence—some by choice, some by force—would leave an indelible mark on what was to become the United States.

Transitional Franco-American Cultures. The phenomenon of the "Acadian Exile" of French speakers from Canada, as well as the changing status of France's control of vast areas south of the Canadian border, brought repercussions that could be felt well into the the twentieth century.

While the ACADIANS are best known for their settlement of Louisiana, they also set up communities along the Atlantic coast. This lesser known aspect of Acadian American history was marked by attempted "forced assimilation" of Acadians into British-ruled colonies such as Delaware and Maryland. While many French-speaking Canadians who found themselves without a homeland were able to implant themselves in the pre-1776 Colonies, as in Maine, they often did so at the risk of being treated as "foreigners" by the English-speaking colonists. In a number of documented cases, English-speaking colonists practiced discrimination in employment and shunned the predominantly Catholic religious heritage of the French. Such factors may have contributed to Acadian immigrants' apparent willingness to abandon their distinct cultural and ethnic trappings (as in the Chesapeake area) or to relocate a second time by moving on to French Louisiana, particularly in the 1770's and 1780's. French status there would change again with the LOUISIANA PURCHASE by President Thomas Jefferson in 1803.

When Napoleon I consented to sell the Louisiana Territory, this involved much more land than what later became the state of Louisiana. Socio-cultural ASSIMILATION among Acadians or other French who had settled in parts of the vast Louisiana Territory was similar to that of Acadians who migrated down the Atlantic coast, resulting in many surviving French place and local family names throughout the Mississippi Valley—and not much else. On the other hand, the state of Louisiana retained many characteristic features of its French antecedents. These French influences came into Louisiana not only down river from the north, but also—at least until the American Civil War—on ships from French Caribbean island possessions. French import-export interests in the Caribbean included human cargos of African slaves, whose first European language was and would remain French, not English.

As early as 1804, the inhabitants of Louisiana sent a formal declaration to the U.S. Congress requesting retention of French as their language. This concern would still be reflected over a century and a half later when the Louisiana legislature passed a bill in 1968 guaranteeing that French would be a part of the curriculum of public schools throughout the state.

Cajun Culture. Such concerns are of particular importance among the actively French-speaking population known as the Cajuns in rural southern Louisiana. These racially mixed descendants of ACADIANS came to Louisiana at the end of the eighteenth century through an offer from the Spanish king, Charles III. They have maintained an ethnic and cultural distinctness that is atypical of most contributors to the Ameri-

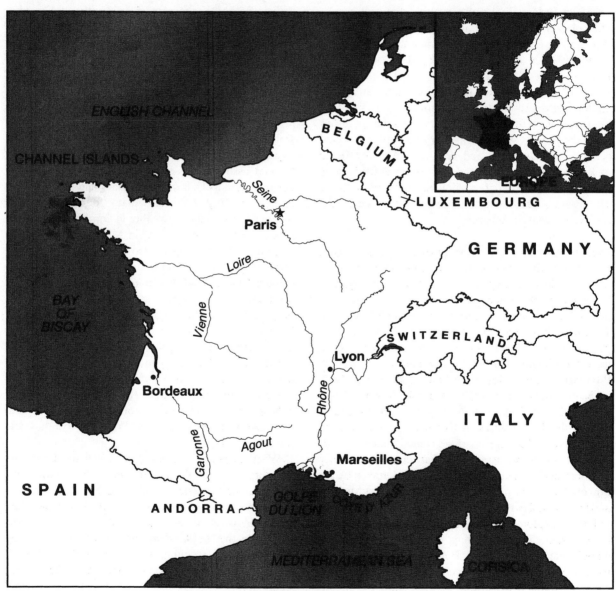

FRANCE

Several houses, farm buildings, and churches have been relocated to re-create the French-influenced environment of an early Cajun bayou village in Louisiana. (Louisiana Department of Tourism)

can "MELTING POT. " This distinctness is maintained in their unique dialect of French—not always an advantage in a majority English-speaking environment—and a rich tradition of rural FOLKLORE, particularly in music, dance, and cuisine.

Cajuns have remained somewhat withdrawn from mainstream society in Louisiana and have often suffered from prejudicial biases against their perceived "backwardness." Yet the creation by the legislature of the Council for Development of French in Louisiana (CODOFIL) in 1968 on the initiative of former U.S. Congressman James Domengeaux, placed their community in a new perspective. CODOFIL aimed essentially at "upgrading" Louisianans' French-speaking heritage by encouraging native-speaking teachers from France, Québec, and elsewhere to work in the local school system. Pride in "upgrading" language tended to bring pride in other aspects of Cajun culture, adding another dimension to the ethnic heritage revival that has come to mark a number of ethnic communities in the United States.

French Dispersion and Assimilation. Other than special cases such as Louisiana where the heritage of French settlement remains visible in subregions, the general pattern of French immigration to the United States reveals a high degree of ASSIMILATION. In most urban areas of the country, one finds French names, never in very large numbers, and seldom concentrated in one section of a given city. On the other hand, one can find traces of previous occupational specialization that tended to bring French immigrants to certain areas. Among these were a once-prosperous silk weaving industry in Paterson, New Jersey, that attracted significant numbers of French skilled workers in the late 1800's. Another obvious example of geographical attraction for specialized work by the French is the development of the grape vineyards and wine making industry of California.

French Cultural Events, Organizations, and Media. The most important impact of the French presence in the United States can be found either on a more popular "folk" level, or on a higher level of elite cultural institutions. In the first category, a number of towns in the Mississippi Valley celebrate festivals recalling some form of French heritage in their history. The Fort de Chartres Rendezvous Festival in Prairie du Rocher, Illinois, or the Jour de Fête in Sainte Genevieve, Missouri, are smaller versions of St. Louis' own Fête de Normandie.

French influence may also be seen in American literary and professional associations, as well as in specialized publications. From the most specialized national organization of the American Friends of Lafayette (a key revolutionary war ally), to the Huguenot Historical Society in the historically unique French Protestant community of New Paltz, New York, to the Société Historique et Folklorique Française, or the more scholarly Society for French Historical Studies, one finds a number of gathering places for people interested in French subjects tying the mother country to extensions of its history and culture in the United States.

A few popular French publications have existed for many years, such as *La Liberté News*, published in Fitchburg, Massachusetts, since 1909, or the extraordinary *France-Amerique: Le Courrier Français des États-Unis*, published in New York City since 1827. By far the most widely circulating organ of news of general interest to French speakers in the United States, *France-Amerique* was founded in 1941. It has subscribers in every state.

In 1976 seventy American radio stations offered several hours of broadcasting each week in French. Some but certainly not all of these have some affiliation with educational institutions dedicated to formal instruction in French. A surprising number are located in small towns not only in Louisiana but also in states of the Mississippi Valley or the Northeast Atlantic coast, where descendants of historical French settlers still live.

SUGGESTED READINGS. Essays in *Frenchmen and French Ways in the Mississippi Valley* (1969), edited by John Francis McDermott, portray the French heritage of various Mississippi Valley towns. Rodolphe L. Desdunes' *Our People and Our History* (1973) is a reprint of a 1911 book which documents contributions made by Creoles who were of mixed French, black, and other ancestry. Christopher Hallowell's *People of the Bayou* (1979) is a series of ethnographic sketches of the French-speaking Cajun community of Louisiana. Finally, a general text by William J. Eccles, *France in America* (1972), covers French contributions to religion, exploration, and politics in the United States since colonial times.—*Byron D. Cannon*

French and Indian War (1756-1763): Last of four colonial wars, which tested the strength of British and French colonial influence in North America. Specifically at issue was whether the upper Ohio Valley was a part of the British or the French empire. Both empires sought the support of as many Indian tribes as possible in order to increase their share of territory in North America, but the French were generally more successful in gaining Indian allies. This led the British, in 1755, to decrease its control over Indian affairs. The diminished control, along with more vigorous efforts against the French, resulted in eventual victory for the British.

French Canadians in the U.S.: French colonization of the North American continent was sporadic, unfocused, and essentially exploratory or evangelical in nature until the eighteenth century. North Americans owe much to the early French explorers and missionaries who mapped and traversed the vast territories of the continent's interior with their American Indian guides. Many early French contributions to North American culture can be found in place names, folklore, music, and dance, as well as cuisine and fashion. The two strands of French Canadian influence discussed here came from Acadia in the 1700's and Quebec in the 1800's.

The Acadian Exodus. The colonization of Acadia, the territory that included Nova Scotia, New Brunswick, Prince Edward Island, and part of the state of Maine, began in the late sixteenth and early seventeenth centuries when colonists from Normandy, Brittany, and the Loire Valley were recruited to farm the rich valleys and fish the plentiful waters of the Bay of Fundy and the Grand Banks. The settlers were Roman Catholics of peasant or sea-faring origin and carried with them the rich folk tradition of their Celtic and Norse ancestors. The farming and fishing communities established by these hardworking colonists were self-contained, self-sufficient, and largely self-governing. Following the Peace of Utrecht in 1713, the ACADIANS, as they had begun to call themselves, fell under English rule and were ordered to swear al-

According to Louisiana tradition, the majestic oak tree shown here marks the location where the Acadian heroine of Long-fellow's epic poem Evangeline *was reunited with her beloved Gabriel.* (Louisiana Department of Tourism)

legiance to the British crown or to withdraw into English territory. This they did willingly enough in 1730, becoming "French Neutrals," in an act that prevented them from having to bear arms against their former compatriots or their Indian allies.

In 1740, the British began an intense effort to colonize Acadia with Protestant refugees from Europe and Scotland, granting them huge tracts of land as incentives for permanent settlement. Tension between these new immigrants and their French Canadian Catholic neighbors grew, and, in 1755, the English king forced six to eight thousand Acadians into exile. The tale of their forced march is movingly captured in Henry Wadsworth Longfellow's Acadian American epic, *Evangeline*.

Acadian settlements in Louisiana date from 1756. Most of the emigres made their way there from Maryland, South Carolina, or French and Spanish colonies in the Caribbean where they had taken religious refuge. Some Acadians had returned briefly to their homeland, but made their way back across the Atlantic to rejoin their kindred in the Louisiana territories, establishing the townships of St. Martinville, Delcambre, Lafayette, Broussard, St. Landry, and Abbeville in St. James and Ascension parishes. By the late 1700's, Acadian (soon corrupted to "Cajun") towns and villages had spread as far west as Lake Charles. In these backwater territories, the Acadians continued their former occupations of fishing and farming, including large-scale production of sugar cane, sweet potatoes, and rice. Like their forebears, they maintained friendly relations with local Indian trappers and fishers, as well as their Spanish *VAQUERO* neighbors, from whom they learned livestock farming and ranching. These pursuits remained the mainstay of the Cajun economy until the twentieth century when large agricultural combines encouraged the development of the staple crops of rice, sugar cane, cotton, and corn.

Cajun American Cultural Contributions. The Cajuns have long been noted for their spicy, seafood-based foods and cooking. Cajun cuisine enjoyed nationwide popularity in the last quarter of the twentieth century, when it was featured at restaurants specializing in regional American cookery. Cajun festivals, music, and dance have similarly proliferated beyond the bayou while bringing tourists from around the globe to participate in local *fais-dodo* and *boucherie de campagne*, country dance and hog-killing contests that date from medieval French practice. Perhaps the least known contribution of the Acadian FOLKLORE to

American culture is that of the American Northwoods legendary hero, Paul Bunyan, whose attributes and exploits were borrowed directly from the hero of the mock epic, *Gargantua* by the French author Rabelais. While the Acadian communities of northern Maine are smaller, less isolated, and less well known than those in Louisiana, they have undergone a new appreciation and understanding of their cultural experience since the 1970's, and they are transmitting that appreciation to the people of Maine and New England.

Quebec and French Canadian Emigration. Jean de Monts, a French HUGUENOT, who obtained his letters of patent from his friend and sponsor, Admiral de Coligny, colonized the Northern Territories now known as the Province of Quebec, which once extended west to the Great Lakes and south to Louisiana. Because of his religion, de Mont's contributions to the founding of Quebec have been subsumed into the history of his lieutenant and partner, the great French Catholic explorer, Samuel de Champlain. Together, they established the colony of Quebec in 1608. Its purpose was twofold. It was to serve as the center for the fur trade from which the early *voyageurs* or trapper-adventurers would depart to ply their trade and explore the interior of the vast new continent for the glory of their French King, Henry IV. It was also to serve as the religious and civil center of the rapidly expanding territories of New France. From there, the Recollects, an order of Franciscan monks, and later the Jesuits, would begin the attempt at conversion of the American Indian tribes of Canada to Christianity.

Emigration from France, however, was virtually nonexistent following the earliest settlements. The ban on Huguenot immigration by Cardinal Richelieu eliminated a flow of educated and freedom-seeking pioneers from the mainland that might otherwise have sought refuge in North America, as their English counterparts had done. Life in French Canada took on a similar character to the rural areas of mainland France. It was feudal in character, ROMAN CATHOLIC in religion, and conservative in social custom.

These characteristics followed the French Canadians as they immigrated to the United States in great numbers in the nineteenth century, when the marginal economy of Quebec could no longer provide a living for the impoverished large families of the countryside. Most of these emigrants settled in the New England area. In new industrial towns such as Manchester, New Hampshire; Lewiston, Maine; Lawrence, Massachusetts; and Woonsocket, Rhode Island, they pro-

Many French Canadian immigrants, such as this dairy farmer, settled in rural New England; others found employment in New England textile mills. (Library of Congress)

vided the cheap labor to run the textile mills and established thriving ethnic communities that still flourish.

French Canadian–American Indian Relations. The Indian tribes' relations with the early French settlers differed radically from their relations with Spanish and Anglo-Saxon settlers. The French viewed the American Indian population as differing in religion and custom but otherwise equally subject to and subjects of the French monarchy. Relationships were generally friendly as Champlain and his followers explored the interior and depended upon the native peoples for sustenance and companionship. Early hostile encounters of Champlain with the Algonquin and Huron tribes on the banks of Lake Champlain and his championship of the Iroquois Nation embroiled the French settlers in tribal warfare and shaped the outcome of the struggle for dominance between the French and the English over control of the interior and the Northwest territories of North America. In response to Champlain's alliance with the Iroquois, the Hurons and the Algonquins sided with the Dutch and the English in their

contests, assuring the British of long-term victory and control of New France in the FRENCH AND INDIAN WAR.

Slavery. Three forms of slavery existed in New France as they did in New England, New Spain, and the Virginia territories: term indenture (as with INDENTURED SERVANTS), villeinage (in which peasants were slaves to their feudal lords but free in relation to others); and lifetime indenture (as in the system that enslaved Africans for life). Owing to the harsh climate, few African slaves were imported to Quebec or Acadia. Many American Indians were enslaved, however, and white bondservants abounded. In the New France Census of 1784, 304 persons are identified as slaves, the greater number of whom were Panis (or Pawnees), Western Plains Indians purchased from the Huron and Algonquin tribes. For the most part the French Canadians had little sympathy for slavery of any kind. The institution had virtually disappeared by 1794, although it was not formally abolished until 1833. The migration of the Acadians to the West Indies and the rigors of southern plantation life made them adapt more readily to the tradition of lifetime tenure for African slaves than their counterparts who migrated to New England or the North Central Great Lakes Territories.

Women Immigrants. Women were extremely rare in the first century of French colonization in North America. Nevertheless, they played an influential and formative role in the settlement of French Canada and, later, in the emigration of French Canadians to New England and Louisiana. Two women in particular were especially influential in the pioneer effort of the French in the New World: Marie de Vignerod (Madame de Comballet, Duchesse d'Aiguillon, the niece of Cardinal Richelieu) and Marie Madeleine de Chauvigny, (Madame de la Peltrie). These women, with their companions Mère de Saint Ignace, Mère de Saint Bernard, and Mère de Saint Bonaventure, cooperated to form the Ursuline Order in New France, which undertook the education of the faithful and the conversion of Indians throughout the colony. They were also instrumental in establishing the first hospitals in Quebec and Montreal. Mademoiselles Jeanne Mance and Margaret Bourgeois, in turn, were the founders of Ville Marie (Montreal), a colony originally envisioned as a celibate community of religious missionaries. Women thus established traditions of nursing, education, and parochial service that would assure the maintenance of French cultural identity in North America as first the ACADIANS and then the Quebecois were forced into political, religious, or economic exile. Even after immigration to the United States, French women continued to be viewed as the repositories of tradition, education, and religion within the family and the community. They enjoyed a cultural equality with men that was rare among their fellow European immigrants of the eighteenth and nineteenth centuries.

SUGGESTED READINGS. See James Hill Parker's *Ethnic Identity: The Case of the French Americans* (1983) for studies of French-speaking immigrants to the U.S. from Canada. Among valuable sources on Acadians, see William Faulkner Rushton's *The Cajuns: From Acadia to Louisiana* (1979) and an anthology edited by Glenn R. Conrad entitled *The Cajuns: Essays on Their History and Culture* (1978).—*Barbara Langell Miliaras*

Friedan, Betty (Betty Goldstein; b. Feb. 4, 1921, Peoria, Ill.): Feminist leader and writer. Friedan was married with three children when in 1963 she wrote *The Feminine Mystique,* a book that catapulted her into fame as a leading theorist for contemporary American feminism. In 1966 she helped organize the NATIONAL ORGANIZATION FOR WOMEN (NOW), and was its president until 1970. In 1971 she helped establish the NATIONAL WOMEN'S POLITICAL CAUCUS and headed the National Women's Strike for Equality. She was present when the International Feminist Congress convened in 1973 and helped set up the First Women's Bank that same year. Other works by Friedan include *It Changed My Life* (1977), an anthology of articles on the feminist movement, and *The Second Stage* (1981), a reassessment of American FEMINISM.

Friends, Religious Society of. *See* **Quakers**

Friends of the Indian: Group that began meeting at Lake Mohonk, New York, in 1883, and thereafter met annually for some years. It was among a number of groups formed in the late twentieth century by well-meaning if misguided white liberals; many of those at the Lake Mohonk conferences had been staunch abolitionists. One objective of such groups was to help bring justice as well as "civilization" to the Indians. The reservation system was thought to be impeding this goal, and allotment—breaking up reservations into individually owned parcels—was believed to be the solution. When put into effect, however, allotment proved disastrous.

Frontier wars and African Americans: Of the African Americans who participated in the westward expansion of the United States, perhaps the most famous were those soldiers who fought in the Indian wars in the trans-Mississippi West after the Civil War. They were called "BUFFALO SOLDIERS" by the Plains Indians because the African Americans' "woolly" hair reminded the Indians of the sacred buffalo, which furnished the tribes' entire sustenance.

In the post-Civil War era the United States needed a military presence in the West where conditions were most unsettled because of continuing white encroachment on Indian lands. In 1866 Congress created four African American regiments—the 9th and 10th Colored Cavalry and the 24th and 25th Colored Infantry—under the command of white officers to reinforce white units in the West.

From 1867 to the end of the nineteenth century, buffalo soldiers served all over the West in many different garrisons. In all, they made up 25 percent of all troopers in the West. They soldiered from Texas to Montana, and they fought in most of the major Indian campaigns: Red Cloud's War (1865-1868); the Red River War (1871-1875); the second Sioux War (1876-1878); and the Apache uprisings (1878-1890). Later, they also fought in the SPANISH-AMERICAN WAR and in WORLD WAR I. In all their campaigns African Americans and whites fought together, with the buffalo soldiers proving their mettle and usually getting the harder, more dangerous assignments. They came to be known as some of the best men in the U.S. Army. They also did many jobs that whites did not want to do such as garrison duty for the infantry and scouting for the cavalry.

Despite their valiant service, the African American soldiers were nevertheless victimized by racial discrimination. The buffalo soldiers tended to get cast-off equipment and horses, inferior arms and ammunition, and poor rations and quarters. Further, for many of the years that they served in the West, the army established a wage "differential" that awarded African Americans less pay than their white counterparts.

In time, the buffalo regiments won national recognition as the best units to serve in the INDIAN WARS. Whereas whites tended to serve one "hitch" and then move on, many African Americans re-enlisted because they viewed army life as better than what they would face as civilians in a white man's world. For the same reason, fewer buffalo soldiers deserted. They eventually became "crack" veterans. In the 1870's the army

Members of the 10th Colored Cavalry—known as "buffalo soldiers"—served with distinction in various military campaigns in the American West. (National Archives)

began allowing a small number of African Americans to serve as junior officers with the buffalo detachments. One was Henry O. Flipper, the first black graduate of West Point; another was Charles YOUNG, who eventually attained the rank of colonel.

With their bravery, toughness, and intelligence, the buffalo soldiers occupy a unique place in American history. More important, at a time when many whites were proclaiming "Negro inferiority," the buffalo soldiers were busy disproving such racist ideas.

SUGGESTED READINGS. Brief coverage of this topic is found in W. Sherman Savage's *Blacks in the West* (1976). For more detail see William Leckie's *Buffalo Soldier: A Narrative of the Negro Cavalry in the West* (1967) and Arlen L. Fowler's *Black Infantry in the West, 1869-1891* (1971). Another volume that puts the soldiers in a broader context is William Katz's *The Black West* (1973).

Fugitive Slave Act (1793): Series of federal laws empowering slaveholders to capture escaped slaves who had fled to the North. The original Fugitive Slave Act was passed in 1793 and did not actually mention SLAVERY at all. It simply prohibited one state from helping people avoid labor that they were legally required to perform in another state. Nevertheless, the intention behind the law—to prevent slaves from escaping to the North—was never in question.

Under the law, a slaveholder could capture fugitive slaves and return them to the South without a warrant. All he needed to do was appear before a judge and state his intention. No jury was called and fugitives had no opportunity to present their case. They were not permitted legal representation, or the right to call witnesses on their behalf.

Northerners opposed the law, saying it violated the basic right to a fair trial and created opportunities for abuse. They cited several incidents of free African Americans, living peacefully in border states, being captured and forced into slavery. Many Northerners simply believed that slavery—and any law supporting the institution—was immoral.

As antislavery feeling grew in the North, most people chose to ignore the act. Some actively and openly defied it, helping slaves to escape and sheltering them. Others chose passive resistance, neither actively helping slaves nor taking steps to return them to the South. By 1850, as many as twenty thousand escaped slaves were living in the North, with no serious effort being made to turn them in.

This resistance angered Southerners. In 1850 Congress passed the Compromise of 1850, intended to calm tensions between North and South. One part of the compromise reaffirmed and strengthened the Fugitive Slave Act. Under the new law, federal marshals were sent to capture escaped slaves, and local citizens were required to help with the arrests. Heavy fines and stiff sentences could be given to those who refused. These provisions enraged Northerners. Even those who did not find slavery in the South especially objectionable had no desire to become personally involved in aiding slaveholders.

Abolitionist Frederick Douglass, himself a former fugitive slave, fought to overcome the harsh provisions of fugitive slave legislation. (AP/Wide World Photos)

Northern resistance led to an expansion of the UN-DERGROUND RAILROAD. Instead of transporting small numbers of slaves to the North, the network of contacts and safe houses began to move larger numbers all the way to Canada. In response to the law, Harriet Beecher STOWE was also inspired to write her famous antislavery novel, *Uncle Tom's Cabin* (1862) in response to the 1850 law. Several states passed their own "personal liberty laws," which directly nullified the act.

Southern reaction to northern defiance was predictably hostile. The tensions on both sides over this law and other issues regarding slavery were uncontainable and eventually led to the CIVIL WAR.

SUGGESTED READINGS. For further reading see Stanley W. Campbell's *The Slave Catchers: Enforcement of the Fugitive Slave Law, 1850-1860* (1970) and Thomas D. Morris' *Free Men All: The Personal Liberty Laws of the North, 1780-1861* (1974). One of the finest studies of American slavery is Kenneth M. Stampp's *The Peculiar Institution: Slavery in the Ante-Bellum South* (1956). See also *Prologue to Conflict: The Crisis and Compromise of 1850* (1964) by Holman Hamilton.

Fuller, Margaret (May 23, 1810, Cambridgeport, Mass.—July 19, 1850, off Fire Island, N.Y.): Writer, transcendentalist, and feminist. As a child she was said to be a prodigy. After 1835 she kept company with writer Ralph Waldo Emerson and educator Bronson Alcott in the Boston area. She was known for her "Conversations," meetings with other contemporary intellectuals which included discussions of philosophy, education, and women's rights. In 1840 she and Emerson began *The Dial,* a magazine she edited until 1842. In 1845 she wrote her most influential feminist work, *Woman in the Nineteenth Century and Kindred Papers Relating to the Sphere, Conditions, and Duties of Woman.* She died five years later in a shipwreck.

Funk music: Form of African American popular music that is highly syncopated, danceable, and dominated by the bass. As a genre, funk was inspired by a renewed interest in African musical forms and aesthetics in the late 1960's, although the term "funk" first appeared in 1953 in jazz pianist Horace Silver's "Opus de Funk." As a popular musical genre, funk is basically rhythm-driven dance music in which the bass plays an important role (unlike disco, in which drums are the most important instrument).

Horace Silver, Art Blakey, and other JAZZ artists propagated "funky" music as a counter to the heady intellectualism associated with bebop, cool, and West Coast jazz. Just as the earthy expressiveness of SOUL MUSIC countered the lovelorn predictability of RHYTHM AND BLUES in the early 1960's, so the harsh rhythms of funk countered the slick commercialism

James Brown's 1965 hit "Papa's Got a Brand New Bag" marked the beginning of his transition into a funk music style. (AP/Wide World Photos)

of DISCO in the 1970's. Of all the artists who figured in the development of funk in this period, the most important were James Brown, Sly Stone, and George Clinton.

For Brown, the shift from soul music, which emphasized the performer, to funk, which emphasized the backbeat, began in 1965 with his hit single "Papa's Got a Brand New Bag," a song whose title and theme heralded the transformation in music style. Brown followed this hit with a number of other funk songs, including "Cold Sweat," "Ain't It Funky," and "Make It Funky."

Sly Stone formed the Family Stone, a seven-piece

band that included his brother and sister, and found success with his first single, "Dance to the Music," in 1968. This and his other hits, such as "Everybody Is a Star," and "Hot Fun in the Summertime," were pure entertainment, their only social conscience a certain vague utopianism. With "Family Affair," from his 1971 album, *There's a Riot Goin' On,* Stone's music became overtly political and extolled BLACK NATIONALISM.

If Brown is the "Godfather of Soul," George Clinton is the "Godfather of Funk." Dressing his bands, Parliament and Funkadelic, in outlandish psychedelic costumes with colorful wigs, emphasizing the electric guitar and synthesizer as much as the bass and drums, writing playful lyrics that were alternately cartoonish and political, Clinton elevated funk to a bizarre mul-

tidimensional post-1960's art form. His major hits include "(I Wanna) Testify," "Atomic Dog," and "One Nation Under a Groove."

Other important funk stars who lasted into the 1980's include the Isley Brothers ("Who's That Lady"), Rick James ("Super Freak"), and Chaka Khan ("Jive Talking"). In the 1980's and 1990's, Prince combined funk with ROCK AND ROLL in such hits as "When Doves Cry".

SUGGESTED READINGS. Information on funk music can be found in Nelson George's *The Death of Rhythm and Blues* (1988), Arnold Shaw's *Black Popular Music in America* (1986), Charles T. Brown's *The Art of Rock and Roll* (1983), and Michael Haralambros' *Right On: From Blues to Soul in Black America* (1974).

G

Gadsden Purchase (1853): Referred to in Mexican history as the Treaty of La Mesilla, in which the United States acquired 29 million acres of territory in southern Arizona and New Mexico (the Mesilla Valley) for $15 million. The treaty recognized land claims protected under the TREATY OF GUADALUPE HIDALGO but only for land with titles recorded in Mexican archives. Mexican President Antonio López de Santa Anna was pressured to accept the agreement when U.S. troops were sent to "preserve order" along the New Mexican border.

Galarza, Ernesto (Aug. 15, 1905, Jalcocotán, Nayarit, Mexico—Jun. 22, 1984, San Jose, Calif.): Mexican American activist and writer. Galarza and his family fled the Mexican Revolution and came to the United States in 1911. He studied at Occidental College and earned his M.A. degree from Stanford University in 1929. He later earned his Ph.D. in education at Columbia University in 1944. From 1936 to 1947, he worked in the Education and Labor divisions of the Pan-American Union (later the Organization of American States) and from 1947 to 1963 held leading positions with the National Farm Labor Union (affiliated with the AMERICAN FEDERATION OF LABOR) and the National Agricultural Workers Union, where he lobbied strenuously for workers' rights. He taught and lectured widely, advised congressional committees and foreign governments, and wrote sixteen books, including *Merchants of Labor: The Mexican Bracero Story* (1964), and his autobiography, *Barrio Boy* (1971).

Gall [Pizi] (1840, near Moreau River, S.Dak.—1894): Hunkpapa Sioux war chief and chief lieutenant of SITTING BULL in the defeat of GENERAL GEORGE ARMSTRONG CUSTER and his troops at Little Bighorn (1876). Although Gall had been one of the most aggressive Sioux leaders, after his surrender he became a farmer on the reservation. With his friend, Indian Agent James McLaughlin, Gall spent the rest of his life promoting better relations between Indians and Caucasians.

Gangs and crime: Crime is a fact of life in modern, industrialized nations, and it affects people of all ethnicities. Yet while crime and gang activity are undeniable realities, general perceptions of such illegal activities are often exaggerated, being based more on exploitation of fears by the media than on an understanding of the realities of crime. Historically, the DOMINANT CULTURE of the United States has tended to brand various ethnic or racial groups as particularly vicious purveyors of violence and corruption. Among the reasons marginal groups traditionally are accused of criminality and criminal association, according to sociologists, is the dominant society's desire to interpret other groups' differences, control their actions, or justify their exclusion.

Whether attributed to ethnic culture, social deprivation, or race, characterizations of illegality, immorality, or ignorance have denigrated AFRICAN AMERICANS, IRISH AMERICANS, CHINESE AMERICANS,

Lou Rivera (front) coaches baseball and basketball teams for youth in Brooklyn, N.Y., providing them with an alternative to gang involvement. (Hazel Hankin)

Samoan Americans, and CUBAN AMERICANS, among other groups. Moreover, the specter of clandestine or uncontrolled organization, whether street gangs among youths, tongs among Chinese, or the Mafia among Italians, has served to justify police controls, media sensationalism, missionary reform, and a range of urban policies from renewal to enclosure.

The people defined by these negative characterizations are in reality quite diverse. Criminal behavior most certainly exists, although less as an innate characteristic than as a product of complex social forces. Luc Sante, in his book *Low Life: Lures and Snares of Old New York* (1991), suggests that "the basic unit of social life among young males in New York in the nineteenth century was (as it perhaps still is and ever more shall be) the gang." Yet in many cases, the neighborhood, community, or ethnic group categorized by the criminal actions of a few has been deeply divided by these activities, a situation apparent in African American community campaigns against contemporary black-against-black violence or the protests of ITALIAN AMERICAN associations against identification of their ethnic tradition with organized crime.

In other cases, behavior that is considered criminal by the dominant culture represents misunderstanding or stereotyping imposed upon a community. For example, the identification of JAPANESE AMERICANS as subversive criminals in WORLD WAR II by reason of race/nationality led to their confinement in internment camps and also marked a watershed in community identity. Some actions marked as conspiratorial may also be considered revolutionary—whether slave revolts or the civil disobedience that has characterized the struggles of women, blacks, the poor, gays and lesbians, and other marginalized groups in the twentieth century.

The study of gangs and crime itself has been shaped by these contradictions. In 1927, sociologist Frederic Thrasher explored Chicago gangs as organizations serving vital needs on urban frontiers. By the 1960's, gangs and crime research sought deeper understanding of social issues and possibilities for change. Since the 1970's, cutbacks in social services and subsequent wars on drugs and crime have situated gangs once again as problem groups in even more marginal areas plagued by unemployment and decay. Some contemporary analysts suggest that metropolitan gangs comprise ethnic and CLASS-based adaptations to police provocations as much as purely criminal activities.

Historical Origins and Associations. The identifica- tion of ethnic diversity and criminality originated in the foundations of American identity. Whether in Puritan Massachusetts or the royal colony of Georgia, the boundaries of colonial communities often relied on negative STEREOTYPES of those who differed from the mainstream. Witches and dissenters were called criminals in New England, while southerners suspected Catholics, slaves, and American Indians of aiding nearby Spanish colonists. Conspiratorial behavior was identified as a threat in terms that foreshadowed later depictions of ethnic and class-based groups.

Later, in the antebellum South, the idea of black criminal conspiracies overshadowed real resistance in the minds of slave-holding communities. Meanwhile, as northern cities received European immigrants, these, too, became suspect for their associations, whether carry-overs from their nations of origin or adaptations to new environments. Nineteenth century advocates of NATIVISM decried the secretive quality of rites and fraternities as well as differences of language, culture, and mores that made Irish, Italians, and JEWS appear suspect. These views underpinned destructive urban riots from Boston to Louisville as well as tensions in everyday intergroup relations.

In response, some immigrants assimilated to extralegal roles and associations, especially in American cities. Groups with names such as the Bowery Boys (white) and Fly Boys (black) appeared in New York by the end of the eighteenth century. Irish gangs were well established there by the 1830's, peopling slum tenements with the Roach Guards, the Plug Uglies, and the Dead Rabbits. These groups, including women as well as men, were based on ETHNICITY and occupation, although actively differentiated by territory, costume, and rivalries—traits that still characterize modern gangs. Apart from some in the dock areas, few of these groups were actually criminal, although such activities increased with the draft riots of the mid-1800's. By this time, gangs were also associated with political bosses such as those of TAMMANY HALL, who organized immigrant communities in ways that went against the prevailing political morality. Gang members voted (frequently), intimidated opposing voters, and even battled physically for their candidates.

Throughout the nineteenth century, depictions of illicit activity and organization as well as official response were shaped both by perceived differences and "shared" cultural values. Thus African Americans were a highly visible group in North and South to whom immorality as well as illicit activities were easily imputed. Among Chinese Americans, both traditional family associations and clandestine TONGS were set apart by language, race, and culture. The tongs gained notoriety in wars for control of Chinese enclaves, which they waged for decades. These, in turn, strengthened Orientalist stereotypes of danger and mystery imputed to all Chinatown residents.

ticated as new geographic and ethnic communities took over urban avenues. The Irish villains of earlier outraged newspapers gave way to Jews, Italians, and others. By 1890, for example, New York's Five Points gang had fifteen hundred members, headed by Paul Kelly (born Paolo Antonio Vaccarelli). Urban youth survived, assimilated, advanced, and even transmuted

Chinese American tongs controlled a host of criminal activities, including opium dens in various Chinatowns. (Asian American Studies Library, University of California, Berkeley)

Early gangs and criminal behavior nonetheless exemplified fundamental American beliefs. Virtue, for example, was defined in loyalty to groups and localities, although gangs promoted strong individualism as well as collective spirit. They also participated in the gendering of crime; gangs were strongly associated with males while females, although likely to belong to associations, became mythologized as isolated criminals, hysterics, or fallen women. Finally, gangs came to symbolize negative traits of urban disorder in contrast to rural tranquillity and the safety of the small town, and later, the protected suburb.

Social and Organizational Changes. Organizational structures evolved by the late nineteenth century. Extralegal associations became larger and more sophis-

their experience into popular comedy in the Marx Brothers or the Bowery Boys. In Harlem, black associations handled numbers and other services that, while technically illegal, were not viewed askance within their social networks. On the western frontier, the heroism of the outlaw took on divisive meanings epitomized by the many legends associated with the James Brothers or, later, Gregorio Cortez among MEXICAN AMERICANS and local Anglos. Gangs became violent in racially divisive riots when more-or-less organized groups terrorized any people whom they saw as different.

Frederic M. Thrasher's classic 1920's study, *The Gang*, surveyed 1,313 groups in Chicago to understand what they offered males on frontiers of race, ethnicity, and class in the industrial city. Admiring the resilience, democratic integration, and function of many gangs, Thrasher suggested broad-based social reform that would build on the strengths as well as the weaknesses of such organizations.

Yet while reformers considered policies for youth, criminal associations reached a new organizational level with Prohibition. The sale of prohibited alcohol offered tremendous profits for large and better-managed criminal activities and syndication among cities from coast to coast. Although emerging from earlier roots, these groups tended to include older figures in their leadership and to be more violent and organized, as was their opposition at local, state, and federal levels. By the early 1930's, wars and treaties had winnowed older crime families, although new youth gangs continued to spring up in changing environments. During and after the GREAT DEPRESSION, these organized criminals sought new power through legalized gambling, entertainment, and tolerated vices as well as political influence in Washington, D.C., while facing occasional investigations such as the Kefauver trials of the 1950's. Meanwhile, gangsters gained popular, even heroic, representation in films from *The Public Enemy* (1931) to the *Godfather* trilogy (1972, 1974, 1990), *Miller's Crossing* (1990), *GoodFellas* (1990), and *New Jack City* (1991).

The Post-World War II Era. The transformations of American society after WORLD WAR II, however, changed the ideological landscape of gangs, crime, and fear. White flight to suburban havens and the security of cars, tract housing, and the family underpinned middle-class imagery in the 1950's. The city became more readily identified as a realm of hoodlums or ethnic criminals. As hotrodders, however, gangs turned the hallmarks of new suburbia—the car and the nurtured teenager—into problems. This became evident in cinematic antiheroes such as the motorcyclists of *The Wild One* (1954) or James Dean's alienated teenager in *Rebel Without a Cause* (1956).

By the 1960's, youth gangs evoked renewed concern in the literature of social sciences. Authors detailed portraits of young men in gang nations such as Chicago's Vice Lords or the street-corner networks of Boston and Washington, D.C. Blacks, and later, Latinos, figured prominently among depictions of urban problems, while Leonard Bernstein recast *Romeo and Juliet* as a clash between mixed-ethnic and Puerto Rican gangs in the musical *West Side Story* (1961). Some white gangs, such as the Chicago Vice Lords, actually

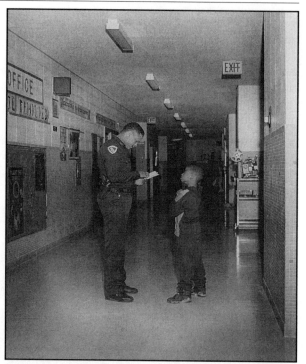

Police presence in a community can sometimes act as a deterrent to gang activity and crime, but it can also provoke violence. (James L. Shaffer)

participated in programs aimed at urban renovation and neighborhood/racial pride.

As marginal urban residents demanded equality in various protests including urban RACE RIOTS, however, problems beyond gang organization became apparent. Shifting family patterns and urban decay emphasized the social crises facing new generations, which public policy had failed to resolve. By the 1970's, systematic statistics on gangs as well as organized opposition to them increased, along with more general attacks on organized crime. The problems of cities, however, grew with the VIETNAM WAR, as well as economic recession and restructuring. Cycles of drug trafficking and new weaponry, which linked organized crime and local gangs, further heightened the panorama of urban violence in the 1980's and 1990's. As media consumerism has indoctrinated people with limited access to resources, as government cutbacks and a recession have meant a continual loss of jobs and opportunities, drugs and associated crimes have proved tempting despite their immediate dangers and long-term consequences.

New immigrant groups still tend to leave behind these associations that facilitated their assimilation to American society to characterize others as antisocial.

Thus established, for example, Chinese American communities may complain about the violent incursions of Southeast Asian and PACIFIC ISLANDER AMERICAN gangs. PUERTO RICANS in New York and Cuban Americans in Miami have been vilified by images associating Latinos with drugs and violence in staples of popular culture such as the television program *Miami Vice*. In these cases, complex ethnic categories and communities of Asian American and Latino

the United States. The Los Angeles riots in 1992 and response around the country showed a range of frustrations in which the notorious gang nations of the city, Crips and Bloods, emerged as potential peacemakers. Meanwhile, mass media and policymakers continue to face a range of representations and realities focused on drugs, corruption, and drive-by violence, strongly associated with cities but increasingly visible in suburbs and rural areas as well.

Members of rival Los Angeles gangs the Bloods and the Crips tie their gang bandannas together as a symbolic gesture to represent a truce in the aftermath of the 1992 Los Angeles riots. (AP/Wide World Photos)

urbanites are divided by issues and images of origins, class, and ASSIMILATION.

At the same time, recent decades have witnessed new patterns of multicultural crime. Women, for example, had been sex objects, tomboys, or auxiliaries for nineteenth century gangs (as well as victims). Anne Campbell, however, has underscored women's increasingly public roles and associations in their own gangs. As the boom of the 1980's ended, white-collar conspiracies and corruption in political office also challenged perceptions of the criminal "other" across

The picture that emerges from centuries of an American experience of gangs is not so clear as the fervent national rhetoric of wars against crime might suggest. Crime and associations around illegal activities have multiple meanings and interpretations that have to do with assimilation, social protest, and solidarity in addition to mere gain. Gangs and crime develop from strength as well as weakness, from valuable solidarities and alliances as well as divisions. As such, they entail neither simple problems nor simple solutions.

SUGGESTED READINGS. For historical perspectives on gangs and perceptions of gangs, see *Low Life: Lures and Snares of Old New York* (1991) by Luc Sante and *The Gang* (1927, rev. ed. 1960) by Frederic M. Thrasher. More recent events are discussed in *City of Quartz: Excavating the Future in Los Angeles* (1990) by Mike Davis and *The Girls in the Gangs* (1984) by Anne Campbell. Organized crime is examined in *Organized Crime: The Fifth Estate* (1979) by August Bequai and *Chinatown No More* (1992) by Hsian-shui Chen.—*Gary W. McDonogh*

Garifuna: Descendants of Caribs (original residents of the Caribbean) and African slaves who were transported to the island of St. Vincent in the sixteenth and seventeenth centuries. Also known as Black Caribs, most Garifuna were exiled from St. Vincent and were dispersed to Ruatan; Trinidad; Trujillo, Honduras; and Mosquitia. As a result of natural disasters (such as volcanic eruptions and a hurricane in St. Vincent) and fighting between British, Spanish, and French over territories in which they lived, the Garifuna continued to move from place to place. In the twentieth century, they came to inhabit small communities in British Honduras, Nicaragua, and Guatemala. Their culture is a blend of Carib, African, French, English, and Spanish elements.

Garment industry: Prototype for immigrant enterprise in the United States. It has been dominated by immigrants since the massive tide of Jewish and Italian immigration to NEW YORK CITY around the beginning of the twentieth century, which occurred just as the demand for factory-made clothing began to surge. The garment industry has served many minority groups, primarily Jews from what was once the Russian Empire, Italians from the south of Italy, Chinese, Southeast Asians, and Latinos. From its beginnings, the industry has provided immigrants with jobs, introductions to their new culture, and opportunities for entrepreneurship.

Historical Background. Urbanization, the development of a national market, and the rapid population growth of the 1880's spurred a demand for ready-made clothing that quickly supplanted both individually tailored and homemade clothes. New York City became the center of the garment industry because it had both the labor force and access to the raw materials. It was the funnel through which Russian Jews, fleeing poverty and persecution, poured into the United States and was also home to 390,000 Italian immigrants around the turn of the century. Equally important was New York City's status as the nation's leading port and as a center for the sale of textiles, both foreign and domestic. Textiles were available at better prices and in greater variety there than anywhere else in the country.

The immigrants of this period were poor and industrious but were often lacking in industrial skills. Among Jews, however, there was a long tradition in the needle trades, which was an outgrowth of religious custom in the Old Country. ORTHODOX JEWS were forbidden to wear clothing made of mixed wool and linen, and they trusted only Jewish tailors to know and observe the rule. Their services soon gained a wider clientele, so much so that the Russian census of 1897 showed that 17 percent of all employed Jews worked in the making of clothes.

Both before and after immigration, Russian Jews considered the garment trade a respectable occupation for women. Both men and women worked in the trade—the men in coats and suits, the women in shirtwaists (blouses), undergarments, and children's clothes. By contrast, newly arrived Italian men were mainly drawn into heavy labor jobs such as construction. Because these jobs were unstable and low-paying, many Italian women were compelled to continue working after marriage and motherhood. Most of these women entered the garment industry after 1900.

Before this massive immigration, most clothing was made in large workshops or factories owned by German Jews of earlier migrations. With the influx of poor Russian Jews, a new production system emerged. Small contractors housed their workshops in the same tenements in which the immigrants lived. Themselves Russian Jewish immigrants, contractors had an advantage over manufacturers in recruiting laborers who often came from the contractor's hometown. Since the job opportunities of new immigrants were limited by language and economic need, contractors could push their former neighbors to heights of productivity that larger manufacturers could not rival. This tendency to divide functions between manufacturing and small-scale contracting has remained a feature of the garment industry. It often led to exploitative conditions in New York's infamous sweatshops.

The Rise of Socialism and Unions. SOCIALISM was a vigorous idea in Jewish immigrant life during the opening years of the twentieth century, but it had little effect as an organized movement. By 1910, primarily as a result of the failed Russian Revolution of 1905, a large number of Bundists had reached New York.

Inclined to the left wing of international socialism, these Russian Jews aimed to create a Jewish working class with a sense of its own worth, since many workers continued to live passively and in constant fear, much as they had in the Russian Empire. The Bundists joined the American socialist movement and provided vigorous new leadership in the unions.

The INTERNATIONAL LADIES GARMENT WORKERS UNION (ILGWU) was organized in 1900 at a New York conference of East Side delegates and the AMERICAN FEDERATION OF LABOR. After a false start, the ILGWU gained momentum toward the end of its first decade. The years 1907 and 1908 saw a severe national depression. Partly in reaction, a series of major strikes broke out, representing an outburst of rage and yearning within the Jewish community that was to have far-reaching consequences.

The most important of these strikes started on November 22, 1909, when twenty thousand shirtwaist makers went on strike. Most were women in their teens or early twenties. About two-thirds were Jewish, one third Italian. While physical conditions tended to be better in the relatively new shirtwaist part of the industry, the female workers were subject to many tyrannies. They were taxed for the chairs on which they sat and charged for needles, electric power, and other supplies.

The strike wore on until mid-February, 1910, and was finally settled with improvement in working conditions but without the formal union recognition which the ILGWU had demanded. By the strike's end, Local 25 had grown to ten thousand members and many immigrants had discovered a new sense of dignity and self-worth on the picket lines.

Five months after the end of the shirtwaist makers strike, the Cloak Operators Union, Local 1 of the ILGWU, declared a general strike. They asked for a forty-nine-hour work week; the employers offered fifty-three hours. The workers demanded that employers hire only union members in what is called a "closed shop." Louis D. Brandeis, a prominent Jewish attorney and later U.S. Supreme Court Justice, acted as negotiator. He negotiated a compromise settlement: a fifty-hour week, wage increases, and a "preferential union shop" in which union standards prevail and the union receives preference. This last concept would later be used nationwide in settling industrial disputes.

The workers were jubilant. Their success demonstrated the rise of a new Jewish working class that was structured, disciplined, and more strongly tied to

socialist politics than other American workers. Through their struggle the garment workers had given hope to other immigrants as well as native-born workers. A new national consciousness was developing.

Changes in the Industry. New York City's garment industry continued to grow in the 1920's, but by the 1930's other centers had become important. Boston, Philadelphia, Chicago, and Baltimore all gained sizable concentrations of clothing manufacturers. By 1941, only 39 percent of all garment workers were employed in New York City. Reasons included higher labor costs in New York (as a result of unionization by the ILGWU), faster highways for the transportation of materials, and the ease in relocating garment shops, which can operate in rented lofts and storefronts. The South beckoned to the industry with its supply of surplus rural labor and poor towns offering benefits to new industries. By the 1950's, first the South and then the far West had become centers of industry growth.

By this time, the United States' clothing needs were increasingly being met by foreign producers. As the market for imported clothing grew, the number of countries exporting clothing grew as well. Japan and Hong Kong were the first to woo American consumers, but eventually every country with a developed

Laotian refugee working in a Queens, N.Y., clothing factory. (H. Gloaguen/UNHCR)

New York City garment workers march in a 1985 Labor Day parade. (Odette Lupis)

clothing industry tried, and usually succeeded, in gaining a piece of the U.S. market. Because of higher labor and capital costs, U.S. makers were often unable to compete.

Renewal. From 1965 to 1985, a new immigrant garment industry developed in New York. Russian Jews had been the dominant group among manufacturers since 1914, with Italians also well represented. Yet most owners were pleased when their children chose other pursuits, and many actively dissuaded their children from entering the business. This attitude opened the way for other groups of immigrants to enter the industry.

The garment industry is one in which small, new firms have a chance to succeed. It utilizes immigrant owners' informal connections to their broader ethnic community. Start-up capital is usually pieced together from a variety of sources: savings, loans from relatives, and advances from friends as well as the traditional financial community. Success, however, even once won, is sometimes short-lived. Of the large influx of newcomers from the Caribbean and Asia in the 1970's, two groups stand out for their role in the New York City garment industry: the Dominicans and the Chinese.

Dominicans seized the opening when fashion trends suddenly changed in the 1970's to favor pleated skirts. Since Dominicans had previously been the key work group in New York's dominant pleating industry, they were well positioned to profit. In the late 1970's, scores of Dominicans set up pleating shops using simple, labor-intensive techniques. The same market forces that facilitated the Dominicans' entry into pleating, however, left the new shops vulnerable to changing consumer demand. According to union officials, half the garment firms owned by Dominicans had gone out of business by the early 1980's.

The opportunity for the Chinese came with the precipitous downturn in New York's economy in 1969. The vacancy rate in the industrial-loft supply soared; in the lower Manhattan district that borders New York's traditional Chinatown, space emptied out abruptly and rents dropped dramatically. Chinese entrepreneurs took advantage of these conditions to open garment factories. They organized ethnic business associations, just as the Dominicans had, but participation was limited in the Latino associations. The Chinese firms had a greater impetus to organize, greater collective resources, and strong associations of their own within the unions.

The ethnic and kinship ties that were so important to their Jewish and Italian predecessors were even more essential for the Chinese. "Relatives are a must," noted one owner who immigrated from Hong Kong in 1981. "You need people to take care of all the departments, and when you start out you don't have enough money to hire as many people as you need." Chinese owners from Hong Kong recruited other arrivals from Hong Kong, while new owners from mainland China tended to hire workers from the mainland. Dominican owners invariably recruited other Latinos, but Dominicans furnished the majority of their labor force.

With the tremendous influx of Asian and Latino immigrants to the West Coast in the 1970's and 1980's, Los Angeles saw a boom in the garment trades. Refugees from El Salvador, Guatemala, and Southeast Asia were among the new recruits. Immigrant owners saw network recruiting as a way to screen out unqualified or inappropriate workers, gain trust, and reduce the likelihood that workers would leave. Such kinship and friendship networks assure a paternalistic (and sometimes exploitive) relationship between immigrant owners and their employees.

The history of the garment industry is a history of the hard work, grit, and determination of American immigrants. The process by which new immigrants replace older ethnic groups will continue to provide newcomers with opportunities. History shows that the businesses founded by new ethnic groups do not simply add to the existing businesses, but tend to replace them. They, in turn, are displaced by the next wave of aspiring immigrants. Yet because of an uncertain American economy, no one can predict the future of the garment industry. Immigrants will continue to get ahead, but whether they do so as garment capitalists is a matter largely beyond the newcomers' control.

SUGGESTED READINGS. For a cultural and social study of women workers in the early days of New York's garment industry, see Susan A. Glenn's *Daughters of the Shtetl: Life and Labor in the Immigrant Generation* (1990). For the men's part of the story, see Harry A. Cobrin's *The Men's Clothing Industry: Colonial Through Modern Times* (1970). Irving Howe's nicely illustrated *World of Our Fathers* (1976) places the garment industry in a national context and describes in detail the ups and downs of the early labor movement. *Through the Eye of the Needle: Immigrants and Enterprise in New York's Garment Trades* by Roger D. Waldinger (1986) offers a theoretical overview based on numerous studies and statistics.—*Sheila Golburgh Johnson*

Garvey, Marcus (Aug. 17, 1887, St. Ann's Bay, Jamaica—June 10, 1940, London, England): West Indian black nationalist. Jamaican-born Marcus Garvey founded the UNIVERSAL NEGRO IMPROVEMENT ASSOCIATION (UNIA) in Kingston, Jamaica, in 1914. Its goals were to promote the spirit of racial pride and love, to establish a universal confraternity among the races, and to conduct a worldwide commercial and industrial enterprise.

Influenced by the work of Booker T. WASHINGTON, Garvey migrated to the United States in March, 1916, settling in Harlem. He saw American blacks as progressive industrially, financially, educationally, and socially, aiding the cause of race development. Garvey soon realized that black business could be a major step up for the black race everywhere.

Marcus Garvey founded the Universal Negro Improvement Association and promoted black-owned and operated businesses. (Library of Congress)

By 1918, Garvey had set up UNIA in NEW YORK CITY, claiming 1,500 members, and founded the widely circulated weekly *Negro World*. Editorials in the paper recalled blacks' racial heritage and the greatness of civilizations in ancient Africa, and urged readers to write and speak for social equality and unity.

In 1919, Garvey organized the Black Star Line steamship company, owned and operated exclusively by blacks. Thousands of shares of stock were sold to blacks all over the country as well as abroad. In June, 1920, Garvey declared the line solvent, raising black pride everywhere.

Many blacks saw Garvey as a new Moses who would rescue them from oppression. His weaknesses, however, soon appeared, particularly when he met legal difficulties. Lawsuits crippled the Black Star Line, which had been plagued by mismanagement and financial insecurity. In 1922, Garvey and three associates were indicted on twelve counts of fraudulent use of the postal system. The Black Star Line filed for bankruptcy. At the third annual convention of the UNIA in 1922, anti-Garvey meetings sprang up.

In May, 1923, Garvey was found guilty of fraud and sentenced to five years in prison. During the appeal he pushed plans for a colonization program to resettle American blacks in Africa. A group of UNIA delegates was sent to Liberia in December, 1923, to complete plans for repatriation of 20,000 to 30,000 African American families. Opposition grew both in the United States and in Liberia, however, and the project was dropped.

On February 8, 1925, Garvey was imprisoned, having lost his appeal. President Calvin Coolidge commuted his sentence in late 1927 but had Garvey deported as an undesirable alien. Back in Jamaica, Garvey revitalized the local UNIA and visited other branches in the West Indies and Central America. In 1929 he called an International Convention of the Negro Peoples of the World in Kingston. His keynote address focused on African redemption, the emancipation of a downtrodden race. The same year also saw the end of the Garvey organization, as dissension increased in the ranks and Garvey continued to face legal challenges. By 1940, his dream of a worldwide organization of blacks devoted to African liberation was dead—partially because of the outbreak of World War II. Chronic asthma and bouts with pneumonia weakened Garvey. In 1940 he suffered a severe stroke, from which he soon died. Friend and foe alike admitted that Garvey was a master propagandist, stimulating black race consciousness as no one before him. He remains a tragic figure whose failings overwhelmed his movement's high hopes.

SUGGESTED READINGS. A scholarly and balanced analysis of Garvey's life is given in Theodore G. Vincent's *Black Power and the Garvey Movement* (1971). Less scholarly, but very detailed and clear is *Black Moses* (1955) by Edmund D. Cronon; reprints 1962, 1964, 1966, and 1968. See also John H. Franklin's *From Slavery to Freedom* (1947) and *The World of Marcus Garvey* (1986) by Judith Stein.

Gavin, John (b. Apr. 8, 1932, Los Angeles, Calif.): Latino actor, diplomat, and corporate executive. Gavin graduated from Stanford University in 1952 with a degree in the economic history of Latin America. From 1955-1974, he was a noted film performer, serving as president of the Screen Actors Guild from 1971 to 1973. At the same time, Gavin was an adviser to the Secretary-General of the Organization of American States from 1961 to 1974. He served as president of Gamma Services Corporation from 1968 to 1981, leaving that post when President Ronald Reagan appointed him to serve as U.S. Ambassador to Mexico from 1981 until 1986. There-

John Gavin during his acting career. (AP/Wide World Photos)

after, he assumed major positions as vice president with Atlantic Richfield Co. (ARCO) and president of Univisa, Inc. For his dedication to inter-American understanding, Gavin received the Order of Balboa from the Republic of Panama.

Gay and lesbian activism: Organized efforts toward social justice for American homosexuals and public education about homosexuality have their ideological and cultural roots in late nineteenth century Europe. The theory that homosexuality was abnormal, espoused by German psychiatrist Richard von Krafft-Ebing in 1876, was tempered by the scientific neutrality in *Sexual Inversion* (1897) by English physician and sexologist Havelock Ellis and challenged by the radical, positive celebrations of homosexuality of English socialist Edward Carpenter. Homosexuality (and sexuality in general) was thrust into general consciousness internationally in the monumental psychoanalytical theories of Sigmund Freud in the late 1800's and early 1900's. The first organization founded to discuss and promote inquiry into these ideas was the Scientific Humanitarian Committee, whose German members addressed groups throughout Europe and the United States, but whose end came with the rise of the Nazis.

In The United States, activist Emma GOLDMAN championed homosexuality among her various causes, and in 1908, Edward Prime-Stevenson published his unprecedented study, *The Intersexes*. Still, little activism was evident until Henry Gerber founded a small and short-lived emancipation group, the Society for Human Rights, in Chicago in 1924. Conditions were not yet right for organized social protest and action.

The Postwar Era. WORLD WAR II uprooted and mobilized unprecedented numbers of young people, depositing them in unfamiliar and often urban environments that were frequently segregated by gender; an opportunity for change and redefinition of self presented itself to an entire generation. The postwar years also evolved into the rigidly conformist COLD WAR, and homosexuals as a group became targets for institutionalized identification and discrimination. The Kinsey Reports in 1948 (on men) and 1953 (on women) domesticated Freud and legitimized sexuality as a topic of discussion and study; Kinsey objectively presented the first American numbers and percentages for homosexuality. In 1951 Donald Webster Cory published *The Homosexual in America*, his pioneering study of what he argued was a significant minority group in American society. Conditions were now ripe

Latino gays and lesbians celebrate with pride on a march through San Francisco, Calif. (Robert Fried)

for organization and resistance: Gays and lesbians were no longer invisible.

In 1950, five gay men, all with some Communist associations, met in the home of Harry Hay in Los Angeles. By the next year the Mattachine Society was founded, organized for the discussion of "homophile" issues, a term chosen to embrace the emotional and political dimensions ignored by the specifically sexual and clinical associations of "homosexual." This group grew and expanded along the West Coast and in New York, and their 1953 convention drew five hundred representatives. Allied organizations included ONE, Inc., still vital today as the ONE Institute, and the publication *ONE,* issued 1953-1972, which became the leading voice for the new homophile movement and whose right to publish was affirmed by a 1955 Supreme Court decision. Subsequently, *The Mattachine Review* was published by the New York chapter. In San Francisco in 1955, Del Martin and Phyllis Lyon founded a lesbian organization, the Daughters of Bilitis, which published *The Ladder.* As awareness of homosexuality spread, these groups began using the

courts to fight for their rights and to congregate in public establishments to forge the beginnings of solidarity. Homosexuals were no longer isolated individuals but were instead asserting their presence and defending their civil liberties as an emerging social force and movement. This presence was noted by the Federal Bureau of Investigation (FBI), which conducted extensive surveillance of homosexual groups and their leaders for more than two decades beginning in 1953.

Homophile Activism. The initial emphasis on education and research that propelled the early gay organizations began to shift toward social and legal change in the midst of the growth of the CIVIL RIGHTS MOVEMENT and PEACE ACTIVISM in the 1960's. Activism became the mode for various gay groups. The Society for Individual Rights was formed in San Francisco in 1964; gays attending a fund-raising ball in San Francisco clashed boldly and publicly with police in 1965; the NATIONAL ORGANIZATION FOR WOMEN (NOW), with a significant lesbian presence, was formed in 1966; students at Columbia University received the first authorized campus charter for a gay group in

1967; Rev. Troy Perry organized the gay Metropolitan Community Church in 1968. Also in 1968, delegates from twenty-six groups gathered in Chicago for the North American Conference of Homophile Organizations (NACHO), endorsing the slogan "Gay Is Good" and issuing a five-point "Homosexual Bill of Rights." In July of that year, *The Wall Street Journal* brought gay issues into the mainstream media by publishing "U.S. Homosexuals Gain in Trying to Persuade Society to Accept Them."

Vocal and visible, four hundred gay and lesbian organizations formed alliances with and gained energy from other social justice movements. At the same time, bitter internal battles divided the community of gay organizations. These years marked a period of growth, but a unified gay activist identity and an effective agenda eluded national focus.

Gay Liberation. The watershed event and defining moment for gay activists arrived in June of 1969 with two nights of militant opposition to attempted police harassment of the patrons of a gay bar, the Stonewall Inn, in New York City. A crowd of two thousand battled four hundred policemen. The event galvanized the disparate activist groups, awakened a national sense of anger and gay pride, and provided a unifying symbol for action to end social marginalization and oppression. Thus, radicalism proved to be the method and direction for a fully national activist movement.

Soon after, the Gay Liberation Front (GLF) emerged in New York as a consciousness-raising effort. Loosely organized and nonhierarchical, it was dedicated to the credo that "personal is political." The GLF spread rapidly across the country, particularly on college campuses. It was decidedly radical, calling for fundamental social change and relying on dramatic public demonstrations with a new language and style from its homophile predecessors. GLF also transformed "coming out," or publicly acknowledging one's homosexuality, into an overtly political act. Later in 1969, a dissatisfied faction splintered off to form the Gay Activists Alliance (GAA), dedicated to working with and within established systems while still attempting to end oppression. Militant but nonviolent, the GAA took a more structured approach to civil rights, adopting the Greek letter lambda as its symbol and publishing *The Gay Activist.* GAA organized an active speakers bureau and promoted the concept of Gay Pride as a means of both personal and social liberation. In 1972, GAA formed the Lesbian Liberation Committee, which became separate the fol-

lowing year as Lesbian Feminist Liberation. Although many lesbians continued to work within GLF and GAA, among other groups, the issues and concerns of gay women were seen as fundamentally different from those of men. This gulf was to grow and to separate gay and lesbian activist groups and efforts into the 1980's.

With the maturity of the movement as gays and lesbians became undeniable social forces and presences in the United States, the focus of activism began to shift away from liberation and toward a reform orientation. By 1974, close to one thousand gay American organizations flourished based on a variety of professional, social, political, and religious interests. Their primary focus was immediate and local causes and issues, and their strategies for reform grew increasingly pragmatic. For example, in 1972, Dignity was formed by gay Catholics, as was Integrity by Episcopalians, and educators organized the Gay Academic Union. With the decline of radicalism came the rise of community centers and legal aid agencies, such as the National Gay Rights Advocates. Gay and lesbian activism had become a potent, pervasive, and wide-ranging social presence.

Successes were many and varied. Two openly gay delegates spoke at the 1972 Democratic National Convention. Also in 1972, the first of many openly gay politicians was elected to public office after the Alice B. Toklas Gay Democratic Club—the first of many such political groups—was organized in 1971 in San Francisco. The National Gay and Lesbian Task Force and the Lambda Defense and Education Fund were founded in New York in 1973, the same year that the American Psychiatric Association responded to unprecedented lobbying and removed homosexuality from its list of mental disorders, thus freeing gays and lesbians from the stigma of "sickness." The first gay rights bill was introduced into Congress in 1975, the same year that the Civil Service Commission dropped its ban on the employment of gays. In 1977, activists met with White House officials and staged a national gay rights march on Washington (repeated in 1987 and 1993), which drew thousands of committed gays and lesbians, as well as significant media attention. In 1978, the Briggs initiative to ban homosexual teachers was soundly defeated in California.

The achievements were tempered by adversity and resistance from various sectors of American society. Elected to the San Francisco Board of Supervisors in 1977, activist Harvey Milk was assassinated the following year, sending thousands into the streets of San Francisco and other cities in shocked disbelief and protest. In 1977, Anita Bryant mounted her "Save Our Children" campaign (countered by gays with "We Are Your Children") that successfully repealed the gay rights ordinance in Dade County, Florida; her efforts also inspired the Rev. Jerry Falwell's "Moral Majority" and a fundamentalist antigay movement. These setbacks, however, served to jar many groups out of complacency and brought splintered special interest organizations together to work in coalitions.

The AIDS Era. The mainstream press began reporting the presence of new and serious diseases in the gay community beginning in 1981. With the identification of ACQUIRED IMMUNE DEFICIENCY SYNDROME (AIDS) and the growth of the AIDS epidemic, a new era in gay activism began. Discrimination issues were thrown into sharp focus, homophobia took new and dangerous forms, and hate crimes began to rise. The movement's old goals and usual approaches proved inadequate. A general lack of knowledge about the new disease frightened all Americans, casting activists' policies and procedures into doubt. Scientific in-

sight and public education about AIDS grew at a glacial pace. Famous people began to die, and fundamentalists garnered increasing attention with moral explanations. Moreover, the Supreme Court affirmed the constitutionality of antisodomy laws with *Bowers v. Hardwick* in 1986. Established activist organizations shifted gears. Lesbians and gays reunited in concern over health care issues, and the Gay and Lesbian Alliance Against Defamation was formed in 1985 to attempt to address increasingly negative public attitudes that were threatening to eclipse all the advances made in the postwar years. A new generation of gay and lesbian activists, facing new social and medical problems, created new organizations.

Playwright Larry Kramer sparked the genesis of the confrontational AIDS Coalition to Unleash Power (ACT-UP) in 1987, a group whose dramatic and aggressive tactics split activists by generation and philosophy. However debatable its methods, ACT-UP's message could not be ignored; indeed, its agitation was responsible for many advances in research and treatment of the disease. In 1990, Queer Nation evolved, self-consciously discarding established cate-

Cultural organizations such as the Gay Men's Chorus of Los Angeles pictured here promote greater awareness and acceptance of homosexuals as individuals who make positive contributions to American society. (Gay Men's Chorus of Los Angeles)

gories of behavior and activism. Men and women, particularly the young and ethnic, chanted in unified chorus, "We're Here! We're Queer! Get Used to It!"

The infusion of youthful, iconoclastic concern and angry mobilization served as an important spark to reinvigorate gay and lesbian activism. Established organizations renewed their efforts in familiar arenas while new groups helped address an expanded agenda. Political involvement became a collective concern, even a matter of life and death. For example, political activism exploded in 1991 in California after Governor Pete Wilson vetoed gay rights legislation; spontaneous demonstrations erupted around the state and spread nationally, lasting for weeks. Gays and lesbians became a potent political force in the 1992 U.S. elections, proving to be a significant factor in the election of President Bill Clinton. As in the past, adversity provoked an activism that adapts and endures on behalf of gay rights.

SUGGESTED READINGS. Among the most balanced historical accounts of gay and lesbian activism are John D'Emilio, *Sexual Politics, Sexual Communities: The Making of a Homosexual Minority in the United States, 1940-1970* (1983); Donn Teal, *The Gay Militants* (1971); and Toby Marotta, *The Politics of Homosexuality: How Lesbians and Gay Men Have Made Themselves a Political and Social Force in Modern America* (1981). Also illuminating is Eric Marcus, *Making History: The Struggle for Gay and Lesbian Equal Rights 1945-1990, An Oral History* (1992). For more thoughtful analyses, see D'Emilio's *Making Trouble: Essays on Gay History, Politics, and the University* (1992), and Margaret Cruikshank's *The Gay and Lesbian Liberation Movement* (1992).—*Rodney Simard*

Gay and lesbian rights movement: Organized efforts to generate changes in sexual values and public opinion, with the goals of ending discrimination against homosexuals and granting them equal access to benefits commonly enjoyed by all U.S. citizens.

Michel Foucault's intellectual history of sexuality described a nineteenth century expansion of sexual discourse that created new categories of sexuality. A Hungarian physician named Karoly Benkert, writing in 1896 under the pseudonym Kertbeny, devised the label "homosexual," while seeking to decriminalize homosexuality. English dramatist Oscar Wilde was imprisoned for homosexuality in 1895, and American novelist Willa Cather, a lesbian, believing Wilde de-

servedly punished, called the homosexual's part in history "the thing not named."

Seventy-five years later, gay and lesbian Americans responded to the rallying call to "come out" openly as homosexuals. Stigma had not ended, but lesbians and gay men experienced social visibility and new opportunities to find each other. "Gay" named an isolated minority historically subject to discrimination and, simultaneously, a distinct social group with its own lifestyle. Gay liberation groups opened vigorous, even vituperative debate about sexuality and family life. In 1992, this resulted in positions on gay and lesbian rights in both major political parties' presidential platforms.

Historical Background. The criminalization of homosexuality in the Western world drew on legal precedents of Rome, the ancient Jews, and Christian canons. Using medical language, early sex reformers attacked sodomy laws as irrational and outdated. This shift to science and reason emphasized civil rights and civil liberties, which the American and French revolutions had promoted. The emphasis on the findings of embryology, biology, psychology, and other disciplines countered religiously oriented moral arguments against homosexuality; however, it also influenced an equation of homosexuality with deviance. Conditions grew more favorable for movements to abolish anti-sodomy laws.

By 1900, a distinct male homosexual identification and urban gay subculture had emerged in the United States. In the early twentieth century, women such as Lillian Wald, a public health pioneer and founder of New York City's Henry Street settlement house, and Jane Addams of Chicago's Hull House and her particular friend Mary Rozel Smith, built independent support networks in order to live and work in equal relations with heterosexuals. This foreshadowed the late twentieth century emergence of gay neighborhoods in large cities with ample white-collar jobs.

Organizational Development. In Germany a forerunner of Dr. Alfred Kinsey, Magnus Hirschfield, founded a Scientific-Humanitarian Committee to seek gay and women's rights, arguing that to criminalize a sexual orientation established at birth was both irrational and unjust. In Chicago in 1924 a parallel organization, the Society for Human Rights, formed and quickly ran afoul of the law. Fascism interrupted the groups' activities in 1933.

Impressed by the 1948 Kinsey report, the International Bachelors Fraternal Orders for Peace and Social

Lesbians participate in a gay pride festival in New York City in 1989. (AP/Wide World Photos)

Dignity formed in 1950 from a Los Angeles foundation called Citizens' Committee to Outlaw Entrapment. It intended to fight the persecution of "androgynes" as the Mattachine Society (MS). It reverted to a more conservative tone when the forces of McCarthyism subpoenaed founder Henry Hay because of his communist affiliation. Yet chapters continued to form across the nation, including one in Buffalo, New York, that in 1972 sponsored Madeline Davis as the Democratic presidential nominating convention's first openly lesbian delegate. For twenty years, MS struggled to defeat employment and housing discrimination, protested police raids on gay bars, and supported sympathetic candidates for public office. The organization continues today but is far less active.

Lesbians' roles have been less well documented than those of gay males because of sexism in the gay liberation movement and homophobia in the women's liberation movement. Lesbians found themselves in conflict over and personally conflicted by which movement took precedence. Daughters of Bilitis (DOB) formed in 1955 as a voice for lesbians to assist them in improving their self-image and social consciousness. Barbara Grier, a.k.a. Gene Damon, edited its groundbreaking publication, *The Ladder.* In 1970 DOB convened the first national lesbian conference. Chapters participated in electoral campaigns, and the New York City and San Francisco chapters engaged in direct action protest. The national organization refrained from protest demonstrations, but helped strategize bar raid cases, one of which resulted in judicial affirmation of homosexuals' right to free association. The onset of the contemporary women's movement coincided with a feminist surge in DOB and, eventually, internal division and the organization's demise.

By 1968 the gay San Francisco Society for Individual Rights had a thousand members and sponsored an array of political and social activities. Lesbians were increasingly receptive to political organization; founders of separatist groups, they also participated in the founding of the NATIONAL ORGANIZATION FOR WOMEN (NOW) in 1968. That same year, the Metropolitan Community Church formed to serve gays and lesbians who felt excluded from mainstream Christian churches. Estimates of the total lesbian and gay organizations in 1973 range from fifty to eight hundred.

The late 1960's to 1980's were a time of intense citizen activism on many fronts, and saw the formation of several major gay rights organizations. The first was the National Gay Task Force, founded in 1973 to fight discrimination and antigay violence. Its first victory was pressuring the American Psychiatric Association to rescind its classification of homosexuality as a disorder. The U.S. Health, Education, and Welfare Department regulations for the Rehabilitation Act still defined homosexuality as a handicap. In 1975 the National Gay Task Force became the National Gay and Lesbian Task Force; in 1992 half its officers were women, as were one-third of its members.

Early in the 1970's, the U.S. Supreme Court began supporting homosexuals' First Amendment-based right to free association, although it rejected claims related to the right to privacy. In 1972 Lamba Legal Defense and Education Fund formed to advance gay and lesbian status, fourteen years before the AMERICAN CIVIL LIBERTIES UNION (ACLU) established its Lesbian and Gay Rights Project. Jill Johnson, writing in the June, 1975, issue of *Ms.* MAGAZINE, urged women to overcome the barricades dividing them and asserted lesbians' significance as "women-identified women." Despite a lesbian-straight split, and more yet to come, NOW at its 1975 conference voted to devote 1 percent of its first $1 million budget to lesbian rights. In 1977 the Lesbian Rights Project formed in San Francisco.

Mass Protest. In 1963 twelve picketers at Whitehall Induction Center in New York protested a failure to honor the confidentiality of draft records containing information about sexual orientation. There was a sizable protest against Los Angeles bar raids in 1967, the year after the North American Conference of Homophile Organizations proclaimed that "gay is good." That same year, some ACLU chapters took a position against gay discrimination in government employment, immigration, and police harassment; the next year, the ACLU represented gay activists trying to end harassment in Chicago, Houston, and Philadelphia. Illinois in 1961 and Connecticut in 1969 decriminalized consensual sex between adult gay men. When police raided the Stonewall Inn in Greenwich Village two nights running in 1969, they confronted the "Stone Wall," a week-long response, sometimes violent, by gays and lesbians that gave birth to gay power. Stonewall's anniversary is celebrated on the last Sunday in June as Lesbian/Gay Pride Day with parades and other festivities in major cities.

In 1977, Dade County, Florida, passed a gay rights ordinance that gay-bashing singer Anita Bryant opposed with scare tactics. A successful repeal initiative followed. Ordinances in St. Paul, Wichita, and

Gay Pride Day festivals like this one in Los Angeles, Calif., commemorate the anniversary of the Stonewall riots. (Bob Myers)

Eugene, Oregon, survived because of strong popular support. San Francisco passed an ordinance in 1978 after the election of Harvey Milk, who was gay, to the Board of Supervisors in 1977; that same year Californians en masse defeated the John Briggs amendment to prohibit public school hiring of gays, lesbians, and their supporters. A former San Francisco supervisor assassinated Milk and Mayor George Moscone in late 1978. After learning that a jury had convicted the assassin only of voluntary manslaughter, thousands protested at City Hall, breaking windows and burning police cars on the scene. In retaliation, police raided the Elephant Bar in the gay Castro district.

Harbingers of Change. Waves of stigma accompanied the massive spread of the ACQUIRED IMMUNE DEFICIENCY SYNDROME (AIDS) EPIDEMIC in the gay male community in the 1980's. With right-wing encouragement, AIDS became known as a homosexual disease or gay plague, promoting misperceptions about risk. Community organizations to confront the crisis sprang up alongside gay rights groups, first at its epicenters, then in medium-sized cities. In 1987 playwright Larry Kramer pushed for the formation of the AIDS Coali-

tion to Unleash Power (ACT-UP) to respond to the politics of AIDS; the group pressured the Food and Drug Administration with protests. Lesbians formed an ACT-UP Women's Caucus to access clinical trials and treatments for women with human immunodeficiency virus (HIV), lesbians among them. Women were seen as "vectors of transmission" instead of individuals in their own right, and lesbians, inaccurately, as a no-risk population. Some lesbians resented the support given gay male communities and felt they were the victims of gender discrimination. Lesbians nevertheless joined gay men in force as protesters, caregivers, and supporters.

Public opinion about the immorality of same-sex sexual relations seemed unrelenting. In 1985 the Gay and Lesbian Alliance Against Defamation formed to combat the hostile climate the media fostered. A year later, in *Brown v. Mardwick*, the U.S. Supreme Court upheld Georgia's antisodomy law as based on perceptions about majority beliefs; the Court originally voted 5-4 to overturn it, but Justice Lewis Franklin Powell changed his mind. After he retired in 1987, he said he had made a mistake. In 1989 the National Coalition of Black Lesbians and Gays introduced a five-year agenda to promote positive images of homosexuals and an accountable media.

On August 27, 1992, *Newsweek* magazine reported that 51 percent of respondents did not find lesbians and gays a threat to family values, and 78 percent favored equal employment opportunity for them. After President Bill Clinton's election in 1992, a *Washington Post*-ABC News opinion poll reported that 55 percent of Americans favored lifting the ban on gays and lesbians in the military, as Clinton had promised to do. The Ninth Circuit Court of Appeals refused to countenance antigay prejudice as a basis for excluding them from service, and the Supreme Court did not interfere with a lower court's decision to let a lesbian's discrimination lawsuit progress after her discharge from the Army Reserve. In a suit brought by Martina Navratilova, the ACLU, and the cities of Aspen, Boulder, and Denver, a 1993 court decision held back a popularly ratified amendment to the Colorado constitution that would have forbidden the passage of gay and lesbian civil rights legislation. Organizations such as the American Association of Physicians for Human Rights and the SOUTHERN CHRISTIAN LEADERSHIP CONFERENCE joined a boycott against the state of Colorado, which the Atlanta City Council, among others, also approved.

President Clinton's vow to end the military's ban on gays in the armed forces created a storm of controversy during the early months of his administration and met with strong resistance both from the military and in Congress. In July, 1993, Clinton finally proposed a compromise plan (which he termed "not a perfect solution"). People entering the military would no longer be asked about their sexual orientation, but the possibility of investigation and discharge of individuals for openly gay behavior remained. Meanwhile, homosexuals staged what they claimed was the biggest civil rights demonstration in American history in Washington, D.C., in 1993, making the case for gay

Perry Watkins served in the U.S. Army for fifteen years before he was discharged because of his sexual orientation. Gays in the military became a major issue of American debate in 1993. (AP/Wide World Photos)

rights as the last vanguard for progress in civil rights. As the twenty-first century approached, gay and lesbian civil rights were not guaranteed, but at least they were securely on the American public agenda.

SUGGESTED READINGS. The classic comparative work is Vern L. Bullough's *Sexual Variance in Society and History* (1976); see especially part 6, "The Twentieth Century: Trends and Assumptions." John D'Emilio and Estelle B. Freedman offer a well-researched history of American sexuality in *Intimate Matters* (1988), which integrates gay and straight experiences to provide context for both. *Hidden from History: Reclaiming the Gay and Lesbian Past* (1989), edited by Martin Bauml Duberman, Martha Vicinus, and George Chauncey, Jr., is a collection of essays grouped by time period. Dennis Altman's *The Homosexualization of America, the Americanization of the Homosexual* (1982) is a provocative work on gay men that is not always accurate. Lillian Faderman's *Odd Girls and Twilight Lovers: A History of Lesbian Life in Twentieth Century America* (1991) provides chronological organization and diversity. See also Madeline Davis on the Mattachine Society and Genie Stowers on Daughters of Bilitis in *Women's Groups: Institutional Profiles* (1993), edited by Sarah Slavin.—*Sarah Slavin*

Gay and lesbian studies programs: The period of the 1960's and 1970's was marked by the rise of a number of different, yet related, social movements concerned with the rights of African Americans, Chicanos, American Indians, women, youth, and homosexuals and lesbians. Through these social movements, Americans' attitudes (though not necessarily their behavior) toward various groups have moved—if only to a small degree—in a more positive, accepting direction. These changes are a result, at least in part, of individuals being introduced to information about the accomplishments and concerns of each of these groups as well as being made aware of the societal discrimination the group has faced. An outgrowth of these various civil rights movements of the 1960's and 1970's was the birth of various "specialized studies programs," such as WOMEN'S STUDIES PROGRAMS, AFRICAN AMERICAN STUDIES PROGRAMS, CHICANO STUDIES PROGRAMS, and, among others, gay and lesbian studies programs.

Several general types of gay and lesbian studies programs exist. Among them are collegiate "academic" programs, including traditional academic departments (or other units) offering courses, majors, and minors that carry college credit. Another type of academic program involves centers or research projects that support scholarly activity but do not grant degrees or offer courses. A different type of approach is taken by "nonacademic" collegiate programs such as institutes that are not affiliated with accredited academic institutions; they may offer courses for which there is no college credit. Another type of program involves conferences or meetings at which research papers are presented.

Perhaps no specialized program has met with as much resistance as gay and lesbian studies programs have. Despite the apparent willingness of large segments of American society to be more tolerant, many individuals remain steadfastly opposed to both civil rights for and the study of lesbians and gay men. Indeed, many otherwise rational people exhibit homophobia and label lesbians and gay men as "abnormal," "perverted," "sick," and "sinful," among other categorizations, based upon biases such as fundamentalist religious beliefs. In both higher education and public schools, attempts to design and implement gay and lesbian studies programs or even single courses with gay and lesbian content have faced considerable resistance. Even where such programs do exist, they are often relegated to a marginalized status.

Collegiate Departments, Programs, and Centers. The only officially recognized full-fledged gay and lesbian studies department at the collegiate level is the department of gay and lesbian studies established in 1989 at City College of San Francisco, the largest two-year institution in the United States. The departmental offerings are multidisciplinary, with courses from the departments of gay and lesbian studies, anthropology, English, film, health, labor studies, theater arts, and interdepartmental studies. Examples of courses include "Anthropology of Homosexualities," "Survey of Gay and Lesbian Literature," "Film Expression: Homosexuality in Contemporary Film," and "U.S. Gay and Lesbian Reform and Liberation: World War II to Present." Enrollment continues to grow each year, perhaps because of the accepting atmosphere toward gays and lesbians in San Francisco. At other colleges and universities around the country, such as University of California at Santa Cruz, Harvard University, University of Minnesota, and University of Michigan, there are courses in a variety of departments (usually English and the social and behavioral sciences) whose contents are expressly lesbian/gay. There are also courses with lesbian/gay content that are not specifically designated as such in their titles.

Probably because of strong adherence to the traditional, conservative academic canon in higher education and to a sense of public conservatism about gays and lesbians, departments of gay and lesbian studies do not exist at any four-year college or university in the United States. There are, however, a number of programs, centers, or research projects whose purpose focuses on scholarly pursuits concerning gays and lesbians.

Perhaps the most well known of the centers is the City University of New York Center for Lesbian and Gay Studies (CLAGS), a graduate program and center founded in 1991. Its goal is to form an ethnically diverse intellectual community of scholars committed to gender parity. It offers an institutional "home" and networking base for scholars working on lesbian and gay-related topics and for lesbian and gay scholars themselves. CLAGS offers opportunities for independent research, sponsors colloquia and panels, and supports a fellowship program.

The Lesbian and Gay Studies Center at Yale University is another well-known locus of scholarly activity related to lesbians and gays; it was established in 1986. Its purpose is to include a wide diversity of perspectives and viewpoints in areas of scholarly inquiry into lesbian and gay issues. The group responsible for daily operations of the center has membership requirements designed to ensure diversity: There must be at least six people of color and no fewer than six members of each gender. The center sponsors a lecture series, annual national conference on lesbian/gay scholarship, and archival and bibliographic projects.

While the latter two programs are initiated or directed by faculty, the Multicultural Lesbian and Gay Studies (MLGS) Program at University of California, Berkeley, founded in 1982, is a student-initiated and student-operated program committed to broad inclusivity in lesbian and gay studies. The program promotes scholarly research and discussion of issues concerning lesbians and gays through sponsorship of lectures, workshops, speakers within the campus and the community, and a resource center. The MLGS assists faculty members in developing courses on gays and lesbians, including content, instructional materials, and plans for active class participation. The MLGS also serves as a consultant body for faculty wanting to incorporate lesbian/gay content into their classes.

While the previously noted programs are all housed within formal post-secondary institutions, the Institute

Included in many gay studies programs is openly gay author James Baldwin, who dealt with the theme of homosexuality in his writings. (AP/Wide World Photos)

of Gay and Lesbian Education, started in 1992 in West Hollywood, California, is an independent, college-level institute devoted to gay themes and issues. The institute was started by Christopher Patrouch and Simon LeVay, the latter best known for his studies on the brains of gay males that established evidence of a biological component in homosexuality. The institute started with eight courses, including "The Psychological Development of Gay Men," "The Science of Human Sexuality," "Lesbian and Gay Fiction Writing," and "Queer Space: Gays and Lesbians and Their Built Environment." Besides eradicating prejudice and improving the welfare of gays, the institute hopes "to improve their self-image and self-understanding while showcasing the talents and contributions of gays [to] heterosexual society," according to the *Lesbian and Gay Studies Newsletter.*

Conferences. Perhaps the largest and best-known conference dealing with gay and lesbian studies is the annual Lesbian, Bisexual, and Gay Studies Conference started at Yale University and held in subsequent years at Harvard University. Recognizing that the lives of gay and bisexual people are connected not only to

Many lesbian activists believe that lesbian issues and achievements receive too little attention in some gay and lesbian studies programs. (Bob Myers)

those communities but also to diverse ethnic, class, and religious communities, a major goal of the conference has been to be broadly representative.

At an increasing number of conferences of professional organizations, such as the American Sociological Association, American Psychological Association, American Educational Research Association, Modern Language Association, and American Library Association, there are special sections of the program in which research and scholarly papers dealing with lesbian and gay issues are presented. There are also often special interest groups within these organizations for those interested in lesbian and gay issues.

Criticisms of Lesbian and Gay Studies Programs. Despite the strong commitment to cultural inclusivity found in the mission statements of gay and lesbian centers or programs, the existing learning materials in gay/lesbian studies are often criticized for focusing primarily on white, middle-age or younger gay males to the exclusion of gay males of a variety of ethnicities, races, religions, classes, and ages and to the exclusion of all lesbians. Another major criticism, not unlike the criticisms leveled at other specialized study programs, expresses skepticism about the academic rigor of any lesbian and gay studies program. Critics doubt that the topic has the capacity to sustain "intellectual independence"—knowledge that is apolitical and separate from an action component. This skepticism arises from the fact that lesbian/gay studies programs grew out of gay and lesbian activism and the gay and lesbian rights movement. There is a great concern on the part of traditional, conservative scholars who claim that lesbian and gay studies cannot contain "pure" knowledge but is highly "politicized." (Rarely, however, is a question raised about the political nature of traditional scholarship that has rejected multiculturalism.)

The debate over the political nature of lesbian and gay studies is not simply a conflict between conservative and gay/lesbian scholars. There is also a rift among gay/lesbian scholars themselves—not unlike rifts in women's studies and other "minority" studies—over the issue of making gay/lesbian scholarship conform to the established standards and canons of the academy, thus running the risk of neglecting the very communities and political concerns that gave birth to gay and lesbian scholarship.

SUGGESTED READINGS. *Looking at Gay and Lesbian Life* (1988) by Warren J. Blumenfeld and Diane Raymond provides an introduction to major concepts and issues related to gays and lesbians. *The Gay Academic* (1978), edited by Louie Crew, offers readings in a number of disciplinary areas. *Lesbian Studies* (1982), edited by Margaret Cruickshank, includes writings by lesbians about experiences in the world of classrooms and research about lesbians. *Coming out of the Closet: Gay and Lesbian Students, Teachers, and Curricula* (1992), edited by Karen Harbeck, is a compilation of readings dealing with background and context for gay and lesbian studies as well as legal issues for gay/lesbian teachers. *In Every Classroom* (1989), edited by Ronald A. Nieverling, is the report of a committee of the president of Rutgers University dealing with lesbian and gay concerns. *The Lesbian and Gay Studies Newsletter*, published three times yearly, contains a wealth of information including book reviews, presentation of course syllabi in lesbian/gay studies areas, and news on scholars in the field.—*M. F. Stuck*

General Federation of Women's Clubs (GFWC): National coordinating organization of local and state women's clubs. When it was founded in 1890, most clubs were devoted to self-education and literary activities. In the early 1900's, they became involved in social reforms such as suffrage, woman and child labor laws, and pure food and drug legislation. In 1916, the GFWC had two million members. The organization encouraged separate clubs of African American women rather than a policy of integration. After World War II, the GFWC retreated from reform and politics entirely to focus again on home life and self-education. Activities later expanded to include service in the arts, conservation, education, and public affairs.

Genocide: Willful, systematic annihilation of a group (racial, ethnic, cultural, or political) by the state or other authority. Although this term is used loosely in common parlance, it is important to note that genocide was coined as a term only in the middle of the twentieth century to refer to the HOLOCAUST during WORLD WAR II. The total

extermination of a victim group is exceedingly rare in world history.

Academic, philosophical, and legal debates continue concerning the precise definition of genocide, especially the problematic nature of defining "political group" and the vast power of the state or central authority to establish such a definition. The first widely used definition was adopted by the United Nations in December, 1948. This definition, though not without problems, includes the criteria noted above as well as measures aimed at preventing births in the victimized groups and the forcible transfer of victimized children to another group.

Genocide has occurred throughout human history. The earliest victims of genocide were generally exterminated because of where they were (trade routes) or what they had (food or other resources). The defeated

At Auschwitz-Birkenau, Nazi soldiers determine the fate of new arrivals to the concentration camp—part of Hitler's "Final Solution." (Simon Wiesenthal Center)

groups were often forced into SLAVERY, but this left open the potential for the vanquished to regroup and fight again. Genocide represented an attempt by the victorious group to ensure that their victory was total and permanent.

Some observers contend that the European American treatment of American Indians throughout most of the history of the United States amounts to genocide. At the beginning of the European conquest, the native population in North America was estimated at nearly ten million. By 1850, their numbers had dwindled to approximately 200,000. This decrease occurred in part because of exposure to new European diseases but also because of a conscious American policy of using superior European firepower and technology to forcibly remove native peoples from their coveted lands.

Thousands of Indians perished as white settlers continuously pushed westward throughout the nineteenth century. The infamous saying, "The only good Indian is a dead Indian"—actually voiced in the hallowed halls of Congress—captured the ideology of the times. By 1900, most Indians had been herded into federal reservations, many of their children had been shipped off to boarding schools where they were forbidden to speak native languages, and their legal status was uncertain (they were denied the right to vote until 1924). This legacy of subordinated status continues today as American Indians rank near the bottom of many quality of life indicators such as poverty rate, infant mortality rate, percentage of the population residing in substandard housing, rates of alcoholism, and infectious diseases.

More contemporary victims of genocide appear to be selected by the state solely on the basis of their ethnic, racial, religious, or socioeconomic identity. Increasingly, modern states have employed genocide as a means of dealing with perceived internal threats. Examples outside the United States include Hitler's "Final Solution," resulting in the extermination of some six million Jews; Joseph Stalin's efforts to eliminate "enemies of the people" in the former Soviet Union; Pol Pot's "killing fields" in Cambodia, littered with the remains of intellectuals, teachers, and foreigners; and attempts at "ethnic cleansing" in the former Yugoslavia. Refugees from genocide elsewhere have been important parts of the history of American immigration.

Charges of genocide have been leveled against government and private birth control advocates who have promoted birth control among American minority groups. While genocide is a highly loaded term, it is easy to understand how episodes of forced sterilization in the past can make African Americans and others suspicious of government motives.

SUGGESTED READINGS. An indispensable reference for those interested in further information about genocide is Frank Chalk and Kurt Jonassohn's *The History and Sociology of Genocide: Analyses and Case Studies* (1990). Two interesting edited volumes that include case studies are Helen Fein's *Genocide Watch* (1992) and Pierre L. van den Berghe's *State Violence and Ethnicity* (1990). For a novel and insightful application of genocide to nuclear warfare, see Robert J. Lifton and Eric Markusen's *The Genocidal Mentality: Nazi Holocaust and Nuclear Threat* (1990).

Genthe, Arnold (Jan. 8, 1869, Berlin, Germany—Aug. 9, 1942, Candlewood Lake, Conn.): German American photographer. Genthe first came to the United States in 1895 as a private tutor, but he soon devoted his full attention to photography. In San Francisco from 1898 to 1911 and thereafter in New York, he was a prominent photographer known for both his studio portraits and his

Arnold Genthe, a photographer of German descent, documented turn-of-the-century urban life in San Francisco's Chinatown. (AP/Wide World Photos)

images of urban street life. The charming, candid photographs included in Genthe's *Pictures of Old Chinatown* (1913), among his only work not destroyed in the 1906 earthquake, became definitive images of the turn-of-the-century immigrant community. Other volumes include *Rebellion in Photography* (1900) and his 1936 autobiography *As I Remember*. Genthe was also an avid collector of Japanese color prints and Chinese paintings and jade.

Gentlemen's Agreement (1907): Agreement between the Japanese government and the United States that Japan would not issue passports to unskilled workers seeking to emigrate to the United States. The government of Japan agreed voluntarily to stop emigration rather than face the international disgrace of having the United States ban immigration. For a time after the agreement went into effect, Japanese men already in the United States were permitted to send for wives and children from Japan. Many men arranged legal marriages with "picture brides" in Japan whom they had never met so that they might begin families in the U.S. Because of anti-Japanese sentiment, picture brides were no longer permitted to emigrate to the United States after 1920.

German Americans: In 1983, the governments of the United States and the Federal Republic of Germany officially celebrated three hundred years of German immigration to the United States. Tricentennial activities focused on the 1683 arrival in Philadelphia of thirteen MENNONITE families from Krefeld in the Rhineland. The Krefelders included weavers, tailors, carpenters, and other craftsmen, and were under the leadership of Franz Daniel Pastorius, a young German lawyer.

They founded the settlement of Germantown, which is now part of Philadelphia.

Germany's Geography and Statehood. The land from which German immigrants came has a tumultuous history. Such basic questions as where Germany is and who the Germans are have provoked much conflict and provided reasons for Germans to seek new lives elsewhere. Germany's boundaries, with the exception of those provided by the Alps to the south and the North and Baltic seas to the north, have been the product of historical pushing and shoving. Geopoliticians have suggested that Germany's geographical situation—having few "natural boundaries"—has made Germany a target when weak but allowed it to expand easily when strong.

The situation was long complicated by the fragmentation of the German nation itself. It developed from a number of early Germanic tribes that began to make an imprint on central Europe as Celtic culture receded

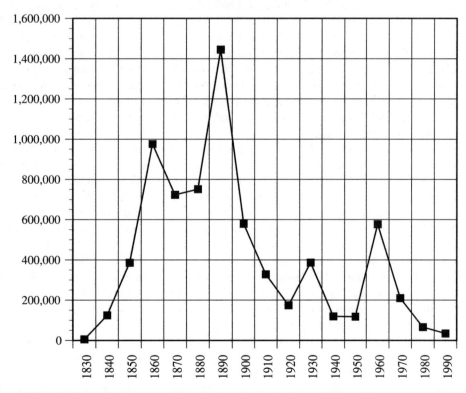

German Immigration to the United States: 1820-1990

Source: From Bernard A. Cook and Rosemary Petralle Cook, *German Americans*. American Voices series, p. 45. Vero Beach, Fla.: Rourke Corp., 1991.

several centuries before Christ. Among the major Germanic tribes were the Bavarians and Swabians in southern Germany, the Franks and Saxons in central Germany, and the Frisians in the lowlands along the North Sea—each with distinctive cultural characteristics, ranging from cuisine to regional dialect.

In this diversity lies much of the problem of "German" nationhood. Swabians overlap the border with Switzerland; most of Friesland belongs to the Dutch. Many people outside Germany speak the German language but do not consider themselves German or part of a German state. The spoken modern German language is still fragmented; Martin Luther's translation of the Bible into German in the 1500's is widely credited with providing a common standard for written German.

Germany's search for an identity can be traced from Charlemagne, through the Holy Roman Empire, to competition between the Hohenzollern family of Prussia and the Habsburgs of Austria to unite the German states under their control. In 1800 there were 314 separate German states and nearly fifteen hundred small estates, producing some eighteen hundred sovereign authorities. Otto von Bismarck is credited with unifying Germany (without Austria) in 1871 to produce the Second Empire, which lasted until 1918. Adolf Hitler's rise to power would add Austria in 1938 to form the Greater German Empire, which was followed, after World War II, by re-fragmentation and zones of occupation by victorious Allied armies. On October 3, 1990, East and West Germany merged, re-unifying the German state.

Immigration. Much early immigration was promoted by the search for religious freedom, but it was also linked to the devastation of war and the simple human search for more land and opportunities. The religious Peace of Augsburg (1555) and the Peace of Westphalia (1648), ending the horrendously destructive Thirty Years' War (1618-1648), set in motion forces that would encourage emigration from Europe for religious reasons. The liberal advertising of the British colonies and the encouraging attitude of the British government toward migration to settle the New World merged with the hopes of those seeking refuge.

German artisans were with Captain John Smith in the Jamestown colony in Virginia in 1607. Peter Minuit from the Rhineland is remembered for purchasing Manhattan Island from the Indians and serving as director of the colony of New Netherland. Jacob Leisler from Frankfurt, governor of New Amsterdam

(New York), was hanged by the British in 1691 for advocating independence from England.

There are varying estimates of the number of Germans who came to the United States in the colonial era; probably between 65,000 and 100,000 Germans arrived before 1776. In the nineteenth century, particularly in the second half, the amount of German immigration to the United States was tremendous. It has been estimated that 5.5 million Germans came to the United States between 1815 and 1914. The two peak years of German immigration were 1854 and 1882; the years 1881-1883 saw the greatest wave of German immigration. An additional 1.5 million have immigrated since World War I. After each world war there was a surge of immigration prompted by conditions in Germany.

Both religious and political persecution have spurred German immigration. A dissident sect known as the Dunkers settled in Pennsylvania in the early eighteenth century. The Amish, a religious movement founded by Jacob Amman, settled in Pennsylvania and the Midwest. The Amish are sometimes misleadingly called the Pennsylvania Dutch; "Dutch," in this case is actually a variation of *Deutsch*, or "German." In different periods, German Jews, Catholics, and Lutherans have all fled to the United States. The failure of the 1848 revolution in Germany drove groups of "Forty-eighters" to the United States as political refugees. Later, the repressive policies of Bismarck, the Kaiser, and Hitler resulted in more immigrants. Hitler's persecution of the Jews, as well as other groups, caused Germany to drive away many of its most creative and brilliant people, including great scientists and artists, in the years preceding and during World War II.

Cultural Contributions. For a number of reasons, contributions by ethnic groups must be kept in perspective: People are often of some mixed ethnic heritage when they immigrate, they may marry someone from a different group following immigration, and their contributions may reflect "personal" as much as "ethnic" achievement. Further, most immigrants from anywhere are common folk simply living out their lives; only a relative few achieve fame.

German contributions to American history began with the revolutionary war. Former Prussian officer Friedrich Wilhelm von Steuben (1730-1794) helped General George Washington mold the Continental Army into a disciplined fighting force against the British army. Many Hessian mercenary soldiers hired by

NORTH
SEA

DENMARK

BALTIC
SEA

EUROPE

NETHERLANDS

Hamburg

Breman

Elbe

Weser

Berlin

POLAND

BELGIUM

Rhein (Rhine)

Düsseldorf

Leipzig

Dresden

RHEINLAND

Frankfurt

LUXEMBOURG

Main

BAVARIA

CZECHOSLOVAKIA

FRANCE

Stuttgart

Donau (Danube)

Munich

SWITZERLAND

AUSTRIA

GERMANY

the British to fight against the colonists deserted to the American side and became part of the diverse fabric of American society.

John Peter Zenger was a German newspaperman, who in the 1700's fought for American freedom of the press. In the world of art, Emanuel Leutze (1816-1868) painted the famous picture *Washington Crossing the Delaware*, and Albert Bierstadt (1830-1902) created startling landscapes with Western motifs such as *The Oregon Trail* (1869). Political caricaturist Thomas Nast (1840-1902) fought political corruption and became famous for creating the elephant and donkey

symbols used for the Democratic and Republican Parties, as well as the popular image of a fat, jolly, bearded Santa Claus.

One of the "Forty-eighters" to flee Germany was Carl Schurz. An opponent of SLAVERY, Schurz served President Lincoln as a major general in the CIVIL WAR. He became a U.S. senator from Missouri in 1869 and served as secretary of the interior under President Rutherford B. Hayes from 1877 to 1881. In this latter capacity he addressed the preservation of the nation's natural heritage, brought stability and dignity to the government's relations with American Indian tribes, and introduced a civil service system to protect civil servants from political influence.

Other prominent Germans' contributions included those of Levi Strauss (1829-1902), whose strong canvas fabric became the basis of the world-famous blue jeans. Johann Augustus Roebling, known for the creation of the modern suspension bridge, built the Brooklyn Bridge with his son, Washington Roebling. Walter Gropius (1883-1969), architect and founder of the Bauhaus school of design, and Ludwig Mies van der Rohe (1886-1969), architect and director of the Bauhaus, were leading figures in modern American architecture.

George Westinghouse (1846-1914), inventor of the air brake; Heinrich Steinweg (1797-1871), creator of the Steinway piano company; H. L. Mencken (1880-1956), outspoken author and journalist; Babe Ruth (1895-1948), baseball legend; Robert Wagner (1877-1953), pioneer of federal labor legislation; Wernher von Braun (1912-1977), rocket and space pioneer; Albert Einstein (1879-1955), renowned mathematician and scientist; and Henry Kissinger (b. 1923), former U.S. Secretary of State and recipient of the Nobel

Nobel laureate Albert Einstein is one of the best-known scientists to have immigrated to the United States from Germany. (AP/Wide World Photos)

Peace Prize in 1973, are but a few examples of the kinds of contributions people of German heritage have made to American, and indeed to world, culture.

All the people of German heritage who made significant contributions to American society could never be adequately recognized. Yet perhaps the very fact that their contributions have been absorbed into the rich fabric of American life is testimony to both their many contributions and the nature of the country that received them.

SUGGESTED READINGS. Don Tolzmann's *German-Americana: A Bibliography* (1975) is an extensive bibliography of the German role in American history, carefully sorted into subcategories. Howard B. Furer has compiled *The Germans in America 1607-1970: A Chronology and Fact Book* (1973), which offers a chronology of German settlement, a collection of translated historical documents, and a bibliography. Victor Wolfgang von Hagen's *The Germanic People in America* (1976) provides a readable history of immigration, with many drawings and photographs. Gerard Wilk's *Americans from Germany* (1976) sketches the biographies of a selection of famous Germans who contributed to American culture. Although academic in format, the two-volume work *America and the Germans: An Assessment of a Three-Hundred-Year History* (1985), edited by Frank Trommler and Joseph McVeigh, offers an excellent, readable collection of papers.—*Forest L. Grieves*

German Jews: Until 1720 the majority of the Jews in colonial America were Sephardic Jews of Spanish-Portuguese provenance. Subsequently central and eastern European Jews predominated. It has been suggested that by the mid-eighteenth century, and most certainly during the first half of the nineteenth century, the typical American Jew was a hard-working, enterprising shopkeeper of German origin who was religiously observant.

The Jewish immigrants of the nineteenth century, classified as German Jews, actually came from different regions in central Europe. Many arrived from places such as Bohemia, Moravia, or Posen, the easternmost province of Prussia, which had been Polish since the late eighteenth century. Perhaps half of all the German immigrants were from Bavaria.

The most significant German immigration to the United States began in the 1830's and has been attributed to the economic restrictions imposed on the Jews in Germany. The German Jewish arrivals were as poor as the millions of Irish, Italian, and other immigrants, yet they were better prepared to climb the ladder of social mobility. Even the poorest of the German Jews, for example, were literate in German, a skill that was soon transferred to English.

The first great wave of German Jewish immigration occurred between 1820 and 1860, when as many as 145,000 persons arrived in the United States. On the eve of the Civil War, German and other central European Jews were no longer confined to the port cities on the eastern seaboard. The normal pattern of the German Jewish immigrant was to send for other members of his family from the region of his origin once he achieved some economic stability. Hence, Jewish communities in the Midwest or South soon represented interrelated families with ties to the same place in Germany. After plying their trade as peddlars, many of these immigrants emerged as important merchants after one or two decades in major American urban centers.

Unlike the Russian/Eastern European Jews who arrived beginning in the late nineteenth century, bitter about discrimination in the Russian Empire and suffering from a siege mentality following centuries of persecution, the German Jews in the United States regarded their identification with Germany as a mark of honor. Many of them were pro-Germany through the early phases of World War I, prior to American involvement in the conflict.

Once German American culture became widespread as a result of the extensive German Gentile immigration since the 1890's, the German Jews became active in German theatrical societies and in the German-language press. The most characteristic contribution of the German Jews to the American Jewish community was their promotion of Reform Judaism. By 1860 several important congregations had adopted this form of religious practice. Its hallmarks were the importance accorded the rabbi, a new role for the sermon, the extensive use of English (or German) rather than Hebrew, and a shortened religious service.

SUGGESTED READINGS. For an important account of German Jews in America, see Arthur Hertzberg's *The Jews in America: Four Centuries of an Uneasy Encounter* (1989). See also Michael A. Meyer's *Response to Modernity: A History of the Reform Movement in Judaism* (1988) and an article on Jews in the United States entitled "United States of America" by Maurice D. Atkin, in *Encyclopedia Judaica* (1972), edited by Cecil Roth and Geoffrey Wigoder, which provides ample data on immigration.

Legendary Apache chief Geronimo led fierce resistance against the U.S. government relocation of his tribe. (National Archives)

Geronimo [Goyathlay] (c. 1827, southern Ariz.- Feb. 17, 1909, Fort Sill, Okla.): Chief of the Chiricahua Apache Indians. Following the abolishment of the Chiricahua Reservation, Geronimo led raids against whites, was captured by General George Crook, escaped, and was recaptured by Captain Henry Lawton. He finally surrendered in 1886 to Colonel Nelson Miles, thus ending Indian resistance to the U.S. Army. Geronimo and his followers were sent as prisoners of war to Florida and then removed to Fort Sill, Oklahoma, where he became a Christian and a well-to-do farmer. He dictated his autobiography in 1906.

Gerrymandering: Division of voting districts so as to favor a particular party or population; often a way of diluting the voting power of a minority group. For example, if there is a large concentration of people of one minority group in one section of a city, the group might organize and try to vote together to elect candidates or approve legislation that supports their own agenda. To prevent this by gerrymandering, the dominant group could redraw the lines that mark out voting districts, breaking the minority population into two or

Western artist Frederic Remington visited the Pine Ridge reservation to create this watercolor depiction of the Sioux Ghost Dance ceremony. (Library of Congress)

more districts, making their success at the polls less likely. In the 1980's and 1990's, minority groups charged that whites did this to block the rise of African American and Latino politicians and voting power. In some cases, areas such as Los Angeles County were ordered by federal courts to do redistricting to counteract the effects of gerrymandering.

Ghetto: Part of a city in which many members of a minority group live. Originally the term meant the Jewish section of a city, but now it refers to the clustering of any minority group. People live in a ghetto largely because the larger society exerts social and economic pressure on them to remain there through the practice of discrimination. "Ghetto" has come to connote impoverished sections of the inner city whose residents are trapped there through continuing poverty and lack of educational and economic opportunities. This is frequently true, particularly for African Americans who live in ghettos. Yet for many minority groups, ghetto life has also helped preserve cultural traditions that might have disappeared had group members been dispersed throughout the dominant society.

Ghost Dance religion (1890-1891): Pacifistic American Indian religion established by Paiute prophet Wovoka. Wovoka grew up on the Nevada ranch of the Wilson family and became known among the whites as Jack Wilson. Some suggest that he was the son of Ta'vibo, another prophet whose Ghost Dance movement in 1870 swept through the tribes in the region. Despite important similarities between the two movements, conclusive evidence to link them is unavailable.

Wovoka's doctrine was revealed to him when he fell into a trance in 1889 during a solar eclipse. Transported to the other world, he saw all the Indians who had ever lived engaged in their traditional pursuits in a bountiful heaven. In his vision, God told Wovoka he must convey a new doctrine to his people. They must keep the peace both among themselves and with the whites. They must work hard and refrain from unethical acts such as lying or stealing. Believers were to dance for four successive nights, then take a ritual bath on the fifth day. If followers adhered to the doctrine and practiced the ritual faithfully, the whites would be destroyed, the buffalo herds would return, and the world would be regenerated as a paradise in which the living would be reunited with their dead relatives. In addition, Wovoka was given power to control the elements.

This pacifistic religion generally urged the preservation and revival of traditional practices, most notably American Indian expressive forms which often were invested with a ritual quality. Because of this focus on an earlier, traditional way of life, the religion has been labeled "nativistic." Yet elements of Christianity were evident in the Ghost Dance, such as the claim by some disciples that Wovoka was, in fact, Jesus Christ.

Promising a return to a distinctively American Indian "golden age," the Ghost Dance religion quickly spread west from the Paiutes throughout the Basin area and into California, north to Wyoming and the Dakotas, and east to the Southern Plains tribes in Oklahoma. Despite growing white fears, the religion generally maintained its peaceful character. In 1890, the religion swept through the Northern Plains tribes. Dismay among white American officials grew into a compulsion to crush this new religion, which appeared not only to work against attempts to wean Indians from their traditional lifestyles but also to generate new hostilities toward whites. Panic led to a series of events (including the fatal shooting of the famed Indian leader SITTING BULL) which culminated in the tragic WOUNDED KNEE massacre of defenseless Sioux by troops of the U.S. Seventh Cavalry. Within a year the Ghost Dance enthusiasm dissipated, discredited by the failure of Wovoka's promises to materialize.

SUGGESTED READINGS. James Mooney's *The Ghost Dance and Sioux Outbreak of 1890* (1896) analyzes the movement, drawing on interviews with Wovoka and his followers. The Paiute messiah's biography can be found in Paul Bailey's *Wovoka* (1957). Descriptions and comparisons of the Ghost Dance to similar movements can be found in Weston LaBarre's *The Ghost Dance* (1970) and Bryan R. Wilson's *Magic and the Millennium* (1973).

Gibson, Althea (b. Aug. 25, 1927, Silver, S.C.): African American tennis champion. Gibson was reared in Harlem, New York. When she was forced to leave school and take a job as a chicken cleaner, a wealthy African American couple paid for her to continue school and eventually earn a degree in physical education. In 1950 Gibson was the first African American invited to play in the American Lawn Tennis Association Championships. In 1956 she won the singles title in both France and Italy,

Althea Gibson broke through the color barrier in 1950 when she became the first African American to play tennis at the U.S. National Championship at Forest Hills. (International Tennis Hall of Fame)

and shared the Wimbledon doubles title. Two years later she was the first African American to win the singles title at Wimbledon. After her tennis career, she became a nightclub singer and professional golfer.

Gilman, Charlotte Perkins (July 3, 1860, Hartford, Conn.—August 17, 1935, Pasadena, Calif.): Writer and feminist. Her first notable work was *The Yellow Wall-Paper* (1892), an emotional short story written in the depths of depression about the state of her first marriage to Charles Stetson. She left her husband shortly thereafter and began lecturing on women's issues. In 1896 she attended the International Social and Labor Congress in London. In 1898 she wrote *Women and Economics,* a sociological explanation of the issues addressed in *The Yellow Wall-Paper*, which held that the economic suppression of women created their so-called inferiority. Before her death she had visions of a separatist utopia for women.

Ginsburg, Ruth Bader (b. Mar. 15, 1933, Brooklyn, N.Y.): Second woman justice (after Sandra Day O'Connor) to sit on the U.S. Supreme Court. Ginsburg was on the law review at Harvard University and finished first in her class at Columbia Law School, yet she failed to receive the job offers that such honors would automatically bring a male law student. She was even rejected for a clerkship with Justice Felix Frankfurter because, as he explained, he was not ready to hire a woman. Ginsburg taught law at Rutgers, Harvard, and Columbia universities while arguing sex discrimination cases for the AMERICAN CIVIL LIBERTIES UNION (ACLU)—five of them successfully before the U.S. Supreme Court. In 1980, she was appointed to the U.S. Court of Appeals, where she became known for judicial restraint rather than activism. In 1993, President Bill Clinton nominated her to the Supreme Court on her strengths as a moderate, marking both the second seat for a woman and the first for a Jewish American justice since 1969.

Girl Scouts of America: Founded in 1912, the organization had more than three million members by the 1990's, including young girls, adult volunteers, and professional workers. The purpose of the organization is to meet the special needs of girls and assist in developing happy, resourceful individuals who can share their abilities to help others as citizens in their homes, communities, country, and the world. Girl Scouts programs emphasize self-awareness and self-esteem, interaction with others, development of responsible values, and service to society. It also works to expand personal interests. Under the influence of the effects of feminism, the organization has also increasingly attempted to encourage new skills, expanded career opportunities, and broader roles for girls.

Giveaways. *See* **Potlatches and giveaways**

Glass ceiling: Invisible barrier that prevents members of minority groups from advancing, particularly in the business world. After legislation by the U.S. government made discrimination in employment illegal, more members of minority groups were hired by corporations. Although these people had good jobs, many of them, including women, soon discovered that they could only "rise" to a certain point in the corporate structure. Hidden obstacles—the glass ceiling—kept them from rising to the top even though they seemed qualified. Glass ceilings result from bias or prejudice on the part of employers and from institutional racism and sexism.

Goizueta, Roberto C. (b. Nov. 18, 1931, Havana, Cuba): Cuban American business executive. Complet-

Cuban American Roberto Goizueta was instrumental in helping Coca-Cola recapture a healthy share of the international soft drink market when he became chief executive officer in 1981. (AP/Wide World Photos)

ing his B.S. in chemical engineering from Yale University in 1953, Goizueta went to work for the Coca-Cola Company in Havana. After the Cuban Revolution, he moved to Nassau, Bahamas, and then to corporate headquarters in Atlanta in 1964. During the ensuing decades, Goizueta worked his way up Coca-Cola's corporate ladder, becoming chairman of the board and chief executive officer in 1981. As the first Cuban American with such corporate power, he helped to turn the company around and recapture the international market during the 1980's. His many honors include the Spanish Institute Gold Medal in 1986 and the NAACP Equal Justice Award in 1991.

Gold Mountain: Name given to California by the Chinese. When news came to China of the discovery of gold in California in 1848, it was very exciting, especially for poor farmers who worked very hard for a small income. They believed that they could travel to California, work for a few years gathering gold, and return home to live comfortably. The stories of gold discovery were so common the Chinese began to refer to California as "Gold Mountain."

Gold Rush: News of the discovery of gold at Sutter's Mill on January 24, 1848, drew peoples of all races, nationalities, and religions to California in search of wealth. In the year that followed the discovery, an estimated twenty-five thousand "forty-niners" came to California over land, by ship around Cape Horn, and through the jungles of Panama. Few great fortunes were made by miners, but farmers, merchants, and other businessmen benefited from the opportunities provided by the rapid growth in California's population. When the mining era died out, vast numbers of these emigrants remained in the West, with the majority in California, particularly in San Francisco.

Goldman, Emma "Red Emma" (June 27, 1869, Kaunas, Lithuania—May 14, 1940, Toronto, Canada): Anarchist. In 1882 Goldman worked in a glove factory in St. Petersburg, Russia. Three years later she emigrated to Rochester, New York, and worked in a clothing factory. In 1889 the self-educated Goldman met anarchist Alexander Berkman. Goldman and Berkman were imprisoned a number of times and were twice suspected of assassination attempts. They were jailed in 1911 for opposing American conscription in World War I and another time for advocating the use of birth control. Together they edited the anarchist chronicle *Mother*

As coeditor of the anarchist journal Mother Earth, *Emma Goldman wrote passionate articles demanding social reforms to improve women's lives.* (AP/Wide World Photos)

Earth from 1906-1918, demanding major social change, especially for women; the journal was eventually banned by the U.S. government. Goldman also wrote *My Disillusionment in Russia* (1923) after deportation to that country in 1919, and her autobiography, *Living My Life* (1931), which explained her passionate belief in individual freedom.

A natural talent who had no formal tennis training, Pancho Gonzales dominated men's tennis from the late 1940's through the early 1970's. (Hearst Newspaper Collection, University of Southern California Library)

Gonzales, Pancho (Richard Alonzo Gonzales; b. May 9, 1928, Los Angeles, Calif.): Mexican American tennis player. Gonzales started playing tennis at the age of twelve. He turned professional at age twenty and stunned the tennis world with consecutive victories at the U.S. National Championships at Forest Hills in 1948 and 1949, also taking Britain's Davis Cup in 1949. He was equally proficient at doubles and held several doubles titles with Frank Parker, Don Budge, and Pancho Segura. Gonzales virtually dominated men's tennis through the 1950's, with the top ranking from 1954 through 1961. After winning the World Professional Championship in 1966, the Tournament of Champions in 1969, and the World Series of Tennis in 1971, he retired from professional play to become a trainer and coach.

Gonzáles, Rodolfo "Corky" (b. 1928, Denver, Colo.): Chicano activist. Born to a family of seasonal farm workers, Gonzáles became a boxer and was at one point considered a contender for the world featherweight title. In 1965, he established the Crusade for Justice move-

las, the Four Tops, and Smokey Robinson and the Miracles. Gordy seeded his phenomenal success in the recording industry with an $800 loan. His background includes featherweight boxing in a Golden Gloves competition, as well as service in the U.S. Army in Korea.

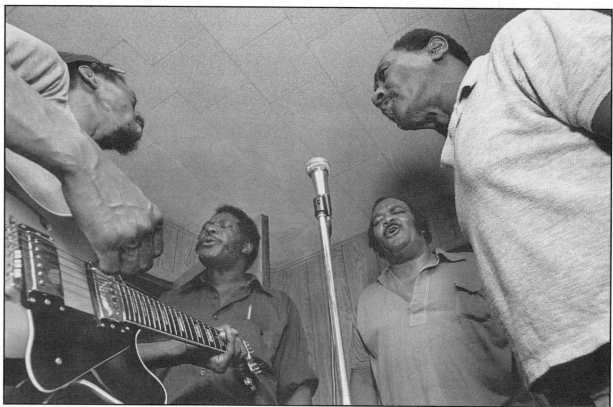

Close harmonies with minimal accompaniment continue to be a hallmark of African American gospel quartets like this one. (Hazel Hankin)

ment in Denver, Colorado, and in 1968 he led the Chicano contingent of the Poor People's March on Washington, D.C. Gonzales organized annual Chicano Youth Liberation Conferences and launched a Chicano political party, La Raza Unida, in 1970. In 1972, he became the party's vice chairman. He is also known for his epic poem, *I Am Joaquín. Yo soy Joaquín: An Epic Poem, with a Chronology of People and Events in Mexican and Mexican American History* (1972).

Gordy, Berry, Jr. (b. Nov. 28, 1929, Detroit, Mich.): African American entrepreneur. Gordy is best known as the president and chairman of the board of Motown Industries in Detroit, a multimillion dollar business that has introduced such famous black performing groups as the Temptations, the Supremes, Martha and the Vandel-

Gospel music—African American: Protestant religious music which developed in the 1930's during the Depression. Though related to white gospel, African American gospel is derived from a much older tradition of African American preaching. This preaching style, which developed in the South, involved a blend of singing and shouting. Though some African American gospel composers may use white gospel hymn texts, the black gospel singing style is more ecstatic and rhythmically forceful. Melodically, African American gospel music is related to both spirituals and blues music, as well as folk-influenced white gospel.

African American gospel music emerged from roots formed by the white gospel tradition, which developed from the revival of Protestant fundamentalism in southern white communities after the Civil War. The messages of white gospel songs of the late 1800's were subdued and compassionate, with rhythms drawn from martial music and melodies from popular songs.

The different function of African American gospel music resulted in the development of its own unique character and style. Its emergence coincided with the appearance of BLUES, ragtime, and JAZZ, as well as the rise of the PENTECOSTAL church. Pentecostal services included dancing, shouting, hand-clapping, and "speaking in tongues," which often brought participants to a trancelike state. The purpose of these services was for the congregation to be taken over by the Holy Spirit. Gospel preachers who had no church gained converts by preaching and singing in the streets.

Early African American gospel performers relied on tambourines, timbrels (tambourines ringed with cymbals), banjo, and guitar. Pianos and even trumpets and trombones were also used. During the 1970's gospel groups began to modernize their instruments, using electric guitars and amplifiers in arrangements typical of rock bands. Such bands typically accompany modern gospel choirs and quartets, though there is also a strong tradition of a cappella gospel singing.

One of the most notable composers of African American gospel music was Charles Albert Tindley (1856-1933), pastor of the Tindley Temple Methodist Church in Philadelphia. Among his most popular gospel songs are "Leave It There" (1910), "Nothing Between" (1905), "By and By" (1905), and "Stand by Me" (1905). His "I'll Overcome Someday" (1900) may have inspired the famous civil rights song "We Shall Overcome." Other distinguished names in black gospel music include singer Mahalia Jackson, the Dixie Hummingbirds, choir director James Cleveland, and, more recently, composer-performers Bill Gaither and Andrae Crouch.

White gospel music gained popularity in the 1930's and 1940's with the recordings of the Carter family and country singers such as the Delmore Brothers and Lloyd "Cowboy" Copas. As African American gospel singing became more popular through recordings and radio and television broadcasts, a number of white gospel groups began to imitate them.

Modern African American gospel music can be heard at both church services and commercial concerts. Gospel singing has been the training ground for many famous black singers, who go on to perform jazz, popular, classical, and other styles. As African American gospel music continues to evolve, its fundamental message remains unchanged: despite the sorrows of life, happiness and joy can still be achieved.

SUGGESTED READINGS. For further study see *Black Gospel: An Illustrated History of the Gospel Sound* (1985) by Viv Broughton and *The Sound of Light: A History of Gospel Music* (1990) by Don Cusic. Paul Oliver's *The New Grove Gospel, Blues, and Jazz: With Spirituals and Ragtime* (1986) offers a thoughtful examination of the genre. *The Rise of Gospel Blues: The Music of Thomas Andrew Dorsey in the Urban Church* (1992) by Michael W. Harris is a thorough study of perhaps the best-known composer of African American gospel.

Graffiti: Writing or drawings on public property, usually done illegally and anonymously. The term is derived from the Italian word *graffiare,* meaning "to scratch," and the singular form is *graffito.* Graffiti is as old as human history, in one sense dating back to prehistoric cave paintings. Contemporary graffiti can be found almost anywhere, from the doors of public bathrooms to

Citizens' groups concerned about rival gang retaliation work together to paint over territorial graffiti marks in their neighborhood. (Aneal Vohra, Unicorn Stock Photos)

street signs, walls, and subway trains in cities around the world. Considered a type of folklore, graffiti is typically anonymous (especially where illegal), traditional (an ancient variant of "John loves Mary" was found in the ruins of Pompeii), marginal, and communal. It is also a distinctly multicultural phenomenon, at least in the United States, because of its very nature.

Graffiti is not the language of power and authority but rather a mode of expression adopted by those whom society has marginalized politically, socially, or economically—particularly the young and the disadvantaged. Governments erect street signs and bridges; young people cover them with spray paint after dark. As such, graffiti is a vehicle for expressing ideas that are not given voice in mainstream society. Common themes of graffiti include sex, politics, relationships, satire, "common sense," and celebrations of personal or communal identity.

Because it is anonymous, graffiti is a safe medium for expressing controversial political opinions, taboo sexual musings, and even racist sentiments. (This is particularly true of "private" graffiti written in public restrooms, as opposed to "public" graffiti found outside on walls and signs.) It can also express ethnic pride and group identification. At its worst, graffiti is considered ugly, obscene, and offensive defacement— even dangerous, when used by urban gangs to mark territory. At its best, graffiti may be artistic or offer valuable insights into the tensions, frustrations, values, and goals of various American cultures and subcultures.

Though the general public often finds graffiti a nuisance, many scholars see it as a worthy subject of academic scrutiny. Archaeologists and historians study graffiti (or records of it) to understand past societies; psychologists and sociologists find in graffiti an uncensored account of individual and group fears, conflicts, and desires. As the study of folklore has gained acceptance within the academic community, the cultural significance of graffiti has been recognized by linguists, anthropologists, and teachers of composition. Many graffiti artists enjoyed gallery exhibits of their work and the interest and admiration of art critics during the 1980's and 1990's.

SUGGESTED READINGS. The extraordinary variety of graffiti, as well as its common themes, is captured in Robert Reisner and Lorraine Wechsler's *Encyclopedia of Graffiti* (1974), which catalogues graffiti by subject and provides copious examples of each type. Those interested in a more in-depth study of the subject will find *The Handwriting on the Wall: Toward a Sociology and Psychology of Graffiti* (1977) by Ernest L. Abel and Barbara E. Buckley both scholarly and accessible. Craig Castleman's *Getting Up: Subway Graffiti in New York* (1982) offers a comprehensive analysis of a particularly prominent form of graffiti. *Student Worlds, Student Words: Teaching Writing Through Folklore* (1990) by Elizabeth Radin Simons considers the relationship of graffiti to the study of folklore and offers teachers advice for incorporating its study into their curricula.

Graham, Katherine (Katherine Meyer; b. June 16, 1917, New York, N.Y.): Newspaper proprietor. In 1938 Graham reported for the *San Francisco News* and in 1939 for the *Washington Post*. In 1940 she and her new husband, Philip Graham, bought the influential *Washington Post*. *Newsweek* was incorporated into the company in 1961. In 1963 her husband committed suicide and Katherine took over the business. She became president, chairwoman of the board, chief executor, and publisher of the Washington Post Company, which grew to incorporate television stations, other newspapers, and

As publisher of the Washington Post, Katherine Graham supported the journalists responsible for uncovering stories about the Watergate scandal. (AP/Wide World Photos)

paper mills. She is known as an executive responsive to the needs of her editors, entrusting them with the editorial freedom necessary for accurate news coverage.

Graham, Martha (May 11, 1893, Pittsburgh, Pa.—April 1, 1991, New York, N.Y.): Dancer and choreographer. Graham, a towering figure in the development of American modern dance, is known for her primitive, mysterious dance style. Her performing group, which she founded in the 1920's, was the first to include African American and American Indian dancers. From 1928 to 1938, many of her pieces were protest dances on social themes, such as *Revolt, Immigrant, Four Insincerities,* and *Heretic.* She also produced a series of renowned pieces on America's heritage, including *Frontier* (1935)

Martha Graham's innovative choreography and unique teaching style inspired numerous young modern dance performers and choreographers. (AP/Wide World Photos)

and *Appalachian Spring* (1944). A number of her dances portray notable women, such as the Brontë sisters, Emily Dickinson (*Letter to the World,* 1940), Joan of Arc, and Mary, Queen of Scots. In the 1960's the U.S. State Department declared Graham's performances obscene and refused to give her government aid. Her teaching, performance, and choreography inspired an entire school of modern dance, which flourished nationwide at the time of her death.

Grandfather clause: Certain laws or constitutional amendments passed by southern states to discriminate against blacks and exempt poor whites in the area of voter qualifications. In 1870 the FIFTEENTH AMENDMENT to the U.S. Constitution made it clear that states could not abridge the right to vote on account of race. Beginning in 1890, however, and extending into the early twentieth century, southern state governments passed an ingenious series of laws that limited the right of poor whites and poor blacks to vote, then provided loopholes for whites.

Typically, southern state voting laws had one or more of these requirements for would-be voters: payment of taxes at a certain level, payment of a special poll tax, or the passing of a literacy test. Many poor whites as well as poor blacks paid few taxes and were barely literate. Southern lawmakers accordingly crafted loopholes that would salvage the right to vote of poor and uneducated whites. One such loophole was the grandfather clause, which in a simplified form said that if a man's grandfather had been qualified to vote, then he was exempt from the literacy or taxation tests for voting. Since no black citizens' grandfathers had been permitted to vote, blacks did not qualify for the loophole.

The precise provisions of the grandfather clauses varied from state to state, but in North Carolina, Louisiana, and Oklahoma, the laws provided exemption from the other voter qualifications for persons who had been eligible to vote in 1866 or 1867 (before black enfranchisement), and their descendants. Alabama and Georgia enacted a variation that became known as the "fighting grandfather clause," waiving voter qualification tests for veterans of any U.S. war and their descendants. Once again, at the time, very few black Southerners were veterans or the descendants of veterans. Other southern states did not pass grandfather clauses, but provided other loopholes to help whites who wished to vote.

Grandfather clauses were enacted into law because southern lawmakers wanted to deny the right to vote to the mass of black citizens, but were unable to do so in a direct way because of the Fifteenth Amendment. Since the grandfather clauses did not mention race but applied equally on their face to both blacks and whites, southern legislators assumed the U.S. Supreme Court would give the laws their blessing. This was not to be. Even in an era when black petitioners before the high court won few victories, the Court struck down an Oklahoma grandfather clause in the case of *Guinn v. U.S.* (1915), saying it was clearly designed to circumvent the Fifteenth Amendment.

Other devices used by white Southerners to reduce black voting were violence, intimidation, fraudulent counting of votes in black precincts, and laws similar to the grandfather clause. While southern lawmakers were ingenious in fashioning ways to limit black voting, they never equaled the grandfather clause as an example of sheer legal discrimination.

SUGGESTED READINGS. For further information, see Paul Lewinson's *Race, Class and Party: A History of Negro Suffrage and White Politics in the South* (1959) and J. Morgan Kousser's *The Shaping of Southern Politics: Suffrage Restriction and the Establishment of the One-Party South, 1880-1910.*

Gray Panthers: Activist, consciousness-raising group working to combat discrimination based on age and change the passive STEREOTYPE of "senior citizens." The

The social activism of the Gray Panthers in the 1970's established a role model for this woman protesting rent increases for fixed-income tenants during the 1980's. (Hazel Hankin)

group, based in Washington, D.C., was founded in 1970 as a way for older Americans to challenge forced retirement at age sixty-five and to join with younger people in resisting the VIETNAM WAR. From these two issues came the central idea that separating old and young people is artificial and counterproductive. Through publications and seminars, the national group helps local groups deal with issues including health care and mentoring. The name "Gray Panthers" was chosen as a humorous variation of "BLACK PANTHERS," a militant civil rights group for African Americans.

Great Awakening: Religious revival movement that swept through the American colonies in the mid-eighteenth century. Between 1739 and 1742 (some scholars consider it to have continued to the 1760's), a religious revival occurred in the American colonies that was part of a larger evangelical movement that was sweeping western Europe. In Europe, the movement was known among Protestants as Pietism or Evangelicalism and among Roman Catholics as Quietism. In colonial America, the revivalists did not so much introduce new doctrines as emphasize the Calvinist principle of regeneration in terms of a "New Birth" (change of heart) experience. In their belief that God had predetermined those who would be saved, these evangelists differed from the METHODISTS, who believed that God's grace was available to all who repented. In all of its manifestations, the revival movement emphasized the role of lay people. Students, merchants, tradesmen, and immigrants bore witness to their own regeneration and distributed books and tracts as they traveled, creating a community of ideas.

Although the exponents of the Awakening in America emphasized their belief that the work of God was preeminently internal (a felt blessing), they were not anti-intellectual. Several of the principal clergymen were, like Jonathan Edwards, Harvard-trained. Revivalism became linked with an uneducated clergy long after the Great Awakening of the eighteenth century. At the meetings, however, there were outbursts of weeping, groaning, and fainting among repentants touched by God's spirit, which gave the movement the reputation of encouraging hysteria or excessive emotionalism. The emotional outbursts alarmed liberal (rational) clergy and became a seriously contested issue as the movement gained momentum.

Causes. The revival movement in Europe and colonial America has generally been explained as a reaction against the Enlightenment. The liberal spirit of

Deism, influenced by the teachings of John Locke and Sir Isaac Newton, freed people from the doctrine that only the "elect" could enter heaven and from the need for salvation. Benjamin Franklin wrote that reading Deistic explanations of the universe had liberated him from the Puritan doctrine of his ancestors. Franklin expressed the views of many exponents of the Enlightenment, for whom reason was the primary way of knowing God and man. Because Deists did not believe in sin, they stressed the importance of virtues, such as honesty and thrift, that enabled people to live prosperous and contented lives.

American churches suffered a decline in attendance and zeal because parishioners turned their attention to commercial matters. As people focused their attention on improving their earthly lives, they were less concerned about church doctrine and personal salvation; church attendance became a social function rather than a religious necessity. CONGREGATIONALISTS, PRESBYTERIANS, and Anglicans did not abandon dogma or deliberately alter their theologies, but their clergy preached liberal doctrines based in reason, implying that prosperity was a suitable form of piety.

Both the rational religious doctrines and the emphasis on material accumulation promoted class differences. Denied access to the learning necessary to comprehend the reasoned concepts of God and equally denied the means of living comfortable lives, the lower classes were drawn to the revival movement. The poor settlers on the frontier, the struggling small farmers in the backwoods, the laborers in the town, the American Indians striving to hold onto their lands, and the enslaved African Americans had no political or social power. Although they could attend church, they heard little from the pulpit that offered them hope or comfort. Thus, social unrest, diminished religious fervor, and an intellectual climate favoring privilege made the 1740's a period in which people were receptive to the revivalists' proclamations.

Revival Leaders. Before the Great Awakening began in the late 1730's, localized "refreshing" occurred in western Massachusetts, where Solomon Stoddard led his parish to seek spiritual renewal, and in New Jersey, where the Dutch Reformed immigrant Theodorus Frelinghuysen warned Dutch merchants against taking their religion for granted. In the middle colonies, Gilbert Tennent (who would join the itinerant evangelists) led the revival movement among Presbyterians, and in the South, Presbyterian minister Samuel Davies led a movement begun by laypersons. The most famous

Jonathan Edwards was one of the leading writers and preachers of the early period of the Great Awakening. (Culver Pictures, Inc.)

of the colonial revivalists was Jonathan Edwards, Stoddard's grandson, who inspired many conversions in Northampton, Massachusetts, between 1729 and 1735 and continued to influence the revival movement of the 1740's through his writings and preaching.

The "Grand Itinerants," as the evangelists who inspired the Great Awakening were called, traveled throughout the colonies preaching to large crowds of people who sometimes walked a day's journey to hear them. The traveling preachers violated one of the customs of traditional denominations by not being attached to a particular church and pulpit. Although they were sometimes invited to speak in prominent Boston churches (such as Edward's at Northampton) as well as frontier missions, their free movement and habit of holding meetings on workdays antagonized both clergy and prominent citizens. A common complaint in Georgia was that laborers neglected the "religion" of work to hear evangelists who encouraged "idleness." New England clergymen voiced similar concerns, objecting to the disregard of precedent such open meetings represented. In spite of opposition, the itinerants were extremely popular, speaking sometimes two or three times in one day to crowds of more than six thousand. These crowds were made up of a

One of the most famous evangelists of the Great Awakening was George Whitefield, an Anglican clergyman, shown here addressing a congregation in the American colonies. (Culver Pictures, Inc.)

cross-section of colonists including slaves, mechanics, young people, American Indians, and representatives of all religious denominations, including ROMAN CATHOLIC.

The most famous of the Great Awakening evangelists, George Whitefield, was an Anglican priest who came to the colonies to establish an orphan home for poor children in Bethesda, Georgia, after winning renown as a powerful orator at English revival meetings. From Georgia, he traveled up the eastern seaboard, soliciting funds for the orphanage and preaching to large crowds along the way. The only southern Anglican to openly welcome him was Commissary James Blair, administrative head of the church in Virginia. Claiming to adhere to the orthodox CALVINIST doctrine, Whitefield focused on the New Birth experience, urging his listeners to repent and receive God's grace as a sign of their election. He preached simple, extemporaneous, emotionally charged sermons that were especially appealing to congregations accustomed to hearing densely textured sermons read from manuscripts. Whitefield's writings stirred up more controversy than his sermons, for he accused New England preachers of having lost the spirit of preaching; worse, he suggested that the religious light of the universities (Harvard and Yale) had turned to darkness. By 1743, Whitefield's popularity had waned, but he remained

the symbol of the Awakening long after his death in 1770. Evidence of his popularity among the people is reflected in "On the Death of the Reverend Mr. George Whitefield" (1773), the first published poem of African American poet Phillis Wheatley, which recalls Whitefield's promise that God was an "Impartial Saviour" who "longed for the Africans, too."

Two other traveling preachers became well known during the years of the Great Awakening. Gilbert Tennent, whose father founded the Log College of New Jersey that later became Princeton University, was persuaded to leave his Presbyterian parish in New Jersey to continue Whitefield's ministry in Boston during the Englishman's temporary absence in 1740. Tennent toured Massachusetts for about three months and returned to his home church, but his influence persisted. He wrote Whitefield that he had been gratified during his brief sojourn to see children, black people, and young people consoled by his sermons.

A third well-known itinerant, James Davenport, was minister to a congregation in Southold, Long Island, when he heard the preachings of Whitefield and Tennent and felt moved to join the evangelical movement. Davenport met with opposition when he denounced his fellow ministers and claimed to be able to distinguish the elect (those chosen for salvation) from the damned. His behavior threatened to discredit the movement, and the furor over his ministry served to intensify the growing resistance, signaling that the revival movement was nearing its end.

Effects of the Awakening. Reports from the period, such as that written by Benjamin Colman, a Boston liberal, for the New England Company, indicate that many American Indians were converted in the New England area during the revival period, some becoming missionaries themselves to other Indians. Additionally, the Calvinists were inspired by the Awakening to expand and create more missions among the Indians. Colman assisted in obtaining funds from England to help sustain the mission to the Housatonic Indians at Stockbridge, Massachusetts. Through Davenport's preaching in New London, Connecticut, Samson Occam, a Mohegan, was converted and became New England's first ordained Indian missionary.

The revival led to ecclesiastical divisions that began in the 1740's as congregations disagreed about the itinerants and their message. Presbyterians split into Old Side and New Side, and Congregationalists divided into Old Light and New Light. These divisions encouraged the growth of BAPTIST, Methodist, and other denominations. The new denominations established colleges to train their ministers: for example, Dartmouth College, incorporated in 1769, was an outgrowth of New Light Eleazar Wheelock's Indian School; Princeton, which began as a Log School for Presbyterians, also served New Light Congregationalists and Baptists; and Brown University began as a college for Baptists in 1764.

Overall, the Great Awakening had a democraticizing effect in both religious and political spheres. By encouraging congregations to oppose authority, it fostered the spirit of independence in the years preceding the American Revolution. Its appeal to the working class and poor, the Indians and the slaves, fostered the ideals of individualism. Emphasizing the power of the spoken word, it encouraged both the political oratory and the emotional enthusiasm that would mark the revolutionary period. Indirectly, the Awakening inspired western expansion and nurtured the politicalization of religious beliefs as clergy and laity took stands on community issues reflecting their denominational biases. The movement's influence was as vital as the liberal views of the Enlightenment in inspiring the Colonies to break with England. Aiming to awaken the religious spirit of the colonists, the revivalists paved the way for the birth of a nation.

SUGGESTED READINGS. The Awakening is treated briefly in most surveys of American colonial history and literature. Comprehensive studies include Alan Heimert's *Religion and the American Mind: From the Great Awakening to the Revolution* (1966) and Edwin Scott Gaustad's *The Great Awakening in New England* (1965). Another source is *The Great Awakening: Documents on the Revival of Religion, 1740-1745 (1970), edited by Richard Bushman.—Bes Stark Spangler*

Great Britain, Treaty of Peace with (1783): Ended the AMERICAN REVOLUTION by establishing the boundaries of the United States, to which the English king and heirs relinquished claim. The treaty declared peace between England and the United States and required the king to remove his armies without "causing any destruction, or carrying away any negroes or other property of the American inhabitants." In other provisions, the treaty gave fishing rights to U.S. citizens in coastal waters; ordered the return of property confiscated during the war and settlement of debts; prohibited prosecuting participants in the war; and released those jailed during it. The Mississippi River remained open to both British and U.S. citizens.

Great Depression: Worldwide economic disaster that forced millions of people out of work and into a life of hardship for more than a decade. In the United States, the Depression began with the collapse of prices on the New York Stock Exchange in October, 1929. Although farm prices had been down since 1921, the American manufacturing economy had grown continuously since the end of World War I; not only entrepreneurs but ordinary citizens joined in the prosperity by purchasing stocks in growing businesses for as little as a 10 percent down payment. When prices finally peaked and brokers made demands for amounts due, many investors could not cover their debts and were financially destroyed.

Frightened by what had happened in the stock market, Americans also spent less money in preparation for hard times. Thus, the manufacturing segment of the economy could not recover from its stock market losses. Industry began firing workers in order to economize, contributing to the downward spiral.

Racial and ethnic minorities and others outside the social mainstream suffered the most. Many African Americans and Latinos who had never been able to climb the economic ladder found themselves pushed off it as they were fired from their jobs or had wages lowered to below subsistence level. Farmers in the South, already pinched by the low farm prices of the 1920's, migrated to other areas in search of work, adding to the oversupply of labor in the North and West and driving wages down. Farmers from the Southwest, hit by the twin disasters of depression and drought, headed for California, changing the ethnic map of that state. The GREAT MIGRATION of African Americans from the South changed the social composition of northern cities. Meanwhile, laborers from South and Central America streamed into the southern United States in search of work.

The failing economy was the biggest issue in the election of 1932, in which Franklin D. Roosevelt defeated Herbert Hoover, who had been president during the stock market crash. Although Roosevelt tried a number of plans to aid the economy, such as public works programs to increase employment and the social security system, unemployment remained high and economic growth was slow until 1940, when the United States began to build its defense industry during World War II. The greatest long term effect of the Depression in the United States was the increased size of government at all levels and the increased impact of government on the lives of the average citizen.

The Great Depression was a global phenomenon.

Long bread lines like this one in New York City were a common sight in many urban neighborhoods during the Great Depression. (Library of Congress)

Inflation had grown in Europe after World War I as warring countries rebuilt their economies. The hard times contributed to the causes of World War II both in inflation-ravaged Germany and in Japan, which sought new sources of raw materials for its expanding economy.

SUGGESTED READINGS. Frederick Lewis Allen provides an introduction to the Depression years in his history of the 1930's, *Since Yesterday: The Nineteen-Thirties in America, September 3, 1929—September 3, 1939* (1940). Harvey Swados presents examples of how various artists responded to the Depression in *The American Writers and the Great Depression* (1966). John F. Bauman and Thomas H. Coode survey contemporary reporters' accounts of the disaster in *In the Eye of the Great Depression: New Deal Reporters and the Agony of the American People* (1988). Paul K. Conkin gives the history of the American political response to the Depression in *The New Deal* (2d ed., 1975).

Great Migration: Major movement of African Americans from the South to the North and Midwest during the first half of the twentieth century, especially during the 1920's and 1940's. For example, from 1920 to 1930, about 750,000 mostly unskilled and poorly educated southern blacks moved north to find better opportunities. The migration was motivated, on the one hand, by the need of black workers to flee racial violence as well as poor wages and a failing cotton crop in the South and, on the other hand, by industrialization and the opening up of factory jobs to blacks after World War I and then again during World War II. Though the North was portrayed as "the promised land," migrating African Americans often found that only low-level jobs, poor schools, and substandard housing were available to them as they encountered a more subtle type of institutionalized racism. The Great Migration not only changed the demography of cities such as Chicago and Detroit, creating the large inner-city black populations that remain in the ghetto today, but also raised the issue of race for all of

American society as African Americans became a force to reckon with throughout the country.

Greek Americans: The Greek Americans are among the most assimilated and successful of immigrant groups in the United States, yet they maintain a proud ethnic identity. Early in the twentieth century, the most visible Greek presence in the United States probably would have been in the mines and railways of the West and in the major cities of the East, where Greek-owned sweet shops, floral shops, and restaurants flourished by the hundreds. Greek Americans became highly visible in American politics in response to the Turkish invasion of Cyprus in 1974, when the "Greek lobby" unsuccessfully pressured Congress to institute an embargo on Turkey.

By the late 1900's, Greek American involvement could be seen in virtually all levels of American business, society, and politics. The U.S. Census of 1980 revealed that the Greek American population of 1,250,000 was divided roughly equally between first-, second-, and third-generation immigrants, with about 100,000 members of the fourth generation.

Both among contemporary scholars of Greek American immigration and among Greek Americans themselves, the debate continues between those who view the Greek American experience as part of the diverse American immigrant experience and those who see Greek Americans in terms of the culture of the worldwide Hellenistic diaspora. Neither side, however, minimizes the importance of Greek ethnic iden-

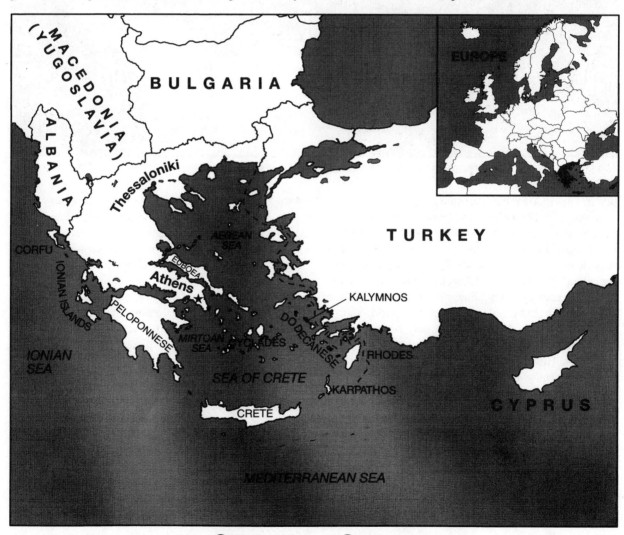

GREECE AND CYPRUS

This Greek American coffee shop proprietor advertises his business to the Greek community in the language of their homeland. (Library of Congress)

tity in Greek American communities.

History. In 1982 historian Charles Moskos, Jr., estimated that more than 700,000 Greeks had come to the United States over the entire course of Greek American immigration, of whom more than two-thirds remained. The majority of Greeks arrived in the early twentieth century, coinciding with the great buildup of American industrialization before World War I. American records show a total of only seventy-seven Greek immigrants in the entire period between 1847 and 1864. However assimilated the Greek American community may have become in American society, their attachment to many aspects of Greek culture and identity remains strong.

The early Greek American experience is well documented. Especially noteworthy were the writings of Athenian journalists who traveled to the United States to report on the conditions of Greek American immigrants. In general, these accounts emphasize hardships, whereas the immigrant writers themselves emphasized "success stories" among the community members. The Greek American press is itself an interesting indicator of the evolution of the community.

Avid readers, the Greek Americans were served by many Greek-language newspapers until late in the twentieth century, when they were replaced by English-language publications. The famous *Atlantis* ceased publication in 1973, although the more liberal *National Herald* continues to be read. Newspapers such as the *Hellenic Chronicle* (Boston) and the *Hellenic Times* (New York) continue to serve an English-speaking Greek readership.

Moskos suggests five distinct periods of Greek American history: the early beginnings before 1890; mass migration (1890-1920); the formulation of Greek American institutions (1920-1940); an era of consolidation (1940-1965); and the contemporary period since 1965. The earliest Greek arrivals in the United States predated 1776. Andrew Turnball formed a colony in Florida on the basis of imported laborers, including many Greeks. Conditions were so poor that riots broke out before the colony was abandoned in 1777. The Greek War of Independence (1821-1828) resulted in the arrival of war orphans in the United States, many of whom would make major contributions in their adult years. Among them were educator

John Zachos and Lucas Miller, the first Greek American congressman.

The mass migration around the beginning of the twentieth century was primarily motivated by economic opportunities. Most Greek immigrants were peasants who came to the United States to escape the uncertain economic lifestyle of peasant farming. Many planned to work briefly and then return with their economic gains to Greece. Typically, men would travel, either leaving their wives and families behind or arriving unmarried.

Some 40 percent of these Greek immigrants worked in mines, on railroads, and in factories, or as peddlers and service providers in major cities. Many of the arriving Greeks were slow to become involved in the labor movement, although this may be at least partly attributed to the discriminatory practices and anti-foreign attitudes in the unions. There were many incidents of anti-immigrant violence directed toward Greeks, sometimes involving the KU KLUX KLAN, sometimes involving local workers who resented the use of Greek American laborers as strike breakers in large mining operations. (Usually the Greeks were unaware they were breaking a strike; they simply trusted a Greek padrone who was dealing directly with the company management.)

When Greek women began to arrive after the beginning of the twentieth century, permanent settlement in the United States began to be a viable option. Furthermore, as immigration legislation became increasingly restrictive, Greek immigrants sought citizenship in dramatically higher numbers in order to reserve their place in the society. Once they gained citizenship, these immigrants could then send for their wives, who could join their husbands despite the rigid quotas on potential immigrants with no family connections. By 1940, American-born members of the Greek American community were the majority.

One of the main institutions of stability for the Greek American community was the Greek Orthodox church. By 1930, there were an estimated two hundred Greek Orthodox churches in the United States. Virtually synonymous with being Greek, the church served to anchor Greek American lives in the traditional rites of passage such as baptism and weddings.

In some parts of the United States, unique Greek communities developed that continue to maintain an appreciation for their Greek roots. Tarpon Springs, Florida, became the national center of the sponge industry when Greek immigrants brought their skills in this industry from the island of Kalymnos and formed a prominent community. There was a strong Greek American working community built around the textile mill industry in Lowell, Massachusetts, as well. In Baltimore, Maryland, Greeks from the isolated village of Olympos on the island of Karpathos maintain their traditional late-night celebrations, complete with improvised folk music and dance. The unique ethnic histories of these communities have only recently begun to gain attention and appreciation.

Politics in Greek American Life. Conflicts in Greece were reflected in divisions in the immigrant community. This was especially true during the first thirty years of the twentieth century, when Greek Americans were either royalist supporters of King Constantine I (who tended to favor the German cause) or more liberal supporters of the statesman Eleutherios Venizelos (who championed the Allied cause during the world wars). This rift even divided the church; archbishops would appoint priests according to their political stand. The priest Athenagoras was a reconciling presence in the Archdiocese of America from 1931 to 1948.

When Greece was brought into World War II, the Greek American community organized in support of the Greek resistance. Yet tensions were evident between supporters of the Communist-dominated resistance and backers of the Greek government-in-exile based in Britain. President Truman finally intervened with support for the non-Communist forces in the Greek civil war, and the defeat of Communists led to a new era of cooperation between Athens and Washington. The two countries have generally maintained a good working relationship except for controversies over the Cyprus issue since 1974 and continuing tensions between Greece and Turkey.

Modern Community Life. The Greek American community shows signs of identity maintenance that are more typical of southern European or Mediterranean peoples than northern European communities in contemporary American society. In traditional Greek life, family feuds were based on the maintenance of honor and the removal of shame. This may have contributed to the strong family ties that persist in the Greek American community, which attaches great value to *filotimo* (honor, pride). In addition to the family, the Greek Orthodox church and Greek American organizations promote solidarity in the Greek American community. They have also been inspired by the ethnic heritage revival to explore oral histories and

Governor Michael Dukakis of Massachusetts, an American of Greek descent, is shown (on right) shaking hands with Republican candidate George Bush at the second presidential debate in 1988. (AP/Wide World Photos)

other aspects of their heritage.

The church remains the center of many Greek American communities. It is a meeting place for organizations such as the fraternal American Hellenic Educational Progressive Association (AHEPA), founded in 1922, and the Greek Orthodox Ladies Philoptochos Society, which raises funds for charitable programs and overseas crisis relief. Many Greek churches sponsor annual bazaars or festivals to introduce Greek food and culture to non-Greeks while raising money for the church. Indeed, Greek churches are instrumental in the preservation of traditional customs through language classes, folk dance troupes, Greek Independence Day celebrations, and other activities.

Modern Greek immigration continues, though at a slower rate. In the visible enclaves of Greek Americans known as the "Greektowns" of New York, Chicago, and other cities, these immigrants might think they were in Athens. Yet in an American suburb where Greek Americans have acculturated, newcomers might not recognize their compatriots as Greeks. Such are the contrasts of the contemporary Greek American community.

Famous Greek Americans. Some aspects of the Greek American contribution to American society can be noted by simply listing a few of the more famous Greek Americans. The most important test for cervical cancer is known as the "Pap smear" for its inventor, Dr. George Papanicolaou. Significant research on Parkinson's disease was contributed by Dr. George Kotzias.

In politics, Greek Americans have produced many senators and members of Congress and at least two candidates for president, Michael Dukakis and Paul Tsongas. During the 1970's, Archbishop Iakovos was honored for his ecumenical work and his support of human rights efforts, which included work with Martin Luther KING, Jr., to promote interracial understanding and coexistence. Greek American contributions to the entertainment industry have also been noteworthy. Spyros Skouras became the president of Twentieth Century studios in 1942. Anthony Thomopoulos was a president of the American Broadcasting Company (ABC). Most major cities feature a Pantages Theater, a legacy of the career of Alexander Pantages, who had built a chain of motion picture theaters by the early 1920's. Dimitri Mitropoulos is a well-known symphony conductor, and John Cassavetes is a renowned actor, film producer, and director. Perhaps the most well-known Greek American actor is the instantly recognizable face of Telly Savalas, popular from the *Kojak* television series of the 1970's.

SUGGESTED READINGS. Two important works on the Greek American community are Charles Moskos, Jr.'s, *Greek-Americans: Struggle and Success* (1989) and Alice Scourby's overview, *The Greek-Americans* (1984). Scourby's work is noteworthy for including comments of an anthropological nature and for highlighting the much-neglected story of women in the Greek American immigration experience. Scourby also edited, with Harry J. Psomiades, the helpful collection *The Greek American Community in Transition* (1982), which contains a detailed and extensive bibliography by John G. Zenelis. The first major scholarly study of the Greek American community was Theodore Saloutos' *The Greeks in the United States* (1964).—*Daniel Smith-Christopher*

Greer, Germaine (b. Jan. 29, 1939, near Melbourne, Australia): Feminist writer and critic. Greer is known best for her first book, *The Female Eunuch* (1970), one of the bibles of the resurgent feminist movement of the 1960's and 1970's, which describes all women as deformed by the demands of male-dominated society. She is also the author of *The Obstacle Race: The Fortunes of Women Painters and Their Work* (1979). Greer has studied, taught, and published in Australia, England, and the United States. She became director of the Tulsa Center for the Study of Women's Literature in Oklahoma in 1979. In 1992, she published *The Change: Women, Aging, and the Menopause*, a major study of the social and psychological effects of menopause.

books include an autobiography entitled *Nigger: An Autobiography* (1964) and a study of the assassination of Martin Luther KING, Jr., *Code Name Zorro: The Murder of Martin Luther King, Jr.* (1977).

Grimké, Angelina, and Sarah Grimké (Angelina Emily; Feb. 20, 1805, Charleston, S.C.—Oct. 26, 1879, Hyde Park, Mass., and Sarah Moore; Nov. 26, 1792, Charleston, S.C.—Dec. 23, 1873, Hyde Park, Mass.):

Author of the landmark feminist book The Female Eunuch *(1970), Germaine Greer published a study on the effects of menopause in 1992.* (AP/Wide World Photos)

Gregory, Dick [Richard Claxton] (b. Oct. 12, 1932, St. Louis, Mo.): African American entertainer and civil rights activist. Gregory first gained attention in the 1960's as a comedian, then as a lecturer and activist. He worked for voter registration in the South and accused the Federal Bureau of Investigation (FBI) of "lying and hiding" the murderers of three civil rights workers in Mississippi (1964). He was jailed in Birmingham, Alabama, for his activities and shot in Los Angeles during the WATTS RIOTS. After the 1960's Gregory became a political analyst and a champion of holistic health. His

Abolitionists and feminists. In 1821 Sarah moved to Philadelphia and joined the QUAKERS. Angelina joined her in 1829. Together they were the first women to lecture for the American Anti-Slavery Society. Despite the hostility they faced, they fought slavery until their retirement in 1867. Among their written works, mostly pamphlets, are *Letters on the Equality of the Sexes, and the Condition of Women* (Sarah, 1838), *An Appeal to the Christian Women of the South* (Angelina, 1836), *Appeal to the Women of the Nominally Free States* (Angelina, 1837), and *Letters to Catherine Beecher* (Angelina, 1838).

Griswold v. State of Connecticut (1965): Landmark U.S. Supreme Court decision that struck down Connecticut's law banning the use of birth control by married couples. In its ruling, the Court recognized a "right of privacy" regarding sexual activity of married couples. Later court decisions extended that right to all persons regardless of marital status.

The controversy had its roots in the nineteenth century. Under the Comstock Act, passed by Congress in 1873, birth control was lumped together with other "obscene, lewd or indecent" material, making it illegal to circulate information about contraception through the mail. Numerous state laws reinforced and extended this ban.

Early twentieth century birth control advocates such as Emma GOLDMAN and Margaret SANGER saw the tragic effects of repeated childbearing on the lives and families of poor women. They braved prosecution and jail to establish birth control clinics and provide contraceptive information in an effort to give women control over their own childbearing. Supporters of birth control also argued that contraceptive devices were a way of preventing the spread of venereal disease, and therefore could be legally justified despite the anti-obscenity provisions of the Comstock Act. The notion of "planned parenthood" gained increasing acceptance during the 1940's and 1950's, although strong opposition to birth control, especially from the Catholic church, continued.

Estelle Griswold was executive director of Connecticut's PLANNED PARENTHOOD League, which deliberately challenged the Connecticut law prohibiting using, or assisting someone else in obtaining, "any drug, medicinal article or instrument for the purpose of preventing conception" for any reason, including to preserve the life of the mother. Together with C. Lee Buxton, a physician who wished to provide contraceptive services to his patients, the league had previously tried to have the law overturned by showing the harm it caused to several married couples. The court refused to rule in that case, claiming that because the couples had not actually been prosecuted, the law was not being enforced. It became clear that in order to be heard by the Supreme Court, the league and Buxton would have to open a clinic and provide birth control information publicly. Within days after the clinic was opened, they were arrested and charged with giving information and medical advice to married persons for the purpose of preventing pregnancy. Planned Parenthood countered that the law violated the FOURTEENTH AMENDMENT which states that no person shall be deprived of "due process" of the law.

In the *Griswold* decision (6 to 2), the majority opinion declared that the Connecticut law violated a fundamental "right of privacy older than the Bill of Rights" by interfering with the sanctity of marital relations. In a subsequent court case (*Eisenstadt v. Baird*, 1972) the right to use and distribute contraceptives was extended to unmarried persons.

SUGGESTED READINGS. For an interesting discussion of birth control in social and historical perspective, see Linda Gordon's *Woman's Body, Woman's Right* (1976). Another excellent source is James Reed's *The Birth Control Movement and American Society: From Private Vice to Public Virtue* (1978).

Guadalupe Hidalgo, Treaty of (Feb. 2, 1848): Formally ended the Mexican-American War between the United States and Mexico. The treaty ceded California and much of the Southwest to the United States. The lands won by the treaty completed the present-day form of the continental United States, along with the GADSDEN PURCHASE (1853) and the Alaska Purchase (1867).

President James J. Polk had dispatched the chief clerk of the State Department, Nicholas P. Trist, to General Winfield Scott's American forces on campaign in Mexico to negotiate a settlement of the war. Trist, a Democrat like Polk, quickly became friends with General Scott, a Whig, leading the president to suspect that Trist might compromise the administration. Polk recalled Trist to Washington in October, 1847, but the diplomat did not receive notice of his dismissal until November.

Technically, Trist had no authority to conclude a treaty, but Scott persuaded him to stay on and forge an agreement with Mexico. Both sides urgently needed his services. Scott had captured Mexico City in September, 1847, effectively ending the war with an American victory. The Mexican government was in disarray, however, and its leader, General Antonio López de Santa Anna, was discredited.

Trist met with representatives of the Mexican government at Guadalupe Hidalgo in central Mexico to hammer out a pact. During the summer of 1847, some Americans had called for the annexation of all of Mexico. Trist wisely ignored that proposal. Under the terms of the treaty, Mexico recognized Texas as part of the United States and ceded more than 500,000 square miles of its territory. The ceded lands comprised what would later become the states of Califor-

Northern Mexico Before the Treaty of Guadalupe Hidalgo

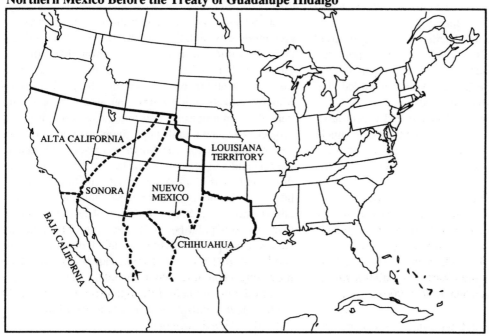

Territories After the Treaty of Guadalupe Hidalgo

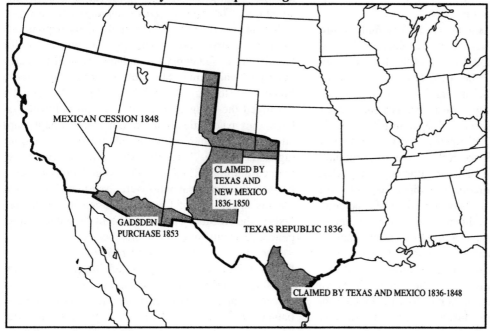

Source: From Paula Lannert, *Mexican Americans.* American Voices series, p. 13. Vero Beach, Fla.: Rourke Corp., 1991.

nia, Nevada, Utah, most of Arizona and New Mexico, and portions of Wyoming and Colorado. In return, the United States was obligated to pay Mexico $15 million and assume the claims of its citizens against Mexico, amounting to $3.25 million.

When Polk received the details of the pact, he was profoundly distressed. He considered Trist a political scoundrel, but that "scoundrel" had succeeded beyond all the president's expectations. Polk forwarded the treaty to the Senate, which ratified it.

The Treaty of Guadalupe Hidalgo had a profound impact. In the short term, the acquisition of so much new land raised the question of the expansion of slavery, further dividing North and South and eventually leading to civil war. In the long term, the infusion of Hispanic culture enriched American society.

SUGGESTED READINGS. A number of general works on the Mexican War and its aftermath cover the treaty. Otis A. Singletary's *The Mexican War* (1960) gives a good overview, as do K. Jack Bauer's *The Mexican War, 1846-1848* (1974) and Charles G. Seller's *James K. Polk, Continentalist, 1843-1846* (1966).

Guatemalan Americans: Guatemala is the northernmost and most populous of the Central American republics. In area, Guatemala is approximately the size of Ohio (42,000 square miles), but it contains tremendous natural and cultural diversity.

Any discussion of Guatemala's history and culture must begin with the basic fact that Guatemala is a divided nation. The capital city and the lowlands are predominantly Ladino (the local term for people of Hispanic descent), while the highlands are largely indigenous (people of Mayan descent). The indigenous Guatemalans include dozens of separate tribes speaking more than fifteen distinct dialects. The largest groups are the Quiché, the Kekchi, the Cackchiquel, and the Mam. Available statistics differ regarding what percentage of the population is indigenous, but most estimates fall somewhere between 50 and 60 percent. The terms Ladino and indigenous are most accurately used in a cultural as well as a racial sense. That is, Guatemalans are considered Ladinos if they have adopted Hispanic customs of dress, religion, and language, and they are indigenous if they maintain Maya customs. These distinctions apply to Guatemalans in the United States as well. Just as there are two distinct groups within Guatemala itself, Guatemalan Americans are generally either very rich or very poor. The rich are primarily people of white, European descent,

and the poor are generally Maya.

The Maya. According to archaeologists, settled village life in Guatemala dates back at least as far as 2000 B.C.E. Between 300 B.C.E. and 250 C.E., the Maya began to build large centers with the monumental architecture for which they are renowned. Their political and economic influence spread throughout the region—south to what is now El Salvador and north into the Yucatán peninsula. During the golden age of Maya civilization (250-800 C.E.), these people embarked on an ambitious and unparalleled architectural project. The Maya built huge pyramids and extensive ceremonial centers. The Maya were accomplished in the arts and sciences; they practiced astronomy, calendrics, and hieroglyphic writing. From 800-1250 C.E., however, the population of these lowland cities declined drastically. Some were completely abandoned. Contrary to popular belief, however, the Maya did not simply disappear, and the so-called mystery of the "collapse" of Maya civilization can be explained by prevailing economic, environmental, and social factors. In the period before the Spanish conquest (1250-1500), Maya civilization had deteriorated into decentralized, regional societies.

History of Guatemala. The long colonial period (1524-1821) was marked by the steady and often violent imposition of Spanish political and economic structures. The Spanish *encomienda* system usurped Indian lands and reduced the indigenous populations to landless serfs who worked on large plantations for Spanish lords. Guatemala remained essentially a slave colony in which migrant, landless natives supported a Spanish aristocracy. Yet while the Spanish gradually destroyed the indigenous economic and political systems, they paid little attention, other than a haphazard attempt at Christianization, to other aspects of the indigenous culture. Thus, the natives in Guatemala remained culturally Indian, unlike populations in other parts of the Americas who were assimilated as mestizos (as in the rest of Central America) or decimated (as in the United States). Guatemala gained independence from Spain on September 15, 1821.

The Twentieth Century and U.S. Relations. During the twentieth century, the United States took an increasingly active role in Guatemalan affairs. U.S.-owned companies expanded operations in coffee and banana production, and the U.S. government influenced the elections that brought to power the dictator Jorge Ubico Castañeda in 1931.

Ubico Castañeda's regime collapsed in 1944 when

students, workers, and reform-minded professionals joined together with an exiled schoolteacher, Juan José Arévalo, in a leftist revolution that brought ten years of democracy and social reform to Guatemala. Arévalo was succeeded as president by his ally, Jacobo Arbenz Guzmán, who extended the government's land reform programs. Wary of communist influence in the government, the United States covertly orchestrated a coup that brought Carlos Castillo Armas to power and effectively ended Guatemala's brief social revolution.

In the decades following the coup of 1954, Guatemala was turned into a killing field. The U.S.-supported military played a direct role in the government. A strong guerrilla movement emerged in the early 1960's, and the nation was plunged into a protracted civil war. Over a thirty-year period, tens of thousands lost their lives in this struggle, most of them indigenous people. In the early 1980's, entire villages were attacked and destroyed by the army. Generally, the U.S. government supported these actions and continued to supply the Guatemalan military with training, equipment, and technical advice.

Because of the civil war, more than 200,000 Guatemalans fled their homeland to become refugees in Mexico or the United States. Although a democratically elected civilian president took power in 1986, the military continued to dominate Guatemalan politics, while paramilitary groups continued a reign of terror in both the capital and the highlands. Worldwide, Guatemala's name came to be associated with

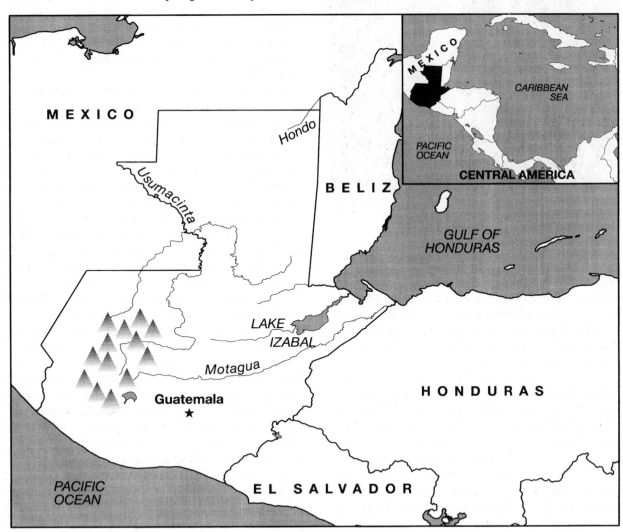

GUATEMALA

Guatemalan nun in Florida helps migrant worker community, including Guatemalan immigrants, adjust to their difficult living conditions. (Michael L. Kimble)

state-sponsored terrorism.

Immigration. Prior to 1970, few Guatemalans immigrated to the United States. Officially, only 19,683 came in the years between 1967 and 1976. The 1970 census counted 26,865 Americans of Guatemalan origin. Ninety percent of these were white, an indication that immigration prior to 1970 was probably for educational or professional purposes.

Since 1970, Guatemalans have immigrated to the United States largely for economic and political reasons. During the 1980's, an estimated 50,000 to 200,000 Guatemalans entered the United States. Most entered illegally. The largest Guatemalan community is in Los Angeles. Houston, Washington, D.C., New York City, Chicago, and San Francisco also have Guatemalan communities. There is, furthermore, a sizable contingent of Guatemalans, primarily indigenous, working as migrant laborers in Southern California's vegetable fields and in south Florida's sugar cane industry.

Because the majority of Guatemalans are undocumented immigrants, these communities remain largely invisible to the general American population. Guatemalan American communities have achieved a measure of stability: Some newcomers, like those in other immigrant communities, have succeeded in opening grocery stores, restaurants, art galleries, and boutiques. For the most part, however, the Guatemalan American communities are only recognized by the "mainstream" population when there are problems. For example, in 1987, a champion soccer team composed of Guatemalans living in Houston was forced to disband when the players were deported. In 1991, a truck carrying Guatemalan sugar cane cutters overturned into a south Florida canal; the fatal accident exposed the degrading circumstances in which the workers were forced to live and work. In 1992, migrant Guatemalans were among the most severely affected people in the deprivation that followed Hurricane Andrew in Dade County, Florida.

Guatemalans have also figured prominently in debates over immigration. In general, the United States has refused to recognize Guatemalans as political refugees. In 1985, Arizona church workers were arrested for giving sanctuary to undocumented Guatemalans. In 1988, the IMMIGRATION AND NATURALIZATION SERVICE (INS) granted asylum status to only 5 percent of the Guatemalans who applied.

In 1992, an indigenous Guatemalan who was denied political asylum, Jairo Elias Zacarias, appealed to the U.S. Supreme Court. Elias claimed that because he had resisted recruitment by the guerrillas, his life was in jeopardy in Guatemala. The Court agreed with the INS that resisting such recruitment was not a political act. This decision further narrowed the grounds by which Guatemalans could qualify for political asylum.

Cultural Contributions. Because of the country's political situation, Guatemalan culture is a culture in exile. At the same time, because the Guatemalan Americans are undocumented, their culture in the United States has remained largely underground.

Still, Guatemalans have distinguished themselves culturally, primarily in literature and the folk arts. Their successes in these areas can be attributed to the unique combination of Maya tradition and Spanish aesthetics that has helped create a distinctly Guatemalan worldview. The most accomplished Guatemalan writer, and the one who best expresses this worldview, is Miguel Ángel Asturias (1899-1974), winner of the Nobel Prize for Literature in 1967. Arturo Arias, a resident of California who carries on the tradition established by Asturias, is the author of several novels, including *After the Bombs* (1979). Arias also co-authored the screenplay for *El Norte* (1983), a film that tells the story of two young Guatemalans who immigrate to Los Angeles and endure POVERTY, oppression, and PREJUDICE.

In 1992, Maya activist Rigoberta Menchú won the Nobel Peace Prize for her work as a spokesperson for indigenous Guatemalans. Her testimony, *I, Rigoberta Menchú* (1983), is the moving story of the destruction that civil war has brought to her community and her family. Menchú's work has focused world attention on the situation in Guatemala and inspired the work of organizations such as *Nisgua* (Network in Solidarity with the People of Guatemala), which provide aid and support for indigenous Guatemalans.

Guatemala's folk art is internationally recognized for its uniqueness and beauty. These qualities are most evident in the rich variety of Guatemalan weaving, a complex art that has been passed down through generations of Maya women. Although the quality of these weavings has been compromised by their increasing popularity with tourists, several cooperatives in Guatemala and the United States have sought to ensure both the survival of the art and a fairer price for the artists. Slowly, the Guatemalan community has set up cultural organizations such as IXIM in Los Angeles to help preserve indigenous arts such as marimba music and folk dance in the United States.

SUGGESTED READINGS. For an account of Maya civilization, see *A Forest of Kings* (1990) by Linda Schele and David Freidel. A good account of the contemporary Maya and their lives is found in Ronald Wright's *Time Among the Maya* (1989). For an overview of Guatemalan society, politics, and culture, see Tom Barry's *Guatemala: A Country Guide* (1989). Issues related to undocumented immigration are treated in *Undocumented Migration to the United States* (1990), edited by F. D. Bean.—*Stephen Benz*

Gullah: African American language. Also called Sea Island Creole and Geechee, Gullah is spoken by African American residents of the Sea Islands and coastal South Carolina, Georgia, lower North Carolina, and northern Florida. Until the 1970's, these isolated inhabitants preserved their language. When Gullah-speaking children were integrated into schools, however, they faced communication problems with teachers. In 1975, the Charleston County School Board began training teach-

ers in Gullah. The 1976 Sea Island Language Project in Beaufort, South Carolina, taught English as a second language to Gullah-speaking adults to improve their chances of getting jobs. By the 1990's, only a few people remained who spoke pure Gullah.

Gutiérrez, Horacio (b. Aug. 28, 1948, Havana, Cuba): Cuban American pianist. At age eleven, Gutiérrez was guest soloist with the Havana Symphony. He emigrated to the United States after the Cuban Revolution and became a citizen in 1967. A graduate of the Juilliard School, in 1970 Gutiérrez took the Silver Medal at Moscow's prestigious Tchaikovsky Competition and then made his professional debut with the Los Angeles Philharmonic Orchestra. He has played under such maestros as Zubin Mehta, Lorin Maazel, and Seiji Ozawa; performed with such orchestras as the Berlin Philharmonic, the Orchestre National de France, and the San Francisco Symphony; recorded several albums with Telarc Records; and won numerous honors including an Emmy Award and the 1982 Avery Fisher Prize.

Cuban American pianist Horacio Gutiérrez took the Silver Medal at the prestigious Tchaikovsky Competition held in Moscow in 1970. (AP/Wide World Photos)

Gynecology: Branch of medicine dealing with the treatment of diseases of the female reproductive organs. It became a separate surgical specialty in its own right in the late 1800's, then merged with obstetrics (concerned with pregnancy and childbirth) in the twentieth century. The nature of gynecology at various points in history has generally reflected the prevailing social attitudes toward and roles of women.

Human societies have always been fascinated by female biology. Many tribal cultures practiced rituals centered around "mysteries" such as menstruation,

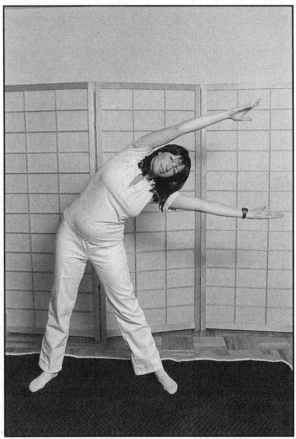

Modern gynecologists have come to recognize the value of low-stress exercise programs for pregnant women. (Hazel Hankin)

birth, and lactation, and women's health problems figure prominently in ancient Egyptian, Hindu, and Hebrew texts. Religious traditions often contributed to the belief that a woman's biological functions were secretive, dirty, and even shameful.

Gynecological practices became more scientific and sophisticated under the Greeks and Romans. Classical texts discuss the female reproductive system, describing beneficial birthing techniques, uterine surgery, and treatment for tumors. During the Middle Ages, both Islamic and Christian religious prohibitions caused medical research, especially gynecological research, to decline.

During the fifteenth and sixteenth centuries, various gynecological and obstetrical treatises—all based on fragments of Roman works—were published. Progress in anatomical studies provided the first accurate definitions of the female reproductive organs, and this facilitated surgical procedures such as induced labor. By the 1700's, cesarean section and surgical repair after delivery were common; after the development of anesthesia and antiseptic procedures in the 1800's, more complicated procedures became routine.

In the nineteenth century, gynecology became one of the pioneering branches of surgery. Indeed, surgery was generally treated as the first rather than the last resort, with gynecologists removing women's organs at will. This aggressive attitude was epitomized in the work of J. Marion Sims, who is known in the United States as the "father of gynecology." He performed numerous surgical experiments without anesthesia on African American women in Alabama in the 1840's, easily exploiting slaves who had no civil rights. He founded the New York Women's Hospital in 1855, where he continued to advocate frequent and radical surgery. By the late 1800's, it was common for gynecologists to remove women's ovaries as a supposed cure for psychological problems.

The medical literature concerning women's diseases often contained attitudes that hindered women's success and fostered a negative female image. Nineteenth century physicians portrayed women as weak, nervous, and chronically ill—all conditions believed to stem from the female organs, specifically the uterus. For example, the term "hysteria," which comes from the Greek word for uterus, was defined as an exclusively female disease. Such "medically based" and male-biased pronouncements were used as evidence that a woman's only healthy functions were marriage and motherhood, denying women such fundamentals as equality in the workplace and the right to vote.

Meanwhile, female midwives, who had been the sole handlers of childbirth until the 1700's and still attended about half of all American births in 1910, were being pushed out of the profession by male obstetricians. In order to establish obstetrics as a medical specialty performed by men, it had to be redefined as something that required knowledge of surgery (such as the use of forceps and cesarean section, both techniques forbidden to midwives). First upper-class and later middle-class women began to put their faith in male physicians, blaming midwives for the high infant mortality rate. By 1920, the American Board of Obstetrics and Gynecology had been formed and women's health was effectively controlled by men for the next fifty years.

Modern obstetrician/gynecologists (OB/GYNs) deal with problems of the reproductive organs, urinary tract, menstruation, and fertility, including cysts and cancer, as well as contraception and both normal and high-risk pregnancies and births.

The emphasis is mainly preventive, encouraging annual checkups, breast exams, and Pap smears. Advancements such as early cancer detection and improved procedures for difficult births improves women's lives, yet the expense of examinations and the often-adverse reaction to some operations cause gynecological practice to be inaccessible and dangerous to many women. Among the many controversies of modern gynecological practice are the high rates of cesarean births and hysterectomies, which critics claim are unnecessary interventions. Government, religious organizations, and women's rights groups vie for control of women's bodies, politicizing such gynecological issues as artificial insemination, contraception, abortion, and health care coverage.

Many feminists in the 1970's rejected established gynecological doctrine, promoting instead a self-help approach to women's health. A growing number of female gynecologists since that time have been transforming the field, contributing a more woman-centered approach. In addition, increasing numbers of nurse-midwives provide routine gynecological care.

SUGGESTED READINGS. Two books by James V. Ricci provide a thorough history of gynaecology: *The Genealogy of Gynaecology: History of the Development of Gynaecology Throughout the Ages, 2000 B.C.-1800 A.D.* (1943) and *One Hundred Years of Gynecology, 1800-1900* (1945). For a more feminist account, see *Clio's Consciousness Raised: New Perspectives on the History of Women* (1974), edited by Mary S. Hartman and Lois Banner, and Barbara Ehrenreich and Deirdre English's *Complaints and Disorders: The Sexual Politics of Sickness* (1974), which discusses nineteenth century and twentieth century gynecological practices among the working classes. *The New Our Bodies, Ourselves: A Book by and for Women* (rev. ed., 1992) by the Women's Health Book Collective exemplifies self-help gynecology, providing practical information concerning women's health.

Gypsies: There are approximately 500,000 to one million Gypsies living in the United States. Since the GREAT DEPRESSION, many have lived in cities such as Los Angeles, San Francisco, New York, Chicago, Boston, Atlanta, Dallas, Houston, Seattle, and Portland. Most other Americans are unaware of the presence of this group in their midst; they were only officially declared a minority group in 1972. Like Gypsies in other countries, American Gypsies live in tightly insulated communities and refuse any type of ASSIMILATION.

Scholars believe that Gypsies originated in northwest India, then migrated to parts of the Middle East, the Balkans, and western Europe. the term "Gypsy" is a misnomer based on the view that they came from Egypt (as in "Egyptian"). In the course of their wanderings, they began to call themselves Rom and their language became known as Romany. They were welcomed in some European countries during the Middle Ages but soon began to be persecuted because of their unusual appearance, nomadic lifestyle, and practices of fortune-telling and entertaining. They first came to North America as a result of deportations. More than 250,000 Gypsies were killed in the HOLOCAUST during WORLD WAR II solely on the basis of their ETHNICITY.

The earliest record of Gypsies in colonial America is in 1695 when legal proceedings were brought against a woman named Joane Scot for having a baby out of wedlock. That same year England deported a group of Gypsies to Virginia. Gypsies were forced to emigrate to the New World from most of western Europe during the colonial period; for example, England sent them to the Georgia penal colonies, France sent them to Louisiana, and Germany sent them to Pennsylvania. Most Gypsies, however, arrived in the United States in the latter half of the nineteenth century from eastern Europe.

Gypsies have always been independent business people who ply a variety of trades to survive. Modern Gypsy women are generally fortune-tellers who set up shop in the front room of the family home. Men play a middleman role by selling used cars, trucks, clothes, and jewelry; repairing car bodies or small machines; salvaging scrap metal; doing roofing, blacktopping, or seasonal farm work; and entertaining at carnivals. Groups of Gypsies join informal working alliances called *kumpaniyi*, which stake out a territory where other Gypsies are not supposed to compete.

There is practically no communication between Gypsies and non-Gypsies, whom they call *gaje*. Their only contact with *gaje* is to transact business and secure special services such as welfare that are unavailable within their community. Because they consider themselves a people apart with a superior way of life, while the *gaje* are, by definition, considered unclean and immoral, many Gypsies feel free to lie to or cheat non-Gypsies. This suspicion and hostile behavior, combined with social isolation, PREJUDICE, and the ignorance of non-Gypsies about Gypsy life, has led to the creation of STEREOTYPES and some intergroup conflict. For example, fortune-telling is illegal in California, although it is widely practiced; when police start to harass Gypsies about this or other issues, they tend to move. In the 1970's, certain state laws still allowed for the legal eviction of Gypsies or special licensing fees required solely of them.

Gypsies in the United States are divided into nations, *kumpaniyi*, clans, and the extended family units in which they live. They are governed by a strict system of social norms called *romania*, meaning the way of the Rom. Central to this is a code of what is pure and acceptable versus what is considered *marime* (impure and punishable). For example, the lower half of the body, the genitals, menstruating women, and non-Gypsies are all seen as impure, and improper contact with any of these can be severely punished. Gypsies have their own court of arbitration, called a *kris*, to enforce these social codes and to settle disputes in relatively rare cases of violence. Punishment is social ostracism for a specified period of time, which places tremendous economic and other hardships on entire Gypsy clans.

Gypsies believe in one God but are neither Christian, Jewish, or Muslim. Many are superstitious and believe in ghosts. They are extremely loyal to their families and clans and believe in non-violence. Dating is prohibited, and all marriages are arranged by the families involved, with a bride price paid by the groom's family. Both weddings and funerals are elaborate occasions lasting three days and attracting Gypsies from other states.

Gypsy children may attend school if it is financially rewarding to the family, but they never attend school after puberty. This is because families wish to minimize *gaje* influence and also need the children's help in the family business. A number of government-supported Gypsy schools have been set up in the late 1900's to deal with their special needs. Gypsies are an illiterate population, but they manage to survive as a distinct minority culture through hard, cooperative work in their separate economic niche and strict enforcement of their codes.

SUGGESTED READINGS. For additional information, read Marlene Sway's excellent sociological study *Familiar Strangers: Gypsy Life in America* (1988). Additional detail on Rom social structure can be found in Anne Sutherland's *Gypsies: The Hidden Americans* (1975), while the article "Gypsies" in the *Harvard Encyclopedia of American Ethnic Groups* (1980), edited by Stephan Thernstrom, is a useful summary. See also *The Journal of the Gypsy Lore Society*, which contains folklore and pertinent articles on Gypsies throughout the diaspora.—*Carol B. Tanksley*

H

Hadassah: American women's Zionist organization. Founded in 1912 by Henrietta Szold, Hadassah is the largest Zionist organization in the world. It is defined by its constitution as "a voluntary, non-profit organization dedicated to the ideals of Judaism, ZIONISM, American democracy, healing, teaching, and medical research." Hadassah sponsors medical education and research, health care, and vocational training in Israel as well as fund-raising and education in the United States. It publishes the monthly *Hadassah Magazine*.

Haitian Americans: Haitian migrants to the United States and Canada differ greatly from other West Indian migrants with respect to history, language, culture, and religion. Population estimates for Haitians in the United States and Canada vary considerably, with a working figure of about 600,000. Although Haitian migration to the United States began as early as the mid-1600's, there has been a tremendous increase since 1965. Haitian-born Americans constitute one of the largest groups of Caribbean migrants living in the United States.

The largest number of Haitian migrants live in the United States, the Dominican Republic (140,000), and Canada (60,000). Major concentrations of Haitians are to be found in New York City, Chicago, Miami, Washington, D.C., Boston, and the Canadian cities of Quebec and Toronto. Haitians may also be found in smaller and medium-sized towns in the West and Midwest and are well represented among university teachers and on hospital staffs throughout the United States.

The majority of Haitians in the United States and Canada consider themselves political and/or economic REFUGEES from the governments of François "Papa Doc" Duvalier, who held power in Haiti from 1957 to 1971, and his son, Jean-Claude "Baby Doc" Duvalier, who was in power from 1971 to 1986. At least 500,000 citizens left Haiti for other parts of the world during the Duvaliers' dictatorial rule.

Haitian migrants represent different regions of Haiti and a range of social classes. Like other Caribbean peoples, large numbers of educated Haitian professionals have migrated. Poor, uneducated peasants, however, constitute the bulk of the migrants as well as the bulk of the population of Haiti, one of the poorest countries in the Western Hemisphere.

History. Haiti was "discovered" by Christopher Columbus in 1492. The nation shares the Caribbean island of Hispaniola with the Dominican Republic. Haiti is unique among Caribbean nations because of its relatively short span of colonial domination and because it was the site of the Caribbean's first and only successful slave revolt. In 1804, the colonial forces of France and Spain were overcome, and Haiti was established as an independent republic under black rule.

The population of Haiti is predominantly composed of the descendants of slaves brought to the Caribbean from the African coast and from the area that comprises the contemporary African nations of Angola, Senegal, Benin, the Ivory Coast, and the Congo. There is also a small elite population who claim mixed black/white heritage. Haitians of mixed heritage and/or mulattos constitute less than 10 percent of the Haitian population and are concentrated in the larger cities of Port-au-Prince (the capital), Cap Haitian, and Gonaives. In addition, there is also a small number of Asians (Chinese and Asian Indians) as well as whites (American and European expatriates, most of whom came to Haiti during the twentieth century). Like mulattos, Asians and whites tend to be concentrated in urban areas.

Patterns of Migration. Migrations of Haitians to the United States began well before the American Revolution. At the Battle of Savannah in 1779, a group of eight hundred "men of color" from Haiti joined American forces in the fight for American independence. During the turbulent years of the Haitian revolution, more than fifty thousand Haitians (white planters, free blacks, and black slaves) migrated to the United States. Philadelphia, Pennsylvania, became a center for the preservation and perpetuation of Haitian culture, and it was in Philadelphia that the white Haitian Mérédic Louis Élie Moreau de Saint-Méry (1750-1819) published his classic two-volume study *Description topographique, physique, civile, politique, et historique de la partie française de l'isle de Saint-Dominique* (1796). Other notable white Haitians of the early period include the naturalist and illustrator John Jacob Audubon, who was born in Haiti in 1785. The grandfather of the eminent black scholar W. E. B. Du Bois was born in Haiti in 1825.

U.S. marines occupied the Republic of Haiti from

1915 to 1934. Black Haitian dissidents, most of whom were urban and highly educated, migrated to the United States during that period and played a major role in what has been called the "HARLEM RENAISSANCE." Following World War II, black Haitian women were recruited for domestic work in Washington, D.C., and Los Angeles.

Major migration from Haiti corresponded to the period of the Duvaliers' rule (1957-1986). Early (pre-1970) migrants were predominantly urban, middle-class, and upper-middle-class professionals. After 1970, however, lower-class peasants began to come to the United States in greater numbers, many arriving illegally. The most famous and/or infamous of post-1970 arrivals received considerable media attention as the "BOAT PEOPLE." For this latter group of migrants, motivations were predominantly economic rather than political.

After the collapse of Jean-Claude Duvalier's regime, there was some repatriation to Haiti, but given continuing political and economic instability, repatriation was not as extensive as social scientists had predicted. For example, some Haitian Americans were encouraged by the election of President Jean-Bertrand Aristide in 1990, but after his ouster in 1991, some forty-thousand Haitains left their homeland in despair. In the early 1990's, the U.S. government policies of intercepting Haitians at sea for deportation or detaining them in camps both provoked controversy.

Cultural Contributions. However long Haitians may have lived in the United States, Canada, or elsewhere, they continue to identify themselves as Haitians and continue what they see as a valiant struggle to keep selected elements of their culture alive in their new land. Total ASSIMILATION into American society is

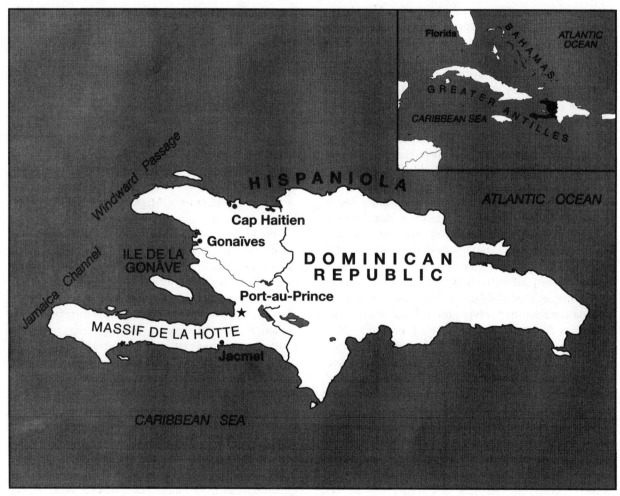

HAITI

A Haitian American Catholic priest working with young people in Florida. (Michael L. Kimble)

rarely stated as a major goal, and most Haitians express a desire to go back to Haiti if and when the political and economic situation changes for the better.

A distinguishing feature of Haitian American culture is the retention of their language. Haitian peasants generally come to the United States and Canada speaking only Haitian Creole. This is not—as widely reported—a bastardized version of French, but a distinct language with a distinct history. Many Creole words are derived from French, while pronunciation and grammatical forms reflect the influence of other European languages and African tribal languages. Many lower-class Haitian migrants are illiterate, but educated mulatto elites in the United States have usually mastered standard, metropolitan French and have a limited command of written and spoken English as well. Creole, which is understood and used by Haitian elites and non-elites alike, remains an important badge of cultural and ethnic identity. It also is a significant barrier to total assimilation to mainstream American life. Haitian Creole (next to Spanish) is the second most common foreign language in the New York City school system. While many Haitian American children learn English in the public schools, their parents usually insist on speaking French and/or Haitian Creole at home.

A second distinguishing feature of the Haitian Americans is their religious beliefs. Most say that they are Roman Catholics, but many Haitians also attend Protestant churches and vodun ceremonies. Religious affiliations in the United States and Canada closely replicate those in Haiti. In New York City and Toronto, there appears to be a marked preference for worship in predominantly Haitian congregations, although some Haitians in New York have been attracted to West Indian Pentecostal groups.

Vodun, sometimes also called voodoo, the folk religion of Haiti, is a complex faith based on family rites and secrets that plays a dominant role in Haitian life. With no seminaries to enforce orthodoxy, there may be as many variants of vodun as there are practitioners of the religion. Many New York City practitioners are non-Haitians, and a growing number of vodun adherents are white. The religion combines selected elements from Christianity and various African tribal religions. African dances were performed by slaves in the western part of Hispaniola as early as the seventeenth century, but the period 1730 to 1790—

Journalist Sarah Hale became famous as editor of Godey's Lady's Book. *(AP/Wide World Photos)*

when African slaves were imported to Haiti in great numbers—is usually interpreted as vodun's formative period. It was during this period that the religious beliefs and practices of Dahomeans, Senegalese, Congolese, Yoruba, and other African groups combined with certain Catholic rituals.

The relationship between the *loa* (vodu spirits) and individual devotees is largely contractual. If one is careful in performance of offerings and ceremonies, the *loa* will be generous in their aid. If one neglects the *loa*, one cannot expect their favors. Neglect of one's *loa* is believed to result in sickness, the death of relatives, crop failures, and other misfortune.

SUGGESTED READINGS. Among the best introductions to the island of Haiti and Haitian religion and culture remain James G. Leyburn's classic *The Haitian People* (rev. ed., 1966) and *The Drum and the Hoe: Life and Lore of the Haitian People* (1960) by Harold Courlander. For information about Haitians in the United States, see *American Odyssey: Haitians in New York City* (1984) by Michel S. Laguerre and *Mama Lola: A Vodou Priestess in Brooklyn* (1991). *Aiding Migration: The Impact of International Development Assistance on Haiti* (1988), edited by Josh DeWind and David H. Kinley III, provides a solid discussion of the Haitian economic and political situation.—*Stephen D. Glazier*

Hale, Sarah (Sarah Josepha Buell; Oct. 24, 1788, Newport, N.H.—Apr. 30, 1879, Philadelphia, Pa.): Journalist. Between 1806 and 1811, Hale wrote for a local newspaper. She wrote *The Genius of Oblivion*, a book of poetry, in 1823, and a novel, *Northwood,* in 1827. In 1828 she edited *Ladies Magazine*, writing half the articles herself. Ten years later she sold the magazine to Louis Godey but stayed on as editor. *Godey's Lady's Book* was a combination of poetry, fiction, fashion tips, and recipes. Hale became a household name. She believed strongly in education for women but had no part in the SUFFRAGE MOVEMENT.

Hale House: Private home that cares for infants of addicted parents. Founded in 1969 in Harlem by Clara M. Hale, Hale House cared for approximately one thousand children up to 1992 when Hale died. Hale encouraged alcoholic- or drug-addicted mothers to leave their babies with her until the women regained their health. With the ACQUIRED IMMUNE DEFICIENCY SYNDROME (AIDS) epidemic in the 1980's, Hale House was among the first institutions to accept and care for the infants born to afflicted mothers. Hale's self-help solution to a major social problem won her the support of many who became contributors and volunteers. Her work followed a long tradition of mutual aid in the African American community. The work of Hale House continues under the direction of Hale's daughter, Dr. Lorraine Hale.

Haley, Alex Palmer (Aug. 11, 1921, Ithaca, N.Y.—Feb. 10, 1992, Seattle, Wash.): African American author. The sensation created by the 1977 televising of his historical novel *Roots: The Saga of an American Family* (1976) made Haley perhaps the best-known writer in America. His own roots were in Henning, Tennessee, where the family he made famous in *Roots* had settled and prospered. After a military career, Haley researched the African background of family stories he had heard as a boy. *Roots* forged a constructive myth of African triumph and inspired people of diverse backgrounds to discover their own family histories. Haley also assisted black leader MALCOLM X with his autobiography (1965).

Hamer, Fannie Lou (Oct. 6, 1917, Montgomery County, Miss.—Mar. 14, 1977, Mound Bayou, Miss.): African American political activist. Hamer worked throughout her life to promote civil rights, voter registration, and social services for blacks. The youngest of twenty children in a poor family, Hamer lost her Mississippi farm job in 1962 when she joined the STUDENT

NONVIOLENT COORDINATING COMMITTEE (SNCC) and tried to register to vote. She helped found the Mississippi Freedom Democratic Party, which challenged white political rule, and made a famous televised speech at the Democratic national convention (1964). Hamer sat briefly in the U.S. House of Representatives in 1965, a first for a black woman.

Handy, W. C. [William Christopher] (Nov. 16, 1873, Florence, Ala.—Mar. 28, 1958, New York, N.Y.): African American BLUES composer. Known as "father of the blues" and honored with a statue on Memphis' famous Beale Street, Handy was a horn player and bandleader who gained fame for writing enduring tunes that popularized the blues. After playing with minstrel groups in the 1890's, he composed "The Memphis Blues" (1909) as a campaign song for the city's political boss. His most famous song was "St. Louis Blues" (1914). After 1918 he worked in the music publishing business in New York City and, despite progressive blindness, authored an autobiography (1941) and other books.

Hansberry, Lorraine (May 19, 1930, Chicago, Ill.— Jan, 12, 1965, New York, N.Y.): African American play-wright. Hansberry's most famous play is her first, *A Raisin in the Sun* (1959), the first play by a black woman to be produced on Broadway. Both funny and serious, it depicts a Chicago family's attempts to improve their lives. Later, *A Raisin in the Sun* was made into a film, and a musical that won a Tony Award (1974). Before this work, black characters tended to be STEREOTYPES, and plays about blacks did not interest general audiences. A second play by Hansberry, *The Sign in Sidney Brustein's Window* (1964), was less successful. Other writings appear in *To Be Young, Gifted, and Black* (1969). Cancer cut her career short.

Hanukkah: Jewish Festival of Lights, an eight-day holiday, usually in December (depending on the Jewish lunar calendar), which commemorates the rededication of the Second Temple in Jerusalem by Judah the Maccabee in 165 B.C.E. According to historical accounts, the Syrians under King Antiochus Epiphanes defiled the Temple's sanctuary with pagan, idolatrous worship. Legend recounts that after defeating the enemy, Maccabee found only one cruse of pure uncontaminated oil, enough to light the menorah (candelabrum) for one day. Miraculously, the oil burned for eight days, which ex-

Alex Haley won the Pulitzer Prize in 1977 for his best-selling book Roots. (AP/Wide World Photos)

The candles of the menorah are progressively kindled on the eight days of Hanukkah. (James L. Shaffer)

plains why the Feast of Dedication is celebrated with candles lit for eight days.

Not a major holiday like ROSH HASHANAH and YOM KIPPUR, Hanukkah (variously spelled Chanukah and Chanuka) is observed in synagogue by reading the Book of the Maccabees in the Torah (the holy scrolls) each day. Hymns of Praise (Psalms 113-118) are chanted, and special prayers are recited. A feast of liberation and survival of the Jewish people, Hanukkah resembles Purim and PASSOVER, which also commemorate religious freedom.

The joy of Judaism brightens the home during Hanukkah. Friends and relatives exchange greeting cards to express best wishes. Special Hanukkah candles made in Israel are progressively kindled on the menorah, beginning with one the first night and culminating in eight the last evening. A candle used to light the other candles also remains in the menorah. Following the lighting of the candles, reciting of the blessings, and singing of songs such as *Rock of Ages*, gifts are exchanged. Children play a traditional game with the dreidl, a small top inscribed with four Hebrew letters standing for Nes Gadol Hayah Sham ("a great

miracle happened there"). This four-sided top is spun after pennies, candy, or nuts are put in the "pot." The letter facing up represents how much is won or lost. Traditional Hanukkah foods include jelly-filled doughnuts and latkes (potato pancakes)—both fried in the symbolic oil.

Although Hanukkah often comes around the Christmas season, Hanukkah is not the "Jewish Christmas." An understanding of Hanukkah means a greater appreciation of Jewish history and cultural heritage.

SUGGESTED READINGS. One of many fine children's picture books that capture the spirit of Hanukkah is Eric Kimmel's *Hershel and the Hanukkah Goblins* (1989), which won the coveted Caldecott Honor Award for its illustrations by Trina Schart Hyman. A collection of fiction for all ages is Isaac Bashevis Singer's *The Power of Light: Eight Stories for Hanukkah* (1980). Other excellent book-length sources on Hanukkah are Elyse D. Frishman's *These Lights Are Holy: A Home Celebration of Chanuka* (1989); Hersh Goldwurm and Meir Zlotowitz's *Chanukah: Its History, Observances, and Significance* (1981); *The Hanukkah Anthology* (1976), edited by Philip Goodman; and Mae S. Rockland's *The Hanukkah Book* (1975).

Harlem Globetrotters: Semiprofessional basketball team. The Harlem Globetrotters have entertained crowds with a mixture of outstanding basketball skill and a humorous presentation since 1927, when Abe Saperstein organized the original five-man group and took them on tour by automobile. At first, the Globetrotters played against other professional teams, but by the 1980's the group had expanded to three touring teams that brought their "opponents," who knew the program, with them. As popular abroad as in the United States, they once played before 75,000 people at Berlin's Olympic Stadium, the biggest basketball audience in history. Many of their players have gone on to become valued players in the National Basketball Association, such as Wilt Chamberlain.

Harlem Renaissance: Although the Harlem Renaissance is considered a milestone in the development of African American social and cultural history, the period has also been viewed as an era in which significant influences from the Caribbean provided a multicultural atmosphere leading to the exchange of political and cultural ideas in Harlem, a section of New York City. The Harlem Renaissance, which spawned developments in music, entertainment, and visual arts, also witnessed the rise of social and political organizations in Harlem dedicated to improving the circumstances of its black residents. Harlem became a cultural nexus for people of African descent from the Caribbean and the United States. The island of Jamaica in particular provided noted political and literary figures. In addition, the influx of immigrants from Puerto Rico and countries in South America led to contributions from intellectuals from those regions.

By the mid-1920's, Harlem, which had been populated by Jewish residents and other European ethnic groups at the turn of the century, had become a predominantly black community as a result of continued black migration to the area. It eventually developed a significant Spanish-speaking population at its southern border in Spanish Harlem, whose residents had migrated from Puerto Rico and other Caribbean islands. As the largest metropolis of black life in the urban North, Harlem was one of the focal points of black social, political, and cultural activities. It became the mecca of black culture, attracting black creative artists and intellectuals from areas throughout the United States and the Caribbean.

Black literary artists in particular have been recognized as prominent exponents of black culture during the Harlem Renaissance. These authors voiced the concerns of the so-called New Negro, which included increased race consciousness, social protest, and recognition of African heritage. The Harlem Renaissance was paralleled by similar cultural developments in Philadelphia, Washington, D.C., and elsewhere which symbolized the rise of black consciousness in the United States.

Various factors led to the rise of Harlem as a cultural center: the migration of African Americans from the rural South to the urban North in the opening decades of the twentieth century, an upsurge of black political protest, and an increase in the number of educated African Americans. The popularity of black creative expression in the arts coupled with the performance opportunities Harlem offered in its theaters, ballrooms, and nightclubs to establish the area as a center of the performing arts. Numerous black men and women contributed to the Harlem Renaissance as political leaders, entrepreneurs, and creative artists.

The Growth of Black Harlem. Harlem gradually became a community with a predominant African American population as a result of fluctuations in the local rental market. During the early 1900's, a large number of housing developments had been constructed in this part of town in expectation of an influx of white residents from other areas of New York City. By the second decade of the 1900's, this influx had not materialized; real estate agents began renting to African Americans, who represented a population on the rise. One of the important black real estate speculators of

James Weldon Johnson, sometimes called an "elder statesman" of the Harlem Renaissance, was a novelist, poet, attorney, and civil rights activist; he published The Autobiography of an Ex-Coloured Man *in 1912. (Library of Congress)*

this period was Philip A. Payton, Jr., whose Afro-American Realty Company was instrumental in encouraging the settlement of blacks in Harlem.

Many blacks who had resided in areas of downtown Manhattan, such as the Tenderloin District between 20th and 53rd streets on the West Side and San Juan Hill above 53rd Street on the West Side, took advantage of the improved housing in Harlem. By 1919, black Harlem, the largest African American community in the country, was geographically defined by the Harlem River on the east, Eighth Avenue on the west, 125th Street as its southern border, and 145th Street as its northern border. Among the first African Americans to come to Harlem after World War I were the prosperous members of the middle class who resided in the Striver's Row area of 138th and 139th streets. By the end of the 1920's, the affluent Sugar Hill district, extending to the 155th Street area, was also populated by people of African descent. The majority of black people in Harlem, however, resided in less affluent neighborhoods in the area known as the Valley. As new black residents moved in, many white residents chose to move out of Harlem, and their population continued to decrease.

The Harlem community became the center for many black FRATERNAL ORGANIZATIONS and social clubs as well as for black churches, such as the Abyssinian Baptist Church led by Adam Clayton Powell, Sr. Harlem also developed entrepreneurs and supporters of the arts such as A'Lelia Walker, whose mother, Madam C. J. WALKER, had become a millionaire through the creation and distribution of hair and facial products for black women. Casper Holstein, a West Indian immigrant whose profits were gained through gambling and real estate, was another influential Harlem resident who supported literary artists.

Political Awareness and Race Consciousness. With peacetime and the return of the black soldiers from Europe at the end of World War I, political awareness was on the increase in Harlem, fueled by the continued persecution of African Americans. In the early 1920's, "race leaders" came to the foreground and developed journals to express their political positions. Marcus GARVEY, the Jamaican-born founder of the United Negro Improvement Association (UNIA); A. Philip RANDOLPH, organizer of the BROTHERHOOD OF SLEEPING CAR PORTERS; and W. E. B. DU BOIS, the Harvard-trained founder of the NATIONAL ASSOCIATION FOR THE ADVANCEMENT OF COLORED PEOPLE (NAACP), represented the diversity of political organizations in Harlem.

Garvey, who had arrived in the United States in 1916, promoted BLACK NATIONALISM through his magazine *The Negro World* and sought to unify people of African descent throughout the world to address common concerns. Randolph, along with Chandler Owen, had founded *The Messenger,* a socialist journal which advocated the unity of black workers. Du Bois' *The Crisis,* sponsored by the NAACP, promoted the philosophy of INTEGRATION, and Charles S. Johnson's *Opportunity,* sponsored by the NATIONAL URBAN LEAGUE, encouraged literary activities. These organi-

zations promoted differing strategies for black ascendancy, and they were often rivals in their garnering of black constituencies. At the same time, black newspapers such as *The New York Age* and *The New York Amsterdam News* published articles relevant to the Harlem community.

Literary Achievements. Harlem became a focal point for the literary activities of black writers, many of whom migrated to Harlem to further their activities as poets, novelists, playwrights, or journalists. Writers of the Harlem Renaissance can be grouped into two categories: the old guard writers, such as James Weldon JOHNSON and DU BOIS, and the prominent younger writers, such as poets Langston HUGHES, Countée Cullen, and Claude McKay, as well as nov-

Zora Neale Hurston, author of Their Eyes Were Watching God *(1937), was an influential figure of the Harlem Renaissance.* (AP/Wide World Photos)

elist Jessie Redmon Fauset and folklorist Zora Neale HURSTON. A Jamaican-born immigrant, McKay had produced poetry collections such as *Songs of Jamaica* (1912) prior to his arrival in Harlem, and his American publications continued to draw upon his experiences in Jamaica.

Other notable writers of the period included Arna Bontemps, Sterling Brown, Rudolph Fisher, Nella Larsen, George Schuyler, Wallace Thurman, Jean Toomer, and Eric Walrond. Like McKay and Garvey, Walrond was also reared in a culture outside of the United States. Born in British Guiana, Walrond spent a number of years in Barbados and Panama. His story collection *Tropic Death* (1926) deals with racial prejudice and imperialism in Panama and the Caribbean. Black female poets included Gwendolyn Bennett, Helene Johnson, and Georgia Douglas Johnson. In 1925, Alain Locke, a Howard University professor of philosophy, published *The New Negro: An Interpretation*, in which he chronicled examples of black achievement in the arts.

The growth of Harlem Renaissance literature was encouraged by key black publications and journals such as *The Crisis, Opportunity, The Messenger, The Liberator*, and *Survey Graphic*, the March, 1925, edition of which was titled "Harlem: Mecca of the New Negro." The short-lived journal *Fire!!*, launched by Richard Bruce Nugent and others, provided an outlet for younger writers and artists. White patrons such as Charlotte Osgood Mason, Julius Rosenwald, Joel Spingarn, and Carl Van Vechten provided financial support and influential connections for many black literary artists. Bibliophile Arthur Schomburg's extensive collection of materials related to black culture housed at the 135th Street branch of the New York Public Library provided a base for scholarly research. As a Puerto Rican of African descent, Schomburg's interest in black culture was reflected in his research involving Phillis WHEATLEY and other African American poets.

Publishing opportunities existed through the prestigious New York publishing houses of Alfred Knopf, Albert Boni, and others who sought promising black writers during the period when "Negro" writing was in vogue. Poetry collections were among the first works to be published. James Weldon Johnson's *Book of American Negro Poetry* (1922) anthologized poets of the earlier generation. McKay's *Harlem Shadows* (1922), Cullen's *Color* (1925), and Hughes's *The Weary Blues* (1926) were significant poetic works that drew on their authors' African American heritage. Toomer's *Cane* (1923), an experimental poetic prose work, received substantial critical attention. Fauset's *There Is Confusion* (1924), the first novel by a black woman to be published during the Harlem Renaissance, investigated the theme of color, as did Fisher's novel *The Walls of Jericho* (1928).

Entertainment. Harlem became a center for musical entertainment, a location where whites ventured from downtown to the numerous uptown nightclubs, ballrooms, and theaters. Jazz Age nightlife was often connected with organized crime, since many of the clubs were owned by white mob bosses who profited from the sale of illegal alcohol to wealthy club patrons. The COTTON CLUB, Barron's, and Small's Paradise were among the prominent nightclubs in Harlem. Other venues included the Savoy Ballroom, the Renaissance Casino, and the Rockland Palace as well as the Lincoln, Lafayette, and APOLLO theaters.

JAZZ MUSIC was performed by numerous ensembles, many of which were led by black bandleaders such as Duke ELLINGTON and featured such artists as Fats Waller, Mamie Smith, Fletcher Henderson, and Louis ARMSTRONG. Other artists, such as Roland Hayes and Paul ROBESON, were featured performers of music in the European classical tradition. Noble Sissle and Eubie Blake, who composed the lyrics and music of the Broadway revue *Shuffle Along* (1921), were notables on the musical stage, as were Fredi Washington, Josephine BAKER, and Florence Mills. BLUES singer Bessie Smith was also active in Harlem during the 1920's.

Painters, Sculptors, and Photographers. Visual artists of the Harlem Renaissance incorporated significant black motifs and images in their works. Elements of African culture, representations of folk life in the rural South, and representations of nightlife in the urban North were common motifs. Many black artists received assistance through the efforts of the Harmon Foundation. Contributors to the visual arts included painters Aaron Douglas, Palmer Hayden, William H. Johnson, and Archibald Motley and sculptors Richmond Barthé, Meta Warrick Fuller, and Augusta Savage. In photography, James Van Der Zee was the prominent black practitioner.

Among these artists, Douglas is the one most often connected with the Harlem Renaissance. Douglas had been greatly influenced by the sculpture of West Africa, and his work appeared in *Fire!!*, *The Crisis*, and *Opportunity* magazines. Douglas' series of paintings

Harlem became an entertainment mecca, and the sophisticated jazz of Duke Ellington was a prime attraction. (AP/Wide World Photos)

in 1927, which included *The Crucifixion,* accompanied James Weldon JOHNSON's *God's Trombones.* Hayden, like Douglas, used African imagery in his work, exemplified by *Fétiche et Fleurs* (1926). William H. Johnson, who visited North Africa, was influenced by folk culture and African crafts.

Black female sculptors also re-created images of African American heritage. Fuller, a forerunner of Harlem Renaissance fine artists, was influenced by PAN-AFRICANISM, as seen in her sculpture *Ethiopia Awakening* (1914). Savage's achievement is notably represented in *Gamin* (1930), which depicts a black youth.

Van Der Zee, who had been an accomplished violinist and founding member of the Harlem Orchestra, turned to photography during the 1920's. As a recorder of Harlem life, Van Der Zee photographed the predominant participants of the Harlem Renaissance. His massive collection has been a storehouse of visual documentation and, along with the works of painters and sculptors, provides a pictorial replica of the Harlem Renaissance and its social, political, and cultural milieu.

SUGGESTED READINGS. The Harlem Renaissance has been a topic of scholarly investigation since the 1920's. Alain Locke's *The New Negro: An Interpretation* (1925) was the first comprehensive anthology and assessment of the writers, social thinkers, and artists of the Harlem Renaissance. David Levering Lewis' *When Harlem Was in Vogue* (1981) places the social, political, and cultural developments of the Harlem Renaissance within a chronological framework. The pictorial representation of the Harlem Renaissance is covered in Allon Schoener's *Harlem on My Mind: Cultural Capital of Black America, 1900-1968* (1968), an edited collection which contains numerous photographs by Van Der Zee, Van Vechten, and others. *Harlem Renaissance: Art of Black America* (1987) contains photographs of the painting and sculpture of black artists during and after the 1920's. The development of jazz, Duke Ellington's early years in Harlem, the role of black classical musicians, and other elements of the musical culture of the Harlem Renaissance are the focus of articles in *Black Music in the Harlem Renaissance: A Collection of Essays* (1990), edited by Samuel Floyd.—*Joseph McLaren*

Harpers Ferry, W.Va.: Town best known as the site of John Brown's raid on a U.S. armory and rifle works in 1859 in an abortive slave revolt. In the mid-nineteenth century, Harpers Ferry (then in Virginia) was the location of a musket factory that was one of the first to implement mass production. Here, in July of 1859, Brown and his followers rented a farmhouse and began planning what they hoped would become a general slave rebellion.

The raid took place on October 16, 1859. Brown's men rode into town, cut telegraph wires, captured the Potomac and Shenandoah bridges, overcame the guard at the armory, broke down the door to the weapons warehouse, and took possession of the rifle works. When townspeople realized what had happened, they sent for help from nearby towns. The raiders, meanwhile, began capturing hostages and sent out a party to recruit slaves to their ranks. Brown assumed that local slaves would flock to join the raiders (among whom were five African Americans), but that did not happen.

News of the raid was telegraphed across the nation, making this incident one of the first national media events. When militia arrived they recaptured the U.S. arsenal and the rifle works, but Brown and a few surviving men holed up in the fire station. The next morning, ninety U.S. Marines under the command of Col. Robert E. Lee arrived. Brown refused to surrender, but he and his men, fatigued and greatly outnumbered, were quickly overcome. The incident lasted little more than thirty hours.

The raid galvanized emotions in the United States,

Abolitionist John Brown, as fancifully depicted in John Stuart Curry's mural The Tragic Prelude. *(National Archives)*

splitting the nation even further on the issue of slavery. Some saw Brown as a Christian soldier, while others viewed him as an unprincipled terrorist, pointing to his earlier involvement in the Pottawatomie massacre as proof.

Eleven raiders were killed, five escaped, and seven were captured, including Brown. His trial lasted six days and drew national publicity. He was found guilty of murder and treason and was sentenced to hang. After his death on December 2, 1859, northern sympathizers glorified Brown, while Southerners villified him. On his way to the gallows, Brown handed his jailor a note which read, "I, John Brown, am now quite certain that the crimes of this guilty land will never be purged away but with Blood."

Harpers Ferry was a frequent battle site during the Civil War. After the war, Storer College was founded there to educate children of former slaves, eventually becoming one of the best preparatory schools for African Americans in the country. In 1906, W. E. B. Du Bois and members of his Niagara movement met at Storer to discuss ways to broaden the still severely restricted rights of African Americans. The fruit of these discussions was the founding of the National Association for the Advancement of Colored People (NAACP) three years later. Harpers Ferry became a tourist attraction after the Civil War and for African Americans, almost a shrine. Today, the Harpers Ferry National Historic Park memorializes the town's profound historic importance.

Suggested Readings. *Harpers Ferry* (1992) by Ray Jones is an overview of the town's place in history. There are many fine studies of Brown's raid, including Stephen B. Oates's *To Purge This Land with Blood: A Biography of John Brown* (1970), Benjamin Quarles's *Allies for Freedom: Blacks and John Brown* (1974), and Jeffery S. Rossback's *Ambivalent Conspirators: John Brown, the Secret Six, and a Theory of Slave Violence* (1982).

Hasidism: Orthodox Jewish religious movement. Hasidism, from the Hebrew word for piety, arose under the mystic Israel ben Eliezer—known as the Baal Shem Tov—in eighteenth century Polish Lithuania. In reaction against the formalism and pedantry of Orthodox rabbinical Judaism, Hasidism emphasizes joy and simple faith as the central elements in Jewish life. Intimate and ecstatic, Hasidic worship expresses itself less through study and scholarship than through song, dance, and story. Close-knit Hasidic communities tend to be iso-

lated from the secular world and led by charismatic, often dynastic, figures called *zaddikim*. Hasids are especially numerous in New York City and Israel, where they have come into conflict with African Americans and secularists, respectively.

Hatcher, Richard Gordon (b. July 10, 1933, Michigan City, Ind.): African American lawyer and political leader. The mayor of Gary, Indiana (1967-1988), Hatcher was the first African American to be elected mayor of a major city in the United States. To gain this position he overcame corrupt machine politics, winning narrowly. Hatcher symbolized the shift "from protest to politics" among African American civil rights leaders in the late 1960's. He was the keynote speaker at the first National Black Political Convention, held in Gary in 1972 to help solidify political gains by establishing a "Black Agenda" for Congress and the nation. Hatcher has been an active Democrat, and president of the National Black Political Council.

Richard Gordon Hatcher addresses the U.S. Conference of Mayors in 1979. (AP/Wide World Photos)

Hate crimes: Acts of intimidation or violence directed at individuals because of their race, ethnicity, national origin, religion, political beliefs, or sexual orientation.

Hate-motivated crimes are committed throughout the United States across various regions; in suburbs, small towns, and rural areas, as well as ghettos; and in schools, homes, and the workplace as well as the street. While typically thought to occur against racial minorities, they may also be directed against whites such as Jews or homosexuals. Some social scientists suggest that criminal acts motivated by prejudice not only affect the immediate victim but also are dangerous to the broader society as well. These analysts fear that hate crimes and intolerance could ultimately lead to major outbreaks of violence between races, religions, or subcultures.

Hate crimes have a long history in the culturally diverse United States, though they have only received systematic attention in the late twentieth century. Authors Michael Newton and Judy Newton have documented more than eight thousand cases of racial or religious violence from the European discovery of America to 1989. The Newtons claim that their historical survey shows that the actions of European explorers in the fifteenth and sixteenth centuries spoke much louder than their statements of humanitarian principles. They engaged in enslavement raids, massacres, and general mistreatment of the native population to advance Christianity in the New World. For four centuries, American Indians were targets for GENOCIDE. Slavery and its aftermath subjected another racial minority to violence. It was not until 1950 that the United States actually had its first year free of LYNCHING. Strong feelings of NATIVISM were expressed by some white Americans when faced with various waves of non-Teutonic and non-Protestant immigration. Chinese immigrants were killed in several midwestern states. Japanese Americans were placed in INTERNMENT camps during World War II, and in the 1970's and 1980's, Vietnamese refugees were harassed and killed in some areas after the Vietnam War; these are only two instances of contemporary anti-Asian violence.

The California Attorney General's Commission on Racial, Ethnic, Religious and Minority Violence issued a detailed and multifaceted definition of hate crimes in its 1986 report: "Hate violence is any act of intimidation, physical harassment, physical force or threat of physical force directed against any person, or family, or their property or advocate, motivated either in whole or in part by hostility to their real or perceived race, ethnic background, national origin, religious belief, sex, age, disability, or sexual orientation, with the intention of causing fear or intimidation,

or to deter the free exercise or enjoyment of any rights or privileges secured by the Constitution or laws of the United States or the state . . . whether or not performed under color of law."

The Federal Bureau of Investigation (FBI) is the major federal agency responsible for investigating and controlling hate violence. The FBI's Domestic Counterterrorism Program uses undercover agents, informants, and court-authorized electronic surveillance to monitor organized groups that unlawfully employ force or violence for political or social ends. The agency's Civil Rights Program focuses on individuals or small groups who commit racially and/or ethnically motivated violent acts that violate federal laws such as the CIVIL RIGHTS ACT OF 1964, the Civil Rights of Institutionalized Persons Act, and the Discrimination in Housing Act. Several private organizations including the ANTI-DEFAMATION LEAGUE (ADL) of B'NAI B'RITH, the Center for Democratic Renewal, the Klanwatch Project of the Southern Poverty Law Center, and the National Gay and Lesbian Task Force (NGLTF) also monitor hate crimes of one or more types and publish various reports on hate groups.

Hate Crime Statistics Act of 1990 and Other Legislation. In order to raise public awareness of hate crimes and prompt public response, the Hate Crime Statistics Act of 1990 was passed by Congress and signed by President George Bush. This legislation is significant as the first federal law requiring the government to collect specific hate crime data and identifying violence against gays and lesbians as hate crimes. The act calls for the U.S. Department of Justice to collect empirical data on hate crimes throughout the United States as part of its regular information-gathering system. The involvement of the police in collecting data may assist them not only in measuring trends but also in developing effective responses, demonstrating sensitivity to victims, and ultimately designing prevention strategies.

The FBI's Uniform Crime Reporting (UCR) Program was given the responsibility of carrying out the directives of the law. Gathering hate crime data was made a part of UCR's ongoing collection of crime information. Because there are numerous types of bias against individuals, the UCR limited its counting process to only those showing discrimination on the basis of the four specifically cited in the law: race, religion, sexual orientation, or ethnic group.

Most states and some cities have some form of antibias laws such as civil rights acts, ethnic intimidation

A Ku Klux Klan cross-burning rally in Georgia. (AP/Wide World Photos)

or malicious harassment acts, civil remedies, data collection acts, or special-purpose statutes such as those outlawing cross-burnings. California law, for example, not only provides criminal punishment for hate crimes, but also requires that perpetrators serve additional prison time for felony hate crime and, in cases of probation, take sensitivity training. Victims of hate crimes can sue for monetary damages for violation of their civil rights.

Problems in Definition and Conviction. While some view hate crimes as being like any other crime against individuals, others suggest that bias crimes have a greater impact because they are done in order to intimidate a whole group of people. Those who prosecute hate crimes identify four particular problems. The first is proving that the crime was motivated by bias. Some general guidelines used to identify hate crimes include the use of language such as racist slurs, the severity of the attack, the lack of provocation, absence of some other likely motive, previous history of similar crimes in the area, and the suspect timing of the act. For example, the burning of a cross in the yard of a minority family, especially if the family has re-

cently moved into a white neighborhood, is likely to be a hate crime. A second problem encountered by prosecutors may be witnesses who refuse to cooperate out of fear of further trouble. Another problem involves special defenses such as claiming self-defense or temporary insanity because of such things as "homosexual panic" or "gay advance." Finally, judges tend to give light sentences to those convicted of hate crimes, especially to avoid giving juveniles serious crime records. Most hate crimes are committed by people in their teens or twenties.

Data and Trends. It is hard to determine exactly how many hate crimes occur in a given year because victims may not report the crime. The National Institute Against Prejudice and Violence and other groups estimate that three out of four, or perhaps four out of five, American hate crimes go unreported. Furthermore, various agencies use different criteria for determination of what is a hate crime. Some may include suspicions of hate crime or so-called minor incidents such as name-calling in their counts, while others require documented evidence of hatred as motivation. Thus it is important to approach the "numbers game" with extreme caution. One thing that does appear clear is that reported hate crimes against various groups have increased, especially from 1988 to 1992.

The FBI's first national report on bias crimes was based on information supplied by only about three thousand of the sixteen thousand law enforcement agencies asked to participate. The study found 4,558 hate crime incidents reported in 1991. Racial bias was identified as the motivating factor in six out of ten offenses reported, religion in two out of ten, and ethnic or sexual orientation bias in one out of ten. African Americans were the most frequent target of attacks (36 percent) followed by whites (19 percent) and Jews (17 percent).

Cross-burnings are often associated with black or interracial couples. According to Klanwatch, there were 101 cross-burnings in 1991, compared to fifty in 1990 and thirty-five in 1989. Nearly half of 289 incidents of racially motivated vandalism and violence Klanwatch documented were related to minorities moving into mainly white neighborhoods.

Regarding incidents of violent ANTI-SEMITISM, in 1989 the ADL found 1,432 actions, an increase of 12 percent from 1988. This was the highest number of incidents in the eleven-year history of ADL's collection of such data. The numbers continued to rise to 1,685 reported cases in 1990 and 1,879 in 1991.

Antigay and antilesbian hate crimes are also on the increase. These occur not only on the street by unknown perpetrators but also in the work place, at schools and colleges, at home, and in prisons. In one study of about two thousand gays and lesbians in eight major cities, one in five reported being punched, hit, kicked, or beaten because of their sexual orientation. The NGLTF reports a 31-percent increase (from 1,389 in 1990 to 1,822 in 1991) in crimes against lesbians and gays in New York City, Boston, Chicago, Minneapolis-St. Paul, and San Francisco. A similar study of these cities and Los Angeles showed an increase of 42 percent from 1989 to 1990. Violence has probably increased against gays and lesbians because of the fear and HOMOPHOBIA generated by the ACQUIRED IMMUNE DEFICIENCY SYNDROME (AIDS) epidemic. Another reason, suggests the NGLTF, is backlash against gays and lesbians who have come out of the closet. As with other groups, homosexual victims of hate crime are also reporting it more freely.

Hate crimes against national groups often fluctuate with U.S. foreign policy. Certainly German and Japanese Americans were victims during World War II.

More recently, Arab Americans experienced violence before and during the Persian Gulf War. Incidents targeted Palestinians, Kuwaitis, and Lebanese as well as Iraqis. The American Arab Anti-Defamation Committee found eight times as many anti-Arab incidents in the last five months of 1990 as in the first seven months, with another increase during Operation Desert Storm. The committee and other groups continue to track and protest not only hate crimes but the biased news coverage and educational materials which they believe set the stage for stereotyping, PREJUDICE, and crime.

White Supremacist Groups. White supremacist organizations are typically equated with hate groups. While the majority of hate crimes are not committed by organized white supremacists, some of the most famous crimes have been. The perpetrators of hate crimes may well share the attitudes of the white power movement. According to the Center for Democratic Renewal, wherever white supremacist groups are active, there are also high levels of bigoted violence. Just as hate crimes are increasing, so, too, there appears to be a small but steady growth in the white supremacist movement.

Klanwatch has identified 346 distinct hate groups that each have their own leadership and structure. These can be grouped into four major divisions. Best known is the KU KLUX KLAN, whose white-robed Klansmen and cross-burnings have signified hatred and intimidation to many for more than one hundred years. In 1987, the United Klans of America were found liable for the lynching of Michael Donald, and the $7 million they were ordered to pay in damages nearly devastated that organization. Another group is the Christian Identity movement, which holds that white Anglo-Saxons are God's chosen people and that Jews are the descendants of Satan. The group is important for unifying racist organizations behind a religious idea and exposing many Christians to the racist aspects of the white power movement. Third are the NEO-NAZI organizations that believe in anti-Semitism and the ideology of Adolf Hitler. Fourth and closely related is the fastest-growing part of the white power movement, the young neo-Nazi skinheads. They often display the Nazi swastika at rallies and provide security for other leaders of the movement. Reports suggest that the skinheads are the most likely group to be involved in violent hate crimes. Tom Metzger, the leader of White Aryan Resistance, was found guilty of inciting several skinheads to kill an Ethiopian immigrant and ordered to pay a large portion of a

Skinheads hosting a 1989 neo-Nazi rally in Idaho hold a press conference. (AP/Wide World Photos)

$12.5 million settlement.

Hate crimes represent the tip of a large iceberg of American PREJUDICE and DISCRIMINATION. Ideologies such as RACISM, ETHNOCENTRISM, NATIVISM, ANTI-SEMITISM, SEXISM, and heterosexism come to the surface and are manifested in acts of violence or harassment. Various tensions, including intergroup rivalry and economic competition, seem to create a favorable atmosphere for hate crimes. Such crimes may also be more common in environments lacking a strong commitment to justice and civil rights.

SUGGESTED READINGS. For a historical view of hate crimes, see *Racial and Religious Violence in America: A Chronology* (1991) by Michael Newton and Judy Newton. *Responding to Hate Crimes* (1992) by the Human Rights Resource Center in San Rafael, California, provides a more contemporary approach. Legislation on hate crimes is covered in articles in law journals such as Joseph A. Fernandez's article "Bringing Hate Crime into Focus," in *Harvard Civil Rights-Civil Liberties Law Review,* no. 1 (1991), pp. 261-293, and Peter Finn's "Bias Crime: Difficult to Define, Difficult to Prosecute," in *Criminal Justice* 3 (1989), pp. 19-23, 47-48. An excellent book is *Hate Crimes: Confronting Violence Against Lesbians and Gay Men* (1992), edited by Gregory Herek and Kevin Berrill.— *Betty A. Dobratz*

Hate-speech codes: Measures taken by many American colleges and universities in the late 1980's and early 1990's to prohibit derogatory language or acts directed at members of particular racial, ethnic, religious, or other minority groups.

In the 1980's, sporadic but alarming acts of violence as well as malicious campus spoofs and satire aimed at minorities triggered the codes. For example, fraternities at the University of Wisconsin sponsored activities such as a slave auction and "Harlem Room" with participants in blackface. At a time when higher education was becoming more diverse and multicultural, partly as a result of landmark CIVIL RIGHTS LEGISLATION and AFFIRMATIVE ACTION programs, the emergence in the 1980's of intolerance and RACISM on some of the most prestigious American college campuses caught many administrators and officials off guard. Such incidents were attributed to antagonistic attitudes toward affirmative action programs or the perceived liberal bias and pressure to be "politically correct" ascribed by some to university and college administrations, faculties, and staffs.

In response, some educational institutions modified existing campus student conduct codes or enacted new codes of behavior to protect minorities. Disciplinary action for those who infringed the codes ranged from public apologies to expulsion. By early 1992, more than one hundred higher education institutions had followed the University of Michigan's lead in banning "hate speech." Manifestations of such speech were racist, sexist, anti-Semitic, and homophobic invective.

Conservatives charged the universities with the introduction of "thought police" and with violations of freedom of speech. The complex issue divided organizations that had been traditional supporters of both civil rights and civil liberties, such as the AMERICAN CIVIL LIBERTIES UNION (ACLU) and the American Association of University Professors. When initially challenged in court, the hate-speech codes were found to be in violation of guarantees of free speech under the First Amendment of the U.S. CONSTITUTION. In the case of Wisconsin, for example, the code that it passed in 1989 and rescinded in 1992 was only applicable to hate speech meant to intimidate individuals rather than actions meant to harass an entire group; thus, it would not have affected the very groups whose racist activities prompted the code.

The heated debate over these codes highlighted difficulties and tensions American colleges and universities experienced in the process of diversifying student bodies and introducing elements of MULTICULTURALISM into campus life and the curriculum.

SUGGESTED READINGS. For information on hate-speech codes, restrictive conduct codes, and related multicultural issues in higher education, see two issues of the journal *Change* that present generally favorable views of these approaches and advocate multiculturalism in academia: *Change* 23 (September/October 1991) contains a number of articles relating to the topic, and *Change* 25 (January/February 1993) contains Lynne V. Cheney's "Multiculturalism Done Right: Taking Steps to Build Support for Change," p. 8. For opposing views, see *The New Republic* 204 (February 18, 1991, a special issue entitled "Race on Campus") and Dinesh D'Souza's *Illiberal Education: The Politics of Race and Sex on Campus* (1991).

Hawaiian ethnic diversity: Hawaii holds an extraordinary place in American history, demographics, and MULTICULTURALISM. The original inhabitants were not American Indians but Polynesians who came to the islands by canoe around the year 300. No one ethnic

Statue of King Kamehameha, who unified the Hawaiian Islands in the 1790's. (National Archives)

group is in the majority there, although Asian Americans/Pacific Islanders combined form 61.8 percent of the population (the highest Asian concentration in the United States). There is much interaction between racial and ethnic groups, and the state has the nation's highest rate of INTERMARRIAGE (about half of all marriages are thought to be interracial). The University of Hawaii is home to the East-West Center, which encourages exchanges between Asia and the United States and symbolizes the state's uniquely Asian role and identity.

Data from the census of 1990 reveal a remarkable diversity. Of a total population of 1,108,229, 61.8 percent were Asian/Pacific Islander, 33 percent were white, 12 percent were native Hawaiian (descendants of the early Polynesians), 2 percent were black, and .5 percent were American Indian. The three largest Asian national groups were Japanese Americans (247,486), Filipino Americans (168,682), and Chinese Americans (68,804). Immigrant cultural ties are strongly maintained: About one in four Hawaiians spoke a language other than English at home.

The first Hawaiians had no contact with non-Polynesian culture until 1778, when the English explorer Captain James Cook reached the islands. At that time, the native population was thought to be about 250,000. King Kamehameha unified the islands in the 1790's, and he and his heirs ushered in a period of prosperity as well as cultural and political development. By the 1820's when the first American Christian missionaries arrived, they found a shrunken population of about 140,000, presumably the result of disease. Missionaries were to have a profound impact on Hawaiian culture, exerting themselves to stamp out traditional religion and customs while introducing a phonetic writing system for the Hawaiian language. By 1853, the population was still 95 percent native Hawaiian, but this was soon to change dramatically.

The growth of sugar plantations in the mid-1800's brought about the need for plentiful labor, and various Asian groups were imported as contract workers, often laboring under harsh, exploitive conditions. The first large group to arrive was Chinese. They were followed by a massive wave of Japanese (180,000 by 1908). Some Japanese soon left Hawaii to pursue their fortunes in the American West. After the GENTLEMEN'S AGREEMENT between the United States and Japan halted the importing of Japanese workers, the plantations began recruiting Filipinos (125,000 between 1907 and 1932). By this time, Queen Liliuokalani had been deposed in an American-led coup (1893), and

Hawaii had been annexed to the United States (1898) and become a territory (1900).

The population in 1900 was already diverse and lacking a majority. Japanese were 39 percent of the total, native Hawaiians were 26 percent, and Chinese were 17 percent. European groups such as the Portuguese were also part of the ethnic mix. By 1910, the native Hawaiian population had dropped to 13 percent

In 1964, Patsy Takemoto Mink of Hawaii became the first Japanese American woman to be elected to the U.S. House of Representatives. (National Japanese American Historical Society)

of the territory's population—a proportion maintained throughout the twentieth century. The word *haole* was originally used to describe any non-Hawaiian, but it eventually came to mean Caucasian.

Haoles and Japanese have dominated public life in the islands for most of the 1900's, although Chinese Hawaiians have been active in commerce. For example, about one-third of the seats in the state legislature are held by Japanese Hawaiians, and Daniel Ken INOUYE became the state's Representative in the House and then one of its senators in the U.S. Congress in 1959. In the same year, Hawaii became the fiftieth state, and the militarization of its lands followed quickly. By 1990, one-fifth of the population (most of them whites and blacks) worked for the military.

Increasing Westernization, militarization, and the phenomenal growth of the tourist industry all had a devastating effect on the native Hawaiian population. They tend to be the poorest, least educated Hawaiians, and have had to fight *haole* authorities to maintain their language, culture, and religion. Although some land reform was attempted in the 1960's, native Hawaiians did not receive what they believed to be their fair share. Since the 1970's, some Hawaiian natives have been active in a SOVEREIGNTY MOVEMENT that would free the state from American domination. Others have been leaders in a Hawaiian cultural renaissance, somewhat akin to the ETHNIC HERITAGE REVIVAL on the mainland, in which masters of the ancient hula dance and chant as well as traditional crafts and other traditions are honored in festivals and museums.

A small number of native Hawaiians continue to worship the gods of their ancestors. The state's largest religious group is Catholics (20 percent); Mormons are the largest Protestant group. Buddhists and Shintoists are also prominent.

SUGGESTED READINGS. For more information, see Andrew W. Lind's *Hawaii's People* (4th ed., 1980) and *People and Cultures of Hawaii: A Psychocultural Profile* (1980), edited by John McDermott, Jr., Wen-Shing Tseng, and Thomas W. Maretzki. On native Hawaiians and militarization, see Francine du Plessix Gray's *Hawaii: The Sugar-Coated Fortress* (1972).

Hawaiian natives and the sovereignty movement:
Since 1980, native Hawaiians of Polynesian origin (locally known as *kanakas*) have been increasingly aware of and vocal about their rights as the original inhabitants of the Hawaiian Islands. A popular political theme among *kanakas* is sovereignty or self-rule, though there are disagreements as to how sovereignty can best be achieved. Some advocates of sovereignty envision a totally separate Hawaiian nation, independent of the United States, in which other Americans would be treated as foreign nationals. Other natives seek the rights now possessed by American Indians to govern their own affairs on reservation or treaty-guaranteed land. Sovereignty advocates seem to agree, however, that land currently owned by the state and federal governments as well as by private individuals who are not *kanakas* should be turned over to native Hawaiians for their own use.

Sovereignty advocates point to the overthrow of the native Hawaiian government of Queen Lydia Liliuokalani in 1893 by a combined contingent of American plantation owners, merchants, and U.S. sailors and marines as the key event in their political subjugation. Though the U.S. government had signed a number of treaties with the Hawaiian monarchy that guaranteed Hawaii's independence, the United States recognized the coup of 1893 and annexed Hawaii as a territory in 1898. The provisional government that took power after the coup seized 1.75 million acres of land and ceded it to the United States at the time of annexation; this holding represents about 37 percent of the Hawaiian Islands. Sovereignty advocates who promote the return of this land to *kanakas* note that while native Hawaiians constitute about 20 percent of the state's population, they own only 2 percent of the land. The major employers in Hawaii—the tourist industry and the U.S. military—provide primarily low-wage work opportunities, leaving many native Hawaiians without satisfactory incomes in an area of soaring real estate prices. Native Hawaiians have the highest unemployment rates, the lowest education levels, and the shortest life expectancies in Hawaii.

In addition, sovereignty advocates seek immediate access to 187,000 acres of land set aside in 1921 by the U.S. government for the use of native Hawaiians; as of 1990, only 32,000 acres had been leased to native Hawaiians while nearly 20,000 applicants remained on a waiting list for the rest. Sovereignty advocates have also asked for native control of several national parks, including Haleakala National Park on Maui and Volcanos National Park on the island of Hawaii, both of which are popular tourist destinations.

SUGGESTED READINGS. On the sovereignty movement in greater detail, see Linda S. Parker's *Native American Estate: The Struggle Over Indian and Hawaiian Lands* (1989) and Melody Kapilialoha MacKenzie's *Native Hawaiian Rights Handbook* (1991). For more information on the history of Hawaii and in particular on the events of 1893-1898, consult Gavan Daws's *Shoal of Time: A History of the Hawaiian Islands* (1974), and Ralph S. Kuykendall's multivolume work, *The Hawaiian Kingdom* (1938-1967).

Hawaiian Sugar Planters' Association: Organization of the major sugar producers in Hawaii who worked to improve the industry. The organization dates back to 1850, when it was called the Royal Hawaiian Agricultural Society. Over the years, sugar became Hawaii's most important crop, and a stable labor force became

S. I. Hayakawa, elected to the U.S. Senate in 1976. (AP/Wide World Photos)

increasingly difficult to obtain. Changing its name to the Hawaiian Sugar Planters' Association in 1895, the group lobbied Congress for legislation to aid the sugar industry, recruited foreign plantation workers, and dealt harshly with efforts by those laborers to unionize. The group also conducted research into ways to improve sugar production and the production of other crops.

Hayakawa, Sessue (Kintaro Hayakawa; June 10, 1890, Naaura Township, Honshu, Japan—Nov. 23, 1973, Tokyo, Japan): Japanese American actor. Hayakawa first came to the United States in 1909 to study political science, but in 1913, while in Los Angeles en route back to Japan, he saw a play at the Japanese Theatre and decided to become an actor. Over the next decade, he appeared in many plays and silent films and even started his own production company in 1918. During the 1920's, Hayakawa returned to Japan and became a Buddhist priest. His most notable films include *The Cheat* (1915) and *The Bridge on the River Kwai* (1957), for which he received a Golden Globe award. A devout Buddhist who spoke eight languages and included religious training at his Tokyo drama school, he called his 1960 autobiography *Zen Showed Me the Way . . . to Peace, Happiness, and Tranquility.*

Hayakawa, S. I. [Samuel Ichiyé] (July 18, 1906, Vancouver, British Columbia, Canada—Feb. 27, 1992, Greenbrae, Calif.): Japanese American semanticist and politician. Hayakawa had a long career teaching English at the University of Wisconsin, Illinois Institute of Technology, University of Chicago, and San Francisco State University, from 1936 through 1973. His central interest was language, and his published work includes *Language in Action* (1941) and *Language in Thought and Action* (1949). As president of San Francisco State University in the late 1960's and early 1970's, Hayakawa was controversial for his adamant refusal to consider the demands being made by student protesters, particularly African American students, who were disrupting the campus; he called in the police to quell demonstrations. He was elected in 1976 to the United States Senate and in 1983 was a special adviser to the U.S. Secretary of State. In the 1980's, Hayakawa was a vocal supporter of making English the official language of the United States.

Hayes, Ira (Jan., 1923, Pima Indian Reservation, Ariz.—Jan. 24, 1955, Sacaton Indian Reservation, Ariz.): Pima Indian U.S. war hero. As a U.S. Marine during World War II, Hayes was one of the six servicemen in the classic photograph of the second flag raising on Iwo Jima's Mount Suribachi on February 23, 1945. He was one of the three who survived the lengthy battle for U.S. occupation of Iwo Jima, but he was unable to cope with postwar civilian life or with the fame the picture brought; Hayes died of conditions related to alcoholism.

Hayworth, Rita (Margarita Carmen Cansino; Oct. 17, 1918, Brooklyn, N.Y.—May 14, 1987, New York, N.Y.): Latina actor. Hayworth began dancing at her father's nightclub at age twelve and began her film career in 1935 under the name Rita Cansino. Married to businessman Edward Judson in 1937, she soon changed her name and image, dying her hair auburn for greater casting opportunities. Films such as *You'll Never Get Rich* (1941) and *You Were Never Lovelier* (1942), both with Fred Astaire, established Hayworth as a major star. During World War II, she was the classic pin-up girl, and her 1946 film *Gilda* consolidated her reputation as a "love goddess." Over the next three decades, Hayworth's long list of credits included *Salome* (1953), *Pal Joey* (1957), *The Money Trap* (1966), and her final film *The Wrath of God* (1972). In her later years, Hayworth suffered from Alzheimer's disease; her daughter Yas-

Latina film star Rita Hayworth (Margarita Carmen Cansino) in a 1940's glamour photo. (Hearst Newspaper Collection, University of Southern California Library)

min was a vocal activist in lobbying for research to combat the disease.

Head of household, female: Increasingly common demographic category and living situation in the late twentieth century, related to the feminization of poverty and changes in American family life. The number of American families headed by women rose from 10.1 percent in 1950 to 17 percent in 1990. This shift was fueled by social changes such as a rise in the DIVORCE rate and the number of women in the workforce, along with the economic independence encouraged by FEMINISM.

By the late 1900's, the trend toward more female-headed households was worrisome to many observers, from religious leaders to social workers to politicians. The people in such households appear to be a population at risk, not because they are headed by a female per se but for various socioeconomic problems associated with that living arrangement. In 1990, female-headed households represented more than half (53.1 percent) of all poor families in the United States. One-third of all female-headed households lived below the poverty line, with consistently higher rates of POVERTY for African American and Latino families in this category. The census of 1990 found that 67.1 percent of the families headed by a woman were white, 31.1 percent were black, and 2.8 percent were of other races. Within racial and ethnic groups, nearly half of African Americans and about one-quarter of American Indians and Latinos, lived in female-headed households, compared to only 14.4 percent of European Americans. Various studies suggest that children from single-parent households are more likely to be poor, have emotional or behavioral problems, drop out of high school, get pregnant as teenagers, abuse drugs, engage in crime, or join gangs.

For some women, single parenthood is a conscious, positive choice of lifestyle. This is more often the case with middle- and upper-class women for reasons such as the lack of eligible partners, the importance of career, or the impact of feminism on their personal values. For most women, however, single parenthood presents numerous challenges and obstacles. The complexities of the female head of household population received much publicity in 1992 as a result of Vice President Dan Quayle's attack on single motherhood as portrayed in the television series Murphy Brown, in which an affluent television news anchorwoman decided not to marry the father of her child. Single mothers of various backgrounds were offended when Quayle decried the show's heroine as setting a bad example, charging him with a lack of understanding of their situation, particularly in view of his disapproval of ABORTION. Quayle and his supporters maintained that the real issue was the dramatic increase in births out of wedlock and that, while a wealthy professional might be able to rear a child alone, teenagers and women with low incomes should not be given a romanticized image of single motherhood.

Childbirth and Marriage. Having a child out of wedlock no longer carries the stigma that it once did in certain American communities. Indeed, more unwed women are having children and remaining single. In the 1960's, 52.2 percent of unmarried women between fifteen and thirty-four who were pregnant with their first child married before the child was born. By the late 1980's, the number had fallen almost by half to 26.6 percent. In 1990, 22.6 percent of American female-headed households were run by women who had never married (17.9 percent represented married women with an absent husband; 23.3 percent were widows; and 36.3 percent were divorced).

There are important variations among racial and ethnic groups in patterns of CHILDBIRTH and MARRIAGE. For example, the percent of African American babies born to single mothers rose from 15 percent in 1959 to 57 percent in 1982. This was at a time when the proportion of African American men who were employed had dropped significantly, from 80 percent in 1930 to 56 percent in 1983. From the point of view of many African American women, there is an alarm-

paths by which a woman can become the head of a family. In addition to bearing children outside marriage, women may assume the position through divorce and widowhood. With significantly rising divorce rates, the chances of a woman experiencing marital disruption have increased considerably. Since divorced women are younger than in the past, there is greater likelihood that they will have children living with them. More than 90 percent of American mothers

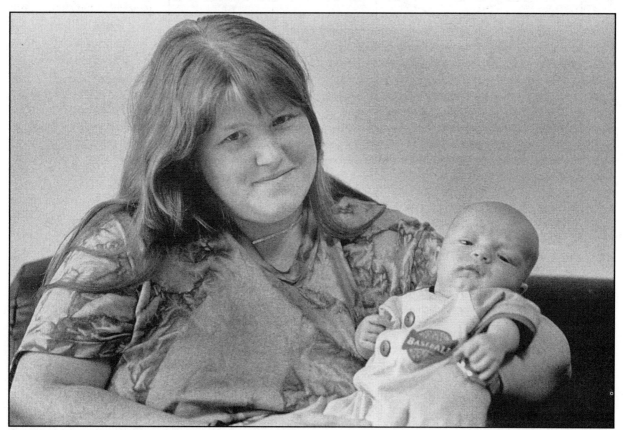

Poverty is a crushing problem for many single mothers. This woman and her child are shown in a Salvation Army shelter. (Mary M. Langenfeld)

ing shortage of "marriageable" males for a complex set of reasons, including the relatively high proportion of young black men who are incarcerated or killed. Other factors that may also favor single-parent household patterns among minorities include male alcoholism or drug abuse, the valuing of childbearing as an attribute of womanhood, the shunning of abortion, the absence of mates left behind by immigrant women, the loss of mates to civil war in one's homeland, and marital tensions among immigrants adjusting to American culture.

Divorce and Child Custody. There are different

receive custody of the children after DIVORCE. While it would seem that either parent could fulfill the role of custodial person, and despite both being on equal footing under the law in any custodial dispute, in practice women prevail. A clearly unfit mother (that is, one who is unstable, negligent, or "immoral") may be denied custody. Yet there is widespread assumption that the best interests of a child lie with the maternal parent. Traditionally, she is supposed to be the parent best suited to protect and nourish the offspring. It is commonly believed that children need their mother's care far more than their father's and that a woman's

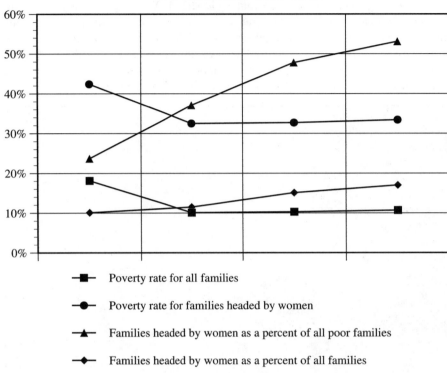

Poverty Rates for Families with Female Heads of Households: 1960-1990

— ■ — Poverty rate for all families

— ● — Poverty rate for families headed by women

— ▲ — Families headed by women as a percent of all poor families

— ♦ — Families headed by women as a percent of all families

Source: Data are from Carol Foster, ed. *Women's Changing Role.* Table 6.9. Wylie, Tex.: Information Plus, 1992.

nature makes CHILD REARING more essential to her than it is to a man. One California court summed it up in *Washburn v. Washburn* (1942): "No one will give such complete and selfless devotion and so unhesitatingly and unstintingly make the sacrifices which the welfare of the child demands as the child's own mother."

A 1982 study reported that 56 percent of the sole-custodial fathers thought that their social status had improved as a result of being the sole-custodial parent while 94 percent of the sole-custodial mothers thought that their status had declined. On the average, divorced women and the minor children in their households experienced a 73 percent decline in their standard of living in the first year after divorce, whereas their former husbands experienced a 42 percent rise in their standard of living.

Divorced women, like unmarried women with children, tend to set up their own households rather than move in with relatives. This phenomenon reflects women's increased economic independence as well as a trend away from extended family patterns throughout American society.

Though single mothers generally have the children living with them, the fathers are mandated to assist financially. The default rate, however, is very high. Nonsupport by absent fathers is not limited to lower wage earners. Seventy-five percent of all delinquents in child support can afford to make payments. Half of the children affected would be out of POVERTY if their mothers received the proper child support checks.

Employment, Unemployment, and Welfare. As early as the 1840's, women used petition campaigns to persuade state legislators to enact married women's property acts to give women control of their earnings and a greater legal say in the custody of their children. Some 150 years later, women are often still in straitened circumstances. Whereas immigrant groups entering the urban labor market at the bottom gradually improved their positions, women as a class have not been as successful.

Among the factors holding single working women back are occupational segregation; employers' view of female employees as temporary or secondary workers; and the absence of high-quality, affordable CHILD CARE. Many of the disadvantages suffered by poor women are compounded by racism and DISCRIMINATION. About one-fifth of employed female family heads earn less than poverty-level income. The unemployment rate of female family heads is more than double that of male family heads.

A trend since the 1960's is for a higher rate of applications for public assistance by eligible families and an increasing acceptance rate on the part of welfare agencies. There has also been a raising of the income eligibility ceilings. In 1964, 29 percent of single mothers received Aid to Families with Dependent Children (AFDC). By 1972, the figure was 63 percent. The proportion dropped to 45 percent in 1988.

Some Americans believe that the "undeserving" poor are taking advantage of and cheating the system. President Ronald Reagan often told anecdotes about the "queen of the welfare cheats." Charles Murray, a neoconservative scholar, asserted that welfare directly encouraged women without husbands to procreate. Others claim that welfare programs actually contribute to the conditions that lead to poverty: illegitimacy, single-parent families, and limited incentives to seek employment.

AFDC. Female-headed families make up 20 percent of families with children, but they comprise 80 percent of those on AFDC; more than 50 percent of food stamp users; and more than 55 percent of households receiving Medicaid. "Welfare" is provided at a grudging, penurious level for most recipients. In 1988 in thirty-one states, the maximum amount for a family of three was less than half the amount fixed as the federally defined poverty level. There are also wide disparities among states. Maximum monthly payments for a family of four in 1991 were $144 in Mississippi and $155 in Alabama, but $824 in California and $990 in Alaska.

AFDC was established in 1935 as part of Social Security to help widows with children. Eventually it came to be the major assistance program for divorced, unmarried, or deserted women with children. In 1990, 41.4 percent of children receiving AFDC were black, 33.1 percent were white, 17.7 percent were Latino, 3.9 percent were Asian American, and 1.3 percent were American Indian.

Despite the popular impression that people stay on the dole forever, by the early 1990's nearly three of every ten AFDC families had received welfare benefits for less than one year, and a majority remained on the rolls for less than four years. Fewer than 8 percent received assistance without interruption for more than ten years.

The system itself has flaws that perpetuate dependence. By restricting its benefits for the most part to female-headed families with children, the system encourages the formation of such living units. The trade-off between what low-skilled working men and women can provide and what welfare can furnish tips

the balance in favor of the latter, especially when other benefits such as Medicaid are included. Some women do not marry because they are concerned about losing welfare benefits.

Other Legislative Remedies. In 1965 Daniel Moynihan of the Labor Department reported that the key to dealing with female-headed families and poverty was to improve the economic status of men so that they would become better providers. Moynihan attributed increases in crime, violence, and social unrest to a

Single parents must struggle to be both wage earners and caregivers. (James L. Shaffer)

system that allowed a large number of young males to grow up in broken families dominated by women. Others denied this causality and attributed the problems to a lack of economic resources for female-headed families with children.

Moynihan's remedy, the Nixon Administration's Family Assistance Plan, which was a guaranteed annual income to replace AFDC, failed to be enacted. It would have put a lower limit on the eligible incomes of all families, working and nonworking, single-parent and two-parent, as other industrialized nations do. It would have removed the penalty against intact and childless families. Instead, the Work Incentive Program of the 1970's placed the training and employment of men first.

Finally, in 1988, Congress passed the Family Security Act. It required states to create job opportunities and basic skills programs for single parents on welfare with children over three years of age. To ease the transition from welfare to work, the federal rules extended eligibility for Medicaid, food stamps, transportation assistance, and child care through the early stages of employment.

A popular remedy, workfare, has the disadvantage of placing recipients in low-skill jobs while increasing public costs with the expense of finding jobs, providing work allowances, and subsidizing CHILD CARE. Poorly paying jobs are unrealistic alternatives to income derived from drugs, prostitution, and other forms of crime.

There have been other proposals aimed at assisting female heads of households who are not poor. One example is Displaced Homemaker legislation, providing spouses who have focused their time and energies on homemaking with an opportunity to receive special occupational training and counseling before entering the labor market.

Social and Psychological Needs. The difficulties of single parenthood are not limited to the economic dimension. CHILD REARING is a full-time obligation. Without a partner, there may be no one to fall back on when there are conflicting obligations, such as attending to a sick child as well as work duties. A role model for a child of the opposite sex from the parent may also be absent. Without a partner, the solo parent may have insufficient private time and space for relaxation. Also, the pressures of single parenthood may cut the parent off from other adults, including prospective marital partners. Organizations and support groups such as Parents Without Partners try to address some of these needs, including the special needs of female heads of household.

SUGGESTED READINGS. For further insights readers are directed to *Rethinking Social Policy* (1992) by Christopher Jencks of Harvard University. Earlier studies of the feminization of poverty include Diana Pearce's "Women, Work and Welfare," in *Working Women and Families* (1979), edited by Karen Wolk Feinstein, and Heather L. Ross's "Poverty: Women and Children Lost," in *Economic Independence for Women* (1976), edited by Jane Roberts Chapman. On the effects of divorce on women with children, see Martha A. Fineman's *The Illusion of Equality: The Rhetoric and Reality of Divorce Reform* (1991) and Lenore J. Weitzman's *The Divorce Revolution: The Unexpected Social and Economic Consequences for Women and Children in America* (1985). Both books argue that current rules for divorce settlements leave most of these women without adequate economic resources to maintain their standard of living. The effects of single parenthood on children are discussed in Marian Wright Edelman's *Families in Peril: An Agenda for Social Change* (1987) and *Contemporary Families: A Handbook for School Professionals* (1992), edited by Mary E. Procidano and Celia B. Fisher.—*Martin Gruberg*

Head Start: One of the oldest and most successful programs developed as part of the WAR ON POVERTY under President Lyndon Johnson. Founded in 1965, Head Start is a comprehensive child development program intended to enhance the academic, social, and physical development of low-income children with the

Pueblo children in a Head Start program in Taos, New Mexico. (Elaine S. Querry)

support and participation of their families. By the early 1990's, about 622,000 children had been involved in this program, and it had become a widely respected model for education reform efforts.

Health and medicine: Efforts to promote health and prevent disease have not closed the gap in health status between Caucasians and racial minorities in the United States. Social, behavioral, and cultural factors, such as POVERTY, unemployment, poor diet, substance abuse, limited education and educational opportunity, and limited access to health care are often associated with poor health and help to explain differences between the state of health of majority and minority populations. Additional, immutable factors—biology and genetics—have brought about major race-specific illnesses such as sickle-cell anemia and Tay-Sachs disease, and have brought increasing attention to the health problems of older citizens.

Sickle-Cell Anemia. Sickle-cell disease (including sickle-cell anemia and thalassemia, a related hemoglo-

bin disorder sometimes termed Cooley's anemia), is one of the most common long-term illnesses in African American children. Although individuals of Greek, Italian, Puerto Rican, Spanish, French, Turkish, Middle Eastern, and Indian ancestry are also at increased risk, the disease appears milder than in Africans and their descendants. The disease occurs in about one in four hundred to five hundred births of individuals of African heritage; one in twelve individuals carries the sickle trait.

A blood hemoglobin disorder first described to the American medical community in 1910, sickle-cell anemia is characterized by distorted red blood cells that resemble sickles in shape. Such cells cannot pass through the small blood vessels, and thus form damaging clots. Any part of the body or any organ may be affected, especially the heart, lungs, kidneys, spleen, pelvic bones, and brain; chronic anemia is typical. The character and severity of the disease differ for various age groups. Only about half the children born with sickle-cell disease survive to adulthood; car-

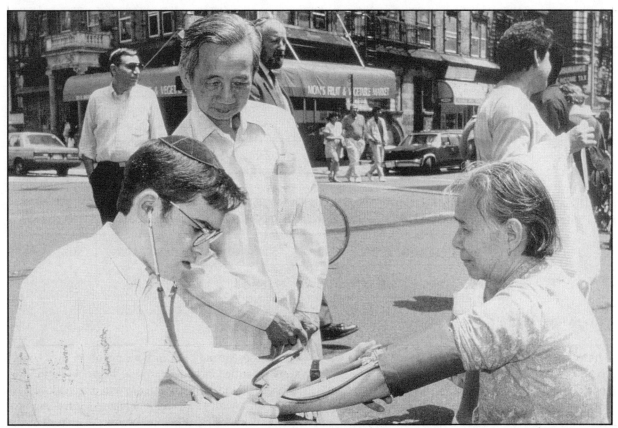

A gap exists between the health of Caucasians and that of minorities in the United States. Here, New Yorkers have their blood pressure tested. (Frances M. Roberts)

Americans Without Health Insurance: 1992

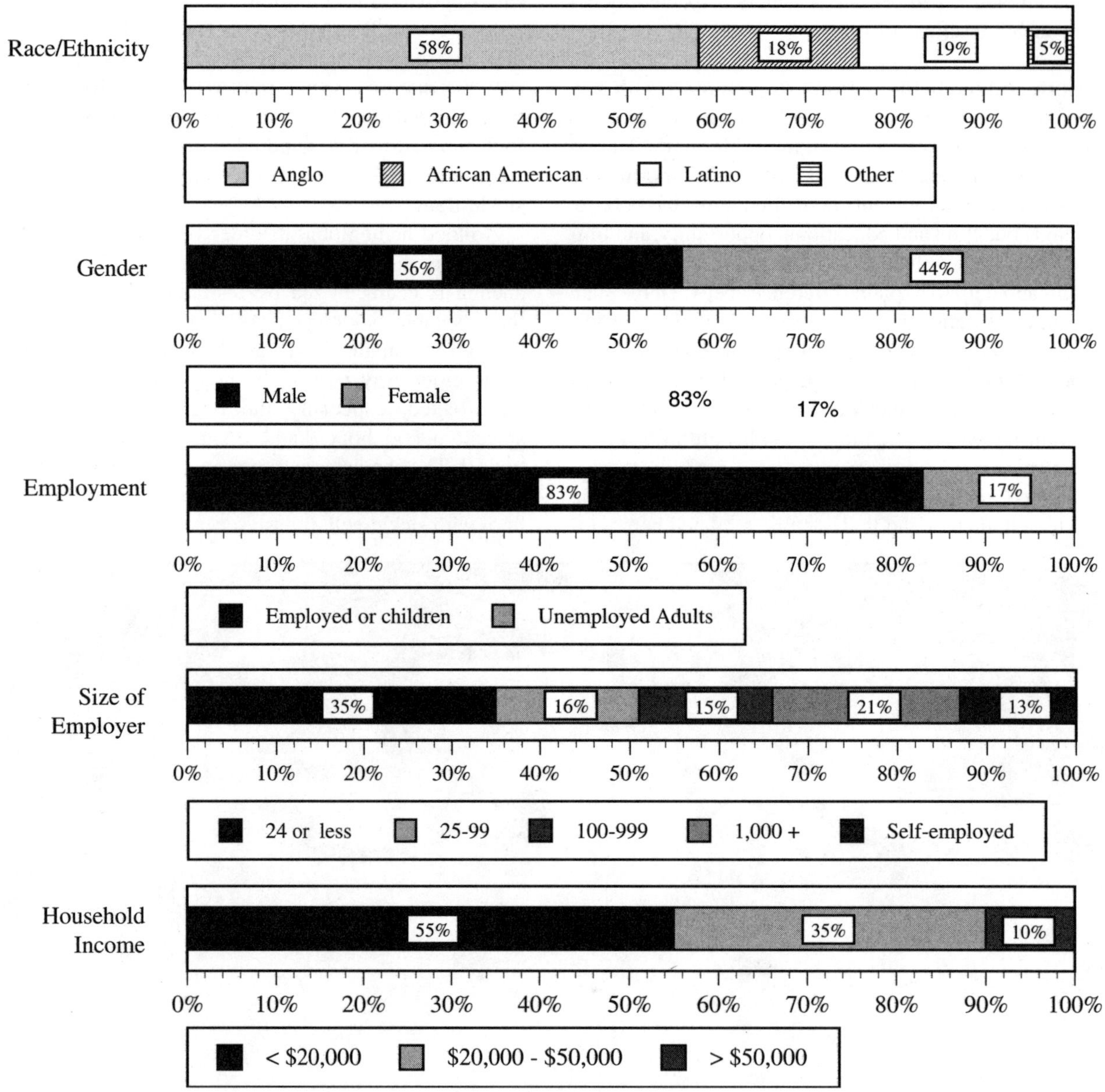

Race/Ethnicity

58% | 18% | 19% | 5%

0% 10% 20% 30% 40% 50% 60% 70% 80% 90% 100%

Anglo African American Latino Other

Gender

56% | 44%

0% 10% 20% 30% 40% 50% 60% 70% 80% 90% 100%

Male Female   83%   17%

Employment

83% | 17%

0% 10% 20% 30% 40% 50% 60% 70% 80% 90% 100%

Employed or children Unemployed Adults

Size of Employer

35% | 16% | 15% | 21% | 13%

0% 10% 20% 30% 40% 50% 60% 70% 80% 90% 100%

24 or less 25-99 100-999 1,000 + Self-employed

Household Income

55% | 35% | 10%

0% 10% 20% 30% 40% 50% 60% 70% 80% 90% 100%

< $20,000 $20,000 - $50,000 > $50,000

Source: Adapted from the *Los Angeles Times*.

riers of the disease, however, are more likely to survive to adulthood and pass their genes onto the next generation. In the early 1970's, media attention focused on sickle-cell anemia as a "neglected disease." Community groups concentrated on remedying that problem. New screening tests were developed, although prenatal diagnosis was not available immedi-

ately. Consequently, when both members of a couple were identified as being carriers, their only option was to forgo childbearing in order to avoid the risk of having a child with sickle-cell anemia. As screening programs were being promoted during a time of racial tension, some African Americans felt that the implication that certain blacks should not have children was racially motivated. Because of inadequate education, being identified as a carrier was mistakenly regarded by many as a personal health threat. Confidentiality problems ensued, and employment discrimination and questions about suitability for military service followed.

In 1972, Congress allocated funds for research and education through the National Sickle Cell Anemia Control Act through fiscal year 1975. In April, 1976, the National Sickle Cell Anemia, Cooley's Anemia, Tay-Sachs, and Genetic Diseases Act broadened the scope of the earlier act, authorizing programs on a wider range of genetic diseases. The act provided for basic or applied research, training, testing, counseling, and information and educational programs. It also contained assurances of "strict confidentiality of all test results, medical records, and other information regarding testing, diagnosis, counseling, or treatment." Testing of parents of newborns with sickle-cell trait has been useful in family counseling and has led to the fetal diagnosis of sickle-cell disease through amniocentesis and fetoscopy. Some states have also included routine sickle-cell screening in newborn testing programs. Those demonstrating abnormal results are transferred to a sickle-cell treatment center for confirmation.

Tay-Sachs Disease. A progressive degeneration of the nervous system, the disease is found primarily in children of Ashkenazi Jews from central and eastern Europe. The incidence of disease is about one in thirty-six hundred; the carrier frequency is one in thirty. The disease was first reported in 1881 by a British opthalmologist (Tay) and several years later by a New York neurologist (Sachs).

Symptoms of the disease increase in severity from infancy to age two. One characteristic sign is a cherry-red spot in the macula of both eyes. Early clinical manifestations are apathy and an excessive "startle reaction" to sound from infancy to six months of age. Gradually the infant loses head control and basic motor skills, as well as sight. After age two, the child remains in a vegetative state with an enlarged head and frequent and severe seizures. Generally death occurs before the child is five.

Other types of this disease exist, referred to as juvenile, adult, and late infantile. There is mental deterioration and progressive blindness in all three, but in the late juvenile or adult form, the life span ranges from five to ten years after onset.

Prior to 1970, couples bearing a child with Tay-Sachs disease who desired more children had limited options: adoption, chance, or artificial insemination by a donor without a family history of Tay-Sachs disease. Many such couples decided against additional children. In 1970 a prenatal screening procedure was developed so that Tay-Sachs disease could be diagnosed early enough to permit termination of the pregnancy. Heightened public and professional awareness created by mass screening and voluntary education and testing programs has led to an increase in counseling and educational information by rabbis, obstetricians, and family doctors.

Older Americans are the fastest-growing segment of the population, and geriatrics is a growing medical specialty. (Robert W. Ginn, Unicorn Stock Photos)

Health Care Issues for Older Americans. People over age sixty-five constitute the fastest-growing group in the American population. The latter decades of the twentieth century saw the growth of interest and medical advances in geriatrics, as well as public policy changes to better meet the health needs of older people.

The SOCIAL SECURITY ACT of 1965 contains the major public policy measures related to health care for older Americans through its health insurance programs, Medicare and Medicaid. The former is a federally administered health insurance program for qualified persons aged sixty-five and over and for persons with disabilities of all ages. Medicare, which is geared toward short-term illnesses and accidents, contains hospital insurance and medical insurance, which cover the major portion of necessary health services. Medicare controls virtually all health care options for many older Americans. Enactment of the Medicare Catastrophic Coverage Act of 1988 provided for chronic care for long-term disability.

Medicaid is a public assistance program for low-income and indigent persons of all ages. As applied to the elderly, Medicaid is designed to defray Medicare premium costs and expenses for those who have exhausted their Medicare benefits. Medicaid coverage varies by state. The Supplemental Security Income plan is a public assistance program available to persons of extremely limited resources.

The Patient Self-Determination Act of 1991 requires all hospitals and other health care facilities participating in Medicare and Medicaid programs to maintain written policies and procedures guaranteeing that every adult receiving medical care is given written information about patient involvement in treatment decisions. The information must describe an individual's rights under state law to accept or refuse treatment and to formulate advance directives (living will or durable power of attorney), and notify the patient about the written policies of the organization concerning these rights.

Members of minorities make up a comparatively small proportion of the rising numbers of older Americans. There are reports that the health of older minorities (especially blacks) is inferior to that of older whites. Minorities generally have shorter life expectancies than the majority population; morbidity data indicate that minorities also tend to have more chronic, debilitating health conditions. Researchers have determined that both socioeconomic and demographic factors unrelated to health contribute in significant part to those distinctions.

Access to Health Care. Differences in access to health care services can generally be traced to differences in insurance coverage. Because minorities are more likely to be poor and unemployed, they are more likely to be uninsured or unable to afford health care coverage. Other differences in utilization of health services by minorities result from cultural and geographic factors, such as the shortage of health care providers

in inner cities and rural areas where many minorities live. Community training programs have been established in an attempt to alleviate such problems. For example, in order to address the problem of lack of prenatal care and the high American infant mortality rate, some communities have advocated low-cost care by trained MIDWIVES in urban and rural clinics.

It has been reported, moreover, that uninsured patients and Medicaid patients tend to receive inferior quality care. A 1992 study found that uninsured patients experienced twice the risk of inferior health care than privately insured patients, particularly in the emergency rooms of public hospitals. Lack of medical insurance was also linked to worse medical outcomes and higher death rates, perhaps because medical problems are less likely to be detected early and treated consistently. The American political agenda in the early 1990's contained a strong commitment to health care reform and a movement toward universal access to health care in order to end past inequities.

SUGGESTED READINGS. *Genetic Variation and Disorders in People of African Origin* (1990), by James E. Bowman and Robert F. Murray, Jr., is one of many books containing detailed medical and clinical information about sickle-cell disease. *Genetic Diseases Among Ashkenazi Jews* (1979), edited by Richard M. Goodman and Arno G. Motulsky, is a thorough resource on Tay-Sachs disease. *Ethnicity and Health* (1988), edited by Winston A. Van Horne and Thomas V. Tonnesen contains a compilation of a variety of articles on problems of minorities.—*Marcia J. Weiss*

Health and medicine—American Indian: As a group, American Indians are among the least healthy people in the United States. Their ancestors were apparently healthy before the arrival of the Europeans. After contact, they were nearly wiped out by disease. Special health problems from diabetes to fetal alcohol syndrome continue to plague American Indians in the late twentieth century, who have access to both traditional healers and modern medicine.

The Precontact Period. Before contact with Europeans, American Indian health care was provided through a variety of traditional, holistic practices. These varied from culture to culture, but generally included the use of medicinal plants, sweat baths, massage, and magical cures to combat the effects of witchcraft, sorcery, or other supernaturally inflicted health problems. The most prominent health care provider was the shaman, a person who specialized in supernatural cures. Shamans would divine the source of an ailment, work countermagic, and engage in elaborate rituals designed to restore the patient to good health. To learn the necessary information required of a shaman often required several years, or even decades, of apprenticeship.

Archaeological and historical evidence suggests that American Indians were generally in good health prior to European contact. Christopher Columbus described the physical beauty of the Carib Indians he encountered in his voyages in the West Indies while Friar Diego de Landa wrote of the children of the Yucatán Peninsula in 1560: "They grew wonderfully handsome and fat during the first two years." This historical commentary is consistent with the findings of medical researchers in the twentieth century working with isolated Indian populations in South America. For example, in 1967 researchers noted the strong musculature, keen vision, lack of dental cavities, slow pulse, and low blood pressure of the Xavante Indians.

This is not to say that American Indians were free from health problems. Both archaeological evidence and modern research point to high rates of infant and maternal mortality. Examination of prehistoric skele-

Causes Of Death: American Indians Compared to All Americans, 1987

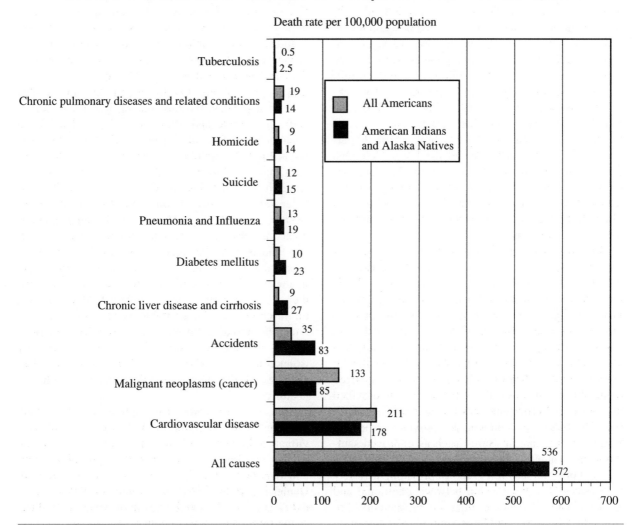

Death rate per 100,000 population

Cause	All Americans	American Indians and Alaska Natives
Tuberculosis	0.5	2.5
Chronic pulmonary diseases and related conditions	19	14
Homicide	9	14
Suicide	12	15
Pneumonia and Influenza	13	19
Diabetes mellitus	10	23
Chronic liver disease and cirrhosis	9	27
Accidents	35	83
Malignant neoplasms (cancer)	133	85
Cardiovascular disease	211	178
All causes	536	572

Source: Data are from Carol Foster, ed. *Minorities: A Changing Role in America.* Table 5.18. Wylie, Tex.: Information Plus, 1992.

tons and burial sites suggests the presence of osteoarthritis and other bone diseases, occasional tumors, kidney stones, and dental abscesses, as well as fractures from accidents or warfare. Evidence of health problems is generally more severe in settled, agricultural populations than in groups dependent on hunting and gathering, as is true worldwide.

The Postcontact Period. After contact with Europeans, large numbers of Indians contracted and/or died from infectious diseases introduced by Europeans. Diseases such as smallpox, measles, influenza, malaria, and yellow fever swept through Indian communities, often decimating them in the process. Having not been exposed to these diseases previously, Indians had no natural immunities or built-up resistance to them, making diseases that were often childhood problems in Europeans deadly to Indians. For example, by 1618, after approximately one hundred years of contact with Europeans, the native population of Mexico had plummeted from twenty million to about 1.6 million people. Similarly, when Hernando de Soto explored the southeastern United States in 1540, he found many towns abandoned because nearly all the inhabitants had died from disease. In the West, 90 percent of the American Indians of the lower Columbia River area had died by 1829, presumably from malaria. As epidemic disease spread among various tribes, traditional medical practices and healers were often discredited by their inability to deal with the new health problems.

The Modern Period. In the twentieth century, most American Indians have a variety of modern and traditional health services available to them. Since 1955, the U.S. government has provided modern health services for Indians living on reservations through the Division of Indian Health of the U.S. Public Health Service. Among the services provided are hospitals and dental clinics often staffed by professionals who are volunteering their time. In many cases, specialized medical care, such as surgical procedures, is provided by contractual arrangements with state or local facilities. The federal government also provides some preventive health care measures, such as improved sanitation and water testing. In addition, traditional healers still practice on many reservations, providing a variety of services. The relationship between traditional and modern health services is often complementary. For example, a Navajo might have a gall bladder operation in a hospital in Albuquerque, New Mexico, but return to the reservation for a Blessing Way ceremony performed by a shaman to restore the patient's harmony and relieve anxiety. Indians who do not live on reservations have to find their own health care—a situation that prompts some urban Indians such as senior citizens to return to the reservation.

In general, contemporary American Indians have poorer health than other Americans. Indians have significantly higher infant and maternal mortality rates and lower life expectancies than the general population. There is also a much higher rate of diseases such as trachoma, tuberculosis, and diabetes among American Indians, as well as gastrointestinal and nutritional disorders that are the results of poor sanitation and diet. While the rate of cancer and cardiovascular diseases are lower than in the general population, these diseases, too, are on the rise. In addition, Indians have notably high rates of ALCOHOLISM AND DRUG ABUSE.

Indian health problems are usually seen as the consequences of POVERTY and culture clashes between Indian and non-Indian society. Per capita incomes for Indians are among the lowest of any identifiable American population, thus making health care, especially preventive and critical care, as well as health insurance, unaffordable for many. Many older Indians speak English imperfectly or not at all, causing communication problems with their health care providers. In addition, many Indians do not share middle-class values about the use of time, efficiency, or other behaviors, prompting problems with keeping appointments and following therapies. Some American Indians who believe that their ailments are caused by a supernatural agent may not seek modern medical care in the belief that it will not prove effective. Finally, there is often a shortage of modern health providers on reservations. These problems are not unique to American Indians, but are shared by other American groups who are impoverished, who live in relatively isolated areas, or who do not share the middle-class attitudes of the dominant culture about health and health care.

SUGGESTED READINGS. Descriptions of pre-contact traditional care are found in most discussions of individual indigenous cultures. Eric Stone's *Medicine Among the American Indians* (1962) provides a general overview while herbal medicine is described in Daniel Moerman's *Medicinal Plants of Native America* (2 vols., 1986). On the health of American Indians at the time of European contact, see *Human Sickness and Health* by Corinne Shear Wood (1979) and *Vectors of Death: The Archaeology of European Contact*

(1987) by Ann Ramenofsky. The health services provided to modern American Indians are described in *Native American Heritage* (1976) by Merwyn Garbarino. Statistical studies comparing American Indian health with that of other American groups are produced annually by the U.S. Public Health Service. The problems of culture conflict in health care are well described in *Caring for Patients from Different Cultures* (1991) by Geri-Ann Galanti.—*David J. Minderhout*

Health and medicine—women's: The subject of women's health is inextricably interwoven with issues of RACE, CLASS, and socioeconomic position. Access to health care, minority status, disability, cultural expectations and practices, urban or rural residence, education, income, and age are among the other factors affecting women's health. Apart from these matters, certain medical conditions are most prevalent among women: osteoporosis, cancer, heart disease, liver disease, thyroid disease, and reproductive disease and dysfunction.

Women's Health Movement. Traditionally, widespread gender distinctions and inequities toward women have prevailed within the American health care system. There has been a definite tendency among physicians to make light of women's complaints, attributing them to menstrual or psychosomatic causes and quickly dismissing them. In the 1970's, the tenets of FEMINISM and consumerism combined as driving forces behind the women's self-help health movement in the area of obstetrics and gynecology. Advocates counseled women to demand serious answers from their doctors and to educate themselves about reproductive health. Many women's clinics opened in cities around the country as health care alternatives for women, particularly as legal

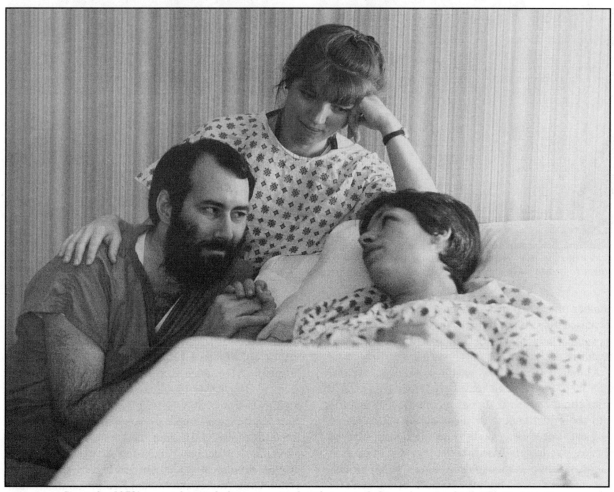

Since the 1970's, more hospitals have permitted midwives to help women give birth. (Photo Agora)

ABORTION and more forms of BIRTH CONTROL became available. The philosophy of this early movement was best expressed in the 1973 manual *OUR BODIES, OUR-SELVES*, by the Boston Women's Health Book Collective.

Some aspects of this feminist approach found their way into mainstream health care, as in the rise in numbers of hospitals allowing MIDWIVES or the provision of more homelike birthing rooms. Meanwhile, the

a study and concern about possible harm to the unborn fetus, as well as potential lawsuits if fetal damage occurred, were also cited as reasons for excluding women. Medications prescribed for both sexes were only tested on males. Although scientists recognized differences in the effect of various drugs on males and females because of metabolic processes, they were not considered of major concern.

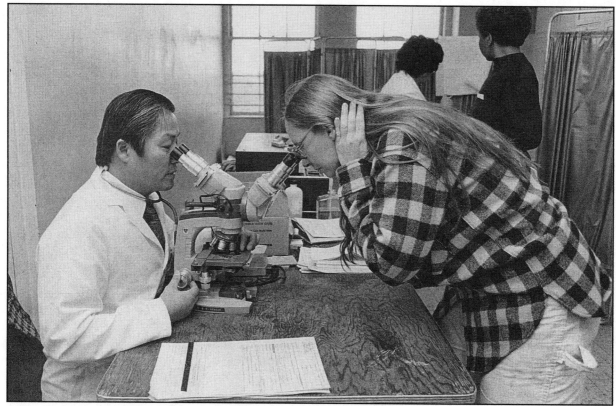

A New York woman and her doctor look at the woman's Pap smear under a microscope; poor women are less likely than others to obtain such screening tests regularly. (Hazel Hankin)

number of women doctors increased, and momentum increased for a more broadly based women's health movement addressing the full spectrum of women's health issues.

Although they utilize health services more often than men, women had long been generally excluded from clinical research studies on disease and inquiries into the effectiveness of medications and medical-surgical procedures. Aside from high costs, this exclusion was largely based on the fear that the participation of fertile women in drug studies would produce inaccurate research findings because of women's reproductive cycles. Fear of pregnancy occurring during

Change came in response to policymakers' recognition of women's health as a public concern and the urgent need for health care programs to address issues central to women's health. Since the 1980's, many hospitals have opened centers devoted to treating women. The early 1990's saw the establishment of various research initiatives to study women's health care services and disease prevention. In 1990, the National Institutes of Health (NIH) issued new research guidelines encouraging inclusion of women and minorities in clinical studies. In 1991, NIH and the Alcohol, Drug Abuse, and Mental Health Administration required research grant applicants to design studies with "gender representation appropriate to the known incidence/prevalence [in the population] of the disease or condition being studied."

Development of a comprehensive women's health specialty has been proposed to resolve the gender gap in health care and eliminate fragmentation. Proponents of the plan assert that it would address the following unmet health care needs of women: reproductive treatment issues that internists are not educated to handle, nonreproductive problems that obstetrician/gynecologists (ob/gyns) are not prepared to address, and other conditions that family practitioners are ill-equipped to treat. Alternative suggestions include altering medical school curricula to incorporate greater emphasis on women's health, retraining physicians, giving physician assistants and nurses a larger role in routine health care, and establishing an interdisciplinary academic graduate program in women's health. Opponents maintain that creation of a women's health specialty might result in "ghettoizing" women's issues by isolating them from mainstream medicine, thereby drawing fewer trainees and lowering earning capacity. They also point to a duplication in care with that of ob/gyns.

Socioeconomic Aspects of Health. Poverty is associated with poor health for both sexes, but the combination of POVERTY and low social status is particularly detrimental to women's health. More women than men are poor, since women's increased longevity causes them to endure on fixed incomes for a greater proportion of their lives. At age sixty-five, women have an average life expectancy of eighteen additional years compared with fourteen years for men. After age eighty-five, there are only forty-five men per one hundred women. Minority women are more likely to be poor than white women, with one-third of black women and more than one-fourth of Latinas living below the poverty line. An increasing number of women are also HEADS OF HOUSEHOLD. Studies indicate that female-headed families tend to be poorer than families headed by a male or a married couple.

Inadequate health insurance is a problem of marked severity for minority women, who are overrepresented among poor women. A 1989 survey conducted by the Bureau of the Census revealed that more than one-third of the Mexican American population, one-fifth of the Puerto Rican population, and one-fourth of the Cuban American population is uninsured, compared with one-fifth of the black population and one-tenth of the white population. Insufficient coverage as well

as lack of insurance affects women's use of health care services generally. The uninsured normally use ambulatory care less than persons with insurance coverage. Routine screening tests such as Pap smears, breast examinations and mammography, blood pressure monitoring, and glaucoma testing are less frequent among uninsured and socioeconomically disadvantaged women.

Lack of employment, income, and education can threaten reproductive health. Unemployed women do not have private coverage for maternity care, and government-provided Medicaid coverage is inadequate. Insufficient dissemination of health care information accounts in part for the fact that nearly 40 percent of African American women and one-fourth of all women in the United States do not receive prenatal care during the first trimester of pregnancy.

Age is another link uniting illness and poverty. The special health care needs of older Americans constitute a heavy burden on the health care system. Older females are twice as likely as older males to be residents of nursing homes. Inadequate Medicare coverage for nursing home care is associated with a higher rate of impoverishment.

Nutritional problems are also greater in women than men, in part because of women's reproductive role and correspondingly greater nutritional requirements. Again there is a strong connection between malnutrition and poverty. Eating disorders such as anorexia nervosa (extreme self-induced dietary restriction resulting in starvation) and bulimia (intentional purging of ingested food) are common disorders among adolescent women in a society in which social pressures and concerns about body image are paramount.

Reproductive Health. Sexually transmitted diseases—ACQUIRED IMMUNE DEFICIENCY SYNDROME (AIDS), caused by the human immunodeficiency virus (HIV), and various reproductive tract infections—are diseases associated with sexual practices. The HIV virus is primarily transmitted through sexual contact, though contact with tainted blood (HIV-contaminated transfusions, intravenous drug use, accidental needlesticks, and contact with an open wound) is another common means of transmission. Infected mothers can transmit the virus to their unborn fetuses as well as to breast-fed infants. Minority women's greater vulnerability to reproductive tract infections and HIV often results from their severely limited means of protection against infection and from strong cultural taboos against denying sex to partners. Many HIV-infected women are drug users or partners of drug users, and their behavior can put their babies at risk of contracting congenital syphilis.

In 1990, the largest proportional increase in AIDS cases occurred in women, who tend to enter treatment programs later than men and at a later state in their illness. AIDS constitutes the leading killer of women between the ages of fifteen and forty-five in several major American cities.

Prior to the legalization of ABORTION with the *Roe v. Wade* case of 1973, many American women suffered health problems, infertility, and even death at the hands of "back-room" abortionists. The availability of oral contraceptives and safe, legal abortion have since combined to make contraception and pregnancy matters of personal choice. Depo-Provera, an injectable contraceptive, and Norplant, a reversible, subdermal (under the skin) time-released hormonal implant with a five-year duration, were approved for use in the United States in the early 1990's.

Infertility rates also vary by race and income group.

Women in a prenatal exercise class. (Hazel Hankin)

Married black women have an infertility rate one and one-half times higher than that of married white women. Factors contributing to infertility include sickle-cell anemia (which primarily strikes people of African American ancestry); pelvic inflammatory disease resulting from certain untreated conditions, ultimately causing tubal damage; and ALCOHOLISM AND DRUG ABUSE. Fetal alcohol syndrome occurs in about one in one thousand live births. Fetal mortality for black babies is one and one-half times higher than for whites, with low birthweight a common cause.

Technological developments have made possible *in vitro* fertilization in previously infertile women, electronic fetal monitoring, increased prenatal detection capability, and surrogate motherhood. Not all these developments are accepted as progress by American women; for example, surrogate motherhood raises complex ethical and legal issues, and some feminists argue that electronic fetal monitoring is inappropriate for low-risk births, tending to disempower women. Low-income women, women of color, and rural inhabitants have restricted access to the new reproductive technology as a result of extended waiting periods, erratic funding plans, uneven distribution throughout various states, and the scarcity of physicians who accept as payment the lower rate of Medicaid reimbursement for prenatal screening procedures (amniocentesis and ultrasound).

Risk of Disease. Coronary artery disease is a leading cause of death among women in the United States, accounting for about one-third of all deaths of women each year. It has been suggested that physicians are less aggressive in pursuing treatment strategies for women than men. That fact has been attributed to the poor accuracy of stress testing in women and a nonrecognition of the high incidence of coronary disease in women. Women are referred for surgery later in the course of their disease than men, increasing their rate of mortality. Fewer blacks than whites undergo open-heart bypass surgery. Angioplasty, an alternative to open-heart surgery, is a technique used to restore blood supply to the heart through insertion of a balloon at the end of a tube into a disease-narrowed, clogged artery. A 1993 study found that women are ten times more likely than men to die after undergoing the procedure. Laser angioplasty has been pioneered as an alternative but has fallen out of favor because of its expense.

Racial and economic distinctions account for some differences in breast cancer mortality rates. Although

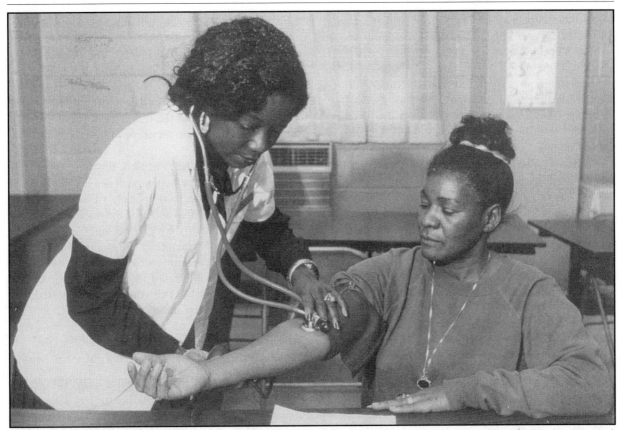

A leading cause of death among women is coronary artery disease. Check-ups and adequate screening help prevent such unnecessary deaths. (Frances M. Roberts)

the incidence of breast cancer appears higher among white women, survival rates are also higher for white compared with black women, who are diagnosed at a more advanced stage of disease. Black women also have higher mortality rates than white women from cirrhosis and diabetes; their risk is likewise increased for tuberculosis, hypertension, and anemia. Latinas have a 38 percent higher mortality rate from diabetes compared with white women.

Osteoporosis, a reduction in bone mass sufficient to increase the risk of fracture, is more prevalent in elderly Asian and white women, many of whom are short and thin with poorly developed musculature. Those prone to heavy smoking or drinking are at even greater risk. Obesity appears to reduce the risk of bone fracture but presents other health risks. Various regimens to prevent bone loss exist with varying success rates. Postmenopausal estrogen replacement therapy may produce a protective effect; calcium supplements are of negligible value. Short-term increases in bone mass produced by exercise and muscle conditioning are rapidly lost when the program is discontinued.

Other conditions more common in women than men include liver damage from alcohol abuse, gallstones associated with pregnancy and obesity in women below age thirty, gallstones associated with estrogen therapy in postmenopausal women, recurrent urinary tract infections, and physical symptoms related to premenstrual syndrome (PMS).

In the 1990's, policymakers were striving for health care reforms within a balanced system in which each person would receive a fair share of resources without discrimination based on gender, age, income, ethnicity, or lifestyle.

SUGGESTED READINGS. There is a proliferation of books and articles on women's health in both popular and scholarly literature. Entire issues of medical journals devoted to the subject include *Journal of the American Medical Association,* volume 268, October 14, 1992, and *Western Journal of Medicine,* volume 149, December, 1988. Useful books include *The Health of Women: A Global Perspective* (1993), edited by Marge Koblinsky, a carefully annotated work discussing the issues addressed in this article and others on an international scale. Charlotte F. Muller's *Health Care and Gender* (1990) contains annotations on the women's health movement and includes a detailed discussion of the differential treatment of women by the medical community. Based on a conference on women, health, and technology, *Healing Technology: Feminist Perspectives* (1992), edited by Kathryn Strother Ratcliff, deals with economic, social, political, ethical, occupational, and environmental considerations in addressing the role of the workplace and technology and their effects on women's health. *The Changing Risk of Disease in Women: An Epidemiologic Approach (1984), edited by Ellen B. Gold, is a compilation of symposium presentations examining gender differences in risk to various diseases.—Marcia J. Weiss*

Heart Mountain Fair Play Committee: Political organization formed in 1944 by Kiyoshi Okamoto in the INTERNMENT camp for Japanese Americans at Heart Mountain, Wyoming. When an insufficient number of Japanese interns volunteered to serve in the U.S. military, a draft was imposed in the camps. Many draftees felt the draft was unconstitutional, since they had been denied other rights of citizenship. The committee attempted to have the citizenship status of the men confirmed in the courts. Eighty-five men from Heart Mountain were jailed for resisting conscription. All had signed their loyalty oaths, but felt that it would be unpatriotic and immoral to support an unconstitutional draft.

Hebrew language: Ancient Near Eastern Semitic language that became the language of Jewish worship and the language of the modern state of Israel. Modern Hebrew is a simplified form of the ancient language, influenced particularly by English and German in vocabulary, although structurally and grammatically maintaining its ancient Semitic roots. Distinctions of Hebrew include a limited alphabet of signs, writing from right to left, and a language built of words that are constructs of basic three-letter ("trilateral") roots.

The oldest forms of Semitic languages are extant in cuneiform (wedge-writing) clay tablets that are more than four thousand years old. Modern Semitic

Store in New York City with signs in Hebrew and English advertising fruits needed for the annual festival of Sukkot. (Frances M. Roberts)

languages include Hebrew, Arabic, Maltese, and Ge'ez (the latter from Ethiopia). Semitic languages, written from right to left, are alphabetic but are unique in being grammatically and morphologically constructed from a three-consonant root, such as S-L-M, from which a field of words is constructed, and in having verbs and nouns that are conceptually and semantically related. Words are generated from the root by the addition of specific vowels and consonants; subjects, actions, and objects can be denoted with a single word with the addition of prefixes and suffixes. Many of these roots are clearly discernible across the entire family of Semitic languages.

Hebrew was originally descended from the Semitic languages of the Canaanites on the eastern shore of the Mediterranean. It has remained a literary language of interest beyond the ethnic identity of the Jews because a form of Hebrew is the language of the Jewish Bible, known to Christians as the Old Testament. Changes are discernible in both structure and vocabulary between older and more recent books within the Hebrew Bible. After the advent of Christianity, Hebrew remained mostly a literary language. Most of the Jewish Rabbinic writings were produced in Aramaic, a Semitic language quite similar to Hebrew but more widely spoken at the time.

Although European Jewry revived Hebrew in poetry and plays in seventeenth century Spain, Portugal, and Italy, the major impetus for the revival of Hebrew came with Jewish nationalism (Zionism). As ZIONISM developed among Jews in Europe in the late nineteenth and early twentieth centuries, moves to revive Hebrew as the language of the Jewish people gathered momentum. Eliezer Ben-Yehuda (1858-1922) was the most prolific lexicographer of the revival of Hebrew in the modern era. American Jews continue to use Hebrew in their worship services and to study the language as part of their cultural heritage.

SUGGESTED READINGS. Volumes have been written on the Hebrew language, both ancient and modern. A modern grammar is Martin Feinstein's *Basic Hebrew: A Textbook of Contemporary Hebrew* (1973). A standard biblical Hebrew grammar is Thomas Lambdin's *Introduction to Biblical Hebrew* (1971). See also Robert St. John's *The Tongue of the Prophets* (1952, repr. 1972).

Hebrew Union College (New York, N.Y.; Los Angeles, Calif.; Jerusalem, Israel): Oldest rabbinical seminary in the United States. Hebrew Union College is dedicated to scholarship and the training of rabbis within the traditions of Reform Judaism. Founded in Cincinnati in 1875 by Isaac M. Wise under the auspices of the Union of American Hebrew Congregations, Hebrew Union College merged with the Jewish Institute of Religion in New York in 1950. A Los Angeles branch was chartered in 1954, and a Jerusalem campus opened in 1963. The college was the first to ordain women as rabbis, beginning in 1972.

Hellman, Lillian (June 20, 1905, New Orleans, La.— June 30, 1984, Martha's Vineyard, Mass.): Feminist, socialist, and playwright. Hellman was a reviewer for the *New York Herald Tribune* (1925-1928) and later worked for Metro-Goldwyn-Mayer Studios. Her first play, *The Children's Hour* (1934), dealt with accusations of lesbianism in a girls' school. Many of her later plays were extremely political, including *Watch on the Rhine* (1941), an anti-Nazi statement. A victim of McCarthyism, she was questioned heavily in 1952 by McCarthy's Senate Committee. Other works include the plays *The Searching Wind* (1944), *The Autumn Garden* (1951), *Toys in the Attic* (1960), two musical librettos, *Regina*

Lillian Hellman's influential plays include The Children's Hour *and* Watch on the Rhine. *(AP/Wide World Photos)*

(1949) and *Candide* (1957), as well as three volumes of autobiography written late in her life.

Henry Street Settlement: Social settlement house serving the lower east side of New York City. Lillian D. Wald and Mary Brewster started the organization in 1893 to provide volunteer nursing services to the impoverished immigrant community. The settlement developed a corps of nurses who provided in-home care to their neighbors. Settlement workers also promoted a wide range of social reforms ranging from better housing conditions to the abolition of child labor. In 1933, Helen Hall became the director of the settlement and continued to emphasize reform and social surveys. During the 1960's, the orientation shifted to delivery of social services to a changing population.

Henson, Matthew Alexander (Aug. 8, 1866, Charles County., Md.—Mar. 9, 1955, New York, N.Y.): African American explorer. An assistant to the Arctic explorer

Shown here at age eighty-one, Matthew Henson was the last survivor of the Peary expedition. (AP/Wide World Photos)

Robert E. Peary for twenty-three years, Henson was the first man to reach the North Pole. He went to sea at age twenty, became an able seaman, and in 1887 first joined Peary, then a U.S. Navy civil engineer, on a trip to Nicaragua. Henson accompanied Peary on eight Arctic voyages, serving as interpreter with the INUITS and in many other necessary roles. On April 6, 1909, Peary, Henson, and four Inuits reached the pole. Peary had sent back five support teams but kept Henson with him for the final dash to their goal.

Hepburn, Katharine (b. Nov. 8, 1907, Hartford, Conn.): Actor. Hepburn began acting on Broadway as an extra but soon moved to films, the first of which was *A Bill of Divorcement* (1932). She became known as a fiercely independent and private person in Hollywood circles. In the 1930's, she won two Academy Awards for *Morning Glory* and *Little Women* and went on to star in many films opposite Spencer Tracy. Her best known pictures are *African Queen* (1951), *Suddenly Last Summer* (1962), *Long Day's Journey Into Night* (1962), *The Lion in Winter* (1969), and *On Golden Pond* (1981), all earning her Academy Awards. In the 1950's, she returned to stage work, taking a number of Shakespearean roles. She published a best-selling autobiography, *Me*, in 1991.

Higher education: Education beyond the secondary school. Higher education programs help prepare men and women for more economically rewarding and socially meaningful lives. At the end of a successful higher education program, the student is awarded a diploma or certificate of achievement indicating a certain level of knowledge in an academic or technical field. The term "higher education" in the United States usually refers to college or university education.

The term "university" stems from the Latin word *universitas*, meaning a group of people organized for a common purpose. By the late fourteenth century, the word defined groups of scholars who were recognized by a local government or the church. Since that time the concept has evolved to the current understanding of a university as an institution of higher education.

In a similar manner, the word "college" originally designated a place where a group of scholars lived. Gradually these communities of scholars became recognized institutions of learning. Today a college is thought of as a four-year undergraduate institution of higher education that emphasizes general education and grants a bachelor's degree upon successful completion of a course of studies. It also can refer to an

These college graduates have surmounted many obstacles to earn their diplomas and honors. (Hazel Hankin)

administrative division of a university that oversees students in a particular field of study, such as the College of Education within a large university.

Historical Background. The first institution of higher education in colonial America was Harvard College, founded in 1636. The young men who studied there were earnest Puritans who pursued a rigorous, religiously inspired curriculum for four years. By the end of the seventeenth century, however, education at Harvard College began to change. The curriculum began to show the influence of secular attitudes, a trend which also was occurring at other colleges. At William and Mary College, founded in Virginia in 1693, Thomas Jefferson was influential in bringing about similar changes and in laying the groundwork for the founding of the University of Virginia in 1819, the true predecessor of the university of today. With the founding of The Johns Hopkins University in Baltimore in 1867, the final element of the modern university was introduced. Modeled on the German university system, this new American educational institution placed considerable importance on research, a dominant feature of today's American universities.

In 1862 the Morrill Act established the federal land grant colleges. The act granted to each state 30,000 acres of land for each senator and representative in Congress (based on the 1860 census) on which to establish an institution of higher education. The primary aim of these early land grant institutions was to train students in agriculture and the mechanical arts without excluding scientific and classical studies. The land grant colleges and universities also provided training in military science. They have played a vital role in developing the design and curriculum of American higher education by giving formal acceptance to disciplines that previously had been isolated in separate professional schools.

The early training of TEACHERS for public schools originally took place in normal schools, which were an extended form of high school. Students continued to learn reading, mathematics, history, and life science. As the public education system grew and the general population became better educated, the demand for better training of teachers caused these schools to evolve into universities and offer full academic programs.

Minorities in Education. Attending a university represents for many Americans a path to widen their professional and social opportunities. Until recently, this path was open primarily to white males. Women and racial minorities were restricted from pursuing higher education. In 1833, OBERLIN COLLEGE was founded in Oberlin, Ohio, to train ministers for the expanding Western frontier. It was the first college to admit both

It has only been in the past twenty-five years that women began to increase their numbers in the professions and break out of the teacher-training programs to which they were restricted for so long.

The African American experience of obtaining access to higher education has been similar to and yet different from that of women. Their opportunity of attending an institution of higher education was first

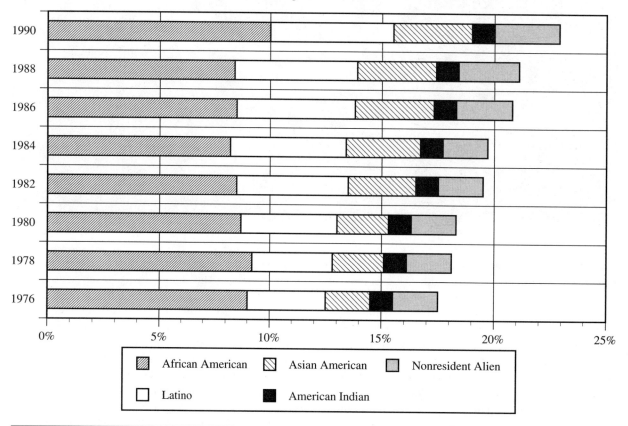

College Minority Enrollment: 1976-1990

Source: Adapted from the 1993 "California College Guide," *Los Angeles Times.*

male and female students. In 1835 the college opened admission to people of any race. In the following decades, more colleges and universities cautiously opened their doors to women, but higher education nevertheless remained largely an institution designed for white males.

In 1861, with the founding of VASSAR COLLEGE, women finally had an institution of higher education available exclusively for them. Other women's colleges were founded and provided increased opportunities for women. Women, however, were socially constrained to a number of acceptable fields of study.

established through the historically black colleges and universities (HBCU). Before the Civil War only Lincoln University in Pennsylvania, founded in 1854, and Wilberforce College in Ohio, founded in 1856, had been established to enable African Americans to obtain advanced education. Following the Civil War, a number of black colleges were founded. With the second Morrill Act of 1890, specific financial provisions were made for the founding of black land grant colleges.

Prior to 1945, almost 90 percent of all African Americans attending college went to one of the

HBCUs, which were for the most part located in the South. These institutions originally played a large role in educating teachers, who in turn would educate the former slaves. American policies of SEGREGATION made these the only educational option in certain periods of history. With the legal mandate for INTEGRATION in the 1950's, and the AFFIRMATIVE ACTION programs of the 1960's which finally began to enact change, African Americans began to have additional options for advanced education. White colleges, responding to the call for affirmative action, began recruiting more minority students.

Few colleges and universities, however, were prepared to deal with the unique problems a minority student faced in the traditionally white educational environment. Racial discrimination, lack of a familiar social environment, and lack of sufficient ethnic faculty to act as role models, mentors, and advisers contributed to (and continue to contribute to) the alienation that minority students often suffer when attending traditionally white universities. African Americans have an unusually high rate of noncompletion of the four-year undergraduate program. It still remains for administrators at universities and colleges to address the needs of minority students to reverse this cycle.

As financial aid has become more difficult to obtain, many minority students have been forced to forgo higher education. This problem has deeply affected both African Americans and Latinos, because both populations have high numbers of families and individuals who cannot afford college tuition and fees. In addition to sharing the problem of alienation at traditionally white institutions and a lack of faculty mentors and role models, Latinos whose first language is Spanish often experience language problems. Anticipation of language difficulties probably leads some Latinos to avoid higher education altogether; for those attending college, language difficulties may exacerbate other difficulties and contribute to dropping out. An additional factor, also present in the African American community, is a perception that obtaining a college education is "selling out" to a white society. Sufficient cultural distinctions exist to leave the impression in a young student's mind that universities are for whites only. This is a problem that can only benefit from the increased emphasis of MULTICULTURAL EDUCATION in higher education in the 1980's and 1990's. The 1993 protest at University of California, Los Angeles (UCLA), calling for the establishment of a CHICANO STUDIES department recalled African American protests of the 1960's demanding BLACK STUDIES programs. The growth of the Latino population and its emerging college-age population continues to underscore the need for an educational process that recognizes the diversity of the United States' student population.

The Asian American population has fared much better than other racial minorities in higher education in the United States. On the average, Asian Americans have higher incomes and more years of education than other minorities and even white Americans.

Proportionately, more Asian Americans graduate from high school, complete college, and become managers and professionals than white Americans. Asian success has been especially prominent in science. Scientific careers have allowed many Asian immigrants to avoid the sort of large hierarchical organizations in which their lack of familiarity with American culture, as well as management's reluctance to put them in highly visible positions, could hinder their advancement. For recent immigrants with incomplete mastery of English, their lack of proficiency does not create a barrier to success in the fields of science and mathematics.

Problems and Challenges. Higher education in the United States is confronting a vast array of visions of its future. Curricular changes are being made in an attempt to include the cultures of all American students—particularly those that have long been undervalued or ignored—in programs of study. Heated debate and controversy has resulted from efforts to design less Eurocentric curricula. Problems have resulted from the fact that in order to add study of the various cultures that now compose multicultural America, classes or areas of study that have long been a part of the education establishment must be dropped or removed from their places of importance.

Universities and colleges are recruiting minority students in larger numbers, and these students require a curriculum that recognizes and respects their cultural heritage, an administration that accommodates their distinct cultural needs, and a faculty that resembles the face of the wider American population. The changes have been slow to come. Universities attempt to recruit minority faculty, but they face a small pool of qualified available minority applicants because of the exclusionary policies of institutions of higher education in the recent past. Efforts are being made to sensitize the academic community to the value of educating more people in a culturally relevant manner; textbooks, for example, are being rewritten to present

Anita Hill returning to teach at the University of Oklahoma after testifying at the Clarence Thomas confirmation hearings. (AP/Wide World Photos)

a more representative point of view about American life, letters, and science.

Not only are traditionally white institutions being challenged by the necessity to educate a multicultural society, but also the historically black colleges and universities as well as women's colleges must cope with a changing educational environment. Their survival in the twenty-first century depends on finding a balance between a segregated and an open educational environment.

SUGGESTED READINGS. For additional information on women in higher education, see Gail P. Kelly and Sheila Slaughter's edited text, *Women's Higher Education in Comparative Perspective* (1991). Michael A. Olivas' edited text, *Latino College Students* (1986), has supplementary information on Latino student achievement and transition from high school to college. *The Education of African-Americans* (1991), edited by Charles V. Willie, Antoine M. Garibaldi, and Wornie L. Reed, contains a historical perspective on the achievements of African Americans. Finally, Dinesh D'Souza's *Illiberal Education: The Politics of Race and Sex on Campus* (1991) discusses some of the controversies and confrontations experienced on college campuses.—*Carol B. Tanksley*

Hill, Anita Faye (b. 1956, Lone Tree, Okla.): African American attorney and law professor who received national attention in 1991 for testifying that she had been the victim of SEXUAL HARASSMENT by Supreme Court justice nominee Clarence THOMAS. Hill, who had worked under Thomas in the Department of Education's Office of Civil Rights as well as at the EQUAL EMPLOYMENT OPPORTUNITY COMMISSION (EEOC) in the early 1980's, testified about the abuse in detail at televised Senate confirmation hearings in a decidedly hostile atmosphere. Americans who watched the proceedings were split as to whether Hill or Thomas, who denied the allegations, was telling the truth. Thomas was subsequently confirmed by the Senate, and Hill became a hero to thousands of women who identified with her experience. Hill's testimony provoked intense debate on the nature of sexual harassment and may have had an effect on both the rise in claims of sexual harassment and the electoral success of women candidates during the YEAR OF THE WOMAN (1992).

Hindus: Adherents of the predominant religion of India. Stemming primarily from the infusion of Asian Indian Hindus and gurus (religious teachers) after 1965, American Hinduism represents an aspect of the broader trend of religious diversification in the contemporary multicultural United States.

Hinduism is a collection of individual regional devotional practices that share a few essential doctrinal similarities. These include belief in the fundamental unity of the universe and the presence in every human being of a divine spark called Atman. Through self-realization, an individual's Atman can merge with the supreme universal force called Brahman. A life of devotion, meditation, and service is the spiritual preparation for the individual Hindu. Hindus frequently worship one or more incarnations, called avatars, of Brahman.

Hinduism was first introduced to the United States in the early nineteenth century by Ralph Waldo Emerson, whose interpretations of the Hindu philosophical texts, the Upanishads, were disseminated in his prose and poetry. With the notable exceptions of missionaries Swami Vivekanda and Swami Yogananda, who arrived in 1893 and 1920, respectively, there was little formal Hindu practice in the United States before 1965. Prior to 1960, fewer than twelve thousand Asian Indians lived in the United States. After 1965 U.S. immigration laws were relaxed, and by 1980 the Asian Indian American population numbered nearly four

Hindus celebrating the Festival of Ganesh at a temple in Queens, N.Y. (Hazel Hankin)

hundred thousand, including several Hindu gurus and their followers.

A significant number of mostly young, white, middle-class Americans have been drawn to various Hindu sects. Numerous Hindu leaders and groups arrived in the United States during the 1960's, each requiring varying levels of commitment from their converts. Members of the International Society for Krishna Consciousness (Hare Krishnas) practiced an ardent devotion to the avatar Krishna, including precise laws of conduct and segregation from society. Other Hindu groups such as the Divine Light Mission, whose members followed a boy guru, required major lifestyle changes but were more moderate in allowing followers to maintain family and worldly connections. Contrastingly, transcendental meditation required only a modest initiation fee and two twenty-minute periods of meditation daily.

Several features were common to most American Hindu groups, including devotion to an avatar or a guru. Most asserted the ultimate perfectibility of humanity through spiritual transcendence and transformation of the self. Usually meditation and yoga were practiced as paths to enlightenment. Both meditation and yoga became well established in mainstream American society in a variety of forms divorced from any real connections with Hinduism. Most Hindu exports maintained a core membership after the initial mass conversions.

Meanwhile, Asian Indian Hindus have established temples and organizations through which they maintain traditions such as the Divali holiday.

SUGGESTED READINGS. An excellent overview of American Hinduism is contained in the *Encyclopedia of the American Religious Experience* (1987), edited by Charles H. Lippy and Peter W. Williams. Roger Finke and Rodney Stark's *The Churching of America, 1776-1990* (1992) describes the diversification of the American religion. A more negative view of eastern religious imports is Harvey G. Cox's *Turning East: The Promise and Peril of the New Orientalism* (1977). In *Religions of Immigrants from India and Pakistan* (1988), Raymond Brady Williams chronicles Asian Indian immigrants and their religious heritage.

Hip-hop culture: Youthful cultural expressions in MUSIC, DANCE, GRAFFITI, and FASHION that were originally developed by teenagers in the ghettos of the South Bronx and Harlem, New York City, in the 1970's. Hip-hop was a response to the social system that paid little attention to the impoverished conditions of the ghetto residents, primarily African Americans and black immigrants from the West Indies, Puerto Rico, and Cuba. Nurtured in an environment rich in cultural traditions, hip-hop culture gave black youth an opportunity to show their creativity and cultural heritage.

Hip-hop graffiti began as simple scribbling of tags (nicknames) on walls. It evolved into elaborate paintings with magic markers and spray paints on entire subway cars as teenagers competed in not only the number but also the style of their graffiti.

Hip-hop music, which also came to be known as RAP MUSIC, originated in break-beats, invented by a Jamaican disc jockey called Kool Herc. Herc manipulated turntables and records at house parties in order to create dance music with strong beats. When break-beats became popular, he hired others to rap to his music. Break-beats, in turn, created break dance with elaborate leg and foot movements. Competitions among dancers, especially Puerto Ricans, added many acrobatic elements such as head and back spins, and break dancing became the rage for many urban youth. Break dancers known as b-boys or b-girls wore casual clothes with bright colors and bold patterns and made it the hip-hop fashion. They also created their own lexicon that reflected street language and ethnic dialects.

Hip-hop culture, which had developed almost unknown to outsiders, began to receive public attention by the end of the 1970's. Graffiti art was featured and sold in galleries. The first rap records, the Fatback Band's *King Tim III* and the Sugarhill Gang's *Rapper's Delight* were released in 1979, and Run-D.M.C. had the first gold rap album in 1984. *Flashdance* (1983) started a break dance craze nationwide. *Yo! MTV Raps* became one of the most popular programs on Music Television. Hip-hop culture continued to dominate the mass media throughout the 1980's, and its influence was clearly observed in fashion design, ballet, modern dance, studio art, and popular musical styles.

Most important, hip-hop culture promoted political and cultural awareness among black youth. When Grandmaster Flash and the Furious Five's *The Message* (1982) presented the hardships of GHETTO life, social and political issues became a theme of rap music. Many rappers have included the voices of civil rights and human rights leaders in their records, and groups such as Public Enemy and the Boogie Down Productions present an Afrocentric view of black experience in the United States. These rappers have changed hip-hop fashion by replacing gold chains and rings with leather medallions featuring the map of Africa, T-shirts with the names and words of civil rights leaders such as Nelson Mandela and MALCOLM X, and other African clothes. Their music, as well as their clothes, has taught black youth to have pride in their cultural heritage and has made hip-hop culture an important source of young African Americans' identity.

SUGGESTED READINGS. For the development of hip-hop music and culture, see David Toop's *The Rap Attack* (1984). Dick Hebdige's *Cut 'n' Mix* (1987) includes a chapter on rap and hip-hop. Craig Castleman's *Getting Up* (1982) is a good source on graffiti.

Hirabayashi v. United States (1943): U.S. Supreme Court decision on whether a Japanese American citizen had to obey a curfew imposed by a military commander. Gordon Hirabayashi was born in Seattle, Washington, in 1918 of Japanese parents who never returned to Japan. He was educated in public schools and was a senior at

Hirabayashi protested the 1942 curfew orders that were followed by exclusion orders; Japanese Americans were forced to pack a few belongings and move to internment camps. (National Japanese American Historical Society)

the University of Washington at the time. He had never been to Japan or had any association with any Japanese people in Japan.

After the declaration of war against Japan by the United States, President Franklin Roosevelt issued Executive Order No. 9066 on February 19, 1942, authorizing the military commander of the Western Defense Command to take appropriate measures to ensure the safety of the area. On March 27, 1942, Congress ratified and confirmed Roosevelt's order. Three days later General J. L. DeWitt of the Western Defense Command issued Public Proclamation No. 3, which imposed an 8:00 P.M. to 6:00 A.M. curfew on all people of Japanese ancestry (about 112,000 persons, including some 70,000 U.S. citizens) in the western coastal states. Hirabayashi believed that his rights as a native-born American had been violated by the imposition of the curfew.

The Supreme Court, in a unanimous opinion authored by Chief Justice Harlan Stone, upheld the curfew as being within the constitutional authority of Congress and the president. It was, the Court said, an emergency war measure, a protective action necessary to meet the threat of sabotage and espionage that could substantially affect the war effort and that might reasonably be expected to aid a threatened enemy invasion. The curfew was a matter of judgment at the discretion of the warmaking branches of government, the Supreme Court said, and the Court should not sit in review of the wisdom of the curfew nor substitute its judgment for that of military authorities.

Stone went on to say that there was no unconstitutional discrimination against U.S. citizens of Japanese ancestry. The Japanese here had intensified their solidarity and in a large measure had prevented their ASSIMILATION as an integral part of the white population. Many sent their children to Japanese-language schools and had little social intercourse with the white population. A group of one national extraction may menace safety more than others. The Fifth Amendment to the Constitution only guarantees due process of law for all persons, not equal protection of the laws. The liberty of citizens can be restricted by war power, Stone stated, and Congress had not unconstitutionally delegated its warmaking power.

As part of a government-sponsored reconsideration of events surrounding the INTERNMENT of Japanese Americans and efforts to give victims reparations, the Hirabayashi conviction was reversed by a federal appeals court in 1987.

SUGGESTED READINGS. The Hirabayashi decision can be read in its entirety in *United States Reports* (vol. 320, 1944), published by the U.S. Government Printing Office. There is an excellent account of the case in *The Courage of Their Convictions* (1988) by Peter Irons.

Hispanic. *Use* **Latino**

Hispanic Chamber of Commerce: Organization established to promote trade and business interests of Latinos. The San Antonio Hispanic Chamber of Commerce, chartered in 1929 as la Camara Mexican de Comercio, is the oldest Hispanic Chamber in the United States. In 1979, the U.S. Hispanic Chamber of Commerce was established to encourage affiliations and agreements with Hispanic chambers, businesses, government agencies, and major corporations. Today the chamber is flourishing nationwide and holds annual conventions that are attended by as many as ten thousand people. It publishes the annual *National Hispanic Business Directory*.

Hispanic Heritage Week: Promotes recognition of the contributions Latinos have made in the United States. It was first established on September 17, 1968, when Congress approved a proclamation of a National Hispanic Week. The proclamation has been repeated annually under various U.S. presidents. In 1989, Hispanic Heritage Week became part of National Hispanic Heritage Month, proclaimed for the period from September 15 to October 15. This period, which includes the Mexican and most Central American independence days, is marked by special education programs, civic ceremonies, and arts events.

Hispanic Policy Development Project (HPDP): Private organization founded in 1982 with headquarters in Washington, D.C., which encourages the analysis of public and private policies and proposals that affect Latinos. HPDP focuses on the problems of Latino youth, especially in education and employment. It sponsors policy-analysis competitions open to Latino and non-Latino scholars as well as to Latino organizations. The findings are brought to the attention of U.S. leaders and are published in reports, bulletins, and books.

Hispanic Society of America: Educational organization founded in 1904 in New York City. The society, which also has a research institute and a reference library, maintains a MUSEUM on Hispanic development from prehistoric times to the present. The library contains more than 200,000 manuscripts and 18,000 books printed before 1701, as well as 150,000 books published since that time in Spain, Portugal, and colonial Hispanic America. The society periodically awards five different medals for creative and scholarly distinction in art and literature.

Hispanic studies programs. *See* **Chicano studies programs**

Hmong Americans: The Hmong are highland agriculturalists who until recently lived in parts of Laos in Southeast Asia. One of the United States' newest ethnic groups, the Laotian Hmong have a history of extensive conflict and considerable migration. Following the termination of hostilities in the VIETNAM WAR, thousands of Hmong migrated to the United States, resulting in further enrichment of its highly pluralistic society.

History and Culture. Most anthropologists believe that the Hmong originally came from central Siberia before migrating to northern China. From the middle of the nineteenth century, they left China and settled in north Vietnam, Laos, Burma, and Thailand, where they lived as isolated ethnic minorities.

The Hmong played a significant role in Chinese history. There is strong support for the notion that they actually occupied the Yellow River basin before the Chinese arrived in that area. Asian historians have chronicled the continuous conflicts between the Hmong and Chinese peoples during the Shang, Chou, Ch'in, and Han dynasties. A Hmong kingdom emerged in China in the mid-sixth century. Some historians have described this period (500-900) as the "glory years" of Hmong history. The kingdom, however, met its demise as a result of increasing numbers of Chinese people, forcing the Hmong to become a tribal people once again in the mountainous areas of China.

Hmong life was relatively peaceful until about the year 1200. After centuries of conflict with the Chinese, the Hmong migrated to Southeast Asia from the Yunnan Province during the middle of the nineteenth century.

Anthropologists refer to the Hmong as having a patrilineal clan structure. Hmong villages usually consisted of a small number of families, with larger villages occasionally composed of up to thirty families. The primary occupation was slash-and-burn farming. One of the main crops was opium. These crops, however, generated only a small income for the Hmong.

Some of the opium was used by the Hmong for medicinal purposes or for spiritual ceremonies performed by the clan shaman.

SHAMANISM has been the primary religion of the Hmong, who believe in a variety of spirits in nature. The shaman is able to communicate with Shee Yee, the first shaman, and through him to Yer Shau, thought to be God's personal representative to humankind who is half-God and half-human. Like many Asian American groups, the Hmong venerate their ancestors and believe that proper attention to honoring the dead helps protect the living from ill fortune.

The Hmong in the Vietnam War. Hmong participation during the VIETNAM WAR is linked to the involvement of the French in that area. By the early 1600's, French Catholic missionaries were attempting to Christianize the Vietnamese. The French were also there for economic purposes. One of the more lucrative enterprises was the opium trade. The French continued to support the Hmong's opium-raising ventures until they departed Indochina and the communists took control of North Vietnam in the mid-1950's.

In 1959, Laos became embroiled in a civil war between the Royal Laotian Army and the Pathet Lao, the Laotian communists' military unit, both of which were active in the highlands. Most Hmong were royalists. General Vang Pao was the only Hmong to become a general in the Royal Laotian Army. By 1961, the United States had decided to support his military efforts since the rest of the Royal Laotian Army appeared to be incapable of containing the communists. The Central Intelligence Agency (CIA) provided strong support for the anticommunist effort through Hmong recruitment and other means for fifteen years. They constructed airfields and trained Hmong pilots in support of the rightist Laotian faction.

By 1972, the United States decided to withdraw all military support for the Royal Laotian Army. When Vang Pao was forced to withdraw in 1975, several thousand Hmong organized a guerrilla resistance effort in an attempt to thwart the communist takeover. Other Hmong—about 100,000—became REFUGEES, crossing the Mekong River to seek asylum in Thailand. Life in the Thai border camps was tenuous at best. For the most part, the Hmong were not welcome, and their presence created a financial burden for the Thais. Also, there was a growing Thai concern about possible retaliation from the Vietnamese for harboring Laotian refugees, especially those who had worked for the CIA.

Immigration to North America. The end of the Vietnam War resulted in a new era of migration for Hmong people. After the victory of the communists, some Hmong refugees chose to settle in Europe and Australia. The vast majority, however, opted to migrate to Canada and the United States.

Vang Pao was granted political asylum in the United States, where he moved to a large cattle ranch in a remote part of Montana. His choice of the United States was instrumental in persuading large numbers of Hmong people to follow his example. Many chose

tance association for the migrating Hmong patterned on those of the Vietnamese Americans. He relinquished his cattle-raising responsibilities in order to provide a much-needed support system for the Hmong, who were now trying to become independently functioning Americans.

Life in the United States. While the Hmong came from a strong agricultural tradition, most tended to live in the larger American cities, where they could find cultural support from one another. Also, the urban infrastructure seemed better-suited to providing the

Groups such as this Hmong dance troupe in Sacramento, Calif., help keep traditions alive. (Eric Crystal)

to reside in urban centers such as Minneapolis, Seattle, and eventually cities in Southern California. In the late 1980's, there were an estimated 50,000 to 70,000 Hmong in the United States. After California, the states with sizable communities included Michigan, Wisconsin, Minnesota, Massachusetts, Rhode Island, Colorado, Texas, Ohio, and Washington.

American social services agencies provided financial support for the nation's newest immigrants, hoping that they would soon become self-sufficient. Vang Pao founded Lao Family Community, a mutual assis-

basic needs of food, clothing, shelter, and moral support. While the tendency of Hmong immigrants to settle in large urban areas was logical, a number of major problems developed.

Coming from small farming villages with no written language, the Hmong found it difficult to adjust to the new "high-tech" society in which they found themselves. Hmong males used to being economically independent subsistence farmers were forced to look for unskilled American industry and service jobs, which required them to work for someone else. The limited

Hmong artisans are well known for their beautiful textile traditions, including work in embroidery, appliqué, and batik, that has become popular with American consumers. (Eric Crystal)

available positions were often sought by applicants from other racial and ethnic minority groups, thus creating a high risk for interethnic strife.

Public assistance funds were initially available to REFUGEES for three years, which meant that within that time period, the Hmong needed to acquire the necessary skills that would allow them to become independent citizens. For most Hmong, this was extremely difficult: They had only recently acquired written language, much less English, and reading had not yet become a part of their way of life. American school systems attempted to serve the needs of Hmong youth, but lacked effective bilingual education programs.

Many Hmong persevered in school and began to enter a variety of professions. Some young Hmong have become certified teachers or social workers in order to ease the struggles of their fellow refugees in adjusting to American life. Others work as computer programmers or even college professors, though the majority of employed Hmong are still in lower-paying jobs. For women, the sale of Hmong needlework to

Americans has been an important supplement to the family income.

Cultural Contributions. While some anthropologists fear a kind of ethnocide of the Hmong Americans, others are more optimistic about their capacity for survival and adaptation.

The Hmong are perhaps best known to other Americans by their exquisite handmade textile arts, such as silk embroidery, batik, and reverse appliqué (in which sewn designs are cut and folded back to reveal the layers below). These forms of FOLK ART represent both a holdover from their highland past and an adaptation to refugee life. In Hmong villages, each clan had its distinctive colors and designs for traditional clothing, and various groups became known as the Green, White, Black, or Striped Hmong. The splendor of Hmong clothing was especially evident at New Year celebrations, which were the high point of the tribal calendar and a time for courtship and marriage. In the refugee camps, Hmong men and women were urged to make "story cloths" that depicted their lost way of life and their wartime experience. These became popular when they were marketed overseas as wall hangings, and many refugee women continued making decorative textiles after their arrival in the United States. In the 1980's, crafts fairs and international festivals across the country often included tables heaped with Hmong *paj ntaub* or *pa ndau* ("flower cloth") for sale. The Hmong artists took note of the more subdued colors preferred by Americans as well as innovative uses for their cloth as handbags and placemats in order to market their work successfully.

The Hmong have made a tremendous impact on the town of Fresno, California, where they were about thirty thousand strong in 1990. They flocked there from larger cities to find work in local agriculture and began to develop their own community infrastructure. New Year celebrations in the region attract tens of thousands of Hmong, including costumed young people playing the ball toss game of Hmong courtship and musicians performing acrobatic dances to the sound of the *gaeng* (a free reed mouth organ with long, curved, bamboo pipes). Traditional healers and religious practitioners can also be found in the area.

The presence of these highland people in American cities is something neither the Hmong nor their American neighbors ever expected. It has made many Americans more aware of the diversity of Asian cultures and the impact of the VIETNAM WAR. Professionals in ENGLISH AS A SECOND LANGUAGE (ESL) PRO-

GRAMS as well as the fields of education and health and medicine have had to make changes in their approach to serve the Hmong, who come from a preliterate culture with animistic beliefs. Increasingly, this young immigrant community with its admirable spirit of survival is building bridges between old Hmong customs and mainstream American ways of life.

SUGGESTED READINGS. A good starting point for information on refugees from various Southeast Asian regions is *Passages: An Anthology of the Southeast Asian Refugee Experience* (1990), compiled by Katsuyo K. Howard. Specific works on Hmong Americans include a recent comprehensive look at children's issues in Henry T. Trueba's *Cultural Conflict and Adaptation: The Case of Hmong Children in American Society* (1990); the story of a Hmong shaman, Paja Thao, with commentary by ethnographer Dwight Conquergood in *I Am a Shaman: A Hmong Life Story with Ethnographic Commentary* (1989), which is associated with the award-winning film documentary *Between Two Worlds: The Hmong Shaman in America* (1989); and an illustrated book on the art of Hmong Americans, *Textiles, Silver, Wood of the Hmong-Americans: Art of the Highland Lao* (1985), edited by Joan Randall. See also the multivolume *The Hmong World* (1986), edited by Brenda Johns and David Strecker. An informative article, "Sudden Unexpected Nocturnal Death Syndrome Among Hmong Immigrants: Examining the Role of the 'Nightmare,'" appeared in the *Journal of American Folklore* (winter, 1991).—*Bruce M. Mitchell*

Hobby, Oveta Culp (b. Jan. 19, 1905, Killeen, Tex.): Government and military official. From 1925 to 1931 Culp was the parliamentarian of the Texas House of Representatives. After her marriage to William Hobby, publisher of the *Houston Post,* she took the position of research editor for the magazine (1953-1955). She is best known for establishing the Women's Auxiliary Army Corps in 1942 under General George C. Marshall; she served, at different times, as director, major, and colonel. In 1953 she was named secretary of the newly formed Department of Health, Education and Welfare, thereby becoming the second woman ever to serve on the Cabinet.

Holiday, Billie "Lady Day" (Eleanora Fagan; Apr. 7, 1915, Baltimore, Md.—July 17, 1959, New York, N.Y.): African American jazz singer. Holiday started performing in Harlem clubs in 1930 and sang with the bands of

Jazz singer Billie Holiday won worldwide acclaim for her unique, emotional style. (AP/Wide World Photos)

Artie Shaw, Benny Goodman, and Count Basie. She became a popular recording artist in the late 1930's and in 1940 began club and theater appearances on her own. Her unique vocal style was personalized, her tone "rough" and emotional, and her subject matter often harshly realistic. "Strange Fruit" and "God Bless the Child" were among her best-known songs. Despite financial success, Holiday suffered from drug and alcohol addiction, as her 1956 autobiography recounts. These conditions hastened her death.

Holidays and festivals: Along with FOODS AND COOKING, holidays and festivals represent one of the most enjoyable, accessible aspects of cultural diversity in the United States. Through celebration, Americans of various backgrounds affirm their identity and learn about the cultures of others. In the history of cultural PLURALISM and MULTICULTURALISM in the United States, holidays and festivals have been used to highlight cultural distinctions, to unify members of groups, and to break down barriers between groups.

These special occasions are intimately related to the arts, FOLKLORE, and belief systems of a community. The celebratory approach to food, music, dance, decoration, symbols, rituals, speeches, parades, pageants, dress, and social customs becomes an important marker of ethnicity as well as a sustainer of group heritage and family life. The multifaceted nature of holidays and festivals makes them popular with a broad cross section of people. It is no coincidence that political leaders speak on television on national holidays and make appearances at local festivals; they gain favor for being symbolically associated with an enjoyable event that is seen as a positive reflection of community or national life.

toms change and exhibit tremendous variety; students should not assume that all customs associated with a holiday are still in use everywhere or that the customs that remain carry their original meaning. To understand a holiday or custom fully, one should study it in the context of general information about that culture, in an effort to seek out the meaning of the holiday practices for the celebrants themselves.

Characteristics. Holidays and festivals are calendar customs—traditional practices that recur annually at a

The traditional Japanese Cherry Blossom Festival celebrates the beauty of the blossoms and the freshness of youth. (Courtesy SFCVB)

Holidays have become an integral part of many MULTICULTURAL EDUCATION programs, especially for young children. This approach has been criticized, however, for perpetuating superficial STEREOTYPES about ethnic groups that do not reflect the range of lifestyles and values found within modern communities. A common pitfall is to attribute customs performed long ago in the land of origin, such as in late nineteenth century Italy, to an immigrant group or their descendants, such as urban Italian Americans in the 1990's. Like other forms of folklore, holiday cus-

particular time of year and mark that time as different from the norm. The date may be set by age-old tradition or by recent laws and community initiative. Some holiday dates are movable, such as CHINESE NEW YEAR, which is based on a lunar (rather than solar) calendar and usually falls in January or February, and Eastern Orthodox church holidays such as EASTER that are based on the old Julian (rather than Gregorian) calendar. The timing of a holiday often reveals its origins. Many celebrations are rooted in the seasons of the agricultural year such as spring planting and fall harvesting. Others commemorate a historic occasion, as with the many national independence days celebrated by immigrant groups in the United States. Still others are tied to high points in a religious calendar associated with a leader (Buddha's birthday, April 8), an event (Jewish PASSOVER for the exodus from Egypt), or a designated saint's day (Our Lady of Guadalupe, December 12).

Festivals are events that are generally more complex, more organized, and more public than holidays. Some festivals are highly elaborated holidays or are planned around a holiday, as when the Nisei Week events in Los Angeles encompass the street dancing traditions of Obon, the Japanese summertime festival of the dead. Yet holidays need not necessarily have a festival attached to them. Some holidays may be celebrated relatively quietly at home, in church, or in a social organization, while others, thrown open to the whole community, take on aspects of a festival, as with a Mexican Independence Day parade.

Not all holidays and festivals are joyous in purpose or in practice. Armenian Americans and Jewish Americans each have remembrance days so as not to forget the tragedies that befell their people in the Armenian Genocide in the early 1900's and the HOLOCAUST during World War II. These days are somber occasions for prayer, speeches, and reflection; Armenian businesses tend to be closed in mourning. Members of the PENITENTES sect in New Mexico observe Good Friday with self-flagellation and the dragging of heavy crosses in procession to commemorate the sufferings of Christ. Observant Muslims are required to fast from dawn to dusk for the entire month of Ramadan while diligently reading the Koran and abstaining from sex, gossip, and other behaviors; this period of privation ends, however, in convivial late-night dinners and culminates in the joyous feasting of Eid ul Fitr.

Both holidays and festivals can be divided into several categories: ethnic, religious, regional, national, and occupational. The first two types are the focus of this essay, as they relate most clearly to multiculturalism. Yet national holidays such as July 4 may have variations according to one's cultural group, while regional celebrations or occupational ones, such as the Cowboy Poetry Gathering in Elko, Nevada, also reflect the nation's diversity.

Another way to categorize celebrations is according to their deep-rootedness in a culture. Folklorists speak roughly of traditional, revivalist, and newly invented holidays and festivals. Traditional holidays include most of those in the religious category and some deriving from ancient ethnic folk custom. THANKSGIVING, though considered traditional and based on the custom of harvest home feasts like that of the Pilgrims in 1621, was not actually declared a national holiday until the 1860's when regionalism gave way to pressures for Americanization. American Indian POWWOWS are another example of a revival type of festival, adapted from elements of Plains celebrations. Governments or communities may invent new holidays or festivals as a self-conscious way of recognizing or promoting a particular culture. In 1964, Norwegian Americans deliberately placed the new Leif Ericson Day (October 9) close to Columbus Day (October 12) to bring greater attention to an earlier explorer of the New World. Over time, some newly invented celebrations take on traditional qualities.

Traditional Holidays and Festivals. There are often surprising links between the ways different groups celebrate. For example, eggs feature prominently in EASTER observances, from the well-known Easter egg hunt on the church lawn to the game of cracking one another's red-dyed eggs among Greek, Armenian, and Russian Americans to the confetti-filled *cascarones* eggs thrown by Mexican Americans. All these customs are holdovers of pagan rituals of spring and rebirth, which coincided with what became the Easter season. Entering a new year likewise holds some similar connotations and obligations among ethnic minorities. At their respective New Year holidays of Tet, ROSH HASHANAH, and Diwali, Vietnamese Americans, Jewish Americans, and Hindu Asian Indian Americans are supposed to settle their debts and start the year with a clean slate—reminiscent of the mainstream practice of making resolutions on December 31. Both the Mexican DAY OF THE DEAD (November 2) and the Japanese Obon holiday (July 12-16) stress honoring the dead through the cleaning and decorating of graves and the offering of favorite foods, though they differ considerably in their style and symbolism. The Mexican holiday falls, significantly, on Catholic All Souls' Day, which follows All Saints' Day (November 1) and All Hallow's Eve (October 31), the latter coinciding with mainstream American Halloween.

One of the most common symbols used in holiday celebration is light, particularly the natural light of candles. In the *kinnara* candelabra of the African American KWANZAA celebration, the seven candles stand for the seven ethical principles that are the theme of the holiday. In the Jewish HANUKKAH menorah, the eight candles represent the miracle of a vial of oil that burned for eight days in the ancient temple in Jerusalem. In the Hindu Diwali, lanterns represent the victory of light over darkness when the god Rama was restored to his throne after a battle with a demon. Thus, material objects along with ritual help to tell the story or teach the lesson that is the point of the celebration.

An especially rich vein of holiday and festival tradition exists around the pre-Lenten season, usually culminating in MARDI GRAS (literally, "fat Tuesday"), the day before Ash Wednesday. Many world peoples and their American communities have customs of masquerading, dancing, and parades on this day. Perhaps the best-known version of this in the United States occurs in New Orleans, where for more than 150 years clubs known as "krewes" have devoted many months and thousands of dollars in the preparation of competitive floats. Among them are the black

More than fifty "krewes" have floats in the annual Mardi Gras parade in New Orleans. (Louisiana Office of Tourism)

"Mardi Gras Indians," who stage their own parade. Acadian (Cajun) Americans in rural Louisiana sponsor riotous festivities for the day, and West Indians in New York take part in huge street celebrations known as Carnival, while the Amish and German Americans celebrate Fastnacht.

Saint's days are marked in a variety of intriguing ways. On St. Joseph's Day (March 19), some Italian Americans construct multitiered, lace-covered altars or tables laden with Lenten foods (such as fruits, elaborate breads, and baked fish) along with candles, Catholic religious objects, and family mementos in a special corner of their house or church hall. They then invite their family and friends for a feast in honor of this patron saint of the poor, an event that is sometimes used as a church fund-raiser. Portuguese Americans take pride in their *festas*, in which community members carry religious statuary through the streets, followed by church leaders, brass bands, and youth in folk costumes; a queen and her court may also be chosen as part of the festivities. Devotees of the Afro-Cuban SANTERÍA religion meet in homes for spirited ritual drumming and song in front of an altar to Santa Barbara, who is associated with music.

Numerous holidays surround the CHRISTMAS season. Las Posadas (December 16-24), as observed by Mexican Americans, reenacts Mary and Joseph's search for a place for Jesus to be born. Singers in a lantern-lit procession, sometimes dressed like Mary and Joseph, stop at houses or churches along the way and end with feasting. Some women set up bright, intricate *nacimientos* (nativity scenes) with Mexican decorative motifs in their homes, around which visitors gather for prayer, singing, and socializing during their season. Some cities, such as San Antonio, Texas, and Albuquerque, New Mexico, also organize large public processions for Las Posadas. Epiphany (January 6) is more important than Christmas itself for many American Christians. Greek Americans, for example, commemorate Jesus' baptism with the Blessing of the Waters. Priests and bishops in their finest robes lead a procession to the nearest body of water and throw in a gold cross; whoever dives in and retrieves it is thought to have good luck. The event has long been a tourist attraction in the Greek enclave of Tarpon Springs, Florida.

Traditions have grown up around historically based holidays as well. Juneteenth (June 19) marks the day that General Gordon Granger arrived in Texas to enforce the EMANCIPATION PROCLAMATION in 1863—

one of many gradual steps leading to freedom for the slaves. Modern African Americans observe the occasion with picnics, church services and suppers, and parades, especially in the South; like other holidays, it is a popular time for homecomings for those who have left the area. In this way, holidays provide an occasion for reunions that help maintain family and community bonds. The holiday has an educational rather than a recreational function and atmosphere when it is celebrated by museums and schools that are trying to raise awareness of African American cultural heritage.

Some traditional holidays have been brought wholesale to the United States by immigrants. In Belize in Central America, Garifuna Settlement Day (November 17) is the biggest holiday of the year. It commemorates the migration of the GARIFUNA Black Carib minority groups from nearby Honduras to Belize, where they eventually built a strong community. The holiday is also the main time that Garifuna immigrants come together in the United States, the women wearing the full skirts and matching headscarves of their homeland. In Los Angeles, their celebration begins with a Catholic Mass in the Garifuna language, followed by feasting and participatory music and dancing in the church parking lot. Some of the most striking AFRICAN CULTURAL SURVIVALS in the United States are in evidence as women lead distinctive call-and-response singing around a group of drummers and flirting dancers, much as they do all night in the Belizean city of Dangriga.

Revivalist Celebrations. Among the most impressive forms of American celebration are the POWWOWS of American Indians, whether those held monthly for a few hundred people in a community center or large outdoor summertime events that attract tens of thousands of Indians from distant states. These occasions were created as a form of intertribal cultural and social exchange that stressed Plains styles of American Indian music, dance, and dress. They draw on traditional elements but differ in both purpose and atmosphere from religiously based celebrations on reservations and in pueblos. They have become an arena for spectacular innovations in Indian dance regalia by young people who participate in dance competitions and by craftspersons and vendors who market costume supplies at the event. Although many simultaneous activities go on at a powwow, the center of attention is the dance, which takes place around the "drum" (a group of singers and drummers) at the center of the circle.

Some dances are participatory while others are the privilege of certain people, such as veterans, and still others, such as the fast, elaborately costumed "fancy dances," are the object of competition for prizes. The

Tribes from all over the United States participate in large events such as this powwow in Taos, N.Mex., where two girls await their dance category. (Elaine S. Querry)

Master of Ceremonies skillfully orchestrates the event, taking note of introductions of new dancers into the community, the honoring of special persons, and the exchanging of gifts.

Sometimes a community organization revives a waning celebration that has previously been observed privately or quietly. For example, in the 1970's and 1980's, groups in the CHINATOWNS of San Francisco and Los Angeles revived the Chinese Moon Festival, which celebrates the most intense full moon of the year. On this day, Chinese people traditionally eat moon cakes filled with a lotus seed and nut paste and preserved duck egg yolks representing the moon. There are long lines for these delicacies at Chinatown bakeries just before the holiday. In Los Angeles, crowds fill the streets, viewing the moon while enjoying moon cakes, Chinese folk music, and dance. In San Francisco, a procession of schoolchildren carries a long papier-mâché dragon.

Newly Created Celebrations. The creation of new holidays and festivals has immense social and political significance. These celebrations are a way of bringing attention to various ethnic groups, regions, traditions, and achievements, among other things. They assert the power of a particular group to define and shape its culture and promote it to the rest of American society.

The African American holiday of KWANZAA (Swahili for "first fruits") was started in 1966 by black studies professor Maulana KARENGA as a means of paying tribute to African heritage. Scheduled for December 26 through January 1, the holiday was also an attempt to develop an alternative or supplement to CHRISTMAS that was symbolically relevant to the lives of black people. Homes or community centers are decorated in the colors of African liberation (red, green, and black) and with harvest fruits. Seven candles, one for each day, represent the seven principles of unity, self-determination, collective responsibility, cooperative economics, purpose, creativity, and faith. These ideas are a starting point for learning about African cultures through speeches and study. Gifts are also exchanged, but the mood throughout is restrained, dignified, and proud. One unique feature of Kwanzaa is ceremonies in which African Americans take on a traditional African name, signaling their connection to the land of their ancestors.

The CIVIL RIGHTS MOVEMENT, the INDIAN RIGHTS MOVEMENT, the CHICANO MOVEMENT, and the ETHNIC HERITAGE REVIVAL of the 1960's and 1970's all had an impact on the nature of American holidays. The federal government declared the birthday of Martin Luther KING, Jr. (January 18) a holiday in 1985, to the delight of some Americans and the chagrin of others. Government has also proclaimed month-long observances celebrating BLACK HISTORY (February), Asian/Pacific Heritage (May), and HISPANIC HERITAGE (September), prompting a wealth of special programs from television documentaries to school assemblies to municipal festivals during that time. While some supporters of MULTICULTURALISM applaud the recognition that these annual observances bring to minority cultural contributions and community concerns, others fault the programming as too superficial because it is done in a tokenistic manner (only once a

This "Healthy High Five" race, part of San Francisco's 1992 Cinco de Mayo festival, shows how such events often grow beyond specific cultural origins. (Robert Fried)

year). They argue that multicultural heritage should be celebrated and explored throughout the year in schools and other areas of public life.

As government and business promote certain ethnic holidays as public events, they appear to become shared cultural property. For example, many people other than Irish Americans wear green and patronize Irish bars on St. Patrick's Day (March 17), and many people other than Mexicans enjoy Mexican food on CINCO DE MAYO (May 5). This sort of cultural borrowing, often motivated by commercial or civic gimmicks, may be seen either as a means of trivializing ethnic holidays or as a way to bring people together.

Another relatively recent phenomenon is the advent of the cultural festival, often billed as a "celebration of diversity." Such events are commonly sponsored by local or state government, ostensibly in an effort to improve intergroup relations. These festivals at their best are models of CULTURAL PLURALISM in action with a juxtaposition of foods, crafts, entertainment, and other activities from a variety of communities. Even the most timid audience members can safely and comfortably sample unfamiliar cultural experiences, at least for the day. Such events can create a sense of harmony between groups as participants and audience members notice their similarities and appreciate their differences.

The sharing of holidays and festivals, whether within cultures or across cultures, is an important tool in MULTICULTURAL EDUCATION and communication. The more positive associations people have with the celebrations of themselves and others, the more receptive they will be to learning about and interacting with people of other backgrounds. Yet for all their value, holidays and festivals represent only one element in a given culture and should be understood as such.

SUGGESTED READINGS. Numerous reference works describe holiday origins and customs, such as George and Virginia Schaun's *American Holidays and Special Days* (1986), but many are dated or insufficiently multicultural in their scope. *The Folklore of American Holidays* (1987), edited by Hennig Cohen and Tristan Potter Coffin, is a broad, relatively diverse compilation of calendar customs. For a fine photographic essay on a distinctly American form of festival, see *Powwow* (1993) by George Ancona. Other useful sources include Judith Young's *Celebrations: America's Best Festivals, Jamborees, Carnivals, and Parades*, Patricia Haseltine's *East and Southeast Asian Material Culture in North America: Collections, Historical Sites, and*

Festivals (1989), and James C. Anyika's *African American Holidays: A Historical Research and Resource Guide to Cultural Celebrations* (1991).—*Susan Auerbach*

Holocaust, the: Systematic extermination of an estimated fifteen million people, including JEWS, Slavs, Poles, Russians, GYPSIES, and homosexuals, as well as infirm, elderly, and mentally ill people, as perpetrated by Nazi Germany in the years before and during World War II. Derived from the Greek word *holokaustos,* meaning "complete destruction by fire," the term is often used more specifically to speak of the attempted destruction of central and eastern Europe's flourishing Jewish population and culture in which six million Jews died.

In describing the Holocaust, Nobel laureate Elie Wiesel said, "Not all victims were Jews, but all Jews were victims." Anguish over the event's effect on their people is a crucial part of the cultural identity of many American Jews, including the assimilated and nonreligious. The Holocaust's horrors helped to discredit ANTI-SEMITISM in the United States and much of the world, while bringing about greater sympathy for ZIONISM and the emerging state of Israel.

Historical Background. The seeds of the Holocaust can be traced to political, economic, and social developments of late nineteenth century Europe. In 1870, the German states were reunited under Otto von Bis-

Nazi SS officer murdering a Jewish mother and child. (Simon Wiesenthal Center)

marck. Nationalism grew steadily, encouraged by waves of westward emigration and a simultaneous influx of immigrants from the east. WORLD WAR I (1914-1918) made conditions worse by displacing thousands of individuals. The severe restrictions imposed upon Germany in 1919 by the Peace Treaty of Versailles angered and humiliated many Germans. Jews and other non-Germans became scapegoats for the nation's political and economic difficulties. There was talk of "the Jewish Problem" and a worldwide Jewish conspiracy. The GREAT DEPRESSION of 1929-1932 also fanned the flames of nationalism and prejudice.

Estimated Number of Jews Killed in the Final Solution

Country	Estimated Pre-Final Solution Population	Estimated Jewish Population Annihilated	
		Number	Percent
Poland	3,300,000	3,000,000	90
Baltic countries	253,000	228,000	90
Germany/Austria	240,000	210,000	90
Protectorate	90,000	80,000	89
Slovakia	90,000	75,000	83
Greece	70,000	54,000	77
The Netherlands	140,000	105,000	75
Hungary	650,000	450,000	70
SSR White Russia	375,000	245,000	65
SSR Ukraine*	1,500,000	900,000	60
Belgium	65,000	40,000	60
Yugoslavia	43,000	26,000	60
Romania	600,000	300,000	50
Norway	1,800	900	50
France	350,000	90,000	26
Bulgaria	64,000	14,000	22
Italy	40,000	8,000	20
Luxembourg	5,000	1,000	20
Russia (RSFSR)*	975,000	107,000	11
Denmark	8,000	—	—
Finland	2,000	—	—
Total	8,861,800	5,933,900	67

Source: From Geoffrey Bar-Lev and Joyce Sakkal, *Jewish Americans Struggle for Equality.* Discrimination series, p. 63. Vero Beach, Fla.: Rourke Corp., 1992.

*The Germans did not occupy all the territory of this republic.

Adolf Hitler, an Austrian-born German soldier decorated for his service in World War I, had helped to found the National Socialist German Workers' Party (the Nazi Party) in 1919. At the party's helm in 1923, he led an aborted coup attempt that landed him in prison. There he wrote his political manifesto, *Mein Kampf* (*My Struggle*), advocating German expansion and the "purification" of the German population.

By 1932, economic hardship and the need for national identity rendered Germany ripe for Hitler's strident message. He ran for the presidency, blaming capitalism, Jewish business, communists, and the Treaty of Versailles for the ills of German society. He lost the election, but the Nazis won a parliamentary victory, and Hitler was appointed to the powerful position of chancellor.

Hitler moved quickly to codify Nazi dogma. He proclaimed the Third Reich, outlawed the Communist Party, organized a secret police force, and obtained the power to rule by decree. He set up concentration camps for the prolonged detention and forced labor of his political enemies. Having long spoken of "removing" Jews from Germany, he initiated hundreds of laws to restrict their social connections, housing and employment options, freedom of movement, and property rights. The government also turned its back on the random outbursts of violence against Jews.

Hitler wanted GERMAN JEWS to emigrate, but there was nowhere for them to go. Surrounding nations had their own "Jewish Problems," and other likely destinations such as the United States and British Palestine had limits on immigration. U.S. President Franklin Delano Roosevelt, anxious to deal with Hitler diplomatically and avoid major international conflict, did little in response to the deteriorating prospects for European Jewry.

In 1938, when Hitler tried to force the repatriation of Polish Jews from Germany, an angry young Polish Jew named Herschel Grynzpan assassinated a German diplomat in Paris. In response, on November 9, 1938, a wave

A synagogue in Berlin burning on Kristallnacht, *Nov. 9, 1938.* (Simon Wiesenthal Center)

of anti-Semitic violence swept across Germany. Synagogues were burned and Jewish businesses were looted and destroyed on *Kristallnacht ("The Night of Broken Glass") which legitimized open violence against Jews.*

In response to *Kristallnacht,* Roosevelt recalled the American ambassador from Berlin. Protest rallies were organized across the United States, including a gathering of twenty-five thousand at New York's Madison Square Garden, and Jews and Christians joined in a Day of Prayer on November 20, 1938. Soon, however, American Jewish response was tempered by German threats to retaliate against German Jews for the public uproar.

World War II. In March, 1938, with the acquiescence of the Western powers, Hitler had invaded Austria, and the attack on Poland on September 1, 1939, started WORLD WAR II. His 1939 nonaggression pact with Russian dictator Josef Stalin lasted until June, 1941, when German forces launched an invasion of the Soviet Republics. The offensive war immediately brought enormous territories and populations into German hands, including Poland's 3.3 million Jews. As the German army moved eastward, ghettos were established in prominent Jewish centers, such as Lodz, Warsaw, Vilna, and L'vov, for the concentration and control of Jews.

The Nazis considered Jews to be nonhumans who were threats to the state by their very existence. Slavs and GYPSIES were considered subhuman, and homosexuals were "socially undesirable." In conquered lands, operational units called *Einsatzgruppen,* consisting of both trained militia and armed civilians, would follow the advancing army and assemble unwanted populations for mass slaughter. Jews, communists, Gypsies, and others would be marched into a forest, ordered to undress, forced into enormous pits already piled high with corpses, and shot in the back of the neck.

While many Americans were shocked by news of such events, ANTI-SEMITISM was also strong at the time in the United States. In one poll, 35 percent of Americans believed that American Jews had too much power, and as late as 1941, 20 percent of those asked said that Jews were a bigger threat than Nazi Germany to the United States.

The U.S. State Department opposed the expansion of existing immigration quotas, as there was still widespread concern over unemployment. Moreover, between 1938 and 1941, quotas allowing 212,000 immigrants from the Nazi-occupied lands were only two-thirds filled because of restrictionist visa practices within the State Department; the 24,000 immigrants accepted in 1943 represented an eighty-year low. In 1939, the *St. Louis,* a ship loaded with German Jewish refugees, lingered off the Cuban and Florida coasts for weeks, where it was refused landing permission, before heading back to Europe. There were calls for the Western powers to accommodate the growing numbers of refugees, but an international conference convened in 1938 at Evian, France, brought minimal results. Hitler publicly justified Nazi actions by the nodding acquiescence of foreign governments and peoples.

The Final Solution. With the cumulative conquest of territory in White Russia, Ukraine, Lithuania, Latvia, Estonia, and Russia, the Nazi invaders had more and more Jews, communists, Gypsies, and war prisoners to eliminate. Hitler and the Nazis needed a solution to the "Jewish Problem." Reinhard Heydrich, charged by Hitler with overseeing forced emigration programs, devised the *Endlosung,* the "Final Solution," to render the German empire *Judenrein,* or "clean of Jews." Hitler convened a Nazi conference in January of 1942 to hone and implement this policy.

The plan provided for the efficient, government-orchestrated extermination of all European Jewry—nothing short of systematic genocide. A number of death camps were added to the network of concentration camps that already existed. In Poland, the camp at Chelmno was opened in December, 1941, followed by Belzec, Sobibor, Treblinka, Majdanek, and, in Austria, Mauthausen. Existing camps at Auschwitz and Dachau added extermination facilities. Through trial and error at the camps, Nazi doctors developed methods for murdering and disposing of thousands of people a day using a poison gas called Cyclon B.

Prisoners arrived by train, after days of traveling in overcrowded livestock wagons. They were inspected to sort out the fittest workers or those with special talents. Some went to barracks and forced labor; most were marched in long lines, forced to undress, given haircuts, and herded into large "showers." Sometimes a Jewish Star of David over the doorway offered false security. Once full, the chamber was locked, and the showers released deadly gas. Once all the occupants were dead—sometimes a matter of minutes, sometimes longer—other prisoners had to pull the corpses apart, extract gold from teeth, and search the bodies for hidden belongings. Victims' hair was shipped back to German upholstery factories; their teeth yielded from eighteen to twenty pounds of gold per day. At first, the corpses were transported to mass graves in nearby forests. Later, pyres and crematoria were built to burn them.

The death camps processed millions of victims. The Nazis pitted Jew against Jew, Gypsy against commu-

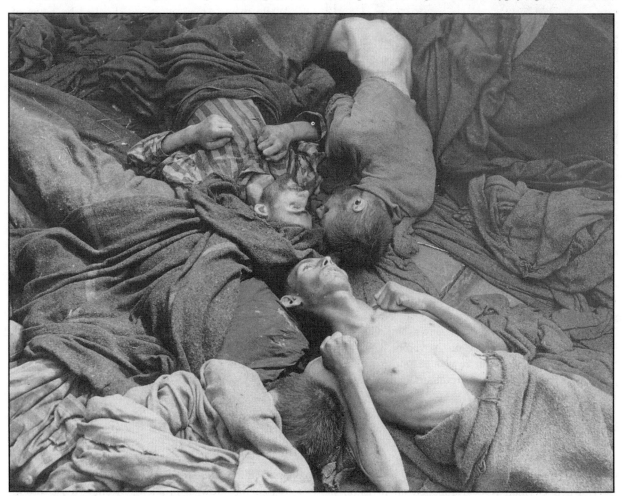

Thousands of Holocaust victims died of starvation while being transported between concentration camps. (National Archives)

nist against homosexual, the fit against the disabled in an effort to break wills and obtain compliance. At Auschwitz, the most notorious of the camps, there was an average of one death per minute, day and night, week after week, for nearly three years. It is estimated that four million people lost their lives at Auschwitz by gas, injections, shooting, hanging, hunger, and disease.

News of the Final Solution reached Allied leaders in mid-1942 and became public that December. Many could not fully believe that such systematic extermination was actually taking place. The United States was one of eleven nations officially to condemn Hitler's government, and there was a public outcry for action to save the millions still in danger. The U.S. State Department, however, opposed diverting war resources to the rescue of civilians, and the assistant secretary of war three times rejected proposals for aerial bombing of railways leading to Auschwitz or of the gas chambers themselves. In January of 1944, President Roosevelt established the War Refugee Board to investigate and address the refugee situation, but no concerted action was ever taken to end the Holocaust itself.

As the Allies gained ground on both the eastern and western fronts, the Nazis accelerated the Final Solution in late 1943 by liquidating ghettos and sending the remaining inhabitants to the death camps. Deportation of Greek Jews began in 1943, and some 400,000 Hungarian Jews, who had been relatively safe during the early years of the war, were transported to Auschwitz in April, 1944.

In November, 1944, Heinrich Himmler, longtime leader of Hitler's Defense Corps, ordered operations at Auschwitz to cease. With enemy forces advancing through the winter, the Nazis closed and dismantled camps and marched the remaining prisoners westward. Thousands who survived the camps subsequently died on the road back to Germany.

The Allied European victory in April of 1945 effectively ended the Holocaust, but even after the war, persecution and anti-Semitism persisted. In September of 1945, President Harry Truman received an official report on the mistreatment of Holocaust survivors by the U.S. military.

Legacy. The final reckoning of the enormity of the Holocaust took years to calculate. Innocent civilians from France, Belgium, Holland, Germany, Poland, Czechoslovakia, Austria, Hungary, Italy, Yugoslavia, Greece, Bulgaria, Romania, and the Soviet Union had been sacrificed to the Nazi death machines. Of an es-timated nine to eleven million European Jews in 1939, six million were killed. Among the victims were 80 percent of the leading European Jewish scholars and rabbis, taking a wealth of culture and knowledge with them. Estimates suggest that 500,000 of 700,000 European Gypsies lost their lives. By nationality, there were some seven million victims from the Soviet Union, including four million civilians; 2.5 million Poles; and 1.5 million Yugoslavs.

Nearly 100,000 European Jews who survived the Holocaust emigrated to the United States after the war through the DISPLACED PERSON'S ACT of 1948, and more arrived in the 1950's with the political upheavals in Poland and Hungary. With the help of such groups as the Hebrew Immigrant Aid Society, they settled mostly in insular communities in New York and other cities. When the Luxembourg Agreement of 1952 mandated German reparations for Holocaust survivors, lawyers and investigators accumulated a body of information on the survivors and their new lives. Psychologists began to recognize patterns of anxiety, depression, guilt, insomnia, and isolation that they called "survivors' syndrome." The insights gleaned from Holocaust survivors have been applied to other collective victims, such as African Americans, American Indians, and Japanese survivors of the atomic bombs. Since the 1960's in the United States and Israel, psychologists have identified certain patterns in the children of Holocaust survivors as well.

In the fields of literature, history, and the social sciences, the Holocaust has become the most extreme model of human atrocity and suffering. American Jews invoke the tragedy in the phrase, "never again," vowing to block all future Hitlers with, for example, a strong Israel. On the other hand, a small group of NEO-NAZIS and academics who call themselves Holocaust revisionists continue to claim that the Holocaust never really happened. Their claims are refuted by the growing field of Holocaust studies and several Holocaust-related museums in the United States, as well as by the chilling testimony of survivors.

SUGGESTED READINGS. An authoritative examination of the Holocaust that focuses on the Nazis is Raul Hilberg's *The Destruction of the European Jews* (1961, rev. ed. 1985). A penetrating view of the Jewish experience is found in Yehuda Bauer's *A History of the Holocaust* (1982). Arthur D. Morse's *While Six Million Died: A Chronicle of American Apathy* (1968) explores the American response to the Holocaust. A classic in the autobiographical literature is *Night*

(1958) by Elie Wiesel, a Romanian-born Jew, international human rights advocate, and winner of the 1986 Nobel Peace Prize. Helen Epstein's *Children of the Holocaust: Conversations with Sons and Daughters of Survivors* (1979) explores the Holocaust's psychological legacy across two generations.—*Barry Mann*

Homelessness: One of the more perplexing social problems facing the United States today is homelessness. In the past the homeless population was generally considered skid row bums, alcoholics, hobos, or social misfits. Since the 1970's, this population has grown to include categories of people that do not fit this description. The exact number of the homeless is unknown. It is estimated that between 250,000 and three million people are homeless in the United States.

POVERTY is the primary cause of homelessness in the United States. The homeless are people of all ages, races, and educational and socioeconomic levels. Groups that are at the greatest risk for poverty as well as homelessness, however, are racial minorities, children, and members of households headed by females.

A number of factors have contributed to the increase in the homeless population since the 1970's. Beginning in that decade, thousands of patients were released from mental institutions. It was believed that community mental health centers could accommodate them. Because of the tremendous numbers released, however, many former patients ended up living on the streets.

A second factor that contributed to the ranks of the homeless was the dramatic rise in the numbers of the unemployed. Many industrial jobs that had helped the United States attain the highest standard of living in the world disappeared through attrition, plant closings, and/or relocation overseas. Many other businesses also opted to relocate outside the United States to take advantage of cheap labor, relaxed regulations on pollution, weak safety regulations, limited health insurance, the absence of workmen's compensation, and the prohibition against labor unions.

A third factor in the 1980's was the purging of the "welfare rolls" by President Ronald Reagan. John E. Farley, in *Sociology* (1990), suggested that the policies

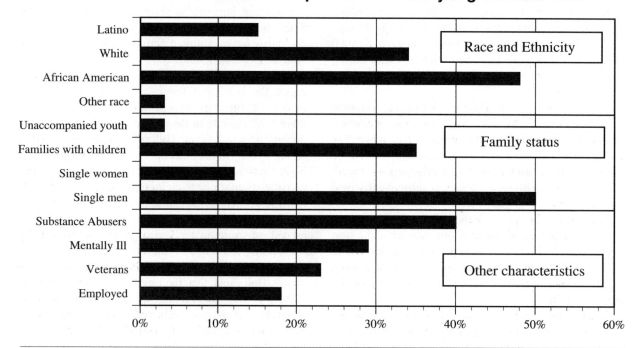

Characteristics of Homeless Population in Twenty-Eight Cities: 1991

Source: Data are from Carol Foster, ed. *Women's Changing Role.* Figure 1.6. Wylie, Tex.: Information Plus, 1992.
Note: These bars total more than 100% because most people fit into several categories. For instance a single man may also be a Latino, a veteran, and employed.

Women and children form the fastest-growing segment of the homeless population; this woman is staying at the Holland Hotel for the homeless in New York City. (AP/Wide World Photos)

of the Reagan Administration aggravated the problems of the poor through cutbacks in antipoverty and social programs, the deregulation of business, and a decrease in the tax rate for the wealthy.

A fourth factor that has contributed to the rise in homelessness has been a lack of affordable housing. The production of new affordable housing essentially ended in the 1980's, while the renovation of old housing has been more inclined toward luxury accommodations for upper-class people.

Numerous projects and organizations, ranging from shelters to advocacy groups, sprang up in the 1980's to help the homeless. Some homeless people took part in demonstrations, encampments, and even theater projects to publicize their plight in cities such as Los Angeles. Some municipalities took steps to ban sleeping on the street or panhandling. Yet no policies or programs seem to have remedied the situation. It appears that the homeless population will continue to rise in the United States. Some experts believe it has already reached epidemic proportions. Perhaps the most disturbing fact is that the fastest growing segments of the homeless population are women and children.

SUGGESTED READINGS. A thorough and unbiased account of homelessness and the social welfare system can be found in *Under the Safety Net: The Health and Social Welfare of the Homeless in the United States* (1990) by Philip W. Bricker. Those interested in improving conditions for the homeless should see *Homes For the Homeless: A Handbook for Action* (1990) by Adam Berger, Hiram Chodosh, and Ronald Slye. For a general understanding of the magnitude of the homeless situation, read *Homeless in America* (1990) by Carol L. M. Caton. A theoretical discussion of the homeless problem can be found in *Sociology* (1988) by Beth B. Hess, Elizabeth W. Markson, and Peter J. Stein.

Homestead Act (1862): Federal act that granted up to 160 acres of land from the public domain to citizens and persons who had filed their intention to become citizens who were either heads of household or over the age of twenty-one, providing that they build a house on the land, reside there for five years, and cultivate the land. The act took effect beginning June 1, 1863, and some later acts modified or waived some of these restrictions. An act of 1872 provided special benefits for Union veterans. The Homestead Act was repealed by Congress in 1976 in all states except Alaska, where it remained in force until 1986.

Homesteaders and exodusters: Settlers who moved westward—to what is now the Midwest—to acquire free land in the second half of the nineteenth century. The HOMESTEAD ACT of 1862 decreed that anyone able to occupy and farm 160 acres of unowned land for five years would own the land at the end of that time. Many homesteaders were immigrants who had little hope of finding good jobs in the eastern cities. The homesteaders, unfortunately, had a very difficult time, and most of them failed. Much of the land available for homesteading was poor, and most homesteaders were both untrained in farming and too poor to finance their efforts adequately. Exodusters was a name given to African American homesteaders, particularly those who migrated in a huge "exodus" from the post-Civil War South between the years 1879 and 1881. Most exodusters (so named because faith largely motivated their migration) moved to Kansas, which had been the home of abolitionist John Brown and had never been a slave state.

Homophobia: Fear and hatred of homosexuals (gays and lesbians) and homosexuality. This fear has often translated into systematic efforts by heterosexuals to discriminate against gays and lesbians.

Though no conclusive estimates exist as to the extent of homosexuality in the United States, most authorities agree that about 10 percent of the population is homosexual. At the same time, national surveys of sexual behavior report that approximately one-third of men and one-fifth of women have engaged in a some form of homosexual behavior. Homosexuality is unquestionably part of the fabric of American culture, but public opinion polls show that gays are viewed as

Marchers in 1986 urging defeat of the "LaRouche Initiative" that would have discriminated against people with AIDS. The AIDS epidemic caused increased homophobia in the 1980's. (AP/Wide World Photos)

outsiders by the dominant heterosexual (or straight) society.

Homophobia may be expressed or reinforced by overt acts of discrimination against gays, perpetuated in large measure by societal institutions such as religion, medicine, law, and the military. The Judeo-Christian tradition equates homosexuality with sin, and biblical proscriptions against the behavior can be found in both the Old and New Testaments. Until 1973, within the field of medicine, homosexuality was considered a form of mental illness, thereby stigmatizing homosexuals as being both "crazy" and sexually deviant. No state legally recognizes marriage between adults of the same sex, thereby denying them the economic, social, and emotional benefits (such as inheritance, spousal insurance coverage, and long term, recognized relationships) that are routinely afforded to heterosexual marriage partners. In addition, gays are often denied employment, promotions, and housing opportunities. Laws against sodomy ("oral-genital sex and/or anal intercourse") are still on the books in twenty-four states. In 1986, the Supreme Court, in a 5-4 decision, ruled in *Bowers v. Hardwick* that (to quote Marshall Kirk and Hunter Madsen) "the Constitution does not protect homosexual relations between consenting adults, even in the privacy of their own bedrooms."

The U.S. military long formally excluded gays, though thousands of gay men and women have served their country while keeping their homosexuality hidden. Ostensibly, the military has seen promiscuous gays as a threat to security and as being contrary to military discipline and lifestyle. In early 1993, President Bill Clinton sought to end the ban on gays in the military, but the idea met strong resistance. He proposed a compromise plan in July, 1993, under which individuals joining the military would no longer be required to state their sexual orientation; the plan fell far short, however, of allowing gays to serve openly.

Homophobia has become even more widespread since the onset of the ACQUIRED IMMUNE DEFICIENCY SYNDROME (AIDS) epidemic in the early 1980's. Originally associated with gay men, the virus reinforced dominant homosexual STEREOTYPES about sexual depravity and deviance—many religious fundamentalists interpreted the virus as God's punishment of homosexuals for their moral depravity—and fueled heterosexual fear and resentment of gays. The problem of AIDS in particular and homophobia in general prompted a new wave of GAY AND LESBIAN ACTIVISM

in the late 1900's. Thousands of gay political organizations such as the Gay Media Task Force, Gay Men's Health Crisis, and the National Gay Task Force, were formed to document and combat discrimination against homosexuals and provide legal, medical, and educational advocacy on behalf of homosexuals.

SUGGESTED READINGS. For a popular account of homophobia, see Marshall Kirk and Hunter Madsen's *After the Ball: How America Will Conquer Its Fear and Hatred of Gays in the 90's* (1989). John D'Emilio's *Sexual Politics, Sexual Communities: The Making of a Homosexual Minority in the United States, 1940-1970* (1983) provides an insightful treatment of the rise of homosexuals as a minority. *Bashers, Baiters, and Bigots: Homophobia in American Society* (1985), edited by John P. De Cecco, is a thought-provoking volume. Randy Shilts's *And the Band Played On: Politics, People, and the AIDS Epidemic* (1987) is one of the most widely cited works on AIDS and homophobia.

Honduran Americans: The relatively small Central American republic of Honduras occupies approximately 43,000 square miles, bordering the Caribbean Sea to the north, Nicaragua to the southeast, El Salvador to the southwest, and Guatemala to the northwest.

Honduras is the poorest nation in Central America, and the second most impoverished nation in Latin America (only Haiti ranks lower). Its infant mortality rate is higher than 10 percent, and more than half of its population is illiterate. The Honduran population is predominantly mestizo and Roman Catholic.

With the passage the IMMIGRATION ACT OF 1965, the United States imposed a ceiling on the number of immigrants legally admitted from the Western Hemisphere. Though Honduran immigration to the United States was slow prior to 1965, after the passage of this restrictive legislation, there was a tremendous influx of Hondurans to the United States. Some immigrated legally, and many entered illegally. From the 1960's to the early 1990's, approximately 100,000 Hondurans relocated to the United States.

To understand the reasons for this migration, one must study the history of Honduras. The impoverished country has had a tumultuous political history, characterized by repeated cycles of abortive elections, military juntas, dictatorships, and coups. Compounding the political instability have been problems related to Honduras' neighbors: El Salvador and Nicaragua.

With El Salvador torn apart by civil war in the late

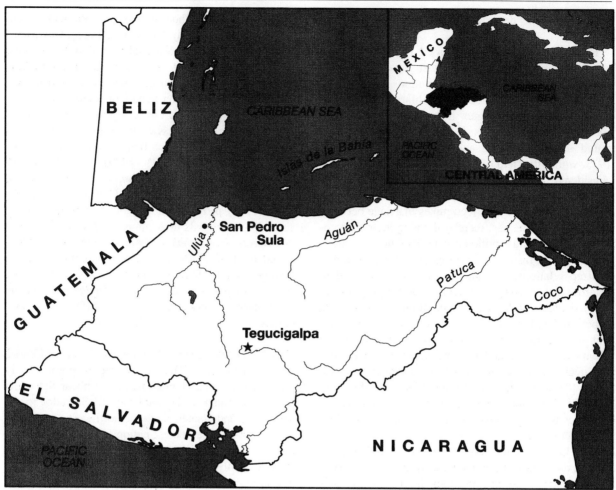

HONDURAS

1970's, throughout the 1980's, and into the 1990's, thousands of Salvadorans took illegal refuge in Honduras, competing with Hondurans for jobs in an economically deprived nation with an already high unemployment rate. Groups of Salvadoran leftists set up strategic bases in Honduras from which to stage their attacks on the right-wing Salvadoran death-squad government.

Nicaragua, too, embroiled Honduras in its own internal warfare and provided the United States with an opportunity to gain a foothold in Honduras. After instituting a revolutionary government in Nicaragua, the Sandinistas were in constant battle against the counter-revolutionaries (Contras). The United States, in return for providing military assistance and financial aid to Honduras, set up permanent military bases in Honduras from which the U.S. government illegally provided military and financial assistance to the Contras.

In the light of these realities, thousands of Hondurans fled to the United States in search of stability, job opportunities, and peace. Great numbers set up residences on the Gulf Coast, in the northeast, and in the southwest. Most remain poor; the majority of those who work are employed as domestic workers.

Hong Kong, Chinese Americans from: Since at least the mid-1800's, Hong Kong Americans have played a significant role in the shaping of American culture and society. Whereas the first large numbers of Hong Kong immigrants were mostly laborers, they were pivotal in building the sugar plantations of Hawaii and the western portion of the first American transcontinental railroad. Both were crucial to the quick and vast economic expansion of the United States. Descendants of these and later immigrants, as well as first-generation immigrants and foreign investors from Hong Kong, have since diversified in other sectors of American business, politics, and community service. The country's oldest Cantonese-speaking Chinese community, in San Francisco, is an example of the evolution of the closed, self-contained Chinatown into a vast Asian American community which includes Japanese, Korean, and Southeast Asian Americans.

One example of how Chinese American businesses have changed the face of American society is the development of entertainment venues that mimic those popular in Hong Kong. These venues include Chinese theaters showcasing imported films from Hong Kong, Asia's largest film-producing country, which have cropped up especially in Los Angeles, the destination of choice for many newer immigrants. Also, Hong Kong-style karaoke singing "bars" (in turn imported from Japan) with private singing rooms are found not in this city's Chinatown but in its outlying, heavily Chinese-populated suburban areas of Alhambra, Rosemead, and Monterey Park. In addition, combination Chinese restaurants/nightclubs serving European-influenced Chinese cuisine that are popular with young residents in Hong Kong have also, in Los Angeles, been favorably attended by Chinese American families as well as the young Hong Kong student and immigrant populations. Video rental stores that stock television shows and films exclusively from Hong Kong have been popular for some time in Chinese American communities and gained more business with the addition of film and karaoke laserdiscs to their inventory. In addition, more well-known Hong Kong singers and entertainers choose to tour major American cities, staging concerts with elaborate sets, lighting, and costumes in large amphitheaters such as the Shrine Auditorium in Los Angeles.

Although Asian Americans in general have not historically been as politically active as other ethnic groups, the first Asian American political organization was formed by Chinese Americans in San Francisco in 1895. Initially called the Native Sons of the Golden State, it is now known as the CHINESE AMERICAN CITIZENS ALLIANCE, which has branches in many cities and is a substantial political action and education organization. In addition, many local Asian American watchdog and community development groups have sprung up, including Asian Pacific Americans for a New L.A. (APANLA) in Los Angeles. Yet, despite such involvement, Chinese American communities have a long history of unfair treatment by the majority society and authorities, which can be traced back through the history of the Hong Kong colony itself.

History of Hong Kong. By the eighteenth century, Europe began to expand trade with China greatly, and oceanic travel lines replaced the Silk Road through central China as the dominant trade route. China, wary of contact with the West, opened only one port for foreign trade in Canton, at the southern tip of China. Canton's close proximity to Hong Kong made the island vulnerable to later foreign hostilities over trade practices.

Britain's fondness for Chinese products, particularly tea, made it China's largest trading partner. British merchants were dismayed, however, with China's lack of interest in British goods, forcing merchants to trade British silver for desired Chinese goods. When Britain finally realized that the Chinese wanted opium for medicinal purposes, the British were only too eager to supply the drug. Recreational use of opium was soon cultivated and fed by Britain's steady supply. Angered by Britain's lack of compliance with attempts to crack down on illegal importation of opium, the Chinese government seized and destroyed twenty thousand chests of British opium in Canton, holding British merchants hostage until the chests were relinquished. Britain's reaction was to move the British community in Canton to Hong Kong, which was soon after occupied by a British naval force. Hostilities between Britain and China continued over Britain's demand for retribution for the confiscated opium. When the British navy took the offensive and threatened to capture Nanking, China agreed to avoid the imminent possibility of war by signing the 1842 Treaty of Nanking.

This treaty forced China to pay compensation for the destroyed opium, open more ports to foreign trade, and—most significantly for Hong Kong—annex the island of Hong Kong to Britain. In 1843 Hong Kong was officially declared a British colony. Greatly weakened economically and militarily, China soon became vulnerable to further Western domination, and by 1899, ceded both the Kowloon mainland peninsula and the New Territories just north of Kowloon to Britain. Thus, Hong Kong, as it is slated to exist until 1997, includes the island, Kowloon, and the New Territories, as well as many adjacent smaller islands.

While Chinese inhabitants initially reacted very negatively to British presence in Hong Kong, their population continued to grow, mainly through the addition of escapees from the growing political unrest and poverty in an increasingly unstable China. Hong Kong also became fully developed as a trading port that became more successful as the population rose, except for the brief interruption of the four-year Japanese occupation during World War II; population dropped as people fled to areas such as Macao and Singapore. When Britain reestablished its rule after the occupation, trade and industrialization expanded again, shaping Hong Kong into the bustling metropolis it is today. Thus, Hong Kong has maintained overwhelming ties to Western cultural influence since the beginning of the twentieth century.

Emigration of Hong Kong Chinese. The rapid population growth and development of Hong Kong as a major port set the stage for the emigration of Hong Kong Chinese. The earliest Hong Kong immigrants to the United States were probably merchants and students. The first Chinese college graduate in the United States, for example, was YUNG WING, a Hong Kong foreign student who received his Yale diploma in 1854.

Hong Kong harbors became a departure point for ships carrying hopeful Chinese gold seekers to the United States, which was referred to as "Gum Saan," meaning GOLD MOUNTAIN. The peak of the GOLD

A side street in the bustling trade center of Hong Kong. New immigration laws brought large numbers of people from Hong Kong to the United States in the late 1900's. (Japan Air Lines)

RUSH years saw a significant increase in the numbers of Chinese emigrants leaving Hong Kong, from 14,638 in 1855 to 26,213 in 1857. In order to pay for expensive passage, many of these young men signed labor contracts, indenturing them to several years of labor in California gold mines, agriculture, or transcontinental railroad construction. Many of these labor recruiters both tricked and physically forced men into signing such contracts in a practice known as the COOLIE trade.

At that time, Manchurian rule in China declared Chinese emigration illegal; thus, these large groups of Chinese who sailed to California generally left from Hong Kong (by then under British rule) rather than Canton, the usual exit port from China. Though it is impossible to determine exactly how many of these mostly young men were Hong Kong natives and how many were from the mainland, it is accurate to surmise that nearly all of them spoke some variation of the Cantonese dialect of Hong Kong and Guangdong province in southern China.

As an adaptive strategy, the early Chinese immigrants were forced to live in marginal communities. Racist hostilities in the West, particularly California, drove many Chinese to the eastern and central states. The Chinese became the scapegoats for the economic depression that followed the Gold Rush bust and post-Civil War Reconstruction.

Restrictionist laws limiting Chinese immigration to a trickle (mainly to teachers, merchants, and temporary visitors), beginning with the CHINESE EXCLUSION ACT of 1882, resulted from these hostilities. This act was continually amended until 1924, when a virtual halt on all Asian immigration was imposed, lasting until the act was repealed in 1965. Between 1924 and the end of World War II, the urban Chinese communities were essentially bachelor ghettos because of laws that prevented immigration of wives and families. Only a few merchants were allowed to bring their families, accounting for the few American-born Chinese before 1940. Thus, the early CHINATOWNS developed self-governing, community-based organizations that acted on behalf of their members in disputes, assisted the illiterate with letter-writing, and generally protected the isolated community. The Chinatowns also remained independent because most Chinatown residents, excluded from vocations that were reserved for whites, worked as employees of Chinatown businesses and industries, such as laundries and restaurants. Other industries included food production,

By the late nineteenth century, there were families from Hong Kong living in San Francisco's Chinatown. This photograph of children with traditional queues *(pigtails) was taken by noted photographer Arnold Genthe.* (Library of Congress)

cigar making, and garment making. The community also depended on Hong Kong merchants to import staple Chinese goods.

HongkongBank is an example of a business with a long American history. It opened its first office in San Francisco in 1875, carving a niche as a commercial bank that financed Asian trade business, especially from Hong Kong to the United States. The bank continues to operate today, and it has the second-largest presence of any American foreign-owned bank (the largest are the Japanese banks). In 1987, the bank moved its headquarters to Los Angeles, reflecting the greater influx of Asian immigrants and Asian American businesses there.

Hong Kong Influence After 1965. When the exclusionary acts were repealed by the IMMIGRATION AND NATIONALITY ACT OF 1965, a large influx of Hong Kong Chinese came into the country. Arrivals have steadily increased since then. Many Hong Kong immigrants gravitated to existing Chinese American communities and infused them with new families,

businesses, and economic vigor. The Chinatown tourist industry was built up during this period as laundries made way for gift stores catering to tourists. Other businesses that serve the Chinese American community such as grocery stores and bakeries also increased. Restaurants serving Cantonese food, including the popular dim sum (afternoon tea), are often staffed with cooks from Hong Kong.

Because of continued RACISM toward Asians, as well as the natural gravitation toward familiar communities and cultures, the first influence of Hong Kong Americans has been and continues to be concentrated in the areas of mostly domestic service industries, as well as local commerce, mainly in the import and export of foodstuffs and other goods from Hong Kong and China, which are in demand in Asian American communities.

Hong Kong immigrants have also sunk capital into Chinatown real estate, raising property values and revitalizing the "ghettoized" communities. In San Francisco, Los Angeles, and Washington, D.C., evidence of this is seen in the erection of multimillion dollar housing projects for low-income seniors, community service and recreation facilities, and large retail centers. In New York, many Chinatown offices are inhabited by first- and second-generation Chinese American professionals such as doctors, lawyers, and accountants, while immigrants seeking lower rents have created Chinese communities both south and north of Manhattan.

Businesses started by Hong Kong immigrants or backed by Hong Kong investment have also branched out from domestic and service industries. The Dah Chong Hong Trading Corporation, a subsidiary of a Hong Kong corporation, operates numerous retail automobile dealerships on the East and West Coasts. Hong Kong investors have also been involved in construction projects such as a large condominium complex in Oakland, California, which houses retail stores and parking structures as well as residences.

Hong Kong investment in the United States has not only invigorated the old urban CHINATOWNS but has expanded the Chinese American community in the suburbs as well, significantly changing city and state demographics. Many immigrants who are middle-class or upper-middle-class have the resources to live and invest in businesses in the suburbs. Monterey Park, California, is one such suburb that has been transformed into a Chinese American business hub. Located ten miles east of downtown Los Angeles, its Chinese American residents make up 85 percent of the Asian population, which is 41 percent of the city's total. The Chinese population in Monterey Park consists of Mandarin-speakers who are mostly first- or second-generation immigrants from Taiwan and China, with somewhat fewer Cantonese-speaking Hong Kong immigrants and their descendants. Monterey Park owes its reputation as a site of superior Chinese cuisine and its dense and diverse number of Chinese and other Asian restaurants to the success of the large, sumptuous Chinese seafood and dim sum restaurants staffed with Hong Kong chefs, established in the early 1980's by Hong Kong investors. Chinese

Businesses owned by Chinese Americans from Hong Kong range from small markets such as this to huge real estate ventures. (Robert Fried)

Hong Kong-born film director Wayne Wang, whose films include Dim Sum *(1984). (AP/Wide World Photos)*

restaurants in Monterey Park are abundant in numbers and variety, and competition is fierce for the large Chinese and American clientele with sophisticated gastronomical tastes. The population has also prompted the establishment of new bilingual churches, schools, theaters, and other services.

Foreign students from Hong Kong continue to attend American universities in large numbers. Hong Kong has been listed as the seventh largest country of origin for foreign students in the United States. Most Hong Kong Chinese students are concentrated in California, New York, Texas, Massachusetts, Pennsylvania, Illinois, Florida, and Ohio. Large Hong Kong student organizations are active on many campuses.

Contributions to American Popular Culture. The film industry in Hong Kong is one of the largest in Asia. Though American films have always found huge audiences in Hong Kong, films starring Hong Kong actors or directed by Hong Kong directors have also made their marks on the American cinematic experience. Most notable is martial artist/actor Bruce LEE, whose four films made during his lifetime were wildly popular with American audiences.

Hong Kong film festivals have also found a growing following in the United States and Canada, which has led to Hong Kong director John Woo's popularity in the United States. Woo's Chinese crime drama films are memorable for their nonstop, intense action scenes, and they have propelled the careers and popularity of actors Jackie Chan and Chow Yun-Fat.

Chinese American filmmakers also deal with themes of immigration and cultural adjustment in Cantonese Chinatown communities. While many are still independent projects that are released through Asian American film festivals and conferences, director Wayne WANG has attracted more mainstream audiences with his films *Dim Sum* (1984) and *Eat a Bowl of Tea* (1989), the latter based on Louis Chu's 1961 novel and featuring many well-known Hong Kong actors, such as Cora Miao.

In the American literary scene, Chinese American writers and playwrights with cultural roots in Hong Kong and Cantonese-speaking Chinese American communities are becoming more widely published and read. A partial list would include poets Marilyn Chin, Nellie Wong, and Russell Leong (who is the editor of *Amerasia Journal* and publications director of the UCLA Asian American Studies program); playwrights Ping Chong and Frank CHIN; and novelists Laurence Yep, Louis CHU, and Maxine Hong KINGSTON.

Hong Kong Americans and their descendants have also made strides in very diverse areas of American life. For example, Gloria Ma, a Hong Kong native, earned her Ph.D. in molecular biology from the University of California San Diego and founded XXsys Technologies, a San Diego-based company which sells and leases laboratory instruments that can perform nondestructive ultrasonic testing of advanced composite materials. Ma has the distinction of being a successful dual minority, a woman and Chinese American, in a male-dominated field of high technology. In the area of agriculture, there is Tom Lam, a native of Canton who grew up in Hong Kong and emigrated to California at the age of twenty. He began working as a farm laborer earning $1.15 an hour and now owns Lam's BLT Farms, which supplies 3 million cartons of produce per year to areas throughout the United States, Canada, Japan, and Hong Kong. The largest Asian-owned printing shop in San Francisco, Fong Brothers Printing, is owned and operated by Tony and Eugene Fong, who, like many former and present Hong Kong residents, were born in China but relocated to Hong Kong at an early age to escape the

Communist takeover. Fong Brothers Printing's clientele consists mostly of large businesses such as Bank of America, General Electric, and Hewlett-Packard.

Chinese American civic organizations and communities have increased the awareness of Chinese traditions and holidays through celebrations such as Chinatown CHINESE NEW YEAR parades. While these celebrations have been highly Americanized to include events such as the controversial Miss Chinatown beauty pageants to attract non-Chinese participants and observers, they have played a role in making these traditions and holidays a recognized part of the American multiethnic culture. A symbol of this recognition by the dominant culture was the release of the first U.S. postage stamp commemorating the Chinese New Year in 1993.

SUGGESTED READINGS. For more detailed accounts of Hong Kong history, see Wai Kwan Chan's *The Making of Hong Kong Society* (1991) and G. B. Endacott and A. Hinton's *Fragrant Harbour* (1968). Roger Daniels gives a comprehensive account of Chinese American history in *Asian American: Chinese and Japanese in the U.S.* (1988), while Gwen Kinkead takes a close look at Chinatown in *Chinatown: A Portrait of a Closed Society* (1992).—*Karen Har Yen Chow*

Hongo, Garrett Kaoru (b. May 30, 1951, Volcano, Hawaii): Writer. Hongo, whose ancestry is Japanese American, studied at the University of Michigan and the University of California at Los Angeles and served as director of the Asian Exclusion Act Theatre Group and the Asian Multi-Media Center, both in Seattle. His first book of poetry, *Yellow Light*, appeared in 1982; his second, *The River of Heaven* (1988), earned him the Lamont Poetry Prize and a Pulitzer Prize nomination. His poetry, which has appeared in *The New Yorker, Antaeus*, and other publications, focuses on the Asian American experience, including the INTERNMENT of Japanese Americans during World War II. Hongo has taught at the University of California.

Hopi–Navajo land dispute. *See* **Navajo–Hopi Land Dispute**

Hopis: Pueblo Indian people who live in northeast Arizona. The westernmost of the PUEBLOS, they speak a Shoshonean language. The name Hopi is derived from "Hopitu," meaning peaceful ones.

The Hopis are descendants of the ANASAZI, cave and later cliff dwellers who, beginning in the second century, settled in the "four corners" region of the southwest where Arizona, New Mexico, Utah, and Colorado join. Before the Spanish arrived, a number of Hopi villages were established in the foothills and terraces of Black Mesa. Oraibi, the oldest Hopi pueblo (adobe communal dwelling) was founded about 1150 C.E., making it one of the oldest continuously occupied villages in the United States. Unknown calamities—possibly outside invaders, but more probably drought—forced the abandonment of the cliff settlements around 1300. Many preserved cliff settlements can still be visited in the Southwest.

In 1540, Spanish explorers under Francisco de Coronado encountered the Hopis. In about 1629, the Spanish established a mission at Awatovi. The Hopis joined the PUEBLO REVOLT OF 1680, but the Spanish returned. The Awatovi mission was reestablished until a massive uprising destroyed it in 1700. Unlike some tribes, the Hopis resisted Spanish influence and maintained their native culture. In 1848, Hopi lands fell under the jurisdiction of the United States, and a Hopi reservation was created by President Chester Arthur's executive order in 1882.

The basic building block of Hopi society was the matrilineal clan, which traced descent through the female. A newly married couple would live with or near the bride's family. The Hopis were—and are—farmers. Unlike some Indian groups, the Hopis considered agriculture to be largely men's work. The Hopis grew several varieties of corn, as well as beans and squash. Dry farming—farming without irrigation—was honed to a fine art. Bred to resist temperature extremes, corn was planted along dry washes, or at the base of cliffs. These were places likely to flood during the infrequent rains. Seedlings were planted deeply to reach available moisture.

Religion has always been an important part of Hopi life. The kiva, a round subterranean chamber, was the place of worship and was entirely a male domain. Women were rarely allowed inside a kiva except for certain ceremonies. The Hopis used the kiva for their practice of the kachina cult. KACHINAS are spirit beings that the Hopi believe live on Arizona's San Francisco Peaks. The kachinas are thought to bring rain and fertility, award gifts, and enforce discipline. During ceremonies, when sacred masked dances are performed, kachinas are said to inhabit the bodies of male Kachina impersonators. According to Hopi legend, the kachinas leave their lofty home in December, around the winter solstice, to reside with humans for about the next six months. The climax of their sojourn is the Niman, or homecoming, when the Hopis bid the kachinas good-bye until the next winter solstice.

The Hopi reservation of some 2,470,000 acres, is completely surrounded by the Navajo reservation. A major Hopi-Navajo land dispute flared in the 1980's. A Joint Use territory claimed by the Hopis but open to both Navajo and Hopi use has been the subject of

the Hopis is Richard Erdoes' *The Rain Dance People* (1976). Walter Collins O'Kane explores Hopi culture in *Sun in the Sky* (1957) and *The Hopis* (1953). Hopi folk tales are recounted in Mando Sevillano's engrossing and entertaining book *The Hopi Way: Tales from a Vanishing Culture* (1986). A chapter in Arrell M. Gibson's *The American Indian* (1980) also deals with the Hopis.

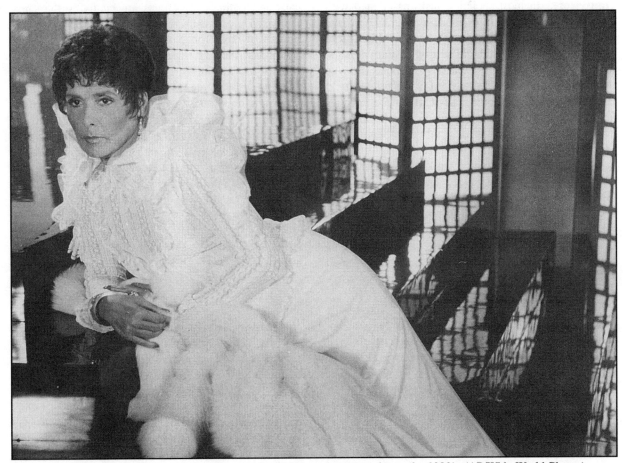

Entertainer Lena Horne's career began in the 1930's and continued into the 1980's. (AP/Wide World Photos)

much intertribal litigation. In 1992, the Bush Administration approved a pact that would give the Hopis 408,000 acres, most of it public land that is not part of either reservation.

By the late 1980's, the Hopi tribe had grown to more than ten thousand individuals. The Hopis have enjoyed something of a cultural renaissance in the twentieth century, especially with the revival of long-lost pottery making and widespread public interest in Hopi culture.

SUGGESTED READINGS. The best general account of

Horne, Lena (b. June 30, 1917, Brooklyn, N.Y.): African American singer and dancer. A durable stage personality, Horne has been called the most beautiful woman in the world. Her career began in the 1930's at Harlem's COTTON CLUB; she also toured as a dancer, sang with bands, cut her first records (including "Haunted Town"), and briefly had a leading role in the stage production *Blackbirds of 1939*. In the 1940's she became the first black woman to sign a long-term motion picture contract in Hollywood, performing in films such as *Cabin in the Sky* (1942),

Stormy Weather (1943), and *Swing Fever* (1943). Thereafter she also performed in clubs and on Broadway and made such popular recordings as "Stormy Weather" and "The Lady Is a Tramp." Horne's one-woman Broadway show in 1981 and her career in general earned important awards, including a Tony Award and a New York Drama Critics Circle award.

Housework: In most societies, tasks associated with housework—preparation of food, maintenance of the home, provision for clothing, and care of children—are assigned to women. Over the past two hundred years, new technologies have significantly changed the way people live, the homes they live in, and the household implements they use there. The marketplace supplies goods once manufactured at home, but the benefits are offset by a decline in the home work force. Servants are relatively rare, family size has decreased significantly, and large numbers of women work outside the home. Some tasks, such as soap making, have disappeared, but have been replaced by other tasks, such as frequent shopping. Clothes washing has been made much easier but is done more often. Technology has provided relief from arduous tasks such as wood chopping and water hauling, but the benefits have accrued to men. Women still have to cook and wash, but men no longer must carry fuel and water.

In essence, before industrialization, households produced goods for consumption and for the marketplace. During the first phase of industrialization (1860-1910), households stopped producing goods for sale, but continued to produce goods for family consumption. During the second phase of industrialization, households continue to produce goods for home consumption, but do so more efficiently.

Despite the many changes in housework brought about by improved technologies, household industrialization lags far behind industrialization in the marketplace. Paid labor in the marketplace is centralized and specialized; the uncompensated labor of housework, however, is decentralized and generalized. That is, wage laborers gather in factories and office buildings, divide their tasks, and perform them for pay. Housewives remain isolated in individual homes, performing myriad tasks for unspecified compensation.

Studies of housework concentrate on white, middle-class women, and general statements regarding housework and technology are most accurate in that context. Technological lag—the time between development of a technology and its widespread accep-

tance—is likely to be much greater for minorities, who are more likely to be poor, than for whites. This was particularly true in the first quarter of the twentieth century. Such special circumstances as slavery, recent immigration, and geographic or social isolation further extend technological lag. While schedules of incorporating technological innovations may vary widely between middle-class women and poor African Americans and Latinas, the effects are relatively the same: increased responsibilities for women, decreased household labor for men.

Pre-Industrial Housework. Until the late nineteenth century brought industrialization to the United States, each household required an adult male, an adult female, and children to do the work necessary to maintain even a moderately comfortable standard of living. Self-sufficiency was the rule, but households had to participate to some degree in a market economy. Metal tools, spices, paper products, and special labor such as masonry had to be purchased. Farm work and housework required the efforts of both sexes. Cooking, baking, and laundry—regarded as women's work—required wood for fuel, grain for flour, and water for washing, all supplied by men. In reality, both sexes had to work together much of the time. Only the very rich were able to divorce themselves entirely from daily household chores, and even the poorest people had help, if only occasionally, from relatives, servants, or neighbors.

Meals tended to be plain, consisting of stews, gruels, and coarse pan or fried breads, all of which could be prepared over a fire in a single pot. CHILD CARE and CHILD REARING were shared among extended family members, and children, not yet the focus of family life, were often apprenticed out or sent to help other relatives. Bodily cleanliness, manufactured clothing, and a variety of foods were the privileges of the very rich until technology lowered costs and increased the availability of manufactured goods.

Early Industrialization. During the nineteenth century, the United States became one of the most industrialized nations in the world. The process took time and required major adjustments in every facet of the society. American business moved from supplying raw materials to manufacturing goods. Young people left the farms and became laborers in factories, working for wages that they used to purchase goods previously made at home. The resultant economic activity fueled further industrialization. For example, coal replaced wood for cooking and heating; homespun cloth gave way to commercial textiles; and candles were replaced by kerosene lamps for household lighting.

Two important early nineteenth century developments, the introduction of the automatic flour mill and the development of the cast-iron cookstove, directly affected American housework. Both relieved men of time-consuming and arduous tasks, but effectively increased women's work.

In the 1780's, Oliver Evans introduced an automatic grain mill that, with subsequent improvements, sepa-

women could bake fine, fluffy, white bread without men's help. White bread became the first status symbol of the industrial age. It proved that a family could afford the luxury of purchased flour.

During that same period, cast-iron stoves, complete with one or more ovens and several burners, replaced open hearths for cooking. Cast-iron stoves burned coal, which was delivered to individual homes, particularly in urban areas. Men no longer had to chop and carry wood. The simple one-pot stew that char-

Increasing numbers of couples share housework chores, using the vast array of appliances and technology available. (James L. Shaffer)

rated fine flour from coarse, increased milling efficiency, and provided automatic removal of bran and germ from flour. Within forty years, vastly improved transportation systems put fine white flour within the reach of most American families at reasonable prices. Men no longer had to pound corn into meal, and

acterized eighteenth century meals gave way to multicourse meals prepared entirely by women. Cast-iron stoves were easier to use, but the trade-off for women was increased preparation time and less help in the kitchen, which was now entirely their domain.

Further industrialization removed virtually all so-

Time Spent on Housework by Gender: 1991

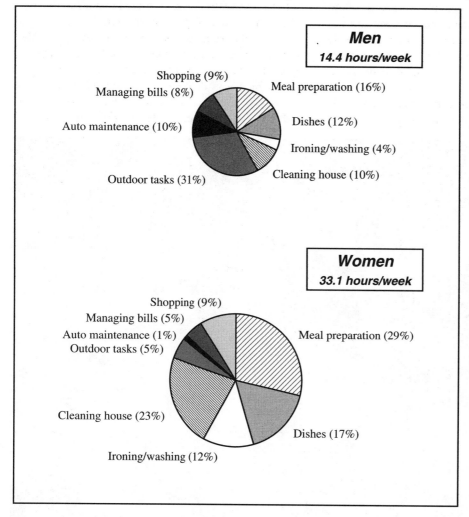

Men
14.4 hours/week

Shopping (9%)
Managing bills (8%)
Auto maintenance (10%)
Outdoor tasks (31%)
Meal preparation (16%)
Dishes (12%)
Ironing/washing (4%)
Cleaning house (10%)

Women
33.1 hours/week

Shopping (9%)
Managing bills (5%)
Auto maintenance (1%)
Outdoor tasks (5%)
Cleaning house (23%)
Ironing/washing (12%)
Meal preparation (29%)
Dishes (17%)

Source: Data are from Carol Foster, ed. *Women's Changing Role.* Table 2.15. Wylie, Tex.: Information Plus, 1992.

called men's work and most of the children's work from the home while defining more separate spheres for men and women. Male tasks such as leather making, wood chopping, and water carrying disappeared and were not replaced as manufactured shoes, coal, and piped-in water became common after the Civil War. Female tasks such as spinning and weaving declined with the advent of manufactured cloth, but time-consuming sewing and laundering replaced them. Ceremonial labor such as needlework and pastry baking added to the burden of housework as children and home life became the focus of female existence.

"True Womanhood." During the nineteenth century, marriage and family roles changed profoundly. Mutual love became the only acceptable basis for marriage and couples were expected to remain in love. The Cult of True Womanhood, also called the "Cult of Domesticity," glorified values of piety, purity, submissiveness, and subservience. The home became the center of efforts to Christianize and civilize American society largely through example and childhood training.

Technological innovations gave many white, middle-class women time to develop their domestic skills while they served their husbands, trained their children, and made their homes sanctuaries from the outside world. Among those domestic skills were both training and directing servants.

The abolition of slavery and the influx of immigrants during the nineteenth century provided a large body of prospective domestic servants for a market hungry for help. Family size declined steadily into the twentieth century and hired help performed much of the manual labor in white households. Social separation between white employers and minority help widened significantly. Separate entrances and back stairs for servants became common. African American, Latino, Irish, and other minority and immigrant women, instructed by their mistresses in the arts of True Womanhood, enjoyed none of its benefits. That Victorian view did empower white women, however, to some extent. They ruled their homes and children despite the absence of real economic power and began to exercise political power beyond their own doors, particularly in the temperance and abolition movements.

Minority women saw no increase in status, worked

long hours for little pay or appreciation, and faced lives without the advantages of rapidly advancing technology.

The Twentieth Century. At the beginning of the 1900's, the vast majority of American women spent most of their time providing for their families. The economic displacement caused by the Panic of 1893 had forced more women into the marketplace, but their responsibilities at home were not diminished. Servants and household help were common and domestic service remained the main opportunity for immigrant and minority women to work. The second phase of industrialization, world war, and the proliferation of household technology soon changed that.

The tremendous increase in manufacturing during the first three decades of the twentieth century provided numerous opportunities for work, particularly for single women who had previously been limited to domestic service. When World War I removed millions of men from the work force, women stepped in. White middle-class married women were forced to find ways to do their own housework and care for their children and husbands.

By 1930, the most important household technologies had evolved, most of them run by electricity. By 1940, urban homes had dependable electricity and even isolated rural areas were equipped with home generators. Small, labor-saving devices proliferated and most middle-class homes had electric vacuums, ranges, refrigerators, and irons. Indoor plumbing and central heating, once the special domain of the very privileged, became necessities, and many families had automobiles.

During the Progressive Era between 1900 and 1920, True Womanhood had declined as the ideal for women. For that brief period, acceptable roles for women expanded beyond the household. With the end of the war and the return of the male workforce from wartime production to peacetime, women were moved back home. Such magazines as *Ladies Home Journal, Life,* and *The Saturday Evening Post* venerated women as homemakers, focusing particularly on child raising, and extolled the virtues of ideal motherhood. For example, when zippers were introduced early in the 1920's, proponents of ideal motherhood seized on them as a way to teach independence to children, something every mother should strive to do.

The renewed focus on motherhood lasted into the 1960's, supported by a cornucopia of labor-saving devices. The woman's labor saved was expended in other important ways in her home. She washed, cleaned house, shopped, and educated her children more intensely and frequently. The emphasis on labor saved had little to do with time saved until 1970's inflation priced the middle-class "American Dream" of home and automobile ownership beyond the reach of many single-income families.

Women continue to work outside the home, but their responsibility for housework remains in what has been termed the "second shift." Prepared foods and microwave ovens may reduce the time needed for cooking; automatic washers, dryers, and wash-and-wear clothes may ease the burden of doing laundry; occasional help from husbands and children who "pitch in and help Mom" with domestic chores may lighten the load. Yet despite the advances of technology and feminism, housework is still primarily seen as women's work. "True womanhood" in the modern sense includes the ability to balance domestic responsibilities and career goals as a "superwoman."

For minority women, technological lag remains. The same inflation that forces middle-class white women into the work force makes economically disadvantaged women, many of them minorities, work to maintain their lifestyles at levels somewhat removed from middle-class ideals. Most have indoor plumbing, central heat, electricity, and such common labor-saving devices as electric stoves and refrigerators, but more expensive time-saving items such as microwave ovens and special fast foods may remain unaffordable. Technological change, which has lowered the price of household appliances and increased their availability, has decreased the apparent distance between economic classes without materially affecting social distance. Despite the growing middle and upper class of people of color, ethnic minorities, for the most part, remain separated from the majority white middle-class population.

Clearly, technology affects housework in major ways. The most important developments—piped-in water, central heating, and electricity—join labor-saving devices in modernizing, but not industrializing, private homes. Industrialization implies centralization. Centralization of housework would spell the end of private homes and the sanctuary provided therein, a possibility adamantly resisted by men and women alike, regardless of their culture or economic status.

SUGGESTED READINGS. Ruth Swartz Cowan's *More Work For Mother* (1983), Carl Degler's *At Odds: Women and The Family in America* (1980), and Glenna Matthews' *Just a Housewife: The Rise and*

Fall of Domesticity in America (1987) are the most useful and balanced works on women and housework. *The Second Shift: Working Parents and the Revolution at Home* (1989), by Arlie Hochschild with Anne Machung, presents case studies of how contemporary men and women of various ethnic groups and backgrounds divide housework. Jacqueline Jones's *Labor of Love, Labor of Sorrow: Black Women, Work, and the Family from Slavery to the Present* (1985) is one of the few books on black women, their work, and their families. David M. Katzman's *Seven Days a Week: Women and Domestic Service in Industrializing America* (1978) is a valuable resource on domestic servants.—*Stephen G. Sylvester*

Housing developments, public. *See* **Public housing developments**

Housing discrimination. *See* **Discrimination—housing**

Howard University: A coeducational historically black university chartered by Congress in 1867. The school was named for General Oliver Otis Howard, head of the FREEDMEN'S BUREAU. Although privately run, the university receives federal support. More than half of the students are African American. Students may earn bachelor's degrees, master's degrees (offered since the 1870's), and doctor's degrees (offered since 1955) in more than two hundred programs including law, divinity, religion, social work, fine arts, pharmacy, medicine, dentistry, engineering, and architecture. Classes are held on four campuses. Howard's library contains extensive African American holdings; the university sponsors research in Liberia.

Howe, James Wong (Wong Tung Jim; Aug. 28, 1899, Guangdong, China—July 12, 1976, Hollywood, Calif.): Chinese American cinematographer. Howe came to the United States in 1904 and was reared in Washington State. He began his career as a cameraman's assistant under director Cecil B. De Mille in 1917 and shot his own first film, *Drums of Fate*, in 1923. Over the next five decades, he earned sixteen Academy Award nominations and two Oscars, for *The Rose Tattoo* (1955) and *Hud* (1963). He also received Look Awards for *Body and Soul* in 1947 and *Picnic* in 1955. He was a member of the Chinese Historical Society and recipient of the Medal of Honor from the George Eastman Festival of Film Artists.

Howe, Julia Ward (May 27, 1819, New York, N.Y.—Oct. 17, 1910, Newport, R.I.): Suffragist and writer. Howe published her first book of poems, *Passion-flowers*, anonymously in 1854. She was, at the time, an unhappy wife and mother of five. Her first play, *Leonora: Or, the World's Own*, was produced by the Lyceum Theater in New York in 1857; it was considered immoral. In 1862 *Atlantic Monthly* published her poem "Battle

Abolitionist and suffragist Julia Ward Howe helped found the New England Woman Suffrage Association. (Library of Congress)

Hymn of the Republic," which was later turned into the famous song. She took advantage of the instant fame by becoming a spokeswoman for the SUFFRAGE MOVEMENT. She founded the New England Women's Club in 1868, and helped found the New England Woman Suffrage Association. In 1870 she founded and edited *The Woman's Journal*.

Huerta, Dolores Fernandez (b. Apr. 10, 1930, Dawson, N.Mex.): Mexican American labor leader and activist. Huerta co-founded the UNITED FARM WORKERS (UFW). She spent most of her early life in Stockton, California. In 1955, she met César CHÁVEZ and began to help organize migrant workers around Stockton and Modesto. She worked in Delano with the central headquarters staff of the United Farm Workers Organizing Committee and later served as a lobbyist, chief negotiator, and vice president of the UFW. In 1988, she was severely injured by police in San Francisco during a demonstration against then Vice President Bush, who opposed the UFW grape boycott.

Hughes, [James Mercer] Langston (Feb. 1, 1902, Joplin, Mo.—May 22, 1967, New York, N.Y.): African American poet, novelist, playwright, columnist, and anthologist. Hughes pioneered black literary realism, using his wit, the black idiom, and blues and folk materials to depict black American life and attack social injustice. He wrote his first book of poems, *The Weary Blues*, in 1926 before graduating from Lincoln Univer-

Langston Hughes in 1953; in the 1930's and 1940's, Hughes was the best-known African American writer. (AP/Wide World Photos)

sity. Hughes's first novel, *Not Without Laughter*, which was published in 1930, rejected romantic STEREOTYPES of black life. Many of his writings in the 1930's focused on racial oppression. His *Chicago Defender* columns after 1940 featured Jesse B. Simple, a fictitious, wisely humorous Harlem resident. Hughes influenced a whole generation of African American writers when his works enjoyed a revival in the 1960's and 1970's.

Huguenots: French Protestants of the sixteenth and seventeenth centuries. After sporadic attempts to settle in South Carolina and Florida failed, French-speaking Protestants from the Channel Islands and what is now Belgium came to Massachusetts and New Amsterdam between 1650 and 1680. Some of these, the Walloons, made their way up the Hudson River and in 1678 founded the town of New Paltz.

The big years for Huguenot emigration to colonial America were from 1680 to 1700, but the record of their settlement is scanty. The main impetus for the Huguenots' coming to America was Louis XIV's revocation in 1685 of the Edict of Nantes, which had guaranteed religious freedom in France. The brutality that resulted from this move is reflected in the drop in the Huguenot population between 1680 and 1690 from around a million to about seventy-five thousand. Many Protestant congregations dissolved, and their churches were destroyed. Two-thirds of the French Protestants joined the Catholic church out of fear, and another one-fifth managed to leave France, most of them for homes elsewhere in Europe. A significant number of Hugenots lived in exile in London for a while before leaving for the New World, and the evidence suggests—not surprisingly—that those who sailed west were younger on the average than the total of those who left France.

The Boston Huguenots were a smaller group than the other main enclaves in New York and Charleston. Their early ASSIMILATION foreshadowed the fate of American Huguenots as an entity. Although by 1690 more than one hundred Huguenot families had settled in Boston, in 1748 the French church in Boston closed down and a unique Huguenot identity was forever lost. Many immigrants had, in fact, come for other than religious reasons; this, in addition to the pull of INTERMARRIAGE and the usual shuffling of church allegiances, contributed to rapid assimilation.

The largest Huguenot settlement in South Carolina, 40 miles north of Charleston on the Santee River,

numbered about sixty families by 1695, with another forty to fifty families in Berkeley County. They practiced all the occupations, including a short-lived silk industry, and were important slaveholders. Friction with the Anglican church helped speed the complete assimilation of the South Carolina Huguenots by 1750.

Huguenots in New York, many of them in New Rochelle, assimilated as swiftly as their brethren elsewhere. They followed diverse paths to success, with half of the New York City Huguenots owning slaves. In 1803 the French church in New York submitted to the authority of the Protestant Episcopal church, and the New York families became part of a nation that they had enriched considerably by their energies and talents.

SUGGESTED READINGS. For the French background of the Huguenots, consult Will and Ariel Durant's *The Age of Reason Begins* (1961). An excellent scholarly study is *The Huguenots in America: A Refugee People in New World Society* (1983) by Jon Butler. Other useful works are George A. Rothlock's *The Huguenots: A Biography of a Minority* (1979) and Arthur R. Hirsch's *The Huguenots of Colonial South Carolina* (1928, repr. 1962).

Hull House Association (HHA): Settlement house in Chicago founded in 1889 by social reformer Jane ADDAMS. Addams, along with Ellen Gates Starr, began the association in order that those more financially able and learned in the arts, education, and social services could assist those less fortunate, such as poor immigrants and urban minorities. Believing that the most creative resources evolved within the community, Hull House associates would "settle" into different communities to assist in meeting the needs of those who lived there. HHA continues to serve some thirty thousand people annually through more than one hundred different programs.

Hungarian Americans: From the time of their original migration into the Ural Mountains between the eighth and eleventh centuries, the Hungarians (Magyars) have suffered the fate of living in a borderland between the older "east" (Turkey) and the more recent "east" (the former Soviet Union) as well as between the older "west" (Austria and German nations) and the more recent "west" (Western European capitalism). The Hungarian language is related to Finnish, Estonian, and Turkish, reflecting this people's mixed political and social history.

Hungarian involvement in the United States began

with a few individuals in the colonial era. The Hungarian scholar Stephen Parmenius Budai chronicled (in Latin) the travels of Englishman Sir Humphrey Gilbert in 1583, accompanying him in his travels to Newfoundland. The Hungarian priest Janos Ratkay did missionary work in New Mexico in the late 1600's, and Ferdinand Konschak was involved in the Spanish missions in California in the 1700's. Substantial numbers of Hungarians did not arrive until the mid-1800's.

The modern Hungarian historian Leslie Konnyu divides the history of Hungarian immigration to the

New Buda, Iowa, named for Budapest (it was subsequently renamed Davis City). Many famous names were among the Kossuth Exiles, such as Joseph Pulitzer (1879-1920), whose publishing interests would eventually lead to the founding of the Pulitzer Prizes in literature and journalism.

The immigrations of 1870 to 1920 resulted in the arrival in the United States of nearly a million Hungarians. Konnyu estimates that Hungarians composed 1 percent of the American population by 1920. Such estimates, however, are problematic given the fact that until the 1920's, Hungarians were often counted by

A view of Hull House, founded in 1889 to assist poor immigrants and urban minorities. (Culver Pictures, Inc.)

United States into three phases: the Kossuth exile of the 1850's, the economic immigrations of 1870 to 1920, and the political and economic immigration of 1921 to 1960.

Nineteenth Century Immigration. Lajos Kossuth was a republican Hungarian nationalist whose struggle for an independent Hungary captured the interest of many Americans. When his revolution of 1848-1849 failed, he and four thousand of his administration and supporters came to the United States to live in exile. These exiles dispersed, forming the nucleus of the early Hungarian presence in the United States in major cities such as New York, Chicago, and New Orleans. At the same time, new towns were formed, such as

U.S. officials as "Austrians." This early immigration was inspired, like so many other waves of immigration from elsewhere, by the hope for a better future among mainly young Hungarian men. They were extremely frugal; U.S. Immigration Commission records comment on the ability of Hungarian youth to save their earnings.

About a quarter of these immigrants returned to Hungary after earning enough to purchase land in the Old Country. Two-thirds of the immigrants of this wave were agricultural workers, with another quarter working in factories or other unskilled labor. By the end of the 1920's, there were more than two thousand Hungarian organizations in the United States to support the new communities of immigrants, serving their social, religious, and medical needs. Dozens of newspapers were started, and in 1907 the American Hungarian Federation was founded as a national advocacy organization for Hungarian immigrants and citizens.

The Political Immigrations of 1920 to 1960. By the end of the 1930's, 82 percent of the Hungarian American community was urbanized—a nearly exact reversal of the rural-urban demographics of Hungary itself. Since Hungary was on the losing side of World War I, a considerable amount of territory of the former

enhower (in excess of the immigration quotas established in the early 1920's) after the failed national revolution in 1956 was put down by the Communists. The earlier political immigrants tended to be more "left wing" in orientation, while the more recent ones were more nationalistic and conservative. Thus, Hungarian Americans can be found on virtually all places along the American political spectrum.

Contemporary Hungarian Americans. Hungarian Americans assimilated slowly into the American dominant culture. By the 1990's, only a dozen Hun-

HUNGARY

Hungarian state was divided into Romania, Czechoslovakia, Yugoslavia, and Austria. The problem with estimating the number of Hungarian immigrants of this period is that after the war, Hungarians were often identified by their new country of origin rather than by their ethnicity.

After World War II, sixteen thousand Hungarian REFUGEES were allowed into the United States, including thousands of Jewish Hungarians who escaped Nazi invasions. Finally, some forty-two thousand Hungarian refugees were admitted by President Dwight D. Eis-

garian Catholic parochial schools still offered courses in Hungarian language. Strong community organizations remain, some with their own folk dance troupes. The legacy of Hungarian immigration is still visible in many aspects of American society such as the names of towns and counties (especially "Buda" and "Kossuth"), and in famous personalities who have contributed to all aspects of American culture.

The Joy of Cooking, probably the most famous cookbook of American publishing, was written by Hungarian Americans Erma and Maryann Rombauer.

The famous composer Béla Bartók made significant contributions to the study and composition of music incorporating Hungarian folk motifs, Eugene Ormandy was the renowned conductor of the Philadelphia Symphony Orchestra, and trumpeter Arthur House played jazz music in the big band era with such

SUGGESTED READINGS. The most prolific writer on Hungarian American immigrant history was Leslie Konnyu (1914-1993), whose many books in both Hungarian and English document various aspects of the Hungarian American experience, including literature, history, and the arts. See his *A History of American*

More than forty thousand Hungarian refugees were admitted to the United States after Soviet Communists crushed the 1956 Hungarian uprising. (National Archives)

greats as Woody Herman and Charlie Parker. Hungarian American actors have made their mark in American films: Bela Lugosi was the best known in a long list of players of the part of Dracula, and Peter Lorre was also famous for roles in horror and mystery films. More recent Hollywood personalities include Tony Curtis, and the Gabor sisters, Zsa Zsa and Eva. Famous Hungarian American athletes include football players George Halas and the celebrated quarterback Joe Namath.

Hungarian Literature, 1583-1987 (1988) and *Hungarians in the United States: An Immigration Study* (1967). See also two older works, *The Magyars in America* (1922) by D. A. Souders and Eugene Pivany's *Hungarian-American Historical Connections from Pre-Columbian Times to the End of the American Civil War* (1927).—*Daniel L. S. Christopher*

Hurston, Zora Neale (Jan. 7, 1891, Eatonville, Fla.— Jan. 28, 1960, Fort Pierce, Fla.): African American

Zora Neale Hurston collected southern folktales; she also wrote four novels and an autobiography. (Library of Congress)

author and folklorist. After studying at HOWARD UNI-
VERSITY and receiving her bachelor's degree from
Barnard College in 1928, Hurston became the most
important female writer to emerge from the 1920's
HARLEM RENAISSANCE, publishing short stories and
four novels (1934-1948); the autobiography *Dust
Tracks on a Road* (1942); and plays, essays, and
collections of southern black FOLKLORE. Hurston was
popular through about 1940 but then largely forgotten;
the feminist movement of the 1970's revived interest
in her work, especially her second novel, *Their Eyes
Were Watching God* (1937), through the enthusiasm
of African American writer Alice WALKER and others.

Hutchinson, Anne (c. 1591, Alford, Lincolnshire, England—c. Aug., 1643, now Pelham Bay Park, Bronx,
N.Y.): Puritan religious leader. In 1636 Hutchinson immigrated with her husband and twelve children to Massachusetts. In 1933 she followed Anglican minister John
Cotton to Boston, taking her family along. There she
espoused the views of Cotton with the addition of her
own doctrine. She established two factions of PURITAN
ministry in Boston, a rift which eventually led to her
excommunication. She and her husband and followers
formed a settlement on an island in Narrangansett Bay.
In August of 1643, she and everyone else except one
child were massacred by Indians.

Hutterites: Survivors of the Mennonite or Anabaptist
("rebaptizer") wing of the Protestant Reformation of
Europe. Some thirty-five thousand Hutterites are found
today in geographically isolated, communal agrarian
settlements called *Bruderhofs,* located mostly in the
Dakotas, Montana, and the prairie provinces of Canada.
Their isolation is by choice, as they seek to minimize
contact with the outside world. Their patriarchal communities blend religious, economic, and social functions. Their everyday language is a Tyrolean German
dialect from their home region of Austria but they increasingly use High German in colony schools and in
worship.

After the Swiss Anabaptist movement of the 1520's
spread to surrounding areas, the Austrian leader Jacob
Hutter began to teach that true Christianity required
communal living and sharing of property. Persecuted
with their fellow MENNONITES for rebaptizing adults,
for their Christian pacifism, and for their refusal to
allow any state control over church affairs, the Hutterites were also seen as dangerous for their practice
of Christian communism.

Civil and state church authorities, usually Roman
Catholic or Lutheran, combined to forcibly break up
Hutterite communal groups, taking their children
away, selling some of the men into slavery, and im-
prisoning others. The Hutterites fled Moravia for Tran-
sylvania in the 1600's, where they again came under
heavy persecution. At one time they were reduced to
fewer than a hundred persons. Fleeing again to Russia
in the 1700's, they were aided by Mennonites who
had preceded them. They left Russia in the late 1800's,
to settle in Dakota Territory near Yankton. Those who
established themselves on private farms were gradually absorbed into the less sectarian Mennonite church
in South Dakota. Those who reestablished the communal *Bruderhof* pattern have successfully resisted AS-
SIMILATION.

Colony Hutterites have retained their identity
through strict endogamy (in-marriage), limited contact
with the outside world, and the self-sufficiency of their
communal agricultural settlements. They permit the
use of modern farm machinery and technology for
business purposes but insist on strict simplicity in personal and family life. Colonies provide dwellings for
all families and work for all individuals, making for
a secure existence.

Large families result in the frequent necessity of
colony division, with mother colonies providing assistance until daughter colonies are well-established.
Hutterite attempts to buy land for new colonies in
large tracts from their neighbors sometimes result in
resentment and hostility. The province of Alberta
passed laws in the 1940's restricting land sales to the
Hutterites. The most severe persecution of the Hutterites by outsiders in North America came during
World War I in South Dakota in response to the sect's
pacifism, Christian socialism, and use of the German
language. Most Dakota Hutterites abandoned their colony lands and facilities and fled to Canada. South Dakota officially invited them back following the war. A
more progressive group of Hutterites called the Society of Brothers has a community in Rifton, New York.

SUGGESTED READINGS. For further reading see John
A. Hostetler's *Hutterite Society* (1974), Hostetler and
Gertrude Edners Huntington's *The Hutterites in North
America* (1967), and Leonard Gross's *The Golden
Years of the Hutterites* (1980).

Hwang, David Henry (b. Aug. 11, 1957, Los Angeles,
Calif.): Chinese American playwright. Hwang studied
English and playwriting at Stanford University and the

Yale School of Drama. His first success came in 1979 with *F.O.B.*, a play about a "fresh off the boat" Chinese American immigrant, for which he won an Obie Award. Other plays include *The Dance and the Railroad* (1981), *Rich Relations* (1986), and *M. Butterfly* (1988), a provocative variation on the Madame Butterfly story that earned the playwright Tony and Drama Desk Awards and status as a spokesperson for Asian Americans in the arts. Hwang received Rockefeller, Guggenheim, and National Endowment of the Arts fellowships, and he has served on the boards of both the Dramatists Guild and the Theatre Communications Group.

David Hwang's plays often examine aspects of the Chinese American experience. (AP/Wide World Photos)

I

Icelandic Americans: Iceland is the most westerly country in Europe, and its northernmost point touches the Arctic Circle. It is a nation-state of about 220,000 people located on an island between Norway and Greenland. The Greek astronomer and explorer Pytheas may have reached Iceland as early as 330 B.C.E. It was not until 825, however, that Iceland entered the modern historical

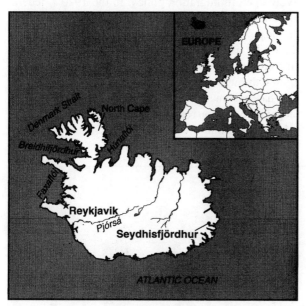

ICELAND

record when the Irish monk Dicuil wrote down first-hand accounts of Irish people who had lived on the island of "Thule." The Norse discovery of Iceland a few years later is credited to Gardar Svavarsson, a Swede (850-875).

Iceland was first settled by Viking chiefs late in the 800's. Christianity was adopted by Icelanders around the year 1000. Iceland was a separate political entity until 1262, when it was taken over by Norway; then, in 1397, both Norway and Iceland were conquered by Denmark. Iceland was under Danish rule until 1918, when it became a kingdom that, though separate, was joined to the Danish monarchy. Finally, in 1944, Iceland became an independent republic. Iceland's location kept it fairly isolated from the rest of Europe, and the modern Icelandic language is remarkably similar to ancient Icelandic.

The ancient Icelandic sagas of the tenth and eleventh centuries are a unique contribution to European culture, and they also contain a record of early exploration of a land called Vinland, now believed to be the North American continent. The Greenland Saga and Eric's Saga tell of Leif Ericsson's discovery of Vinland and of Norse settlement there.

Iceland in the nineteenth century was plagued by economic difficulties, and poverty was widespread; these conditions, as well as political discontent, led to immigration to both Canada and the United States. Yet the first Icelandic immigrants to the United States came for religious reasons: A number of converts to Mormonism began arriving in the 1850's, some moving to Spanish Fork, Utah. (In 1955, Spanish Fork held a festival in honor of the centennial of Icelandic immigration.) The Mormon arrivals generally were skilled artisans, tradespeople, or farmers.

The 1870's saw a larger wave of emigration from Iceland, with most emigrants settling in Canada. Most immigrants to the United States settled in the northern Midwest—Wisconsin, Minnesota, and particularly the Dakotas (then the Dakota Territory). There was even a movement in 1874 to establish Icelandic settlements

Many Icelandic Americans pursued farming as a way of life. (Library of Congress)

in Alaska with the assistance of the U.S. government, but the idea was short-lived. In the 1870's the United States was in a depression, and many of the Icelandic immigrants (as was the case with most immigrant groups) turned to whatever unskilled labor they could find to survive. Some worked in factories, some on the Milwaukee docks. As soon as they were financially able, many then pursued their goal of farming.

Icelandic immigrants were highly literate (in Icelandic), and they quickly established schools in their new midwestern communities. They were active in church, most being LUTHERANS, and in their communities. Icelandic Americans became involved in journalism quite early, and many second- and third-generation Icelandic Americans entered politics. They retained many of their customs but were also eager to ASSIMILATE into American society. The Icelandic National League, designed to preserve Icelandic traditions, was formed in 1919, and there are still Icelandic American organizations in a number of American cities. Icelandic Independence Day, June 17, is celebrated in the larger Icelandic American communities.

SUGGESTED READINGS. For a scholarly yet lively account of the Viking era, see Gwyn Jones's *The Norse Atlantic Saga* (1964). Thorstina Jackson Walters' *Modern Sagas: The Story of the Icelanders in North America* (1953) discusses immigration to the United States and Canada. Louise E. Levathes and Bob Kirst's "Iceland: Life Under the Glaciers," in *National Geographic* (February, 1987), provides information on the inhabitants and language of Iceland.

Immigration—illegal: From colonial times to the late nineteenth century, the United States followed a relatively open immigration policy. In the 1920's, federal law established immigration quotas by country of origin. Public policy focused on determining which immigrants should be admitted legally, rather than on those who entered illegally. Since WORLD WAR II, however, immigration through the "back door" (especially from Mexico) has become a major public issue. In the 1990's, illegal immigration remained controversial in the political and economic life of the United States. The IMMIGRATION AND NATURALIZATION SERVICE (INS), an

Many illegal immigrants—such as this man from Mexico who tried to cross into El Paso, Tex.—take considerable risks to enter the United States only to be turned back by the U.S. Border Patrol. (R. Del Percio/UNHCR)

agency of the Department of Justice, has been criticized from all sides for its enforcement of immigration laws.

Characteristics of Undocumented Immigrants. Figures on the numbers of undocumented immigrants in the United States vary widely and are generally unreliable, considering the difficulty of identifying people whose survival may depend on remaining hidden. BUREAU OF THE CENSUS demographers in the late 1980's estimated a figure of 5 to 7 million people, but the INS claimed a smaller figure of 3.5 to 4 million as a result of its stricter enforcement after 1986. The census of 1980 found that of the undocumented immigrants it counted, half lived in California, with significant concentrations also in New York, Texas, Illinois, and Florida—the same states that also attract most legal immigrants.

Although many Americans equate undocumented immigrants with Mexicans, the Bureau of the Census believes that this group only accounted for 55 percent of that population in the 1980's. About 16 percent came from Central America and the Caribbean, 6 percent from South America, 5 percent from the Middle East, 5 percent from Southeast Asia, and 13 percent from the combined areas of Europe, Africa, Oceania, and Canada. A surprising number of illegal immigrants are foreign students who overstay their visas. In the 1990's, there was growing media attention to illegal immigrants from Ireland and the People's Republic of China in New York City. Government crackdowns on illegal immigrants have focused on the U.S.-Mexico border, since it remains one of the easier ways for any alien to enter the country. In 1988, 95 percent of the undocumented immigrants apprehended were Mexican nationals; the non-Mexicans who made up the other 5 percent amounted to more than fifty-eight thousand people.

Undocumented immigrants are common victims of exploitation, both before and after entering the United States. They are often charged outrageously high fees for transport, as by a Mexican *COYOTE* (guide) who smuggles them in, or by Chinese profiteers, who may collect as much as $30,000 for the journey from Fujian Province through Hong Kong and Mexico to the United States. In June, 1993, a freighter that ran aground off the East Coast caused the death of at least seven of the three hundred illegal Chinese immigrants on board. Incidents have been recorded of Mexican would-be immigrants suffocating in locked boxcars without food or water. Organizations such as the Quaker American Friends Service Committee have

collected data on a pattern of physical and legal abuse of many illegal immigrants at the border by INS authorities.

Undocumented immigrants such as the Chinese are often forced to serve as indentured workers for many years in order to pay off their smuggling debts. Because of their insecure legal situation, they can be compelled to work for low pay and in unsafe conditions by employers who threaten to report them to

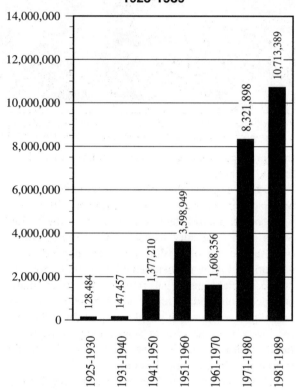

Illegal Immigrants Apprehended: 1925-1989

Source: Data are from Allison Landes, ed. *Immigration and Illegal Aliens.* Table 5.1. Wylie, Tex.: Information Plus, 1991.

authorities if they fail to cooperate. Some labor union leaders such as César CHÁVEZ of the UNITED FARM WORKERS campaigned for reforms that would make workplaces safer for all workers, both documented and undocumented. Yet the most common sources of work for undocumented immigrants—construction, agriculture, restaurants, the garment industry, domestic work, and light manufacturing—remain free of many worker protections. Some communities have tried to ban the soliciting of day-labor jobs on street corners, a com-

The political climate in China has prompted a massive influx of illegal immigrants into the United States. These Chinese were apprehended in the San Francisco Bay in 1993. (AP/Wide World Photos)

mon practice in cities with large enclaves of undocumented workers.

Studies suggest that the typical undocumented Mexican worker is a male in his twenties with several years of schooling. He tends to come to the United States on a temporary or seasonal basis, but returns over the course of several years. He depends on a network of fellow undocumented immigrants for economic, social, and legal support. He often shares crowded, substandard rental housing such as unconverted garages in which people sleep in shifts. Despite his low wages, he tries to send money home to his family in Mexico or, in some cases, to get his family to join him in the United States.

The attitudes of American citizens and legal immigrants toward the illegal immigrants among them are varied. Hostility seems to mount in times of economic crisis, when immigrants generally and undocumented workers in particular are blamed for the nation's woes. A review of immigration history reveals trends that have shaped public opinion on this explosive subject into the 1990's.

Early Immigration Policy and the Restrictionist Movement. As a young nation, the United States welcomed unlimited numbers of immigrants to develop the land, defend the frontier, and work in industry. In the last quarter of the nineteenth century, however, as millions of Europeans entered the country, Congress

defined some immigrants as undesirable: These included convicts, prostitutes, those with communicable diseases, "lunatics" and "mental defectives," polygamists, and anarchists. The CHINESE EXCLUSION ACT of 1882, the first federal law excluding immigrants by national origin, was enacted in response to widespread racial PREJUDICE on the West Coast against Chinese people.

In the mid-nineteenth century, many Americans became alarmed over the possible consequences of unrestricted immigration. Immigrants had always suffered from various persecutions until they became assimilated into the larger society, and strife among immigrant groups was common. The NATIVIST movement wielded considerable political power against "foreign elements," such as Irish Catholics loyal to the pope and Germans who kept their Old Country language and customs.

From 1890 to 1921, some twenty million immigrants entered the country from southern Europe. These people had different appearance and were considered by many Americans, who were primarily of Anglo-Saxon origin, as physically and morally inferior. A growing eugenics movement created public fear that the newcomers would weaken the "native stock."

From 1921 to 1927, IMMIGRATION LEGISLATION restricted entry through QUOTAS based on national origin, intending to maintain the ethnic balance representative of an earlier era when white Anglo-Saxon Protestants were the dominant immigrant group (specifically using the 1790 census as a basis). Until 1972, entrance of immigrants was controlled at two major ports of entry, New York and Los Angeles. After 1927, immigrants could enter the country only after being granted a visa by the American consulate in their country of origin. By this time, the federal government had created the BORDER PATROL within the INS to monitor U.S. borders, especially the vulnerable line to the south over which thousands of Mexicans had been passing since the Mexican Revolution of 1910.

World War II Era Developments. Relatively few immigrants came during the GREAT DEPRESSION of the 1930's. With the Bolshevik Revolution in Russia in 1917 and the rise of fascist and communist powers in Europe, national concern about immigrants shifted from ethnic differences to a fear of subversive political elements. During WORLD WAR II, the INS hunted "enemy aliens" and, until the mid-1960's, deported thousands of illegal immigrants as threats to national security. The IMMIGRATION AND NATIONALITY ACT OF 1952 (the McCarran-Walter Act) changed the emphasis of immigration law from national origin to exclusion of those who threatened the democratic political process.

Meanwhile, in 1942 when many American workers had joined the armed forces in World War II, the United States and Mexico cooperated in the BRACERO PROGRAM. Temporary workers, or *braceros*, were granted American visas to relieve the labor shortage in the Southwest. Many more impoverished Mexican workers, however, began to cross the 2,000-mile border illegally. Called "wetbacks" because they swam across the Rio Grande River, these workers accepted lower pay than the *braceros*. Business and industry defeated attempts by organized labor to regulate this source of cheap labor. "OPERATION WETBACK" in the 1950's used military maneuvers to round up illegal (as well as some legal) immigrants, prompting further controversy.

Illegal Immigration as a Contemporary Political Issue. After World War II, there was national sympathy for refugees from Communism, such as Hungarians in 1956. In 1959, when Fidel Castro established a Communist government in Cuba, thousands of Cubans emigrated, most of them professionals and skilled workers who prospered in American society. Other refugees did not fare so well. In 1980, Castro sent boatloads of criminals, and the mentally ill, as well

as others, to Florida in the MARIEL BOAT LIFT. Interned in camps and prisons, they rioted when threatened with deportation. Southeast Asian refugees from the VIETNAM WAR met a mixed public reception in the 1970's and 1980's. Civil war in Central America led to a flood of Salvadoran and Guatemalan refugees in the 1980's, who generally entered the country without government sanction as undocumented immigrants. The SANCTUARY MOVEMENT, based in a network of religious organizations, offered these people help and refuge but met with stiff government resistance.

Top Ten Sources of Legalization (Amnesty) Applicants: (1986-1990)	
Total amnesty applicants: 1,762,143	
Country of immigrant's citizenship	Number of amnesty applicants
Mexico	1,230,457
El Salvador	143,203
Guatemala	52,583
Colombia	26,392
Philippines	19,089
Dominican Republic	18,285
Poland	16,441
Nicaragua	16,015
Haiti	15,962
Iran	14,649

Source: Data are from Allison Landes, ed. *Immigration and Illegal Aliens.* Table 3.1. Wylie, Tex.: Information Plus, 1991.

The IMMIGRATION AND NATIONALITY ACT OF 1965 removed national quotas. Since then, most immigrants have come from Asia, South and Central America, and Mexico. There has been increasing hostility toward illegal immigrants, who are often seen as an economic threat to American workers. Since most of them are young, single men from poor countries, they are willing to work for lower wages than other Americans. This tends to drive down wages in general, to the dismay of unions, and create competition for low-paying jobs, to the dismay of members of some racial and ethnic minorities. Yet the supporters of undocumented workers believe they are an asset to the economy, filling jobs most Americans would not accept.

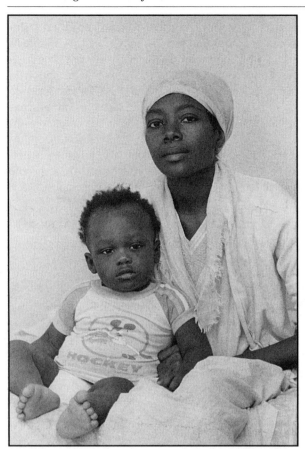

This Haitian woman's temporary work permit has been revoked, but she wishes to remain in the United States to make a better life for herself and her child. (AP/Wide World Photos)

Some American citizens also resent undocumented immigrants' use of public services, such as public schools and hospitals. This has proven to be a burden on the budgets and facilities of border areas and cities such as Los Angeles. In *Plyler v. Doe* (1982), the Supreme Court ruled that the children of undocumented immigrants are entitled to a free education. Moreover, a number of studies suggest that most such immigrants pay more in taxes than they receive in government benefits.

Concern over illegal immigration rose again in the 1980's with a 31 percent increase in apprehensions and a worsening Mexican economy. While the INS stopped at least one million undocumented Mexican immigrants at the border annually, millions more entered illegally. After much debate, Congress passed the IMMIGRATION REFORM AND CONTROL ACT OF 1986, which beefed up border enforcement, offered amnesty to those who arrived illegally before 1982, and made employers responsible for hiring only citizens or documented workers. At least three million immigrants were legalized as a result of this law, but employer sanctions proved difficult to enforce. At the same time, civil liberties groups charged that the law promoted job discrimination against Mexican Americans and other Latinos who are in the United States legally.

Illegal immigrants became the source of several political controversies in the 1990's. In 1992 presidential candidate Bill Clinton made President George Bush's refusal of entry to Haitian refugees a major campaign issue; as president, however, he allowed the Coast Guard to interdict them at sea for return to Haiti. Two of Clinton's women nominees for attorney general were forced to withdraw because they had employed illegal alien immigrants as domestic help or failed to pay their Social Security taxes. The 1993 bombing of the World Trade Center, apparently by illegal immigrants, raised further questions about the enforcement of immigration policy.

Many critics contend that current immigration law is not effectively enforced and demand increased funding for the INS. Others call for revision of current immigration policies to protect the interests of the United States in a competitive world economy. Still others believe that until the United States helps to stabilize and strengthen the Mexican economy, illegal immigration will continue. A conflict is emerging between those who see growing multiculturalism as a positive development in American life and those who say that immigration—both legal and illegal—should be drastically curtailed to ensure the social cohesion of the nation.

SUGGESTED READINGS. *American Immigration Policy, 1924-1952* by Robert A. Divine (1972) presents a historical account of legislation. A collection of essays calling for reform of immigration policy appears in *U.S. Immigration in the 1980's: Reappraisal and Reform* (1988), edited by David E. Simcox. Jack Miles's "Blacks vs. Browns: Immigration and the New American Dilemma," in *The Atlantic* 270 (October, 1992), p. 41, discusses undocumented immigrants in Los Angeles as a threat to the national economy. See also *Immigration and Illegal Aliens: Burden or Blessing?* (1989), edited by Mark A. Siegel et al.—*Marjorie Podolsky*

Immigration Act of 1917: Law restricting immigration to the United States. In a measure specifically aimed at keeping out Asian Indians, it banned immigration from all countries in the Asia-Pacific Triangle except Japan and the Philippines (a U.S. territory). Japan was excluded because Japanese were already prohibited from coming, as were Chinese and Koreans. The act also forbade entry to illiterates, mentally ill people, those entering for immoral purposes, alcoholics, and stowaways. President Woodrow Wilson vetoed the bill because it required would-be immigrants to pass a literacy test, but Congress overrode the veto.

Immigration Act of 1924: Decisively put a stop to the massive immigration that had occurred since 1880 and ensured that most immigration for the next forty years would be from northern and western Europe. The act limited the total number of immigrants and determined national quotas based on 2 percent of the population of that national origin already residing in the United States according to the 1890 census. No country had a quota of less than one hundred. Applicants from Central American, South American, or island colonies belonging to European countries were included in the quotas of the respective European countries. Asian immigration was effectively curtailed.

Immigration Act of 1990: Gave Hong Kong its own immigration quota and doubled the quota of allowable asylees (those granted political asylum). Family-sponsored aliens and those with recognized talents in science, art, education, business, or athletics as well as outstanding professors, researchers, and business executives received preferred status, as did graduates with professional licenses, skilled labor, needed unskilled labor, and employees of U.S. companies operating in Hong Kong. The act contained provisions for nonimmigrant students, protected status for Salvadorans, naturalization provisions for Philippine natives with active-duty service during World War II, and antidiscrimination provisions for immigrant workers.

Immigration and Nationality Act of 1952: Gave each country recognized by the United Nations an immigration quota based on the 1920 census, adjustable to prevent splitting up families. Also known as the McCarran-Walter Act, it continued the exclusion of immigrants from the "Asia-Pacific Triangle" or those of Asian ancestry. Aliens suffering from mental disorders, drug addiction, or serious communicable diseases were also excluded, as were anarchists and members of totalitarian political parties. To be naturalized, immigrants needed to be able to read, write, and speak English (if able), and had to know the principles and history of the United States, in addition to meeting residency requirements.

Immigration and Nationality Act of 1965: Major reform that eliminated the national origins system, which had been in force since the Immigration Act of 1924, and opened the gates to immigration from Asia and Latin America. Visas were issued on a preferential basis to relatives of U.S. citizens and of aliens admitted to permanent residency; to professionals, unskilled laborers, and skilled workers whose services were needed; to refugees from Communist or Middle Eastern countries; and to those displaced by natural disasters. The act established a Select Commission on Western Hemisphere Immigration to study existing and anticipated technological and economic trends related to Western Hemisphere nations, especially Cuba, and report to the president until January 15, 1968.

Immigration and Naturalization Service (INS): Federal agency created in 1891 to regulate and enforce immigration laws. Its function is to keep undesirables out of the United States by deciding which individuals may immigrate, guarding national borders against illegal entry, and capturing and deporting those who do enter illegally. The INS also determines which refugees are permitted to enter. In 1940, the INS was moved from the Department of Labor to the Department of Justice, reflecting the shift from regulating the immigrant influx

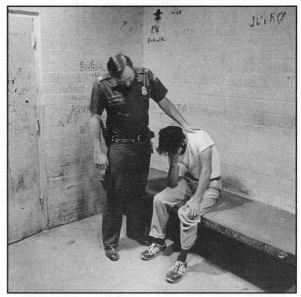

The employees of the Immigration and Naturalization Service have the difficult task of returning illegal immigrants to their country of origin. (AP/Wide World Photos)

into the labor force to combating criminal and subversive elements within the alien population in wartime. In the late twentieth century, the agency has been criticized for ineffective or abusive control of illegal immigration as well as long delays in processing immigrants' applications.

Immigration legislation: United States immigration policy has moved from the open door for would-be entrants to an ever more complex body of regulations. Those regulations include not only limits upon the total of newcomers, but also principles of selection favoring some potential migrants over others. Accordingly, debates over immigration have been, and remain, highly politicized, with the resulting outcome reflecting the balance of forces in the larger political universe.

The shaping of immigration legislation has involved an ongoing tug of war between two conflicting impulses. The idea of the United States as a refuge for the world's poor, downtrodden, and oppressed has exerted a continuing powerful influence. At the same time, however, many longer-settled Americans have viewed immigrants, or at least immigrants who were not of the "proper sort," with varying degrees of alarm as threats to their interests, values, and way of life. "The overall effect has been to close the door partially with one hand and open it selectively with the other," according to E. P. Hutchinson.

From First Settlement to the Civil War. During the colonial period, each colony adopted its own policies dealing with immigration. The demand for labor to exploit the abundant physical resources of the New World made the dominant attitude the encouragement of immigra-

tion. But even during the colonial era there were efforts to exclude "undesirables" such as Roman Catholics, Quakers, convicts, and likely burdens upon the community's taxpayers.

After independence, the states inherited the responsibility for dealing with immigration. State legislatures adopted increasingly stringent legislation requiring bonding of those entering to protect against their becoming public charges. When the growing number of immigrants from Ireland gave rise to a powerful anti-immigrant, anti-ROMAN CATHOLIC movement called NATIVISM, New York and Massachusetts took the lead in imposing head taxes upon entrants to pay for the relief expenses blamed on immigration.

The Constitution left ambiguous the extent of federal governmental authority over immigration apart from granting Congress the power to "establish a uniform Rule of Naturalization." Congress first exercised

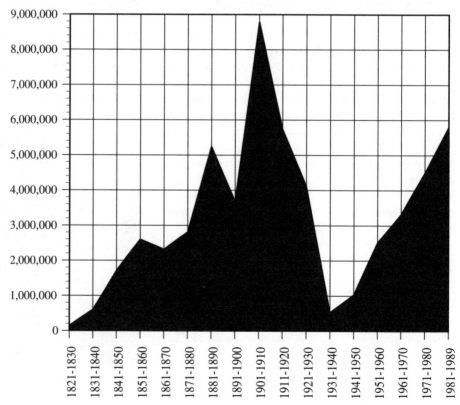

Immigration to the United States: 1821-1989

Source: Adapted from Immigration and Naturalization Service. *An Immigrant Nation: U.S. Regulation of Immigration, 1798-1991,* p. 3. Washington, D.C.: Department of Justice, 1991.

that power in 1790. Alarmed by the pro-Jeffersonian sympathies of many of the newcomers, the Federalist Party majority in Congress adopted the Aliens Act of 1798, giving the president the power to order the deportation of "all such aliens as he shall judge dangerous to the peace and safety of the United States." The legislation carried a two-year time limit, however, and it was allowed to expire without renewal.

Otherwise, the only action taken by Congress before the CIVIL WAR affecting immigration was the passage, beginning in 1891, of so-called steerage laws regulating conditions on ships carrying passengers to the United States. After the Supreme Court struck down the New York and Massachusetts head taxes on immigrants in the *Passenger Cases* (1849), nativists demanded that Congress restrict immigration. Such proposals failed to gain majority support.

The Beginnings of Federal Control over Immigration. The Civil War removed the state rights issue as a barrier to federal government regulation of immigration. Any remaining questions were clarified by the Supreme Court decisions in 1876 in *Chy Lung v. Freeman* and *Henderson v. Mayor of New York*. These struck down state efforts to exclude unwanted would-be entrants by head taxes or regulations upon carriers, and they affirmed the exclusive authority of Congress over immigration under its commerce power.

Congress had undertaken its first direct regulation of immigration in 1875. The major catalyst was the rising clamor on the Pacific Coast against the Chinese. The primary targets of the Immigration Act of 1875 were the two worst evils thought to be associated with Chinese immigration: the so-called coolie trade and the recruitment of prostitutes. Along with prohibiting the bringing to the United States of any Asian person "without their free and voluntary consent," the act barred the importation of women "for the purposes of prostitution." Ongoing complaints about the dumping of criminals led Congress to exclude convicted non-political criminals from foreign lands. Follow-up legislation in 1882 placed two more classes in the excluded category: those judged to be mentally defective (the "idiot" and the "lunatic") and anyone "unable to take care of himself or herself without becoming a public charge."

The same year witnessed the triumph of the agitation against the Chinese with the adoption of the CHINESE EXCLUSION ACT of 1882. The act suspended the immigration of Chinese "laborers" for ten years, barred Chinese from naturalization, and reintroduced

deportation into U.S. immigration law by providing for the deportation of "any Chinese person found unlawfully within the United States." Anti-Chinese sentiment was so powerful that in 1888, Congress invalidated the re-entry permits authorized by the 1882 act for Chinese laborers resident in the United States who had left the country temporarily. When that action was challenged, the Supreme Court in the *Chinese Exclusion Case* (1889) upheld the absolute power of Congress to exclude any foreigner for any reason as "an incident of sovereignty belonging to the government of the United States."

A series of exclusionary immigration acts followed the migration of Chinese laborers into the United States in the late nineteenth century. (Asian American Studies Library, University of California, Berkeley)

From Regulation to Restriction, 1883-1920. Thus given a free hand, Congress responded to the rising tide of immigration in the late nineteenth and early twentieth centuries by expanding and reinforcing the regulatory approach begun in 1875 in order to achieve a more selective admissions process.

The top item on the lawmakers' agenda remained saving the country from the so-called yellow peril. Accordingly, Congress voted in 1892 to continue the suspension of the immigration of Chinese laborers for another ten years. Another suspension—this time, indefinitely—was approved in 1902. In 1904, Chinese exclusion was made permanent. When Japanese immigration sparked a new round of protests from the Pacific Coast, President Theodore Roosevelt averted a confrontation with Japan by arranging in 1907-1908 a "GENTLEMEN'S AGREEMENT" whereby the Japanese government would not issue passports to laborers wishing to emigrate to the continental United States. The final step in the exclusion of Asians was the IM-

The journey to the United States was an arduous one, often characterized by overcrowding and unsanitary conditions. These Europeans arrive on December 10, 1906, aboard the Atlantic liner S.S. Patricia. *(Library of Congress)*

MIGRATION ACT OF 1917 barring the admission of persons from an Asiatic Barred Zone (defined by latitude and longitude to cover South Asia from Arabia to Indochina and the islands adjacent to Asia not possessed by the United States).

At the same time, Congress continued to expand the categories excluded for reasons other than ethnicity and race. Complaints from workingmen's groups led to the passage in 1885 of the first legislation against contract labor. Exclusion of physical and mental defectives was broadened to cover sufferers of "a loathsome or a dangerous disease" (1891); epileptics (1903); tuberculosis victims (1907 and 1917); the insane (1891); "imbeciles" and the "feebleminded" (1907); and those with "constitutional psychopathic inferiority" (1917). The continuing struggle to keep out likely "reliefers" resulted in the exclusion of "paupers or persons likely to become a public charge" (1891), "professional beggars" (1903), and those found by the examining physician to have a "mental

or physical defect . . . which may affect the ability of such alien to earn a living" (1907). The barriers against the criminal and immoral included a ban against "persons who have been convicted of a felony or other infamous crime or misdemeanor involving moral turpitude" (1891, with the adjective "infamous" dropped in 1903) or who "admit having committed" such a crime (1907); polygamists (1891); and chronic alcoholics (1917).

The most important new departure in this area was the exclusion of those deemed politically subversive. In the aftermath of the assassination of President William McKinley by an anarchist, Congress in 1903 prohibited the admission of "anarchists, persons who believe in or advocate the overthrow by force or violence of the Government of the United States or of all government or of all forms of law, or the assassination of public officials" or anyone who "is a member of or affiliated with any organization entertaining and teaching" such views. The Immigration Act of 1917 added to the excludable subversive class those "who advocate or teach the unlawful destruction of property" or "who are members of or affiliated with any organization" advocating or teaching such destruction.

The Supreme Court in *Fong Yue Ting v. United States* (1893) ruled that the power to deport foreigners was "as absolute and unqualified as the right to prohibit and prevent their entrance into the country." Congress proceeded to reinforce exclusion by extending

advocating or teaching anarchy or the overthrow by force or violence of the Government of the United States."

Perhaps most important, there was a subtle but significant shift of emphasis from regulations aimed at promoting more selectivity in admissions to a policy of restriction looking to cap, or even reduce, the number of entrants. The impetus behind the shift was resentment by many older-stock Americans at the grow-

Contemporary Italian American residents of Brooklyn, N.Y., re-enact their ancestors' arrival at Ellis Island. (Odette Lupis)

the time limits for deportability after entry. The Immigration Act of 1917 authorized deportation of an alien convicted of a crime "involving moral turpitude" committed within five years after entry or sentenced for more than one such crime at any time after entry. The same legislation made deportable "[a]ny alien who at any time after entry shall be found advocating or teaching the unlawful destruction of property, or

ing influx of immigrants from southern and eastern Europe beginning in the 1880's. The favored instrument of the restrictionists was adoption of LITERACY TESTING. The literacy test was highly selective. Even its supporters, such as Senator Henry Cabot Lodge of Massachusetts, made no secret of their expectation that the test would discriminate against immigrants from southern and eastern Europe in favor of those from western and northern Europe.

The champions of the literacy test were successful in pushing that requirement through Congress in 1897, 1913, and 1915, only to meet with vetoes by Presidents Grover Cleveland, William Howard Taft, and Woodrow Wilson on the grounds that literacy was a function of opportunity rather than of native ability. In 1917, however, amid fears of an even larger flood of newcomers after World War I, the lawmakers overrode another Wilson veto to exclude "[a]ll aliens over sixteen years of age, physically capable of reading, who cannot read the English language, or some other language or dialect, including Hebrew or Yiddish."

The Closed Door, 1921-1945. War-inflamed anxieties about the dangers of hyphenism (foreign-born Americans), alarm over the new Bolshevik threat, and economic difficulties following World War I reinforced support for restriction of immigration. The explosive jump in arrivals as soon as the fighting in Europe was over made it clear to the restrictionists that the literacy test would not fulfill their goal. In the last days of the Wilson Administration, Congress approved a bill to limit immigration for fifteen months to 3 percent of the number of foreign-born of a given nationality as recorded by the 1910 census, but Wilson pocket vetoed the measure. The same 3 percent quota was readopted at the next session by an even wider margin, this time receiving the signature of the new president, Warren G. Harding. Intended as a temporary stopgap until a permanent plan could be adopted, the 1921 Quota Act was to last until June 20, 1922, subsequently extended to June 30, 1924.

The IMMIGRATION ACT OF 1924 reduced the national quotas to 2 percent and shifted the base from the 1910 to the 1890 census. The result was not simply to reduce the total number of immigrants from 357,801 per year to 161,990, but to discriminate against those from southern and eastern Europe who had been very few in number in 1890. More important, a ceiling of 150,000 immigrants would be imposed after July 1, 1927 (later postponed until July 1, 1929), with national quotas allocated in accord with the newly devised national origins formula: the allowable percentage of immigrants of each nationality was based on the percentage of U.S. residents having that national origin in 1920. All the existing grounds for the exclusion of individuals were retained.

The major loophole in the new quota system was the exemption of immigrants from the Western Hemisphere. The most controversial issue involved the demands from the West Coast for formal exclusion of the Japanese despite the success of the gentlemen's agreement in limiting the number of Japanese immigrants. In 1922, the Supreme Court had ruled in *OZAWA v. UNITED STATES* that Japanese were not eligible for naturalization because of the restriction of naturalization by the 1790 statute to "a free white person." Paying no heed to pleas from the State Department to avoid a needless insult to Japan, the advocates of Japanese exclusion succeeded in writing into the 1924 legislation that "[n]o alien ineligible to citizenship shall be admitted to the United States." The effect was to bar not only Japanese immigrants, but also, because of follow-up court rulings of ineligibility for naturalization, Asian Indians, Koreans, Burmese, Afghans, and Filipinos.

Worries about job competition coupled with ANTI-SEMITISM stymied attempts in the 1930's to gain congressional approval for relaxation of the quota system in behalf of refugees from Nazi persecution. Although the immigration laws left room for administrative discretion, that discretion was typically used in favor of more restrictive policies. Historians have fully documented the extent to which President Franklin D. Roosevelt and executive branch officials were to blame for the failure of the United States to do more to save the victims of Hitler's Holocaust.

Rather than promoting liberalization of the immigration laws, worsening international tensions heightened fears about alien subversives. The result was the adoption of the Alien Registration Act of 1940 for the compulsory registration and fingerprinting of all resident aliens as well as newcomers.

Continued Restrictionism, 1945-1952. The first breakthrough in the attack upon the existing exclusionist framework came during World War II. An effective campaign spearheaded by Pearl S. Buck, author of the best-selling novel about China *The Good Earth* (1931), exploited the wartime alliance with China to induce Congress in 1943 to make "Chinese persons" eligible for naturalization, repeal the Chinese Exclusion Act, and establish a token quota of 105 Chinese per year. The attack on the idea of innate racial differences, begun by social scientists such as anthropologist Franz Boas, had been reinforced and popularized by the war against Hitler. The beginning of the COLD WAR made removal of explicitly racist immigration exclusions appear politically expedient for appealing to Third World peoples. In 1946, Congress approved eligibility for naturalization and annual quotas

With the repeal of the exclusionary and quota-based immigration laws, the U.S. government gradually allowed a more diverse population—seen in the faces of this Ellis Island display—to enter the country. (James L. Shaffer)

of 100 for "persons of races indigenous to India" and "Filipino persons or persons of Filipino descent."

Congressman Walter Judd of Minnesota, a former medical missionary in China who had been the leading congressional champion of the repeal of Chinese exclusion, took the lead in pushing eligibility for naturalization and quotas for all Asian peoples. Congress remained wary, however, about opening the door to a large number of persons of Asian ancestry living in the Western Hemisphere nonquota nations. The compromise solution proposed by Judd, and incorporated into the IMMIGRATION AND NATIONALITY ACT OF 1952 (the McCarran-Walter Act) was the Asia-Pacific Triangle plan to replace the Asiatic Barred Zone. A large triangle was drawn covering most of South and East Asia, including Japan. Most countries within the triangle were given a quota of 100; however, residents of the Western Hemisphere whose ancestry was one-half or more Asian could not come as nonquota immigrants; their slots would be charged to the Asian nation of their ancestry, whether or not they had been born there.

Congress readily voted admission for the spouses, fiancés, and children of U.S. military personnel. More politically divisive was treatment of the large number of homeless refugees left by World War II. The DISPLACED PERSONS ACT of 1948 provided that during the two years following passage, up to 202,000 immigrant visas could be issued without regard to quota limitations, with no less than 40 percent earmarked for those whose homeland had been *de facto* annexed by a foreign power. The upshot was continued protests about admitting too few refugees. A 1950 amendment increased the number of nonquota immigrants only to 341,000 through June 30, 1951.

Resistance to a more liberal policy was partly motivated by the legacy of Depression-era fears about job competition from immigrants. An even more powerful obstacle was suspicion of the loyalty of alien subversives, which had been stirred up by the Cold War. The Internal Security Act of 1950 expanded the excluded subversive class to aliens whose entry would be prejudicial to the interests and security of the United States; who are anarchists; who advocate opposition to or the overthrow of organized government; who are or have been members or affiliates of the COMMUNIST PARTY or associated with world communism; or who engage in or are associated with publication and distribution of subversive writings.

The sheer bulk of the amendments tacked on over the years to the immigration acts of 1917 and 1924 led Congress to undertake a thorough revision and codification of the immigration laws. The resulting Immigration and Nationality Act of 1952 was a defeat for the supporters of a more liberal immigration policy, except for the elimination of the Asiatic Barred Zone. President Harry Truman vetoed the measure because of discriminatory features, but the lawmakers overrode his veto. The new law retained the national origins formula for the allocation of quotas. The annual quota of any country was set at one-sixth of 1 percent of the number of persons of that national origin in the United States in 1920, with a minimum quota of 100. The result was an increase of only a few hundred in total immigration.

At the same time, the previously adopted grounds for individual exclusion—including the literacy test requirement—were retained and even extended. New additions to the excluded list included those suffering from leprosy; those convicted of two or more offenses, whether or not involving moral turpitude, if the actually imposed sentences of confinement totalled five years or more; those who were narcotics addicts, who had been convicted of violating anti-narcotics laws, and who were believed to have been illicit drug traffickers; and those coming to engage in any immoral sexual act. The legislation excluded aliens seeking to enter to perform skilled or unskilled labor if the Secretary of Labor certified that there was an adequate supply of such labor in the United States or that their entry would adversely affect wages and working conditions. Wording changes strengthened the existing provisions for deportation.

The major innovation was the introduction of a strongly weighted occupational preference system for the distribution of slots within a given national quota. The act gave a first preference of 50 percent of each national quota to "qualified quota immigrants whose services are determined by the Attorney General to be needed urgently in the United States because of the high education, technical training, specialized experience, or exceptional ability of such immigrants."

The Struggle for Liberalization, 1953-1965. Despite support for liberalization from Truman's successor, President Dwight D. Eisenhower, the backers of McCarran-Walter retained the upper hand in Congress through the 1950's. The one significant chink made in the status quo was the adoption of the REFUGEE RELIEF ACT of 1953, providing 205,000 special nonquota visas for eligible refugees, their spouses, and their children under twenty-one years of age. A more limited change was approval of special treatment for Hungarian refugees after the 1956 uprising against Communist rule in that country.

After his election in 1960, President John F. Kennedy made reform of the immigration laws a high priority. His successor, Lyndon B. Johnson, made the issue part of his Great Society program. A number of factors contributed to the adoption of the IMMIGRATION AND NATIONALITY ACT OF 1965: the growth of ethnic, religious, and racial tolerance; the general prosperity of the time and the accompanying reduction of fears about job competition from more immigration; the relaxation of Cold War tensions; the lobbying activities of the newer ethnic groups and of voluntary, mostly church-related, agencies involved in refugee assistance; and the large liberal Democratic majorities in Congress after the election of 1964.

The 1965 act imposed an annual limit of 170,000 aliens per year from the Eastern Hemisphere, with an individual nation limit of 20,000; phased out the national origins quota system over a three-year period;

and eliminated the Asia-Pacific Triangle provision of the 1952 law. Yet the new legislation did not significantly alter the rules for individual exclusion and deportation. Most important, congressional alarm over the increase in the number of nonquota immigrants arriving from the Western Hemisphere resulted in the imposition of a 120,000 per year quota for the Western Hemisphere.

A major loophole in these limits upon immigration was a provision for the quota-free admission of "immediate relatives" of United States citizens (children, spouses, and parents). Of even more long-term importance—although its implications were only dimly understood at the time—was the change in the preference system for the distribution of slots within the 170,000 quota for the Eastern Hemisphere from the emphasis upon occupational qualifications in the Immigration and Nationality Act of 1952 (McCarran-Walter Act) to one strongly favoring family unification. Under the new legislation, the 170,000 visas per year for immigrants from the Eastern Hemisphere were to be distributed according to the following pref-

One hundred fifty people from twenty-seven different countries take their citizenship vows at Independence Hall in Philadelphia as part of a 1981 "Freedom Day" ceremony. (AP/Wide World Photos)

erence system: First preference was for unmarried sons and daughters over age twenty-one of U.S. citizens (maximum of 20 percent). Second preference was for spouses and unmarried sons and daughters of aliens lawfully admitted to permanent residence (20 percent plus any not required for the first preference). Third preference was for members of the professions, and scientists and artists of exceptional ability (maximum of 10 percent). Fourth preference was for married sons and daughters over age twenty-one of U.S. citizens (10 percent plus any not required for the first three preferences). Fifth preference was for brothers and sisters of citizens (24 percent plus any not required for the first four preferences). Sixth preference was for necessary skilled and unskilled workers in understaffed occupations (maximum of 10 percent).

There was neither a preference system nor an individual country limit for immigrants from the Western Hemisphere. This opened the door to Mexicans. Yet the requirement for labor certification from the Secretary of Labor worked against would-be migrants from Mexico compared to those from other Latin American countries. In 1977, Congress established a preference system for the Western Hemisphere similar to that of the Eastern Hemisphere, along with a 20,000 per country limit. The following year, Congress voted a single worldwide cap of 290,000 immigrants a year with a uniform preference system heavily weighted in favor of family unification.

Asian and Latin American Immigration after 1965. Although most observers at the time of the passage of the 1965 legislation did not foresee any significant change in the pattern of immigration, they were badly mistaken. The proportion of immigrants coming from Europe fell dramatically, while the numbers from Asia and Latin America saw a quantum increase. The prosperity of most European countries outside the Iron Curtain reduced the number of would-be migrants from those nations. The most important factor in this shift, however, has been the success of Asian immigrants in exploiting the family-unification preference system.

Immigration historian David M. Reimers summarizes the pattern. An Asian student comes to the United States; while finishing his studies, he finds a job, gets Labor Department certification, and becomes an immigrant. As a legal resident, he uses the second preference to bring over his spouse and children. After he and his spouse become citizens, they sponsor their brothers and sisters under the fifth, and largest, pref-

erence, or bring in their nonquota parents. The brothers and sisters, once legal residents, also use the second preference to bring their spouses and children and then expand the immigrant kin network further after they become citizens. "No wonder," Reimers notes, "the 1965 law came to be called the brothers and sisters act."

The number of legal immigrants proved far higher than the numerical limits set by the 1965 act. The nonquota admission of "immediate" family members of U.S. citizens averaged 90,000 per year during the ten years after the 1965 law—more than double the anticipated number—and rose to nearly 150,000 per year by the end of the 1970's. Further ballooning the total of new entrants was the special treatment given favored groups of refugees that resulted in the admission of approximately 360,000 Cubans between 1965 and 1979, and roughly 700,000 Indochinese between 1975 and 1984. Congress sought to regain a larger say in discretionary decisions on refugees in the REFUGEE ACT OF 1980. Although Congress appears to have envisaged an annual limit of 50,000 refugees a year, the number admitted under the new procedures has proved to be far above that level.

An even more controversial issue has been the attempts by Haitians and Salvadorans fleeing their countries to gain asylum in the United States under the United Nations Protocol on Refugees, which was accepted by the Senate in 1968. After long court battles and much political acrimony, Congress established in the Refugee Act of 1980 a statutory right to asylum and accepted the United Nations definition of a refugee as "any person who is outside any country of his nationality . . . [and] is unable or unwilling to return . . . because of persecution, or a well-founded fear of persecution, on account of race, religion, nationality, membership of a particular social group, or political opinion." The administrations of Reagan and Bush took a hard line against Haitian and Salvadoran asylum-seekers by a stringent application of the "well-founded fear of persecution" standard in the 1980's and early 1990's.

Undocumented Aliens and Immigration Reform. What most excited alarm was the rapid growth in the number of illegal immigrants (or undocumented aliens). Although there was a growing influx from Central America and the Caribbean islands, most of the illegals were Mexicans. The flood of Latino newcomers was the more upsetting to many Americans because of what appeared to be their lack of interest in learning English and ASSIMILATING. One widely supported solution was to eliminate the incentive of employment opportunities in the United States by imposing sanctions against employers who hired illegal aliens. That approach became the keystone of the proposed immigration reform legislation sponsored by Senators Alan Simpson of Wyoming and Romano Mazzoli of Kentucky. To overcome the opposition of civil rights and Latino groups, the supporters of employer sanctions had to make the concession of amnesty and legalization for the illegals already present in the United States. The final ingredient that made possible the IMMIGRATION REFORM AND CONTROL ACT OF 1986 (IRCA) was the inclusion of special provisions to assure an ample supply of agricultural labor, which won the crucial support of lawmakers from the West.

IRCA made it unlawful for any person knowingly to hire an alien not authorized to work in the United States and required employers to verify the status of all newly hired persons. The primary sanction was civil fines, but there was a criminal penalty of up to six months imprisonment for a "pattern or practice" of knowingly hiring illegal aliens. To meet complaints that employer sanctions would encourage employers to discriminate against those who sounded or looked foreign, the act created a special office in the Justice Department to investigate and prosecute charges of such discrimination. Although amnesty for illegal aliens in the United States was strongly resisted by many members of Congress, the lawmakers narrowly approved giving legal temporary resident status to illegal aliens who had resided continuously in the United States since before January 1, 1982, and allowing those temporary residents to become permanent residents after eighteen months.

By the time of the deadline for amnesty applications in 1988, more than 1.7 million applications had been filed under the general legalization program and another 1.3 million applications under a special agricultural workers' program. Congress opened the door still wider in 1990 by giving work authorization and possible citizenship to an estimated 250,000 close family members of amnestied aliens; granting protected status to roughly 200,000 undocumented Salvadorans; opening the possibility of protected status for illegally present members of other nationality groups via the device of "extended voluntary departure"; increasing the number of "diversity" visas first authorized by IRCA for favored treatment of the nationals of coun-

The *Immigration Act of 1990 increased legal immigration by approximately one-third. This display at Ellis Island informs visitors of some of the immigrants' struggles.* (Mary Pat Shaffer)

tries underrepresented in the existing immigration flow; speeding the process of naturalization; and narrowing the power of the Immigration and Naturalization Service to exclude aliens on ideological grounds.

The IMMIGRATION ACT OF 1990 increased legal immigration by at least one-third. In 1990, the United States admitted a total of 529,120 aliens. The annual limit for the first three years under the 1990 law was set at 700,000, and thereafter fixed at 675,000. No numerical limitation was placed upon the admission of "immediate relatives" (spouses, minor children, and parents) of U.S. citizens. Illegal immigration continued, with no evidence that employer sanctions have significantly reduced the flow. The multicultural United States continued to undergo a far-reaching change in population composition whose full consequences remain to be seen.

SUGGESTED READINGS. The standard history of United States immigration policies up through the adoption of the 1965 law is E. P. Hutchinson's *Legislative His-*

tory of American Immigration Policy, 1798-1965 (1981). Excellent analyses of the legal status of aliens before and under the McCarran-Walter Act of 1952 may be found in two works by Milton R. Konvitz: *The Alien and the Asiatic in American Law* (1946) and *Civil Rights in Immigration* (1953). David M. Reimers' *Still the Golden Door: The Third World Comes to America* (1985) is informative on post-1965 immigration, legal and illegal, from Asia, Latin America, and the Caribbean. Frank D. Bean, Georges Vernez, and Charles B. Keely's *Opening and Closing the Doors: Evaluating Immigration Reform and Control* (1989) gives a preliminary assessment of IRCA.— *John Braeman*

Immigration quotas. *See* **Quotas—immigration**

Immigration Reform and Control Act of 1986: Controversial act that outlawed the hiring or recruiting of illegal immigrants. Employers were required to verify employability using a combination of identity documents or face heavy sanctions (fines). The act provided for increased border patrols, speedier naturalization process for eligible aliens, and criminal penalties for those who transport undocumented immigrants into the United States. It also established a commission to see how the wages and working conditions of domestic farm workers are affected by the presence of alien farm workers, as well as a joint task force to determine if this law results in discrimination against people who are not illegal immigrants. In its early stages, the law was controversial because it allowed the IMMIGRATION AND NATURALIZATION SERVICE (INS) to raid sweatshops, factories, and farms in "sweeps" of illegal immigrants.

Immigration Restriction League (IRL): Founded by Charles Warren in 1894, this organization was designed to restrict the number of immigrants entering the United States. The league pushed for a literacy test for all potential immigrants, which barred those who could not read or write. Though it claimed humanitarian ideals and a lack of bias, ultimately the group was associated with NATIVISM and XENOPHOBIA.

In Re Ah Moy, on Habeas Corpus (1884): U.S. Circuit Court case which held that the wife of a Chinese laborer was herself a laborer and thus was barred from immigration to the United States. The ruling was one of the many events in the late nineteenth century that restricted Chinese immigration and the growth of Chi-

nese communities in the United States.

Chinese men typically came to the United States in the nineteenth century without their wives or families, because the American construction industry needed a cheap labor force that was mobile and unencumbered. Most of the women who did immigrate were poor, and many of them were prostitutes. Many had been sold as prostitutes even before leaving China: In 1870, of 3,536 Chinese women in California, more than half gave prostitution as their occupation.

In 1875, Congress passed the Page Law, which forbade the entry of Chinese, Japanese, and Mongolian contract laborers as well as women brought in for purposes of prostitution. While this law proved ineffective in controlling male immigration, female entry to the United States dropped significantly thereafter. Between 1870 and 1880, the total male Chinese population in the United States increased from 58,633 to 100,686, yet the number of females only grew from 4,566 to 4,779.

The Page Law was a prelude to the CHINESE EXCLUSION ACT of 1882, which prohibited all Chinese immigration except for diplomats and "teachers, students, merchants, or [those who come] from curiosity, together with their body and household servants." Chinese immigration thus was radically restricted on the basis of class.

Early laws, however, did not specify precisely the measures that were to be adopted with regard to females. This question was tested in 1884 in the U.S. Circuit Court in California. Too Cheong, a Chinese laborer who had gained American residence, had married Ah Moy on a visit to China in 1883 and brought her back to the United States. The court, however, eventually denied her admission, arguing that when a Chinese woman married a Chinese laborer she automatically became a "laborer" herself, and thus she was barred from immigration under the Page Law and the Exclusion Act. The court extended such proscriptions even to women who had not been laborers before their marriage.

This decision, along with continuing restrictions on the Chinese in general, created a continuing gender imbalance in the Chinese American community that lasted for the next eighty years. By 1890, the number of Chinese women had decreased; later ratios were as low as one female for every twenty-seven males, fostering the bachelor society typical of many Chinatowns. Not until the mid-1960's, after early curbs on immigration had eased and the community had reproduced itself over generations, did ratios approach any equilibrium.

SUGGESTED READINGS. The legal structures of Chinese exclusion are dealt with in detail in *Entry Denied: Exclusion and the Chinese Community in America* (1991), edited by Sucheng Chan. Jules Becker considers public opinion on these changes in *The Course of Exclusion: San Francisco Newspaper Coverage of Chinese and Japanese in the United States* (1991). Ronald Takaki puts the event in historical context in his *Strangers from a Different Shore: A History of Asian Americans* (1989).

Indentured servants: People who agree, by contract, to work for another person in exchange for travel or living expenses. In the 1600's and 1700's, many Europeans too poor to emigrate to colonial America on their own made the trip as indentured servants. Some did so by choice; others were forcibly deported as indentured servants. In exchange for the chance to emigrate, they signed a contract to work for the person who paid for their trip. A common practice was to agree to seven years of work. After that time, indentured servants were free to start their own lives.

Independent living movement: Movement whose goal is to enable people with severe disabilities to live outside nursing homes or other care facilities. The independent living movement seeks to obtain and provide services for people with disabilities, and it encourages legislation to make the change from dependent to independent living possible for those people who desire it. The movement has concentrated on helping younger working adults with severe disabilities.

The 1960's and 1970's was a period characterized by a major trend toward the deinstitutionalization of persons with disabilities. Unfortunately, the early phases of this movement occurred without adequate preparation or planning. Large numbers of persons with disabilities were returned to their communities with few survival skills and no community-based support systems. The result was that many were unable to achieve a successful transition from the institution to the community. The independent living movement has sought to rectify this situation by providing the kinds of services that allow persons with disabilities to live in the world of able-bodied persons.

The independent living movement took hold in the 1970's. Ed Roberts and Judy Heumann, both of whom had disabilities caused by polio, are considered move-

ment pioneers. They established the Center for Independent Living in Berkeley, California, in 1972. The Housing and Community Development Act of 1974 was the first legislation to provide financial subsidies for alternative living arrangements for people with disabilities; the act also sponsored eight projects around the country to study various independent living models. In 1978, the Rehabilitation, Comprehensive Services, and Developmental Disabilities Amendments established a four-part independent living program. Central to the program was the creation of an independent living services program to be administered by U.S. vocational rehabilitation centers.

The community living arrangements for persons with disabilities created by this movement are logically viewed as a continuum of placements or options ranging from highly restrictive to independent. Long-term group homes or intermediate care facilities for the mentally retarded provide intensively supervised environments. Supported living in a group home or apartment, frequently transitional in nature, represents a more normalized environmental option for persons with disabilities. Supported living in one's own apartment is an arrangement in which persons with disabilities receive periodic support services as required. Lastly, persons with disabilities may live independently with no support service required, usually because the requisite skills have been acquired in previous supported community placements.

By the early 1990's, more than 500,000 people with disabilities had been helped to live relatively independently through the movement. The movement continues to evolve as American society moves toward acceptance of this population.

Independent Order of B'nai B'rith. *See* **B'nai B'rith, Independent Order of**

Indian Affairs, Bureau of. *See* **Bureau of Indian Affairs (BIA)**

Indian Citizenship Act of 1924: Act granting U.S. citizenship to American Indians. In the early twentieth century, there were several conflicting points of view regarding the gradual or rapid ASSIMILATION of American Indians into the government of the United States. Many Indian tribes were suspicious of the U.S. government's proposal of total assimilation and believed it to be only another step toward the ultimate elimination of tribal values. From several divergent viewpoints came a compromise. Homer P. Snyder of New York introduced a congressional resolution that eventually became the Snyder Act. It stated that all noncitizen Indians born within the United States are to be declared citizens of the United States, provided such citizenship does not impair or otherwise affect the right of any Indian to tribal or other property.

Indian hobbyist movement: Promotes amateur study of and immersion in American Indian cultures by non-Indians. Some Anglos and others have long been fascinated by the ways of life of their Indian neighbors. This interest took institutionalized form in 1910 with the establishment of the BOY SCOUTS OF AMERICA. This organization, which later gave rise to the Cub Scouts, GIRL SCOUTS, and Camp Fire Girls, marked the beginning of an organized, nonprofessional investigation into the lifestyles of the American Indians. Because it is nonprofessional, the term "hobbyist" has been applied to those involved in any of the organizations devoted to the study of American Indians.

Originally, hobbyists were non-Indian boys who had a romanticized idea of American Indians. The movement has grown to include people of all genders, ages, and ethnic backgrounds who show an interest in American Indian cultures. The hobbyist movement gained power in the 1960's when some American Indians joined in its efforts. Until then, it was not held in high regard because of its focus on the superficial notions of American Indian life such as arts and crafts, foods, songs, dances, and powwows. Since that time, a number of hobbyists have declared strong interest in Indian spiritual beliefs and practices. New Age spiritual movements since the 1970's have also incorporated Indian traditions such as the sweat lodge into their activities.

Though no organization of the hobbyist movement exists on the national level in the United States, groups abound on the state and regional levels. These organizations gather for field trips to reservations and powwows, where first-hand knowledge of American Indian culture is obtained. Non-Indian groups also

The Indian hobbyist movement has encouraged understanding of American Indians among nontribal peoples. (Elaine S. Querry)

sponsor their own powwows in order to practice and display their knowledge and crafts.

The hobbyist movement is also popular in Europe, where many hobbyists are organized nationally. British citizens may choose from a number of organizations and publications. The most popular of these are the English Westerner's Society, with its *Brand Book,* and the publication *Tally Sheet.* People in Sweden, Germany, Belgium, France, Holland, Switzerland, Czechoslovakia, Finland, Poland, and Hungary also show an interest in American Indians and the hobbyist movement.

SUGGESTED READINGS. For detailed overviews of the history of the hobbyist movement see "The Indian Hobbyist Movement in North America" by William K. Powers and "The Indian Hobbyist Movement in Europe" by Colin F. Taylor, both in the Smithsonian Institution's *Handbook on North American Indians,* vol. 4 (1978). Many hobbyist groups publish and distribute magazines and newsletters nationally, such as *The American Indian Hobbyist* (changed to *American Indian Tradition* in 1960), *Powwow Trails, American Indian Crafts and Culture, Indian America,* and *Whispering Wind.*

Indian Removal Act of 1830: Legislation that authorized the president to remove American Indians from their tribal lands in the eastern United States. On December 8, 1829, President Andrew Jackson recommended that Congress order the removal of all American Indians from east of the Mississippi River to be relocated on lands west of the river. On February 24, 1830, a bill was introduced in the House of Representatives; on May 28, despite some opposition, the measure was enacted. The president was authorized to create and divide suitable districts west of the Mississippi River to be exchanged for properties held by American Indians living within existing U.S. states or territories east of the river. Although it was declared unconstitutional by the Supreme Court in 1832, the act set in motion a pattern of forced removal of American Indians that was tacitly supported by state and federal officials well beyond the 1830's.

Indian Reorganization Act (1934): Law that ended Indian land allotments by the U.S. government and allowed tribes to form their own governments. Also called the Wheeler-Howard Act, the Indian Reorganization Act (IRA) marked a turning point in U.S. Indian policy. Rejecting the forced assimilation of the previous century and a half, the act inaugurated policies that reformers believed would bring more equitable and progressive administration to Indian affairs by ensuring some measure of self-determination for Indian people.

The Indian Reorganization Act capped a decade of reform inside the BUREAU OF INDIAN AFFAIRS (BIA) after serious revelations of fraud, mismanagement, and poor leadership brought the office under intense scrutiny. John Collier, future Commissioner of Indian Affairs and architect of the act, condemned what he called the "monopolistic and autocratic control over person and property" by the bureau and demanded equal rights for Indian people. Spurred on by the Merriam Report, published in 1928, which revealed shocking conditions on reservations and in Indian communities, the BIA began to address the problems.

When Collier became Commissioner of Indian Affairs in April, 1933, he followed the lead of Franklin Roosevelt's New Deal, engaging in what historian Paul Prucha has called "revolutionary change." Collier proposed four sweeping revisions to U.S. Indian policy in the Wheeler-Howard Bill, introduced into Congress in February of 1934. First, he supported granting tribes the right to organize governments and to write tribal constitutions. Second, eschewing the government's disdain for native culture, the bill called for support of Indian arts and crafts and proposed to end the assault on traditional culture. Third, Collier demanded the end to allotment (as instituted by the Dawes Act of 1887), a practice he and others insisted had been the greatest single disaster in the history of the Indian office. The bill would authorize the Secretary of the Interior to purchase land for the tribes and to reconsolidate tribal holdings in the form of reservations. Last, a special court of Indian offenses would have original jurisdiction over cases involving Indians. In sum, the original bill intended fundamentally to alter the nature of the Indian bureau by making it advisory rather than supervisory for Indian affairs.

Intense congressional and native opposition forced the abandonment of parts two and four, leaving Collier with only half of what he wanted. In its final form the bill ended allotment and authorized limited purchases of land, and it allowed for tribes that voted to accept it to organize tribal governments and write constitutions.

Tribal referendums produced mixed results. By 1936, 181 tribes had accepted the Indian Reorganization Act, while 77 rejected it. When the act was extended to Oklahoma in 1936 under the Oklahoma Indian Welfare Act, a majority of the tribes there rejected it. Yet the act did provide important changes in policy directions. Most significant, the tribal governments created under the act's provisions proved to be the foundation for an unprecedented sense of autonomy and self-determination among Indians. As increasing numbers of Indian people joined the staff of the BIA, policy began to take on a new, more Indian-oriented direction that helped to support the cultural and political resurgence of the postwar years.

SUGGESTED READINGS. A good account of John Collier's work on behalf of Indians is Kenneth Philp's *John Collier's Crusade For Indian Reform, 1920-1954* (1977). Paul Prucha's *The Great Father* (1984) is crucial for an understanding of policy decisions, as is Graham D. Taylor's *The New Deal and American Indian Tribalism: The Administration of the Indian Reorganization Act, 1934-1945* (1980). Able discussions of the act's impact may be found in Stephen Cornell's *The Return of the Native: American Indian Political Resurgence* (1988) and Vine Deloria, Jr., and Clifford Lytle's *The Nations Within: The Past and Future of American Indian Sovereignty* (1984). Donald Parman's *The Navajos and the New Deal* (1976) remains one of the best assessments of the act on a major tribe.

Indian Rights Association: Organization founded in 1882 by Quaker philanthropists and other white reformers who were leading advocates for the immediate citizenship of American Indians as the most effective way to promote ASSIMILATION. In the late 1800's, this group advocated an assimilation plan consisting of Christian conversion, compulsory education of white American values, and the privatization of tribal lands through allocation of land to individual Indians, instilling in them personal initiative. The group, headquartered in Philadelphia, was still active in the early 1990's and working to protect American Indian legal and human rights.

Indian rights movement: PAN-INDIAN movement for individual and tribal rights which began during the WORLD WAR II years. Through various forms of protest and activism as well as through interest-group lobbying efforts, American Indians eventually succeeded in winning a number of policy and legislative victories.

Origins. The World War II experience created an atmosphere of national unity and common cause. Many American Indians, especially those who had served in the military, began thinking of themselves more as U.S. citizens than as members of distinct tribal groups. Some began to work politically for

rights based on U.S. citizenship. They sought inclusion in programs like Social Security and state welfare, and an end to discrimination against Indians such as bans on the purchase of alcohol or exclusion from voting in some areas. In 1944 representatives of tribes throughout the nation formed the National Congress of American Indians (NCAI) to help win fundamental rights of U.S. citizenship. The NCAI did not want to see a further erosion of tribal sovereignty or distinct Indian cultures. It therefore also lobbied to preserve treaty rights and native cultures, and to protect Indian land and resources.

The emerging Indian rights movement received a big boost from Indian efforts to block the government's TERMINATION and URBANIZATION policies of the 1950's. Those policies threatened to curtail federally supplied services and to destroy the special relationship between tribes and the federal government by nullifying tribal government and sovereignty, treaty rights, and the nontaxable status of Indian land. Groups such as the NCAI and reservation Indians from a number of tribes coalesced to fight this newest assimilationist drive. Together with anthropologist Sol Tax, the NCAI organized the American Indian Chicago Conference in 1961 in an effort to defeat controversial termination policies. It went even further, however, by issuing a Declaration of Indian Purpose, proclaiming goals of protecting Indian culture and the remaining tribal land base as well as involving Indians more in political decisions that affected them.

Many Indians by this time had moved into urban areas, where they met Indians of other tribes and forged intertribal ties based on common interests. Influenced by the CIVIL RIGHTS movement in their midst, some urban Indians saw the Chicago conference as too cautious. They formed the NATIONAL INDIAN YOUTH COUNCIL (NIYC) in 1961 to push for bolder action. Beginning in 1964 the NIYC, following the example of civil rights SIT-INS, held "fish-ins" in the Pacific Northwest, where states ignored treaty fishing rights and enforced local game limits. Often joined by celebrities such as Marlon Brando and Dick GREGORY, participants openly fished in violation of state laws. Many were arrested and jailed, but finally in 1966 the U.S. Justice Department intervened in several cases and restored treaty rights.

Red Power. In 1968 some Chippewas in Minneapolis, Minnesota, responded to charges of police harassment and brutality by forming Indian patrols to follow police in Indian neighborhoods and serve as witnesses when arrests were made. George Mitchell and Dennis Banks emerged as leaders of the patrols, and they soon organized the AMERICAN INDIAN MOVEMENT (AIM), the most famous group in what became known as the Red Power movement. AIM became involved in a wide variety of direct political actions. In 1972 it organized a cross-country TRAIL OF BROKEN TREATIES march to Washington, D.C., in protest of historic mistreatment. Publication of Dee Brown's *Bury My Heart at Wounded Knee* (1971) drew national attention to the tragic 1890 massacre at WOUNDED KNEE. In 1973, armed AIM members led by Russell Means occupied the South Dakota village of Wounded Knee in a seventy-day confrontation with federal officials, Pine Ridge Reservation tribal chairmen, and AIM opponent Richard Wilson.

One of the most famous symbolic protests in the Red Power movement took place on ALCATRAZ ISLAND, former home of a maximum security federal prison. In 1969 a small group of Indian students from the San Francisco Bay area, inspired by black and Latino activism, occupied Alcatraz to protest the historical dislocation of Indians. Their removal by authorities drew attention to the issue, and seventy-eight more Indian students formed Indians of All Tribes (IAT) and returned. By this time the action was receiving nationwide publicity and sympathy, and President Richard Nixon, fearing confrontation, did not force a showdown. The demonstrators' demand to turn the institution into an American Indian cultural center was never met, however, and the undertaking was abandoned after two years.

The well-publicized acts of AIM and IAT were not the only examples of Red Power activism. In 1970, about 150 Pit River Indians occupied parts of Lassen National Park and lands owned by Pacific Gas and Electric Company in northern California after the Indian Claims Commission offered the tribe only forty-seven cents per acre for 3,368,000 acres they had lost in the area. That same year, demonstrators briefly took over Ellis Island to draw attention to the expropriation of Indian lands. A few years later, Mohawks seized cabins on state land in the Adirondack Mountains in New York to dramatize claims that the area had been stolen from them.

In the mid-1960's, Dakota Sioux leaders put together the American Indian Civil Rights Council to fight for equal opportunities and fair treatment for all Indians. At about the same time the Indian Land Rights Association was created to work toward restoration of tribal lands. In 1971 tribal leaders on reservations organized the National Tribal Chairman's Association to ensure that reservations would receive adequate attention after the NCAI began directing more of its activity toward urban issues.

Political Victories. After considerable lobbying, Indians won inclusion in President Lyndon Johnson's Great Society programs to combat POVERTY in the 1960's. Tribal councils were able to organize themselves as Community Action Agencies under the 1964

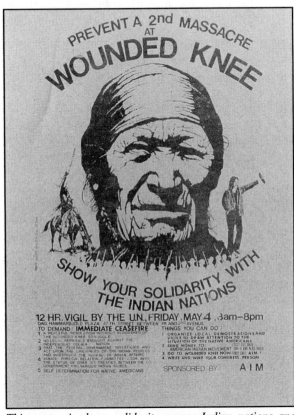

This poster implores solidarity among Indian nations and others, inviting concerned parties to be present at a vigil sponsored by the American Indian Movement (AIM). (Library of Congress)

Economic Opportunity Act and thus to qualify for a wide range of Great Society funding programs that Indians could largely administer themselves. This experience of channeling money and power through tribal councils enhanced the status and power of Indian self-government.

Congress and the White House also contributed to the Indian rights movement throughout the 1960's by launching task forces and investigations that drew attention to the deplorable conditions on reservations.

In 1966 Congress sponsored the Coleman Report on Equality and Educational Opportunity, and the White House initiated a Task Force on Indian Health. In 1969 the Senate Subcommittee on Indian Affairs, led by Senator Edward Kennedy, issued a report on education. President Richard Nixon then handed the Red Power movement its most important victory in 1970 when he issued a message embracing the notion of Indian self-determination and declaring policy goals similar to those championed by Indian activists.

In 1968 Congress enacted the Indian Civil Rights Act, allowing federal courts to review actions by tribal

tual life. The other case involved lands in Alaska, where economic interests had rushed to exploit the rich natural resources after the area gained statehood in 1959. By the late 1960's the federal government, state officials, and corporations all agreed that native claims needed to be resolved before widespread development could occur. In the ALASKA NATIVE CLAIMS SETTLEMENT ACT (1971), the Alaska Federation of Natives received title to 40 million acres and a settlement of $1 billion, which was to be controlled by native peoples and distributed among their own corporations and organizations.

During the 1973 confrontation at Wounded Knee, S.Dak., AIM leader Russell Means speaks to news reporters. (AP/Wide World Photos)

courts and extending most provisions of the Constitution's BILL OF RIGHTS to individual Indians to protect them from arbitrary actions by tribal government. Indian response was divided over this bill, however, illustrating the tension between rights derived from U.S. citizenship versus rights derived from membership in semi-sovereign tribal governments. The bill, in effect, limited tribal jurisdiction by extending the U.S. CONSTITUTION further into tribal matters.

Two important cases in 1971 revealed growing acceptance of Indian rights. After a long, drawn-out legislative struggle, Indians of the Taos Pueblo won the return of Blue Lake, a 48,000-acre tract in northern New Mexico that was important in the PUEBLO'S spiri-

Self-Determination. In 1975 Congress passed the INDIAN SELF-DETERMINATION AND EDUCATION ASSISTANCE ACT, potentially the greatest milestone in the Indian rights movement. The act redefined the relationship between the federal and tribal governments by allowing tribes to set priorities and goals in federal Indian policy. It permitted tribes to take over many social service functions on reservations by contracting directly with the BUREAU OF INDIAN AFFAIRS (BIA) and the Department of Health, Education, and Welfare. The bill also permitted tribes to direct the complete operations of BIA schools on their reservations. Some complained that delays, lack of adequate funding, and BIA resistance in the approval process limited real Indian control, but by the 1980's tribes controlled about one-half of existing programs.

In 1978 Congress enacted the Tribally Controlled Community College Act. The success of the Navajo Community College, constructed in 1969 with some of the first federal grant dollars for Indian HIGHER EDUCATION, had encouraged Congress to provide funding for more colleges founded by tribes or created through cooperative agreements with existing universities. During the 1970's eighteen groups, including the Dakotas, the CHEYENNES, the Blackfeet, and the HOPIS, started colleges that served about five thousand students. Most of these colleges were small and offered vocational courses as well as academic classes, but all were intended to serve the needs of reservation communities.

Two more bills in 1978 furthered Congress' commitment to Indian self-determination and marked the 1970's as a decade of progress toward preserving and expanding Indian rights. The Indian Religious Freedom Act was designed to protect the practice of traditional spiritual life by directing federal agencies to evaluate any policies that might endanger Indian religion, such as the denial of access to sacred sites on federal land. There was little subsequent enforcement and no mandate in the law for changes if problems were found, but it stood as an important statement of principle and a starting point. The Indian Child Welfare Act of 1978 gave tribes jurisdiction over states in child custody proceedings. This was meant to protect tribal rights in the adoption of Indian children, but conflicts developed when individual Indians and tribes disagreed in such proceedings.

Significance. Other ethnic rights movements, especially the black CIVIL RIGHTS MOVEMENT, aided the cause of the Indian rights movement by increasing general awareness of ethnic diversity and by emphasizing equal treatment and opportunity for all. The Indian rights movement was unique, however, since no other group could claim the rights of U.S. citizenship as well as the rights of members of semi-sovereign tribes. This sometimes led to conflict between the rights of tribes and the rights of individual Indians under the U.S. Constitution. The movement, nonetheless, achieved considerable progress for both tribes and individuals.

SUGGESTED READINGS. General works covering the early years of the contemporary Indian rights movement include Stan Steiner's *The New Indians* (1968) and Vine DELORIA, Jr.'s, *We Talk, You Listen: New*

Tribes, New Turf (1970). A similar, but less polemical, general account can be found in Alvin M. Josephy, Jr.'s, *Red Power: The American Indians' Fight for Freedom* (1971). A more recent and complete treatment can be found in James S. Olson and Raymond Wilson's *Native Americans in the Twentieth Century* (1984).—*Larry Burt*

Indian Self-Determination and Education Assistance Act of 1975: Restored tribalism and American Indian sovereignty, reversing policies of ASSIMILATION. The Indian Self-Determination and Education Assistance Act stated that Congress recognized the obligation of the United States to be more responsive to the needs and desires of American Indian communities. It assured maximum participation by the American Indian community in education and other federal services that directly affected their lives. The act established a new relation-

The Indian Self-Determination and Education Assistance Act of 1975 restored tribalism and American Indian sovereignty, reversing U.S. government policies of assimilation. (Elaine S. Querry)

ship between tribal authorities and the federal government. Tribal leaders could negotiate directly with the Department of Health, Education, and Welfare and the BUREAU OF INDIAN AFFAIRS. This act legally restored tribalism and gave American Indians greater control over federal programs.

Indian Territory: Land that now constitutes the state of Oklahoma. Indian Territory was originally defined in the 1820's as all of the United States west of the Mississippi River and not within the states of Missouri or Louisiana or the territory of Arkansas. These exclusions reduced the territory to the land of present-day Oklahoma, minus the panhandle. The FIVE CIVILIZED TRIBES—the CHOCTAWS, Creeks, Seminoles, CHEROKEES, and Chickasaws—were forcibly moved to this area between 1830 and 1843. The western half of Indian Territory was ceded to the United States in 1866 to provide lands for other tribes. Although originally reserved entirely as tribal land, a portion of the territory was opened to white settlers during the land rush of 1889. In 1907, the state of Oklahoma was admitted into the Union.

Indian Wars: Conflicts between American Indians and European (and, later, white American) settlers spanning nearly three centuries of American history. Over this considerable span of time, there was a variety of reasons for the tensions and violence between the two groups.

The Indian and European cultures were so vastly different that, particularly in the early years, some of the problems were caused primarily by the inability of the two cultures to understand each other. Moreover, Indians quickly learned to become suspicious of the demands and promises made by the white colonists. For their part, some white colonists and settlers had a XENOPHOBIC fear of the Indians that made them want to subdue them before the Indians could do damage to them. Under such circumstances, random violent acts (or actions perceived as threatening) on either side would provoke harsh retaliation, and an escalating cycle of violence would result.

In the nineteenth century, as more Europeans arrived and the white American population grew, the Indian population—although it was decimated by the disease, dislocation, and warfare that had resulted from contact with Europeans—increasingly was viewed by whites as an obstacle to American progress. Tribes were forced onto reservations or pushed westward; in the case of the Cherokees, they were first granted a RESERVATION, then forced to leave it and move west to a new reservation in an alien land. The resentments that resulted from these policies fueled the last century of the Indian Wars, culminating with the massacre of hundreds of Sioux by U.S. Cavalry forces at what is somewhat euphemistically called the BATTLE OF WOUNDED KNEE in 1890.

The Indian Wars can be divided into four chronological periods that help shed light on their evolving nature: the early colonial period (until 1689), the period of Anglo-French conflict (1689-1760), the British North American period (1760-1783), and the final period of United States suppression of the Indians (1783-1890).

Early Colonial Period: Pre-1689. The Indian Wars of the early colonial period focused on conflicts between the early European settlers and the American Indians inhabiting the Atlantic coastal areas. Initially, the coastal Indians had greeted the colonists with friendship, but soon the relationship deteriorated and eventually open conflicts erupted. Some of the conflicts stemmed from clashes of cultures. For example, the European colonists brought with them a concept of land ownership alien to the Indian concepts of land usage. While the Europeans often purchased land from the Indians, the European concept of land title and permanently acquired property rights was incomprehensible to the Indians, leading to mutual resentment and conflicts.

More often, however, wars between the colonists and the Indians were the result of what the indigenous peoples viewed as unreasonable, incessant colonial demands. The Indians believed, often with justification, that the Europeans had coerced and/or tricked them into surrendering their rights to the land. Finally, since individual and collective honor were very important to the Indians, motives of revenge for insults or slights of prestige contributed to conflicts with the colonists. For example, even among such groups as the SIX NATIONS of the Iroquois, who had overcome their internal differences to form the powerful IROQUOIS LEAGUE, Iroquois sachems could not prevent individual or small group acts of violence against Europeans while the league itself was formally at peace with the European powers. The Europeans failed to accept this reality and demanded that insults and Indian acts of violence for perceived insults not pass unanswered.

By the end of the seventeenth century, most Indian tribes along the Atlantic seacoast had been suppressed or driven inland. For example, in Virginia, despite persistent conflicts initiated by both the colonists and the

Indians, after 1677 the latter had ceased to be an organized threat to the settlers of the tidewater region. Similarly, in New England, the Pequot War and, later, KING PHILIP'S WAR led to the demise of organized tribal power in the region (except in Maine), even for tribes that had sided with the New Englanders during the earlier of the two wars.

Indian Involvement in the Anglo-French Wars: 1689-1760. By 1689, the French area of control extended from Acadia and the Gulf of St. Lawrence on the Atlantic to Quebec and Montreal on the St. Lawrence River. It then passed into the continent's interior, through the Great Lakes region and across the Illinois

The first of the four wars that would span the period from 1689 to 1760 was the War of the League of Augsburg, known in North America as King William's War. The colonial dimension of this conflict actually began in 1688 when the English authorities attempted to resist the French presence in Maine. This enraged the Abnaki Indians who resided in the disputed area and related well to the French traders. In retaliation, the Abnakis commenced guerrilla hostilities against English frontier settlements. Meanwhile, the Iroquois attacked French settlements such as the village of Lachine, only six miles from Montreal. Eventually, in 1690, the French launched a combined Franco-Indian

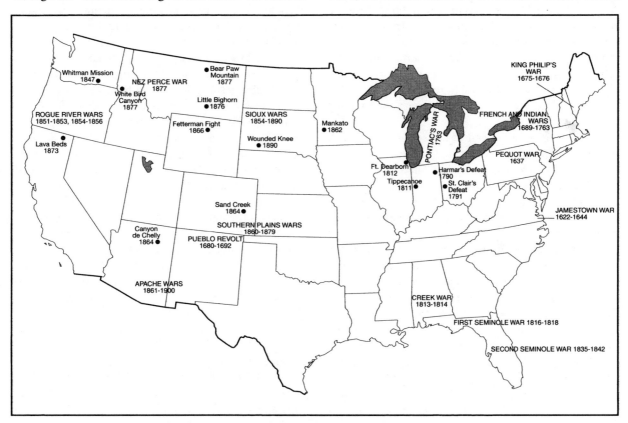

SELECTED SITES OF INDIAN WARS

Source: Adapted from Ronald B. Querry, *Native Americans.* American Voices series, p.38. Vero Beach, Fla.: Rourke Corp., 1991, and *World Book 1993* edition, vol. 10. Chicago: World Book, Inc., 1993.

country to the upper Mississippi Valley. Finally, the French controlled the lower Mississippi to New Orleans and the Gulf coast to Biloxi and Mobile. The English, although more numerous, were concentrated along the Atlantic coast, east of the Appalachian Mountains. Thus, the Woodlands Indians found themselves between two alien, rival European powers.

campaign southward from Montreal into the Hudson Valley, climaxing with the slaughter of some sixty men, women, and children at Schenectady, New York. Although the Treaty of Ryswick of 1697 formally terminated hostilities between England and France, frontier violence continued in North America.

In 1702, the beginning of the War of the Spanish

Succession immediately led to a resumption of formal Anglo-French warfare. Queen Anne's War, as the conflict was known in North America, saw a repetition of the frontier raids that had characterized King William's War. The most notorious of these was the February, 1704, French and Indian attack upon the 270 residents of Deerfield, Massachusetts. Hostilities were formally ended in 1713 with the Treaty of Utrecht, under the terms of which France transferred its holdings in Acadia and Hudson Bay to England.

Periodically between 1713 and 1744, hostilities erupted between the British colonists and the Indians, including the British suppression of the Abnakis in Maine (1721-1725) and protracted fighting between the colonists and the Tuscaroras, the Yamassees, and the Creeks in the Carolinas. The third of the great Anglo-French conflicts, known in North America as King George's War, erupted in 1744. Quickly the familiar pattern of frontier raids reappeared along the New York and New England frontiers; the fighting lasted until 1748.

The beginning of the end of the epic Anglo-French struggle for North America came in the early 1750's as the French moved to occupy the Ohio River Valley, and British colonial forces tried unsuccessfully to rout them. In 1756, as the FRENCH AND INDIAN WAR created renewed hostilities on the colonial frontier, French authorities in Quebec debated strategy. The conventional European approach prevailed. After the British surrender of Fort William Henry and the massacre of the British garrison and their dependents by France's Indian allies, French commander Louis Joseph, Marquis de Montcalm, retrenched the French defenses to Montreal and Quebec. The final French colonial surrender occurred at Montreal in 1760. The concluding conflict of the Anglo-French struggle was formally ended with the Treaty of Paris of 1763.

The Indians and British North America: 1760-1783. The collapse of French power on the mainland of North America led to significant changes for the Indians residing in the interior of the continent. One significant change was the British decision not to follow the French precedent of rewarding loyal tribes with gifts of guns and powder. In addition, the Indians saw troubling indications that the British intended to encroach further upon their lands. Moreover, the Indians felt themselves to be less welcome at the forts which had been transferred from French to British control.

These policies led to reactions among the Indians ranging from those who called only for a rejection of European ways and a return to native lifestyles to those who called for an active crusade to drive the British from the Indians' lands. The latter viewpoint eventually coalesced around the movement led by the Ottawa leader, PONTIAC. In the spring of 1763, in the Ohio region, frontier settlements were raided, and Britain's newly acquired outposts (from Fort Michilimackinac in the west to Forts Venango, Le Boeuf, and Presque Isle in Pennsylvania) fell to the Indian onslaught. The initial success of the attacks led directly to the British Proclamation of 1763, designed to limit colonial settlement west of the Appalachian Mountains. This act, combined with a strong British military response to the attacks and the disintegration of Indian unity, led to the collapse of the Indian offensive by early autumn of 1763.

The following years saw increased colonial pressure to settle west of the line drawn in the 1763 proclamation. Within a short time it had been significantly violated as European settlers entered the Ohio region and Kentucky. The most significant event of the 1770's, however, was the AMERICAN REVOLUTION against the British Crown. While initially the Indians were not asked by either side to aid in the conflict, soon both the British and the Americans solicited Indian assistance. In this conflict, the celebrated unity of the Iroquois was broken as the Mohawks, Senecas, Cayugas, and Onondagas sided with the British, while the Tuscaroras and Oneidas sided with the colonials. Thus, in the late 1770's, violence had broken out again on the frontier. British recognition of American independence in 1783 set the stage for the final century of the wars against the Indians.

The United States and the Suppression of the Indians: 1783-1890. Despite Britain's formal recognition of American independence, for several years following the 1783 Treaty of Paris the British retained their forts south of the Great Lakes. Some Britons fleetingly considered the possibility of supporting the creation of an autonomous Indian Confederation under British protection in the region between the Great Lakes and the Ohio River. Hence, during the first decade and a half following independence, the U.S. government focused much of its attention upon ousting the British from American soil and breaking the power of the Indians of the "Old Northwest." Despite the failure of two military expeditions north of the Ohio in 1790 and 1791, the United States finally defeated the Indians on August 20, 1794, at the Battle of Fallen Timbers. The following year, with the conclusion of the Treaty of Greenville, the government opened significant portions of the region north of the Ohio River for settlement.

The last great combined Indian effort to resist the onslaught of the white Americans east of the Mississippi was orchestrated by the remarkable Shawnee chief, TECUMSEH. Having fought at Fallen Timbers, Tecumseh became a powerful advocate of united Indian resistance to American encroachments onto the remaining Indian lands. His efforts failed both because of resolute and aggressive action by his primary op-

who remained east of the Mississippi were the tragic sequel.

By the mid-1840's, waves of European Americans had already begun to move west of the Mississippi in large numbers. In an effort to protect these pioneers, the U.S. government established a series of military outposts along the routes to Oregon and California. Predictably, as population pressures increased, the resources upon which the Plains Indians depended to sustain life became increasingly scarce. It was in this context that the newly established Department of the

The participants in a Washington, D.C., drill team wear uniforms resembling those of the black "buffalo soldiers" who fought in Indian Wars throughout the American West. (Roy Lewis)

ponent, General William Henry Harrison, and the unwillingness of the various tribes to coordinate their policies and actions. Although other outstanding Indian chiefs, such as the Creek leader William Weatherford, the Seminole leader OSCEOLA, and the Sauk and Fox leader Black Hawk, would later try, unsuccessfully, to resist white American expansion, the failure of Tecumseh heralded the last great hope for effective Indian resistance east of the Mississippi. The forced westward migrations of the eastern tribes between 1820 and 1845 and the suppression of those Indians

Interior proposed, and Congress authorized, the concept of Indian reservations on the Great Plains. Federal government officials told the Indians that if they ceased intertribal warfare as well as warfare against white settlers, relocated to the tribally demarcated reservations, retained limited common hunting grounds, and agreed to permit the passage of trails and eventually railroads westward, the government would provide an annual annuity for a specified period of time.

During the 1850's and following the CIVIL WAR, pressure mounted on the Indians from massive numbers of settlers moving west. In a series of military campaigns prior to, during, and for twenty-five years following the Civil War, the U.S. Army forced the remaining western Indians onto reservations and aggressively punished those who resisted. While some army commanders attempted to deal with the Indians humanely and were respected by the latter as men of honor, others pursued a vicious policy verging upon extermination. It was during this final period of the Indian Wars that RED CLOUD, CRAZY HORSE, and SITTING BULL of the Sioux, CHIEF JOSEPH of the Nez Perce, Quanah PARKER of the Comanche, COCHISE of the Chiricahuas, and GERONIMO of the Apaches, among others, attempted to stop events that had become inevitable.

Three events symbolize the final years of Indian resistance to U.S. policies. One was the 1877 resistance of a group of Nez Perces, under the leadership of Chief Joseph, to placement on a reservation. After a fatal attack by some Indians on white settlers, Chief Joseph led his group on a 1700-mile flight in search of a new home. They were relentlessly pursued by the U.S. Cavalry, however; ultimately the cavalry laid siege to the Nez Perce camp. Realizing that the situation was hopeless, Chief Joseph, in an eloquent speech, finally declared, "My heart is sick and sad. From where the sun now stands I will fight no more forever." The second event was the surrender of Apache chief Geronimo in 1886, which essentially ended significant Indian resistance. The third was the 1890 killing of some three hundred Miniconjou Sioux gathered near Wounded Knee Creek by U.S. forces. The Battle of Wounded Knee, a massacre of mostly unarmed Indians that occurred partly because of a series of misunderstandings, provided final evidence that further Indian resistance was futile.

SUGGESTED READINGS. For excellent overviews of the Indian Wars, see Robert Utley and Wilcomb Washburn's *The American Heritage History of the Indian Wars* (1977) and Wilcomb Washburn's *The Indian in America* (1975). For a superb account of the Anglo-French conflict, see W. J. Eccles' *The Canadian Frontier: 1534-1760* (rev. ed., 1983). Utley's *Frontiersmen in Blue* (1967) and *Frontier Regulars* (1973), focusing on the Western frontier during the periods 1848-1865 and 1866-1890, respectively, provide a comprehensive account of the last stage of the Indian Wars. Finally, Dee Brown's *Bury My Heart at Wounded Knee* (1971) provides a fascinating contrast to Utley's military histories.—*Howard M. Hensel*

Indochina Resource Action Center (IRAC): Organization assisting refugees from Southeast Asia. From its national headquarters in Washington, D.C., the center produces reports relating to Indochinese refugees, including employment, health care, and social adjustment. IRAC is a strong force for the protection of its constituents' human and civil rights. It also acts as a national clearinghouse for information on Indochinese refugees. IRAC shares this information with more than eight hundred refugee organizations across the country and offers training workshops and technical assistance for dealing with Indochinese refugees. It was formerly known as the Indochina Refugee Action Center.

Indochinese refugees and post-traumatic stress disorder. *See* **Post-traumatic stress disorder—Indochinese refugees**

Indonesian Americans: Indonesia, the largest and most populous country in Southeast Asia, is composed of more than 13,600 islands of which approximately 6,000 are inhabited. Formally known as the Republic of Indonesia, this country includes the islands of Java, Sumatra, Bali, part of Borneo, and thousands of smaller archipelagos that were formerly referred to as the East Indies. Indonesia's neighbor to the north is Malaysia, and to the east, Papua New Guinea. The Indonesian population is a blend of Malayan and Papuan peoples, with a mixture of Chinese and Indian—the result of past invasions.

During the seventeenth century, the Dutch East India Company asserted control over this area, particularly Java—placing great value on the spices from these islands. Indonesia was ruled by The Netherlands until the mid-twentieth century. The native population suffered economically and socially under the Dutch, and by the late 1920's, a nationalist movement had formed under the leadership of Sukarno. During World War II, the islands were overrun by Japanese troops. Following Japan's surrender to the Allies, Sukarno declared the independence of Indonesia; formal independence was achieved in 1949 despite Dutch attempts to reassert control. Indonesia then entered a period of great political instability marked by the usurpation of power by President Sukarno and eventually a military coup d'état that placed General Suharto in charge. These events caused many Indonesians to flee their country.

By the early 1990's, there were approximately thirty thousand Americans of Indonesian descent living in the United States, many of whom were former Dutch

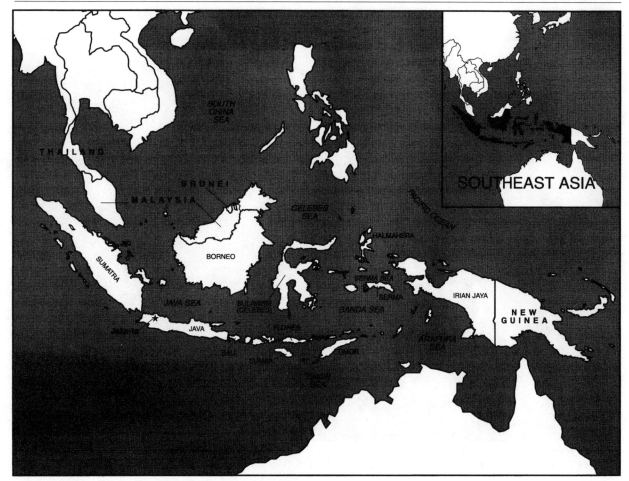

INDONESIA

colonials who immigrated in the 1960's. In the 1970's—1990's, immigration to the United States was more common for family groups. Most of these immigrants were professionals or skilled workers, and students.

Industrial Revolution: In the one hundred years between 1820 and 1920, the United States underwent a transformation from a largely rural, agricultural society to an industrial and increasingly urban one. Over the course of that period, the Industrial Revolution contributed to a revolution in science and its practical application through mechanization. Power-driven machines replaced hand tools, and the rise of large scale factories, major technological innovations, and new managerial strategies for the division, control, and exploitation of labor dramatically increased productivity and industrial output. The Industrial Revolution's impact on American life was thorough and profound, involving changes in

the goods Americans produced and consumed, as well as the techniques for producing them.

Demand for Labor. If the Industrial Revolution required scientific and mechanical advances, infusions of capital, and the cooperation of government, it also required large quantities of labor. Specifically, it demanded wage labor. In the United States, nineteenth century industrialization was part of the larger process of capitalist development. Before the slow rise of the factory system (after 1820), independent artisans and small manufacturers—mostly men who were native-born Anglo Americans or British immigrants—produced goods in their homes or small workshops, drawing upon the labor of family members, apprentices, journeymen, and sometimes slaves. The production of goods for sale in larger or more distant markets, the subdivision of labor into more discrete tasks, the assembling of larger groups of workers under one roof, the commercialization of agriculture—all were

This old town in Oregon, complete with smokestacks, textile mills, and factories, is representative of the changes that took place as the United States underwent an Industrial Revolution. (Culver Pictures, Inc.)

based on capitalist values and were part of a market revolution that at times preceded, and at other times accompanied, the rise of the factory system. The Industrial Revolution and the attendant spread of capitalist social relations concentrated ownership and contributed to the decline in the independent status of the producer. The 1870 census revealed that the United States was becoming a nation of employees, with 67 percent of productively engaged Americans working for someone else.

Sources of Labor. The labor required by the growing economic enterprises came from a multitude of sources. Native-born white Americans, African Americans, French Canadians, Mexicans, Japanese, Chinese, and immigrants from western, southern, and eastern Europe all joined the intermittent flows of people across oceans and borders in search of employment. By the early twentieth century, the Industrial Revolution had transformed the nation's (and the world's) economic landscape and had brought into existence

an extremely diverse labor force, a multiracial and multiethnic working class.

The Industrial Revolution in the United States first began in the textile industry of the Northeast. Beginning in the 1790's, textile manufacturers utilized English technology to build water-powered factories in the rural New England countryside. In Massachusetts, manufacturers in the 1820's drew upon a large reserve of native-born, rural white women from the surrounding countryside. The so-called LOWELL MILL GIRLS, for example, were young and single, and they sought mill work in order to supplement their families' farm income or gain a degree of personal or economic independence.

The relative ethnic homogeneity of the textile mill labor force began to change by the 1840's. By mid-century, Irish immigrants constituted nearly a third of one large company's work force in Lowell; ten years later, they constituted almost one half. This was only the first of many ethnic shifts that the New England textile labor force would experience. In 1912, as many as twenty-five different nationalities were represented among the thirty thousand immigrants who participated in the "Bread and Roses" strike against the American Woolen Company in Lawrence, Massachusetts. They included seven thousand Italians, six thousand Germans, five thousand French Canadians, twenty-five hundred Poles, two thousand Lithuanians, eleven hundred Franco-Belgians, and one thousand Syrians. Out of this veritable tower of Babel, union organizers from the Industrial Workers of the World (IWW) managed to forge a unified force that, at least temporarily, compelled management to improve conditions.

The experiences of the New England textile industry were by no means unique. Virtually all the nation's major industries assembled a racially or ethnically heterogeneous labor force over the course of the nineteenth and early twentieth century. By the early 1900's, the coal companies of southern Colorado employed Mexican migrants, MEXICAN AMERICANS,

Slavs, Italians, Poles, Greeks, and native-born whites; the steel mills of western Pennsylvania relied upon native-born whites, Italians, African Americans, Croatians, Slovenes, Serbs, and Bulgarians; and the packinghouses of Chicago employed Poles, Slovacks, African Americans, Lithuanians, IRISH AMERICANS, and Bohemians.

The Industrial Revolution generated employment not only in the new, modern factory system but also in infrastructural development and extractive industry as well. The emergence of water and rail-based transportation networks enabled producers to secure raw materials from greater distances and sell goods in new markets. From the 1810's through the 1840's, a wave of canal building linked markets and people in inland cities to key waterways. The construction of canals required the unskilled labor of thousands of workers. Irish male immigrants in particular made up the bulk of the work crews, suffering high mortality from disease and accidents. Even more important than canals was the expansion of railroad networks after 1830.

Young girls and women operate cotton presses and other machinery in this 1829 depiction of work inside the cotton mills. During the Industrial Revolution, women sought employment to supplement their family income and to gain greater personal or economic independence. (Culver Pictures, Inc.)

These networks linked geographically disparate regions, vastly expanded consumer markets, and facilitated an exchange of goods and people on a truly continental scale. The first transcontinental railroad, completed in 1869, relied overwhelmingly upon roughly twelve thousand Chinese coolies to lay track, build bridges, and dig tunnels through the High Sierra mountains. Railroad construction and maintenance-of-way gangs remained a realm of common labor, composed of gangs of Japanese, Mexican, African American, and Eastern European workers well into the twentieth century.

The Industrial Revolution and Slavery. African Americans stood in a paradoxical relationship to the Industrial Revolution. On the one hand, they were largely excluded from jobs created by expanding industry in the North and Midwest during the period from 1820 to 1920. Employer preference ran to white immigrants; trade unions often barred blacks from

African Americans were largely excluded from jobs created by the expansion of industry. Employers preferred to hire white immigrants, as seen in this glimpse of a northern factory. (Culver Pictures, Inc.)

membership; and African Americans often lacked the skills—and the opportunities to acquire skills—needed to compete successfully in the marketplace. On the other hand, in the seven decades before the CIVIL WAR, African Americans raised a crop—cotton—that helped to fuel the growth of the textile industry that stood at the forefront of this Industrial Revolution in the North and in Great Britain. Thus, the most modern sector of the American economy, textiles, was fueled by its most backward institution, American slavery. Yet not all African Americans were field workers raising cotton, sugar, or rice. Before the Civil War, as much as 10 percent of southern slaves worked in "industrial slavery"—laboring in salt and coal mines as well as iron foundries, and working as carpenters and common laborers in the cities of the South. In southern urban centers before and after the Civil War, tens of thousands of blacks worked as longshoremen, teamsters and loaders, railroad track laborers, building tradesmen, and domestic servants.

Accompanying the Industrial Revolution's technological and organizational achievements were changes in ideology that contributed to the ultimate demise of SLAVERY. Industry and capitalism in the North generated a set of beliefs about the nature of the individual's relationship to the economy and society. While abolitionists attacked slavery on moral grounds, a larger group of white northerners advanced a critique of the South's "peculiar institution"—as slavery was called—based upon a "free soil ideology." Free soil advocates glorified the economic, material, and cultural achievements of northern society—its factories, productivity, schools, and internal improvements. Above all, this view celebrated the opportunity that the North supposedly provided free white workers to achieve upward social mobility. This belief in free labor/free soil, reflecting the aspirations and experiences of some members of American society, contrasted sharply with the social and economic ethos generated by slavery. While the North industrialized on the basis of free labor, the South remained grounded in a labor system in which some human beings owned other human beings. The western migration of white Northerners and Southerners into new territory produced a clash between worldviews and economic/social systems centered on the expansion of slavery and its consequences. In the ensuing clash (the Civil War, 1861-1865), the North's victory ended chattel slavery in the United States. The Industrial Revolution, which had long depended upon slave-produced cotton, had generated ideological currents that contributed to slavery's ultimate downfall.

The Changing Ethnic Composition of the Labor Force. The ethnic composition of the labor force changed radically over time in most major industries. In various periods, different immigrant groups responded to deteriorating conditions in their homelands and the availability of work in other lands. The United States was hardly the only destination of migrants: Within Europe, population flows reflected "push" and "pull" factors. Seeking economic security or advancement (and at times political or religious liberty), migrants sought work in extractive or industrial labor wherever jobs were to be found within Europe itself. Outside Europe, destinations included Canada, the United States, Brazil, Argentina, and Australia. Between 1820 and 1860, about five million immigrants, largely from Ireland and Germany, arrived in the United States. Between 1880 and 1890, Germany, England, Ireland, and Scandinavia provided about two-thirds of European immigrants. After 1890, the geographical origins of European immigration shifted to the east and south, with two-thirds coming from Russia, Italy, and Austria-Hungary. Between 1900 and the outbreak of World War I in 1914, some nine million Europeans, mostly Slavs and Italians, immigrated to the United States to take up unskilled jobs at the bottom of the nation's economic hierarchy. Immigrants from Asia—particularly China and Japan—and from Mexico worked as unskilled factory laborers, railroad construction gang members, agricultural hands, domestics, and as miners, primarily in the West and Southwest. By 1910, immigrants constituted as much as 60 percent of the labor force in manufacturing and mining.

SUGGESTED READINGS. On the multiethnic character of the labor force in two industries (steel and meatpacking), see David Brody's *Steelworkers in America: The Nonunion Era* (1960) and James R. Barrett's *Work and Community in the Jungle: Chicago's Packinghouse Workers, 1894-1922* (1987). David Montgomery's The Fall of the House of Labor: The Workplace, the State, and American Labor Activism, 1865-1925 (1987) includes a discussion of unskilled labor in factory and other settings. Elizabeth Gurley Flynn's first-hand account, *The Rebel Girl: An Autobiography: My First Life (1906-1926)* (1973), explores the working conditions of numerous immigrant groups and efforts by the Industrial Workers of the World to organize them in the early twentieth century.—*Eric Arnesen*

Inner city: Since the foundation of the thirteen colonies, American cities have been places where people of diverse social and cultural backgrounds have come together. Whether one looks at the Spaniards, Africans, and American Indians of early St. Augustine or at the multiple languages, lifestyles, beliefs, and associations of contemporary cosmopolitan centers, the city represents both the successes and the failures of the American experience. The failures are apparent in the urban conflicts, decay, and flight that divide metropolitan populations.

Defining the Inner City. Sociologists have attempted to define and delineate urban areas according to such elements as status, function (such as a central business district), and distance (central city versus suburbs). Areas can also be categorized simply according to the rich ethnic or neighborhood identities of everyday conversation—New York's Harlem, Los Angeles' Little Tokyo, or Miami's Little Havana. Since the 1960's, the term "inner city" has transcended its purely geographic or functional definitions to become a shorthand designation for an urban area with both intense problems and recurrent conflict. Nevertheless, the centers of American cities often remain those areas that most richly embody the meaning of contemporary MULTICULTURALISM.

The idea of an inner city as an expression of social divisions has grown out of the processes of urban immigration and social differentiation. In early American cities, despite differences among the inhabitants in status and wealth, neat separations often proved impossible. Commerce and industry stood beside the residences of all social groups. In Philadelphia, for example, the crowded streets near the Delaware River brought together artisans, stevedores, merchant wives, and former black slaves. Even in areas of strict social division such as the antebellum South, blacks and whites in the city were often brought together by adjoining (if unequal) residences.

As waves of immigrants poured into American cities in the nineteenth century, their diversity encouraged neighborhood divisions, often in areas surrounding the urban core, which offered work and transient housing. In some cases, the new residential areas took on racially marked names, such as the Chinatowns of New York and San Francisco. In other cases, these areas became associated with socially defined vices such as alcohol abuse, prostitution, and gambling. This association caused certain urban areas to be considered unlawful places in need of intense police control and their residents to be seen as lost souls in need of help from social reformers. Yet to many people, especially the immigrants and other minorities who lived there, these areas were also symbols of freedom and way stations on the path to becoming "real Americans."

The City and the Suburbs. Technological innovations in transportation and communication allowed American cities to expand in the later nineteenth century, causing a remapping of the geography of wealth, culture, and race. Horse cars dominated this process from the 1850's to the 1880's, giving way to cable railways, railroads, streetcars, and finally the automobile. Each alternative permitted people to move farther away from the urban workplace, redefining the core left behind by its new metropolitan context.

By the 1920's, social scientists recognized different functional zones of the city. Robert Park and E. W. Burgess' studies of Chicago, for example, identified a central district that contained political, economic, and cultural services for the city and limited places of residence. Around this stood factories and service centers such as train stations. These in turn were linked to an outer circle of working-class immigrant homes through a transitional zone in which formerly wealthy residences were abandoned by people who moved outside the city. In this transitional zone the sociologists identified both urban diversity—Chinatown and Little Sicily, for example—and the beginning of the "black belt" as well as an urban underworld. This model suggested that the inner city was constantly renewed by new populations, including immigrants, while those who assimilated gradually moved through a sequence of better neighborhoods to the suburbs.

Those left behind in the urban core developed important ties that adapted to urban expansion as well as internal migrations. As residents of similar backgrounds clustered together, they created other institutions such as churches and synagogues, cultural associations and fairs, and even workplaces—which became symbols of their complex identities. Where New York's Little Italy had its Madonna and campanile, for example, Tampa's Ybor City formed communities of Cubans, Spanish, and Italians around cultural associations, political clubs, and the cigar factories that had brought many there. At the same time, schools, civic associations, and political bosses introduced immigrants to the language and

Children in Brooklyn, N.Y., cool off in spray from a fire hydrant, a common summertime recreation for inner-city residents.
(Hazel Hankin)

values of the dominant culture.

After the beginning of the twentieth century, new urban populations arrived and established themselves in the transition areas around the urban core. In the first decades of the century, for example, rural African Americans from the South flooded many northern cities, attempting to escape PREJUDICE and find better opportunities in EMPLOYMENT, EDUCATION, and housing. The results included the growth of Harlem as the African American capital of the United States. Harlem soon had a million black residents and possessed a cultural vitality that belied the oppressive living conditions of many of its residents.

Relations among groups living and working in the urban core were not always friendly or even peaceful. After one ethnic group had become established in an area and had obtained an economic foothold, it often viewed newer arrivals as invaders who threatened to take jobs away. Ethnic groups jealously and fearfully guarded their own turf, keenly aware that their position in the American hierarchy was only one precarious step above that of the new arrivals. Prejudice and DISCRIMINATION against immigrant groups as well as against African Americans came from both established generations of American citizens and from various immigrant ethnic groups themselves.

Urban Renewal and Gentrification. Many aspects of the inner city as a problem zone were exacerbated by urban renewal projects in the 1960's. Various government and private agencies often worked at cross-purposes, fixing one urban problem but generating others. Highways as routes between central areas and suburbs, for example, often cut through and disrupted vibrant areas around the business district. Urban renewal plans, with their extensive elimination of decaying houses and factories in the urban core, sometimes created vast open areas, some of which still remain as ravaged holes in the once tightly knit fabric of the city.

Not all inner city areas fell into decay or were disrupted or leveled by urban renewal projects, however. Gentrification movements brought in many predominantly white suburbanites to restore older homes at the center of the city that previous generations had abandoned. Unfortunately, this often forced the eviction of populations who then could find no new housing near the center and could not afford to move farther out. Still, "success stories" such as Philadelphia's Society Hill and Savannah's Historic District enriched the inner city alongside new corporate towers and public buildings.

Inner cities have also been stages for the agitation for social and cultural change. These areas saw violent group action in the past, such as the anti-Catholic riots in the nineteenth century and the race riots and violence around the time of World War I. They also provided a place for more peaceful protests, whether by SUFFRAGISTS demanding the vote for women or by African Americans marching for civil rights. In the 1960's, however, urban conflagrations broke out, from the WATTS RIOTS in Los Angeles to the DETROIT RIOTS, often laying waste whole sections and driving out businesses, employers, and residents. These riots and their aftermath, both in sparking governmental investigations and programs and in feeding popular fears about urban life, have left a painful legacy for contemporary urban cores.

Continuing Problems of the Inner City. Inner cities have continued to age. Their residents and leaders face eroding tax bases and further urban problems even as new groups make their way there. Immigrants from around the world continue to use these areas as their entry into the United States, whether they are represented by an Iranian driving a cab in New York or a Korean family opening a small grocery store in Los Angeles. Illegal immigrants find safety in numbers as well as familiar cultural and linguistic patterns in the inner city, although they can also become victims of exploitation because of their isolation and their avoidance of authorities. In some cities, plans for new uses for urban areas, new community facilities, and sponsorship of new social forms (such as New York's SoHo lofts for artists) have provided new hopes for the urban core. In other cases, squatters have reclaimed abandoned housing or fashioned the empty wastelands of urban renewal into urban gardens.

Nevertheless, many groups, especially African Americans, have been deeply affected by the ongoing POVERTY, discrimination, and lack of opportunities that make the inner city a place of confinement as well as a residence. Ongoing tensions among the city's many groups have also become more dangerous as drugs, crime, and GANGS have proliferated, seeming to pit Asian Americans, Latinos, African Americans, and European Americans against one another on an urban battleground. The 1992 LOS ANGELES RIOTS highlighted the pain and anger of those who feel trapped by both the myths and the realities of the inner city.

Modern theorists have argued that postindustrial cities, defined by services and information rather than by heavy production, no longer require the spatial concentrations of the past. Government offices, corporate headquarters, and even sports teams have left the aging infrastructures behind in order to be closer to a larger group of suburban consumers. Even ethnic communities have reproduced themselves outside the central city, a process exemplified in Los Angeles' suburban Chinese communities in Alhambra and Monterey Park. In some cases, inner cities are defined by metropolitan residents in terms of "special" places and events, such as museums, theaters, restaurants, or markets. These cities have accommodated to changing times by creating projects specifically designed to refurbish areas of the urban core as tourist centers. Among such projects are Baltimore's Inner Harbor and San Francisco's Ghirardelli Square. Yet in other cities, the inner city is associated with danger, poverty, and homelessness by those who avoid it, and with hopelessness and rage by those who inhabit it.

As the core of the city—a place where diverse Americans have always met, where first-generation Americans have established their claims on the country, and where men and women have found freedom in their individual choices—the inner cities have been the cradle of a multicultural experience. Yet these areas have also been identified with the worst urban nightmares of the present and future. The resolution of this contradiction lies in rethinking both the differences and interdependences among the peoples and areas that constitute contemporary cities.

SUGGESTED READINGS. Among many sources chronicling the changes in American cities is Maurice H. Yeates and Barry J. Garner's *The North American City* (3d ed., 1980). The troubles of the 1960's are explored in the *Report of the National Advisory Commission on Civil Disorders* (1968), prepared by the United States Kerner Commission. This provides an interesting comparison with the Institute for Alternative Journalism's 1992 collection *Inside the L.A. Riots*, edited by Don Hazen. A range of other examinations and solutions to the questions of the modern inner city can be found in Larry Bennett's *Fragments of Cities* (1990); *Inner-City Poverty in the United States* (1990), edited by Laurence Lynn and Michael McGeary; Thomas Stanback's *The New Suburbanization: Challenge to the Central City* (1991); and William Goldsmith's *Separate Societies: Poverty and Inequality in U.S. Cities* (1992).—*Gary W. McDonogh*

Lacking green and open spaces, these Harlem youths congregate on a rooftop playground. (Photo Agora)